STUDY GUIDE

FOR USE WITH

FINANCIAL ACCOUNTING

——

FIFTH EDITION

Roger H. Hermanson
Georgia State University
James Don Edwards
University of Georgia

IRWIN
Homewood, IL 60430
Boston, MA 02116

Printed in the United States of America.

ISBN 0–256–09258–3

2 3 4 5 6 7 8 9 0 VK 9 8 7 6 5 4 3 2

CONTENTS

THE ACCOUNTING ENVIRONMENT

Learning Objectives

1. *Define accounting.*
2. *Describe the functions performed by accountants.*
3. *Describe employment opportunities in accounting.*
4. *Differentiate between financial and managerial accounting.*
5. *Identify several organizations that have a role in the development of financial accounting standards.*

REVIEW OF INTRODUCTION

ACCOUNTING DEFINED

1. Accounting is defined as "the process of identifying, measuring, and communicating economic information to permit informed judgments and decisions by the users of the information."[1]

---

[1]American Accounting Association, *A Statement of Basic Accounting Theory* (Evanston, Ill., 1966), p. 1.

EMPLOYMENT OPPORTUNITIES IN ACCOUNTING

2. Accounting is now recognized as an important profession and offers various types of employment.

PUBLIC ACCOUNTING

3. The public accounting profession offers accounting and related services for a fee to companies, other organizations, and the general public.

    a. An accountant may become a certified public accountant (CPA) by passing an examination and meeting other requirements.

    b. Some CPAs are hired as auditors by companies to conduct an examination of their accounting and related records.

    c. Auditors give independent opinions or reports indicating whether or not the financial statements fairly report the economic performance of the business.

    d. CPAs also often provide expert advice on the preparation of federal, state, and city tax returns as well as on tax planning.

    e. Management advisory or consulting services are also performed by CPAs to provide clients with suggestions on how to improve their operations.

PRIVATE (OR INDUSTRIAL) ACCOUNTING

4. Private or industrial accountants provide services for one business; they may or may not be CPAs.

    a. Some private accountants, regardless of whether or not they are CPAs, pass the Certified Management Accounting (CMA) exam.

    b. Some private accountants conduct internal audits to determine if policies and procedures established by the business are being followed; these accountants may pass the Certified Internal Auditors (CIA) exam.

GOVERNMENTAL AND OTHER NOT-FOR-PROFIT ACCOUNTING

5. Other accountants, having similar educational backgrounds and training, may be employed by governmental agencies and other not-for-profit organizations.

HIGHER EDUCATION

6. Academic accountants teach accounting courses, conduct scholarly and applied research, and perform services for the institution and the community.

FINANCIAL ACCOUNTING VERSUS MANAGERIAL ACCOUNTING

7. Accounting is divided into two categories, financial and managerial accounting, based on the parties for whom the information is prepared.

FINANCIAL ACCOUNTING

8. Financial accounting information is prepared for external users such as stockbrokers and creditors.
9. Financial accounting information relates to a company as a whole, while managerial accounting focuses on the parts of a company.

MANAGERIAL ACCOUNTING

10. Managerial accounting provides special information for the managers of a company ranging from broad, long-range plans to detailed explanations.

DEVELOPMENT OF FINANCIAL ACCOUNTING STANDARDS

11. These organizations—the American Institute of Certified Public Accountants, the Financial Accounting Standards Board, the Governmental Accounting Standards Board, the Securities and Exchange Commission, the American Accounting Association, the Financial Executives Institute, and the Institute of Management Accountants—have each contributed to the development of Generally Accepted Accounting Principles (GAAP).

AMERICAN INSTITUTE OF CERTIFIED PUBLIC ACCOUNTANTS (AICPA)

12. The AICPA Committee on Accounting Procedures issued 51 *Accounting Research Bulletins* recommending certain principles or practices during a 20-year period, ending in 1959.
13. The Committee's successor, the Accounting Principles Board (APB), Issued 31 *Opinions* that CPAs generally are required to follow.
14. Through its monthly magazine, the *Journal of Accountancy,* the AICPA continues to influence the development of accounting standards and practices.

FINANCIAL ACCOUNTING STANDARDS BOARD (FASB)

15. The Financial Accounting Standards Board replaced the Accounting Principles Board in 1973.
16. The FASB is an independent, seven-member, full-time board that has issued numerous *Statements of Financial Accounting Standards.*

GOVERNMENTAL ACCOUNTING STANDARDS BOARD (GASB)

17. The Governmental Accounting Standards Board was established in 1984 to develop new governmental accounting concepts and standards.

SECURITIES AND EXCHANGE COMMISSION (SEC)

18. The SEC has the power to prescribe accounting practices for companies under its jurisdiction.
19. The SEC also indicates to the FASB the accounting topics it believes should be addressed and works closely with the accounting profession.

AMERICAN ACCOUNTING ASSOCIATION (AAA)

20. The American Accounting Association is composed largely of accounting educators and has sought to encourage research and study into the concepts, standards, and principles of accounting on a theoretical level.

FINANCIAL EXECUTIVES INSTITUTE (FEI)

21. Through its Committee on Corporate Reporting (CCR) and other means, the FEI is effective in influencing the decisions of the FASB, SEC, and other regulatory agencies.

INSTITUTE OF MANAGEMENT ACCOUNTANTS (IMA)

22. Through its Management Accounting Practices (MAP) committee and other means, the IMA provides input on financial accounting standards to the FASB, SEC, and other regulatory agencies.

OTHER ORGANIZATIONS

23. Other organizations, such as the Financial Analysts Federation, the Security Industry Associates, and CPA firms, provide input to the FASB.

ETHICAL BEHAVIOR OF ACCOUNTANTS

24. Several accounting organizations have formulated codes of ethics that govern the behavior of their members.

COMPLETION AND QUESTIONS

---

1. Accounting is primarily an information system with three objectives—to _____, _____, and _____ economic information that is relevant to users for their decision-making needs.

2. The four major employment fields in accounting are _____, _____, _____, and _____.

Introduction

3. Financial accounting information generally relates to a company as a _____ and is usually _____ in nature.

4. Accounting deals primarily with information regarding _____ activities of a business and is expressed in _____ terms.

5. Accountants who offer their services solely to a single profit-seeking organization are said to be in _____ or _____ accounting.

6. An independent, professional accountant, licensed by the state to practice as a certified public accountant (CPA), may offer clients three types of services, namely, _____, _____, and _____ services.

7. The decisions that must be made by the management of a business generally fall into four major categories: (a) _____, (b) _____, (c) _____, and (d) _____ decisions. That part of the accounting discipline called upon to provide information for such internal decision making is called _____ accounting.

8. The two tests that information supplied by managerial accountants must meet are:
   1. _____
   2. _____

9. The dominant influence over the past half century in the development of financial accounting standards is the _____.

10. A governmental agency having the power to prescribe the accounting practices of most large business corporations is the _____.

11. The major influence in the private sector in the development of new governmental accounting concepts and standards is the _____.

12. An accountant's most valuable asset is his or her _____.

SOLUTIONS

Completion

1. identify; measure; communicate
2. public accounting; private accounting; governmental and other not-for-profit accounting; and higher education
3. whole; historical
4. economic; monetary
5. private or industrial
6. auditing; management advisory; tax
7. (a) financial, (b) resource allocation, (c) production, (d) marketing; managerial
8. 1. It must be useful.
   2. It must not cost more to gather than it is worth (this test is known as the cost/benefit test).
9. American Institute of Certified Public Accountants
10. Securities and Exchange Commission
11. Governmental Accounting Standards Board
12. reputation

1 ACCOUNTING AND ITS USE IN BUSINESS DECISIONS

Learning Objectives

1. *Identify and describe the three basic forms of business organizations.*
2. *Distinguish among the three types of activities performed by business organizations.*
3. *Describe the content and purposes of the income statement, statement of retained earnings, and balance sheet.*
4. *State the basic accounting equation and describe its relationship to the balance sheet.*
5. *Using the underlying assumptions or concepts, analyze business transactions and determine their effects on items in the financial statements.*
6. *Prepare an income statement, a statement of retained earnings, and a balance sheet.*

CHAPTER OUTLINE

FORMS OF BUSINESS ORGANIZATIONS

1. A business organization is referred to as an accounting or business entity; the three basic forms of business organizations regarding ownership are single proprietorship, partnership, and corporation.

SINGLE PROPRIETORSHIP

2. A single proprietorship is a business owned by one individual.
   a. This business is often managed by the owner.
   b. No legal formalities are necessary to organize a single proprietorship, and usually only a limited investment is required to begin operations.
   c. In a single proprietorship, the owner is solely responsible for all debts of the business.
   d. The business is considered an entity separate from the owner.

PARTNERSHIP

3. A business owned by two or more persons associated as partners is a partnership.
   a. Partners often manage the business.
   b. A partnership agreement creates the partnership and sets forth the terms of the business.
      1. The partnership agreement itemizes the duties of each partner, the initial investment of each partner, and the means of dividing profits or losses between partners.
      2. A written partnership agreement is preferred over an oral agreement.
   c. Each partner may be held liable for all the debts of the partnership.

CORPORATION

4. A corporation may be owned by a varying number of persons and is incorporated under the laws of a state.
   a. Owners of the corporation are called stockholders or shareholders.
   b. Stockholders elect a board of directors which then selects officers who manage the corporation.

TYPES OF ACTIVITIES PERFORMED BY BUSINESS ORGANIZATIONS

5. Instead of classifying business entities according to the type of ownership, they can be grouped according to the type of business activities they perform—service companies, merchandising companies, and manufacturing companies.
   a. Service companies perform such services as accounting, cleaning, or legal work for a fee.
   b. Merchandising companies buy goods that are ready for sale and sell them directly to customers.
   c. Manufacturing companies purchase materials and convert them into a different product for sale to other companies or to final customers.

FINANCIAL STATEMENTS OF BUSINESS ORGANIZATIONS

THE INCOME STATEMENT

6. The income statement reports the profitability of a business organization for a stated period of time.
   a. An income statement may be called an earnings statement.
   b. An income statement indicates the revenues earned and the expenses incurred. The difference is net income (if revenues exceed expenses) or a net loss (if expenses exceed revenues).
      1. Revenues are defined as the inflow of assets resulting from the sale of products or the rendering of services to customers.
      2. Expenses are the costs incurred to produce revenues.

THE STATEMENT OF RETAINED EARNINGS

7. The statement of retained earnings explains the changes in retained earnings that occurred between two balance sheet dates.

   a. Usually these changes consist of adding net income and deducting dividends.
   b. Dividends are payments to the stockholders representing distributions of income.

THE BALANCE SHEET

8. The balance sheet reflects the company's solvency. Solvency is the ability to pay debts as they become due.
9. A balance sheet lists the company's assets, liabilities, and stockholders' equity at a specific moment in time.
10. A balance sheet is sometimes called the statement of financial position.

ASSETS

11. Assets are things of value owned by a company.
12. Assets are known as resources and include such items as cash, land, and buildings.

LIABILITIES

13. Liabilities are debts or obligations owed by a company and usually must be paid by a specific date.
14. Liabilities include amounts owed suppliers for goods purchased with a promise to pay the amount owed at a later date.

STOCKHOLDERS' EQUITY

15. Stockholders' equity reflects the owners' interest in a company.
16. Stockholders' equity is equal to assets minus liabilities.
17. Stockholders' equity consists of the owners' original investment in a company plus cumulative net income earned through operations minus total dividends distributed to the stockholders.

THE FINANCIAL ACCOUNTING PROCESS

18. The process of accumulating data to include in financial statements reflects the relationship of assets, liabilities, and stockholders' equity.

THE ACCOUNTING EQUATION

19. The accounting equation is: Assets = Liabilities + Stockholders' Equity.

   a. The equation must always be in balance.
   b. The right-hand side of the equation (Liabilities + Stockholders' Equity) reflects the equities, since liabilities can be viewed as creditors' equity.

      1. Equities are claims to or interests in assets.
      2. The right side of the equation shows who provided the funds to acquire existing assets.

ACCOUNTING ASSUMPTIONS

20. Accountants rely on five underlying assumptions or concepts.

   a. The *business entity concept* assumes that each business has an existence separate from its owners, creditors, customers, and employees.
   b. The *money measurement concept* refers to the form of common monetary unit of measure in which economic activity is initially recorded.
   c. The *exchange price (or cost) concept* indicates that most assets are recorded at their acquisition cost measured in terms of money paid.
   d. The *going-concern (continuity) concept* allows the accountant to assume the business entity will continue operations into the indefinite future unless strong evidence exists to the contrary.
   e. The *periodicity (time periods) concept* allows an entity's life to be subdivided into time periods for purposes of reporting its economic activities.

ANALYSIS OF TRANSACTIONS

21. Exchanges of goods and services are called transactions.

   a. Transactions provide much of the raw data entered in an accounting process because a transaction is an observable event that occurred at an agreed-upon price, which is objective.

   b. The evidence of the transaction is usually a source document.

TRANSACTIONS AFFECTING ONLY THE BALANCE SHEET

22. Typical transactions affecting only the balance sheet are described below.

   a. Owners invested cash—Increase in cash (asset) and increase in capital stock account (stockholders' equity).

   b. Borrowed money—Increase in cash (asset) and increase in loan payable account (liability).

   c. Purchased equipment (or land) for cash—Increase in equipment (or land, both are assets) and decrease in cash (asset).

   d. Purchased equipment (or land) on credit—Increase in equipment (or land, both are assets) and increase in loan payable (liability).

   e. Paid liability—Decrease in cash (asset) and decrease in accounts or loan payable (liability).

TRANSACTIONS AFFECTING THE INCOME STATEMENT AND/OR BALANCE SHEET

23. In its effort to use its assets to generate greater amounts of assets, a business typically encounters the following transactions involving revenue and expenses.

   a. Earned service revenue and received cash—Increase in cash (asset) and increase in revenue (retained earnings).

   b. Service revenue earned on account—Increase in accounts receivable (asset) and increase in revenue (retained earnings).

   c. Collected cash on accounts receivable—Increase in cash (asset) and decrease in accounts receivable (asset).

   d. Paid expenses such as wages or rent—Increase in expense (which decreases retained earnings) and decrease in cash (asset).

   e. Received bill for expense incurred during a period such as utilities—Increase in expense (which decreases retained earnings) and increase in accounts payable (liability).

SUMMARY OF BALANCE SHEET AND INCOME STATEMENT TRANSACTIONS

24. Illustration 1.3 in the text shows the summary of all of the balance sheet and income statement transactions.

DIVIDENDS PAID TO OWNERS (STOCKHOLDERS)

25. When owners (stockholders) receive assets (such as cash) from the company, the company's assets are decreased and the Dividends account is increased.

   a. Dividends do not appear on the income statement.

   b. Dividends are considered a distribution of earnings to the owner.

DEMONSTRATION PROBLEM

Asset, liability, and stockholders' equity titles for The Martin Service, Inc., are given in equation form below. At the left of the equation is a partial list of transactions completed during the month. Indicate the effect of each transaction on the items in the equation by writing a plus sign (+) below the item that is increased and a minus sign (−) below the item that is decreased.

	Assets				= Liabilities	+ Stockholders' Equity	
	Cash	+Accts. Rec.	+Equip- ment	+Land	=Accts. Pay.	+Capital Stock	+Retained Earnings
1. Stockholders invested cash by buying capital stock.							
2. Purchased land for cash.							
3. Performed services for cash customers.							
4. Paid rent for month.							
5. Purchased equipment on account.							
6. Performed services for charge customers.							
7. Paid for equipment purchased earlier on account.							
8. Received payment from charge customers.							
9. Sold equipment at cost for cash at no gain or loss.							
10. Paid dividends to stockholders.							
11. Returned defective equipment (purchased earlier) for cash.							
12. Made cash payment for monthly wages.							
13. Paid utilities for the period.							

SOLUTION TO DEMONSTRATION PROBLEM

	Assets				= Liabilities	+ Stockholders' Equity	
	Cash	+Accts. Rec.	+Equip-ment	+Land	=Accts. Pay.	+Capital Stock	+Retained Earnings
1. Stockholders invested cash by buying capital stock.	+					+	
2. Purchased land for cash.	−			+			
3. Performed services for cash customers.	+						+
4. Paid rent for month.	−						−
5. Purchased equipment on account.			+		+		
6. Performed services for charge customers.		+					+
7. Paid for equipment purchased earlier on account.	−				−		
8. Received payment from charge customers.	+	−					
9. Sold equipment at cost for cash at no gain or loss.	+		−				
10. Paid dividends to stockholders.	−						−
11. Returned defective equipment (purchased earlier) for cash.	+		−				
12. Made cash payment for monthly wages.	−						−
13. Paid utilities for the period.	−						−

MATCHING

Referring to the terms listed below, place the appropriate letter next to the corresponding description.

a. Accounting equation
b. Assets
c. Corporation
d. Dividends
e. Liabilities
f. Manufacturing company

g. Merchandising company
h. Net income
i. Net loss
j. Profitability
k. Salary expense

l. Service company
m. Single proprietorship
n. Solvency
o. Stockholders' equity
p. Transactions

_____ 1. Ability to generate earnings.
_____ 2. Cash paid to stockholders as distribution of income.
_____ 3. Exchanges of goods and services which are objective and which occur at an agreed-upon price.
_____ 4. An organization owned by stockholders and managed by officers who generally are people other than the owners.
_____ 5. Land, buildings, cash, and other resources owned by the business.
_____ 6. This type of business acquires materials and converts them into products to sell to other companies or final customers.
_____ 7. Creditor's equity or claims on assets.
_____ 8. An organization owned by one individual who is solely responsible for all debts of the business.
_____ 9. The resulting figure when expenses exceed revenues.
_____ 10. This type of business acquires goods and sells them in the same form to customers.
_____ 11. Ability to pay debts as they become due.
_____ 12. Stockholders' Equity = Assets − Liabilities is one form of this equation.

COMPLETION AND EXERCISES

1. The _____ _____ (sometimes called the statement of financial position) reflects a firm's solvency while the _____ _____ shows profitability.

2. Accounting deals primarily with information regarding _____ activities of a business and is expressed in _____ terms.

3. _____, _____, and _____ are the three forms of ownership of business organizations.

4. The balance sheet of a business corporation usually shows three classes of items, namely (a) _____, (b) _____, and (c) _____ _____; while the income statement shows two classes, namely, (a) _____ and (b) _____.

5. In its most basic form the accounting equation is simply _____ = _____. This is usually expanded to _____ = _____ + _____ _____.

6. Changes in the financial position of an organization are brought about by events, exchanges, and other real-world happenings that accountants measure and record and which they call _____.

7. To show your understanding of the effects of each of the named transactions on the assets, liabilities, and stockholders' equity of a business, fill in the blank in each column with either + (for increase), − (for decrease), or 0 (for no change).

	Assets	Liabilities	Stockholders' Equity
a. Stockholders invested cash in the business	_____	_____	_____
b. Borrowed money from a bank	_____	_____	_____
c. Purchased equipment on credit	_____	_____	_____
d. Rendered services for cash	_____	_____	_____
e. Paid creditor in (c)	_____	_____	_____
f. Paid monthly rent	_____	_____	_____
g. Rendered services for which the customer promised to pay at a later date	_____	_____	_____

8. Indicate, by letter, which of the above transactions would be reported in the income statement: _____, _____, and _____.

9. The inflows of assets for services rendered or goods delivered (as measured by the assets received from customers) are called _____, while the assets surrendered or consumed in this process are called _____.

10. The statement that shows the assets and equities of an entity as of a point in time is called the _____ _____.

11. The specific unit or organization for which accounting information is accumulated and reported is called the _____. The basis for valuation of assets in accounting is _____.

12. The _____ concept in accounting refers to the fact that the amounts entered in an accounting system are the objective money prices determined in the exchange process.

13. If expenses for a period exceed revenues for the same period, the entity is deemed to have suffered a _____ _____.

14. An income statement is prepared for a _____, while a balance sheet is prepared as of a _____.

15. Under the _____ concept, the accountant assumes that a business will continue more or less indefinitely.

16. Indicate the effect each of the following transactions has on the basic accounting equation by indicating one of the following:

A. Decrease in an asset, decrease in a liability.
B. Increase in an asset, increase in stockholders' equity.
C. Increase in one asset, decrease in another asset.
D. Increase in an asset, increase in a liability.
E. None of the above.

_____ 1. Purchased equipment on account.

_____ 2. Returned an item of defective equipment purchased in (1).

_____ 3. Paid cash to the supplier of equipment purchased in (1) for the remainder of the equipment.

_____ 4. Received cash on account from customers.

_____ 5. The stockholders invested additional cash in the business.

TRUE-FALSE QUESTIONS

Indicate whether each of the following statements is true or false by inserting a capital "T" or "F" in the blank space provided.

_____ 1. Assets are generally recorded at cost because this amount is the objective price determined in the exchange process.

_____ 2. The laws of incorporation of each state require that the partnership agreement list the duties of each partner and the distribution of income and loss to the partners.

_____ 3. Liabilities represent things of value owned by the business and are also known as resources.

_____ 4. Each partner may be held liable for the actions of other partners when they are acting within the scope of the business.

_____ 5. All increases in cash and accounts receivable represent revenues, which increase retained earnings.

_____ 6. Cash is increased when an outstanding account receivable is collected.

_____ 7. A creditor of the partnership has a claim against an individual partner's personal assets if the partnership has no cash.

_____ 8. The creditors of an organization are the companies and individual customers who owe the business for goods and services purchased on account.

_____ 9. Claims to or interests in assets are referred to as equities.

_____ 10. For an exchange to occur that is recorded as a transaction in the accounting records, both sides of the accounting equation must be affected.

_____ 11. Another way to express the accounting equation is: Assets − Stockholders' Equity = Liabilities.

_____ 12. Equities are composed of assets and stockholders' equity.

_____ 13. The accounting equation should be in balance only at the end of the year when the income of the period is determined.

MULTIPLE CHOICE QUESTIONS

For each of the following questions indicate the best answer by circling the appropriate letter.

1. The purchase of equipment for cash would:
   A. decrease an asset and decrease a liability.
   B. increase an asset and increase a liability.
   C. increase one asset and decrease another asset.
   D. increase an asset and increase stockholders' equity.
   E. None of the above.

2. The payment of cash to the supplier of services previously accounted for as a purchase on account would:
   A. increase an asset and increase a liability.
   B. increase an asset and increase stockholders' equity.
   C. increase one asset and decrease another asset.
   D. decrease an asset and decrease a liability.
   E. None of the above.

3. The return of defective equipment to the supplier before it is paid for would:
   A. increase an asset and increase stockholders' equity.
   B. decrease an asset and decrease a liability.
   C. increase an asset and increase a liability.
   D. increase one asset and decrease another asset.
   E. None of the above.

4. The receipt of cash on account from customers would:
   A. decrease an asset and decrease a liability.
   B. increase one asset and decrease another asset.
   C. increase an asset and increase stockholders' equity.
   D. increase an asset and increase a liability.
   E. None of the above.

5. Investment of additional cash in the business by the stockholders would:
   A. decrease an asset and decrease a liability.
   B. increase an asset and increase a liability.
   C. increase an asset and increase stockholders' equity.
   D. increase one asset and decrease another asset.
   E. None of the above.

6. In accounting, the resources of a business organization are called:
   A. assets.
   B. proprietorship.
   C. creditors' equity.
   D. stockholders' equity.
   E. None of the above.

7. The payment of business debts:
   A. increases a liability account.
   B. increases stockholders' equity.
   C. has no effect on stockholders' equity.
   D. increases assets.

8. If liabilities have increased by exactly the same amount that assets have increased, stockholders' equity will have:

   A. remained the same.
   B. decreased.
   C. increased.
   D. decreased more than increased.

9. A financial statement that has a date line similar to "For the month ended June 30, 19X1," is a:

   A. Schedule of accounts receivable.
   B. Balance sheet.
   C. Income statement.
   D. None of the above.

10. Gomex Company collected $600 of its $12,000 accounts receivable. How is the balance sheet affected?

   A. Cash increased $600, and Retained Earnings increased $600 because revenue was received.
   B. Accounts Receivable is decreased by $600, and Retained Earnings is decreased by $600.
   C. Total assets are decreased, but liabilities and stockholders' equity remain the same.
   D. There is no change in total assets, liabilities, or stockholders' equity.
   E. There is no change in any of the balance sheet items.

SOLUTIONS

Matching

1.	j	7.	e
2.	d	8.	m
3.	p	9.	i
4.	c	10.	g
5.	b	11.	n
6.	f	12.	a

Completion and Exercises

1. balance sheet; income statement
2. economic; monetary
3. Single proprietorship, partnership, and corporation
4. (a) assets; (b) liabilities; (c) stockholders' equity; (a) revenues; (b) expenses
5. Assets = Equities; Assets = Liabilities + Stockholders' Equity
6. transactions

7.

	Assets	Liabilities	Stockholders' Equity
a.	+	0	+
b.	+	+	0
c.	+	+	0
d.	+	0	+
e.	−	−	0
f.	−	0	−
g.	+	0	+

8. (d), (f), and (g)
9. revenues; expenses

10. balance sheet
11. entity; cost
12. cost
13. net loss
14. period; date
15. continuity

16. 1. D
    2. A
    3. A
    4. C
    5. B

True-False Questions

1. T
2. F   The partnership agreement lists the duties of each partner and the income and loss distribution. Each state's laws of incorporation apply to corporations.
3. F   This statement is the definition of assets; liabilities are debts of the business.
4. T
5. F   Cash received from a customer on account does not necessarily represent revenue; revenue is recognized at the time the service is performed, not when cash is received. However, it is true that revenues increase retained earnings.
6. T
7. T
8. F   The creditors are the companies and individuals to whom debts of the company are owed. This statement describes customers.
9. T
10. F   A transaction may occur that involves only one side of the equation; for example, cash received from a customer in payment of an account receivable.
11. T
12. F   Equities are composed of liabilities (creditors' equity) and stockholders' equity.
13. F   The accounting equation should be in balance at all times.

Multiple Choice Questions

1. C
2. D
3. B
4. B
5. C
6. A
7. C   Cash is decreased and liabilities are decreased; thus, there is no effect on stockholders' equity.
8. A
9. C
10. D   Cash and accounts receivable are both assets, and total assets do not change.

2 RECORDING BUSINESS TRANSACTIONS

Learning Objectives

1. *Use the account as the basic classifying and storage unit for accounting information.*
2. *Express the effects of business transactions in terms of debits and credits to different types of accounts.*
3. *Record the effects of business transactions in a journal.*
4. *Post journal entries to the accounts in the ledger.*
5. *Prepare a trial balance to test the equality of debits and credits in the journalizing and posting process.*

CHAPTER OUTLINE

THE ACCOUNT AND RULES OF DEBIT AND CREDIT

1. Steps in recording and posting the effects of a business transaction are:
    a. The company enters into a business transaction.
    b. The business transaction is evidenced by a source document.
    c. The source document serves as the basis for preparing a journal entry.
    d. The journal entry is posted to accounts in the ledger.

THE ACCOUNT

2. An account is used to classify and summarize measurements of business activity.
    a. Accounts are established where it is necessary to provide useful information about particular business items.
    b. A variety of formats can be used for accounts such as a printed format in a bound book or an invisible encoding on magnetic tape.
    c. Every account format must provide for increases and decreases in that particular item.
    d. The number of accounts will vary in an accounting system.
    e. The primary requirement is that the account provides useful information.

THE T-ACCOUNT

3. The T-account format is used in the textbook for illustration, with increases recorded on one side and decreases on the opposite side of the T-account.

DEBITS AND CREDITS

4. Debits are entries on the left side of the ledger account.
    a. Dr. is the abbreviation, and another name for debit is "charge."
    b. A debit entry simply means an entry on the left side.

5. Credits are entries on the right side of the ledger account.
    a. Cr. is the abbreviation for a credit.
    b. The right side of *all* accounts is the credit side, and the left side is the debit side.

DOUBLE-ENTRY PROCEDURE

6. *Increases* in *assets* are recorded on the debit or left side, while decreases are recorded on the credit or right side.

7. Since liabilities and stockholders' equity are on the opposite side of the accounting equation, increases and decreases are recorded opposite to assets.
    a. Increases in liabilities and stockholders' equity are credits.
    b. Decreases in liabilities and stockholders' equity are debits.

8. Expenses and revenues could be recorded directly in the Retained Earnings account; but the volume of transactions involved prevents this approach from being recommended.
    a. Instead, expense and revenue ledger accounts are established.
        1. Increases in revenues are recorded as credits and decreases as debits. (Note that revenues increase retained earnings.)
        2. Increases in expenses are recorded as debits, and decreases as credits. (Note that expenses decrease retained earnings.)

9. Distribution of assets to the stockholders are recorded in a separate account and have the same effect as expenses on stockholders' equity.
    a. The Dividends account is increased by debits and decreased by credits.

DETERMINING THE BALANCE OF AN ACCOUNT

10. The balance of an account is determined by subtracting the smaller sum of the debit or credit side from the larger total; if the sum of the credits exceeds the debit total, the account has a credit balance.

NORMAL BALANCES

11. The normal balances follow the pattern of increases in the account:

Type of Account	Normal Balance
Assets	Debit
Expenses	Debit
Dividends	Debit
Liabilities	Credit
Stockholders' Equity	Credit
Revenue	Credit

RULES OF DEBIT AND CREDIT SUMMARIZED

12. The double-entry procedure, which keeps the accounting equation in balance, requires that an entry must have equal debit and credit amounts.

THE JOURNAL

13. A journal is a record of business transactions arranged in order of time.

   a. A journal entry reflects the effects of a business transaction expressed in debits and credits.
   b. A journal is called the book of original entry because each transaction is recorded here first.

THE GENERAL JOURNAL

14. A general journal contains:

   a. Date column—the first entry on a page contains year, month, and day; for other entries, only the day is shown until the month changes.
   b. Account titles and explanation column—the first line shows the account debited and the second line shows the account credited. An explanation is included on the next line if needed.
   c. Posting reference column—shows the account number to which the debit or credit amount has been posted in the ledger.
   d. Debit column—where the debit amount is placed.
   e. Credit column—where the credit amount is placed.

JOURNALIZING

15. Journalizing is the recording in terms of debits and credits of the effects on specific accounts of business information from source documents.

FUNCTIONS AND ADVANTAGES OF A JOURNAL

16. The functions and advantages of using a journal are:

   a. Records each transaction in chronological order.
   b. Shows the analysis of each transaction in terms of debit and credit.
   c. Supplies an explanation of each transaction when necessary.
   d. Serves as a source for future reference to accounting transactions.
   e. Removes lengthy explanations from the accounts.
   f. Makes possible posting to the ledger at convenient times.
   g. Assists in maintaining the ledger in balance.
   h. Aids in tracing errors.

THE LEDGER

17. The ledger contains all the company's accounts, which are classified into balance sheet accounts and income statement accounts.
    a. Balance sheet accounts are called *real* accounts because they are not subdivisions of other accounts.
    b. Income statement accounts are called *nominal* accounts because they are subdivisions of stockholders' equity accounts.
    c. A complete listing of all accounts in the ledger with their titles and account numbers is known as the *chart of accounts*.
    d. The typical sequencing of the accounts in the ledger is: assets, liabilities, stockholders' equity, dividends, revenues, and expenses.

THE ACCOUNTING PROCESS IN OPERATION

18. The text contains a detailed illustration of the accounting process in operation.

THE RECORDING OF TRANSACTIONS AND THEIR EFFECTS ON THE ACCOUNTS

19. Examples of transactions and their effects on accounts are given on pages 65-75 of the text.

THE USE OF THREE-COLUMN LEDGER ACCOUNTS

20. In practice, companies normally use three-column ledger accounts rather than T-accounts.

POSTING TO THREE-COLUMN LEDGER ACCOUNTS

21. Posting is recording in the ledger the information contained in the journal.
    a. Posting carries out the instructions in the journal.
    b. Posting may be made to a three-column ledger account, which has columns for debit, credit, and balance.

CROSS-INDEXING (REFERENCING)

22. Cross-indexing is a means by which the journal and the ledger are tied together; it involves placing the account number in the journal's posting reference column and placing the journal page number in the ledger account.

COMPOUND JOURNAL ENTRIES

23. A *compound journal entry* has more than one debit and/or credit, while a simple journal entry has only one debit and one credit.

POSTING AND CROSS-INDEXING—AN ILLUSTRATION

24. Illustrations 2.6 and 2.7 in the text illustrate the journalizing and posting process.

THE TRIAL BALANCE

25. A trial balance lists the ledger accounts and their debit and credit balances to determine that debits equal credits.
    a. A trial balance is a means of checking the equality of debits and credits.
    b. An inequality of debit and credit column totals signals an error; however, an error may be present even if these totals are equal.
    c. A trial balance may be prepared at any time, but one is usually prepared before financial statements are prepared.

DEMONSTRATION PROBLEM

Dexter Company informs you that the following business transactions occurred in 1994:

May 1 Stockholders exchanged $15,000 cash and equipment with a value of $4,000 for capital stock.

1 A building costing $39,000 and land costing $20,000 were purchased. Cash in the amount of $5,000 was paid and a mortgage note was given for the remainder.

2 Premiums for property insurance were paid in the amount of $1,500 for May.

3 Supplies costing $500 and equipment costing $6,000 were purchased on account.

15 Cash received for professional services performed, $5,600; other clients were billed for services in the amount of $2,430.

16 Paid cash to creditors on account, $1,800.

20 Returned portion of the supplies costing $240 since they were not of the proper grade.

22 Received $1,880 cash from clients on account.

31 Paid utility bill for May, $500.

31 Paid monthly salaries, $3,000.

31 Recorded additional amount owed by clients for services performed in May, $4,900; payment is due within 30 days.

Required:

a. Open three-column ledger accounts for Dexter Company using the following accounts:

Cash	Mortgage Note Payable
Accounts Receivable	Capital Stock
Supplies on Hand	Service Revenue
Equipment	Salaries Expense
Buildings	Utilities Expense
Land	Insurance Expense
Accounts Payable	

Use the account numbers shown in the chart of accounts on the inside cover of your textbook.

Record the above transactions in a general journal. (Omit explanations)

b. Post the journal entries to the ledger accounts. (Omit explanations)

c. Prepare a trial balance as of May 31, 1994.

d. Determine the following:

(1) Total revenue for the month.

(2) Total expenses for the month.

a.

GENERAL JOURNAL

DATE		ACCOUNT TITLES AND EXPLANATION	POST. REF.	DEBIT	CREDIT

b.

			ACCOUNT NO.		
DATE	EXPLANATION	POST. REF.	DEBIT	CREDIT	BALANCE

			ACCOUNT NO.		
DATE	EXPLANATION	POST. REF.	DEBIT	CREDIT	BALANCE

			ACCOUNT NO.		
DATE	EXPLANATION	POST. REF.	DEBIT	CREDIT	BALANCE

b. *(continued)*

ACCOUNT NO. _____

	DATE		EXPLANATION	POST. REF.	DEBIT	CREDIT	BALANCE

ACCOUNT NO. _____

	DATE		EXPLANATION	POST. REF.	DEBIT	CREDIT	BALANCE

ACCOUNT NO. _____

	DATE		EXPLANATION	POST. REF.	DEBIT	CREDIT	BALANCE

ACCOUNT NO. _____

	DATE		EXPLANATION	POST. REF.	DEBIT	CREDIT	BALANCE

ACCOUNT NO. _____

	DATE		EXPLANATION	POST. REF.	DEBIT	CREDIT	BALANCE

ACCOUNT NO. _____

	DATE		EXPLANATION	POST. REF.	DEBIT	CREDIT	BALANCE

ACCOUNT NO. _____

	DATE		EXPLANATION	POST. REF.	DEBIT	CREDIT	BALANCE

b. *(concluded)*

ACCOUNT NO.

DATE	EXPLANATION	POST. REF.	DEBIT	CREDIT	BALANCE

ACCOUNT NO.

DATE	EXPLANATION	POST. REF.	DEBIT	CREDIT	BALANCE

ACCOUNT NO.

DATE	EXPLANATION	POST. REF.	DEBIT	CREDIT	BALANCE

c.

d. (1)

(2)

a.

DEXTER COMPANY
General Journal

Page 1

DATE	ACCOUNT TITLES AND EXPLANATION	POST. REF.	DEBIT	CREDIT
1994				
May 1	Cash	100	15,000	
	Equipment	170	4,000	
	Capital Stock	300		19,000
1	Buildings	140	39,000	
	Land	130	20,000	
	Cash	100		5,000
	Mortgage Note Payable	218		54,000
2	Insurance Expense	512	1,500	
	Cash	100		1,500
3	Supplies on Hand	107	500	
	Equipment	170	6,000	
	Accounts Payable	200		6,500
15	Cash	100	5,600	
	Accounts Receivable	103	2,430	
	Service Revenue	400		8,030
16	Accounts Payable	200	1,800	
	Cash	100		1,800
20	Accounts Payable	200	240	
	Supplies on Hand	107		240
22	Cash	100	1,880	
	Accounts Receivable	103		1,880
31	Utilities Expense	511	500	
	Cash	100		500
31	Salaries Expense	507	3,000	
	Cash	100		3,000
31	Accounts Receivable	103	4,900	
	Service Revenue	400		4,900

b.

DEXTER COMPANY
General Ledger

Cash   ACCOUNT NO. 100

DATE	EXPLANATION	POST. REF.	DEBIT	CREDIT	BALANCE
1994					
May 1		G1	15,000		15,000 Dr.
1		G1		5,000	10,000 Dr.
2		G1		1,500	8,500 Dr.
15		G1	5,600		14,100 Dr.
16		G1		1,800	12,300 Dr.
22		G1	1,880		14,180 Dr.
31		G1		500	13,680 Dr.
31		G1		3,000	10,680 Dr.

Accounts Receivable   ACCOUNT NO. 103

DATE	EXPLANATION	POST. REF.	DEBIT	CREDIT	BALANCE
1994					
May 15		G1	2,430		2,430 Dr.
22		G1		1,880	550 Dr.
31		G1	4,900		5,450 Dr.

Supplies on Hand   ACCOUNT NO. 107

DATE	EXPLANATION	POST. REF.	DEBIT	CREDIT	BALANCE
1994					
May 3		G1	500		500 Dr.
20		G1		240	260 Dr.

Land   ACCOUNT NO. 130

DATE	EXPLANATION	POST. REF.	DEBIT	CREDIT	BALANCE
1994					
May 1		G1	20,000		20,000 Dr.

Buildings   ACCOUNT NO. 140

DATE	EXPLANATION	POST. REF.	DEBIT	CREDIT	BALANCE
1994					
May 1		G1	39,000		39,000 Dr.

Equipment   ACCOUNT NO. 170

DATE	EXPLANATION	POST. REF.	DEBIT	CREDIT	BALANCE
1994					
May 1		G1	4,000		4,000 Dr.
3		G1	6,000		10,000 Dr.

b. *(continued)*   DEXTER COMPANY

Accounts Payable   ACCOUNT NO. 200

DATE	EXPLANATION	POST. REF.	DEBIT	CREDIT	BALANCE
1994					
May 3		G1		6,500	6,500 Cr.
16		G1	1,800		4,700 Cr.
20		G1	240		4,460 Cr.

Mortgage Note Payable   ACCOUNT NO. 218

DATE	EXPLANATION	POST. REF.	DEBIT	CREDIT	BALANCE
1994					
May 1		G1		54,000	54,000 Cr.

Capital Stock   ACCOUNT NO. 300

DATE	EXPLANATION	POST. REF.	DEBIT	CREDIT	BALANCE
1994					
May 1		G1		19,000	19,000 Cr.

Service Revenue   ACCOUNT NO. 400

DATE	EXPLANATION	POST. REF.	DEBIT	CREDIT	BALANCE
1994					
May 15		G1		8,030	8,030 Cr.
31		G1		4,900	12,930 Cr.

Salaries Expense   ACCOUNT NO. 507

DATE	EXPLANATION	POST. REF.	DEBIT	CREDIT	BALANCE
1994					
May 31		G1	3,000		3,000 Dr.

Utilities Expense   ACCOUNT NO. 511

DATE	EXPLANATION	POST. REF.	DEBIT	CREDIT	BALANCE
1994					
May 31		G1	500		500 Dr.

Insurance Expense   ACCOUNT NO. 512

DATE	EXPLANATION	POST. REF.	DEBIT	CREDIT	BALANCE
1994					
May 2		G1	1,500		1,500 Dr.

c.

DEXTER COMPANY
Trial Balance
May 31, 1994

Acct.
No.

100	Cash	10,680	
103	Accounts Receivable	5,450	
107	Supplies on Hand	260	
130	Land	20,000	
140	Buildings	39,000	
170	Equipment	10,000	
200	Accounts Payable		4,460
218	Mortgage Note Payable		54,000
300	Capital Stock		19,000
400	Service Revenue		12,930
507	Salaries Expense	3,000	
511	Utilities Expense	500	
512	Insurance Expense	1,500	
		$90,390	$90,390

d. (1) $12,930
   (2) $5,000 = ($3,000 + $500 + $1,500)

MATCHING

Referring to the terms listed below, place the appropriate letter next to the corresponding description.

a.	Charge	f.	Double entry	k.	Posting
b.	Compound journal entry	g.	Expenses	l.	Real accounts
c.	Credit side	h.	Journal	m.	Simple journal entry
d.	Cross-indexing	i.	Journalizing	n.	Trial balance
e.	Debit side	j.	Nominal accounts		

_____ 1. Synonym for debit.

_____ 2. Cost of the use of services or consumption of assets for the purpose of generating revenue.

_____ 3. Entry involving more than one debit and/or credit.

_____ 4. Recording in the ledger the information contained in the journal.

_____ 5. Entering of a transaction in the book of original entry.

_____ 6. The right side of an account.

_____ 7. This procedure is related to the duality concept indicating that every transaction has a two-sided effect.

_____ 8. Revenue and expense accounts that appear on the income statement.

_____ 9. Placing of the ledger account numbers in the posing reference column of the journal and placing the journal page number in the posting reference column of the ledger account.

_____ 10. A chronological record of all business transactions that may also be called the book of original entry.

_____ 11. Entry involving only one debit and one credit.

_____ 12. Provides a proof of the arithmetic accuracy of the recording process by listing the ledger accounts and their debit or credit balances.

1. The act of entering a transaction in a journal is called _____. After a transaction is so entered, it is _____ from the journal to the _____, at which time a process known as _____ _____ also takes place so that amounts in the accounts can be readily traced to the original record of each transaction.

2. Accountants do not speak in terms of increases and decreases. Rather, they use technical terminology. Thus, to _____ an account means to place an entry on the left side of the account; to _____ an account means to place an entry on the right side of the account.

3. The _____ _____ procedure requires that an entry has equal debits and credits, which keeps the accounting equation in balance.

4. For each of the following T-accounts, indicate on which side increases are recorded and on which side decreases are recorded:

Assets	Liabilities	Stockholders' Equity

5. From Question 4 it follows that assets, which appear on the left side of a balance sheet, will have balances on the _____ side of the account. Conversely, liabilities and stockholders' equity items will appear on the right side of the balance sheet and have balances on the _____ side of the account.

6. Fill in the blanks below with the word *debits* or *credits*:

Type of account	Increased by	Decreased by
Asset	_____	_____
Liability	_____	_____
Stockholders' equity	_____	_____
Revenue	_____	_____
Expense	_____	_____

7. A _____ _____ contains a listing of the ledger accounts and their debit or credit balances to determine that _____ equal _____ in the recording process.

8. Collectively, all of the accounts in the accounting system are referred to as the _____. The list of accounts in an accounting system (often together with their numbers) is called the _____ _____ _____.

9. The basic unit in which data are stored in an accounting system is called an _____. These storage units should be so constructed as to readily receive money measurements of the _____ or _____ in the items for which they are established.

10. Whether or not an account is established is determined largely by whether or not it will provide _____ _____.

11. The difference between the amounts entered as increases in an account and those entered as decreases is called the _____ of the account.

12. Since revenues increase Retained Earnings and increases in Retained Earnings are recorded on the _____ side of the account, it follows that increases in revenues are recorded on the _____ side of the account.

13. Since expenses decrease Retained Earnings and since decreases in Retained Earnings are recorded on the _____ side of the account, it follows that increases in expenses are recorded on the _____ side of the account.

14. Prepare journal entries for the company that engaged in the following transactions:
Jan. 1 Stockholders invested $10,000 cash in the business.
10 Paid the rent for January, $100.
13 Performed services for customers who promised to pay later, $125.
20 Purchased equipment for $2,000 with a promise to pay later.
30 Received payment for the services rendered on January 13.

GENERAL JOURNAL   Page 1

DATE	ACCOUNT TITLES AND EXPLANATION	POST. REF.	DEBIT	CREDIT

15. Post the journal entries prepared in Question 14. Use the chart of accounts on the inside covers of your text to assign account numbers.

DATE	EXPLANATION	POST. REF.	DEBIT	CREDIT	BALANCE

DATE	EXPLANATION	POST. REF.	DEBIT	CREDIT	BALANCE

DATE	EXPLANATION	POST. REF.	DEBIT	CREDIT	BALANCE

DATE	EXPLANATION	POST. REF.	DEBIT	CREDIT	BALANCE

DATE	EXPLANATION	POST. REF.	DEBIT	CREDIT	BALANCE

DATE	EXPLANATION	POST. REF.	DEBIT	CREDIT	BALANCE

DATE	EXPLANATION	POST. REF.	DEBIT	CREDIT	BALANCE

16. A _____ is often called a book of original entry and contains a chronological record of the transactions of a business. Before a transaction can be entered in this book of original entry, its effects on the business must be determined and encoded in terms of _____ and _____ .

17. The properties used by a business are known as _____; whereas the rights in the properties of a business are known as _____ .

18. A sale made to a customer or client is recorded as an increase in a revenue account and an increase in an _____ account.

19. The total assets of the Miller Service Company are $22,000 and the total liabilities are $10,000. Therefore, the total stockholders' equity is $ _____ .

20. An entry on the left side of an account is known as a _____ .

21. At the start of a year a company had liabilities of $35,000 and stockholders' equity of $150,000. Net income for the year was $50,000, and $11,000 cash was distributed to the stockholders as dividends. Compute stockholders' equity at the end of the year and total assets at the beginning of the year.

    Stockholders' equity at end of year: _____

    Total assets at beginning of year: _____

22. Explain each of the sets of debits and credits shown in the accounts below. There are twelve transactions to be explained. Each set is designated by the small letters to the left of the account.

Cash

(a)	75,000	(c)	20,000
(d)	1,500	(e)	1,000
		(g)	500
		(j)	1,800
		(k)	200

Accounts Receivable

(b)	2,600	(d)	1,500
(i)	5,000		

Supplies

(f)	800	(h)	100

Service Equipment

(c)	20,000		
(l)	40,000		

Accounts Payable

(g)	500	(f)	800
(h)	100	(l)	40,000

Capital Stock

	(a)	75,000

Service Revenue

	(b)	2,600
	(i)	5,000

Salaries Expense

(e)	1,000

Rent Expense

(j)	1,800

Utilities Expense

(k)	200

23. At the beginning of 1994, the total assets of Hardy Corp. were $2,500,000, the total liabilities were $1,500,000 and the stockholders' equity was $1,000,000. Hardy has earned $500,000 in 1994 and paid dividends of $50,000. The only transaction that affected Hardy's liability accounts was the redemption of its notes payable, $100,000. Compute total assets, total liabilities, and stockholders' equity at the end of the year.

TRUE-FALSE QUESTIONS

Indicate whether each of the following statements is true or false by inserting a capital "T" or "F" in the blank space provided.

_____ 1. Liabilities represent claims against the company's assets and may be in the form of accounts payable or notes payable.

_____ 2. Posting a transaction requires more knowledge than journalizing a transaction.

_____ 3. The primary function of the general ledger is to store transactions by account classification and to provide a balance for each account.

_____ 4. Since a particular journal entry has equal debits and credits, this entry must be correct.

_____ 5. A debit to the Dividends account would indicate an increase in expenses.

_____ 6. Expense accounts usually have debit balances and show the cost associated with producing revenue during an accounting period.

_____ 7. A purchase of land or equipment for cash would cause total assets to increase by the cost of the land or equipment.

_____ 8. One of the purposes of a ledger account is to record the complete effect of a transaction in one place.

_____ 9. Assets are recorded at cost for accounting purposes because cost is subjective and market value is objective.

_____ 10. Transactions are recorded in the journal in chronological order.

_____ 11. The trial balance would automatically reveal the following error: Land was purchased for cash but instead of crediting cash, the credit was made to Accounts Receivable.

_____ 12. Account numbers are entered in the posting reference column of the two-column general journal at the time the transactions are recorded in the ledger accounts.

_____ 13. If only two liability accounts are affected by a transaction, the balance of one account must be increased and the balance of the other decreased in recording this transaction.

_____ 14. The Office Equipment account normally has a credit balance.

_____ 15. Revenue is the difference between the selling price of a service and the cost of providing such service.

_____ 16. A trial balance proves that no errors were made in recording transactions, posting, and in preparing the trial balance.

_____ 17. A journal aids in the division of labor by allowing one person to journalize entries while another individual may post these entries.

_____ 18. Every transaction always affects two or more accounts in a double-entry accounting system.

_____ 19. All of the accounts of a specific business enterprise are referred to as a ledger.

_____ 20. Even though an expense is recognized on the income statement, it may not require an equivalent outlay of cash in that same period.

_____ 21. A general journal entry having two debits and a credit is a compound entry.

_____ 22. A purchase of an asset for immediate consumption that will not be paid for until next month would cause liabilities to increase and stockholders' equity to decrease this month.

_____ 23. A liability account normally has a debit balance.

_____ 24. A journal provides a complete collection of all of the accounts of an entity.

_____ 25. A cash expenditure for insurance and utilities would cause assets to increase but stockholders' equity to decrease.

MULTIPLE CHOICE QUESTIONS

For each of the following questions indicate the best answer by circling the appropriate letter.

1. The determination of periodic net income involves comparing (1) the revenue recognized during the period and (2) the expenses to be allocated to the period. This procedure is frequently referred to as:
   A. cost accounting.
   B. double-entry accounting.
   C. balancing the accounts.
   D. matching of revenues and expenses.
   E. None of these.

2. A company returned for credit a portion of the office supplies purchased previously for future use on credit. What entry is required?
   A. Debit Office Supplies on Hand; credit Cash
   B. Debit Cash; credit Office Supplies on Hand and Office Equipment
   C. Debit Accounts Payable; credit Office Supplies on Hand
   D. Debit Office Equipment; credit Office Supplies Expense

3. A company purchased equipment for $1,000 cash; the journal entry to record this purchase is:

   A. Equipment 1,000
      Accounts Payable   1,000
   B. Cash 1,000
      Equipment   1,000
   C. Supplies on Hand 1,000
      Cash   1,000
   D. Equipment 1,000
      Capital   1,000
   E. None of the above.

4. A company received $600 for services performed in the current period. What is the entry?

   A. Cash 600
      Service Revenue   600
   B. Accounts Receivable 600
      Cash   600
   C. Cash 600
      Accounts Payable   600
   D. Service Revenue 600
      Accounts Receivable   600
   E. None of the above.

5. Which of the following is(are) descriptive of an asset?
   A. It is something of value because it can be used to produce products of the business.
   B. It has value because it has service potential.
   C. It is owned and/or under the control of the business.
   D. (A), (B), and (C) are all correct.

6. A company purchased office equipment and office supplies on credit from Doug Equipment Company. What is the entry?
   A. Debit Office Equipment; credit Accounts Payable
   B. Debit Equipment; credit Office Supplies Expense
   C. Debit Office Equipment and Office Supplies on Hand; credit Cash
   D. Debit Office Equipment, debit Office Supplies on Hand; credit Accounts Payable

7. Expenses for an accounting period are:
   A. the costs of goods and/or services consumed in the earning of the revenue of the period.
   B. former assets whose usefulness expired this period in the earning of revenues.
   C. only the amounts actually paid for services used during the period.
   D. (A) and (B), but not (C).

8. Stockholders' equity is the term applied to which of the following?

   A. Amount of cash the stockholders invested in the company 10 years ago.
   B. Residual claim against the assets of the business after the total liabilities are deducted.
   C. Is also referred to as net worth.
   D. Residual cash of the business after the total liabilities are deducted.
   E. B and C are correct.

9. A law firm completed legal work for Public Service Company on credit. What entry should be made on the law firm's books?

   A. Debit Accounts Receivable; credit Legal Fees Revenue
   B. Debit Legal Fees Revenue; credit Cash
   C. Debit Cash; credit Capital Stock
   D. Debit Cash; credit Legal Fees Revenue

10. If $500 cash and a $2,000 note are given in exchange for a delivery truck for use in a business:

    A. the stockholders' equity is increased.
    B. total assets are decreased.
    C. total liabilities are decreased.
    D. None of the above.

11. Which of the following is *not* a business asset?

    A. Cash
    B. Capital stock
    C. Equipment
    D. Accounts receivable
    E. All of the above are business assets.

12. A $150 debit to Office Equipment was entered in the account as a $150 credit. This error caused the trial balance to be out of balance by:

    A. $75
    B. $150
    C. $450
    D. $300
    E. None of these.

13. Debit entries:

    A. increase assets; and decrease expenses, liabilities, revenues, and stockholders' equity.
    B. increase assets and stockholders' equity; and decrease expenses and revenues.
    C. decrease assets and expenses; and increase liabilities, revenues, and stockholders' equity.
    D. decrease assets and revenues; and increase expenses, liabilities, and stockholders' equity.
    E. increase assets and expenses; and decrease liabilities, revenues, and stockholders' equity.

14. Which of the following statements about the accounting equation is *not* true?

    A. A transaction may add to both sides of the equation.
    B. A transaction may add to two items on the same side of the equation.
    C. A transaction may transfer between the terms on one side of the equation and have no effect on the other side of the equation.
    D. A transaction may subtract from both sides of the equation.

SOLUTIONS

Matching

1.	a	7.	f
2.	g	8.	j
3.	b	9.	d
4.	k	10.	h
5.	i	11.	m
6.	c	12.	n

Completion and Exercises

1. journalizing; posted; ledger; cross-indexing
2. debit; credit
3. double-entry
4.

Assets		Liabilities		Stockholders' Equity	
increases	decreases	decreases	increases	decreases	increases

5. left; right
6.

Type of account	Increased by	Decreased by
Asset	Debits	Credits
Liability	Credits	Debits
Stockholders' equity	Credits	Debits
Revenue	Credits	Debits
Expense	Debits	Credits

7. trial balance; debits; credits
8. ledger; chart of accounts
9. account; increases; decreases
10. useful information
11. balance
12. right; right
13. left; left

14.

Page 1

DATE		ACCOUNT TITLES AND EXPLANATION	POST. REF.	DEBIT	CREDIT
Jan.	1	Cash	100	10,000.00	
		Capital Stock	300		10,000.00
		Cash invested in business.			
	10	Rent Expense	515	100.00	
		Cash	100		100.00
		Rent for January 19—.			
	13	Accounts Receivable	103	125.00	
		Service Revenue	400		125.00
		To record fees earned for services.			
	20	Equipment	170	2,000.00	
		Accounts Payable	200		2,000.00
		Purchased equipment on credit.			
	30	Cash	100	125.00	
		Accounts Recievable	103		125.00
		Received cash on account.			

15.

Cash   ACCOUNT NO. 100

DATE		EXPLANATION	POST. REF.	DEBIT	CREDIT	BALANCE
19—						
Jan.	1		G1	10,000.00		10,000.00
	10		G1		100.00	9,900.00
	30		G1	125.00		10,025.00

Accounts Receivable   ACCOUNT NO. 103

DATE		EXPLANATION	POST. REF.	DEBIT	CREDIT	BALANCE
19—						
Jan.	13		G1	125.00		125.00
	30		G1		125.00	0

Equipment   ACCOUNT NO. 170

DATE		EXPLANATION	POST. REF.	DEBIT	CREDIT	BALANCE
19—						
Jan.	20		G1	2,000.00		2,000.00

Accounts Payable   ACCOUNT NO. 200

DATE		EXPLANATION	POST. REF.	DEBIT	CREDIT	BALANCE
19—						
Jan.	20		G1		2,000.00	2,000.00

Capital Stock

ACCOUNT NO. 300

DATE	EXPLANATION	POST. REF.	DEBIT	CREDIT	BALANCE
19— Jan. 1		G1		10,000.00	10,000.00

Service Revenue

ACCOUNT NO. 400

DATE	EXPLANATION	POST. REF.	DEBIT	CREDIT	BALANCE
19— Jan. 13		G1		125.00	125.00

Rent Expense

ACCOUNT NO. 515

DATE	EXPLANATION	POST. REF.	DEBIT	CREDIT	BALANCE
19— Jan. 10		G1	100.00		100.00

16. journal; debit(s); credit(s)
17. assets; equities
18. asset
19. $12,000
20. debit
21. Stockholders' equity at end of year: $150,000 + $50,000 − $11,000 = $189,000
    Total assets at beginning of year: $35,000 + $150,000 = $185,000
22. (a) Investment of cash in business by stockholders
    (b) Services performed on account
    (c) Service equipment purchased for cash
    (d) Cash collected on account
    (e) Salaries paid in cash
    (f) Supplies purchased on account
    (g) Cash paid on accounts payable
    (h) Supplies returned for credit
    (i) Services performed on account
    (j) Cash paid for rent expense
    (k) Cash paid for utilities expense
    (l) Service equipment purchased on account
23. Stockholders' equity at the end of the year = $1,000,000 + $500,000 − $50,000 = $1,450,000
    Total liabilities = $1,500,000 − $100,000 = $1,400,000
    Total assets = $1,450,000 + $1,400,000 = $2,850.000

True-False Questions

1. T
2. F Journalizing requires the knowledge of determining the effect of the transaction on the accounting equation, while posting involves transferring the data from the journal to the proper accounts.
3. T
4. F A wrong ledger account could have been used.
5. F A debit to the Dividends account indicates payments of cash or other assets to the stockholders. Dividends are not expenses.
6. T

7. F Total assets would remain unchanged because cash would decrease by the same amount land or equipment increased.
8. F A journal records the complete effect of a transaction in one place.
9. F Cost is objective, and market value is subjective.
10. T
11. F The trial balance would be of limited assistance in locating this error because the total of the debit balances would equal the total of the credit balances. The trial balance does not call attention to errors of this type.
12. T Account numbers are entered when the journal entries have been posted to ledger accounts.
13. T
14. F Assets normally have debit balances.
15. F Revenue is the selling price of a service; net income is the difference between revenue and expenses.
16. F A trial balance only proves that debit balances equal credit balances.
17. T
18. T
19. T
20. T Using the accrual system, expenses are recognized in the period in which incurred rather than when cash is paid.
21. T
22. T An expense and a liability have been incurred; expenses decrease stockholders' equity.
23. F A liability account normally has a credit balance.
24. F A ledger provides a complete collection of all of the accounts of an entity; a journal provides a source of reference for the future by providing a chronological record of all financial events.
25. F Assets would decrease by the amount of cash expenditure; stockholders' equity would decrease because of these expenses.

Multiple Choice Questions

1. D
2. C
3. E The correct entry is to debit Equipment and credit Cash for $1,000.
4. A
5. D
6. D
7. D
8. E There is no direct relationship between the amount of cash a company has and the balance in the stockholders' equity account.
9. A
10. D Total assets are increased by $2,000 ($2,500 delivery truck − $500 cash given up), and total liabilities are increased by $2,000.
11. B Capital stock is not a business asset.
12. D $150 × 2 = $300 error; $150 was missing from the debit side that should have been there, while $150 was included on the credit side that should not have appeared.
13. E
14. B

3 ADJUSTING THE ACCOUNTS

Learning Objectives

1. *Describe the basic characteristics of the cash basis and the accrual basis of accounting.*
2. *Identify the reasons why adjusting entries must be made.*
3. *Identify the classes and types of adjusting entries.*
4. *Prepare adjusting entries.*
5. *Determine the effects of failing to prepare adjusting entries.*

CHAPTER OUTLINE

CASH VERSUS ACCRUAL BASIS ACCOUNTING

1. Using the cash basis of accounting, revenues are recognized when cash is received and expenses are recognized when cash is paid out.

   a. Small business firms and professional persons may account for their revenues and expenses on a cash basis.

   b. The cash basis of accounting is acceptable only if the results obtained approximate those obtained under the accrual basis of accounting.

2. Using the accrual basis of accounting, revenues are recognized when sales are made or services are performed, even though cash has not yet been received. Expenses are recognized when incurred, regardless of the time of cash payment.

   a. Adjusting entries are needed under the accrual basis of accounting to bring the accounts up to date for economic activity that has occurred but has not yet been recorded.

THE NEED FOR ADJUSTING ENTRIES

3. Adjusting entries are needed so that the income statement and balance sheet of an entity will be complete and accurate.

   a. In order to prepare financial statements, accountants arbitrarily divide an entity's life into time periods.

      1. These time periods are normally equal in length and are called accounting periods.
      2. A fiscal year or accounting year is an accounting period of one year.

         (a) A calendar year accounting period is a fiscal year that ends on December 31.
         (b) Other fiscal years continue for twelve consecutive months but do not end on December 31.

   b. This division of an entity's life into time periods requires the preparation of adjusting entries.

4. The need for adjusting entries is based on the matching principle which requires that expenses incurred in producing revenues be deducted from the revenues they generated during an accounting period.

5. Adjusting entries must be prepared whenever financial statements are to be prepared.

   a. Adjusting entries may be recorded more frequently, but must be recorded annually in keeping with annual reporting.

   b. If monthly financial statements are prepared, monthly adjusting entries are required.

CLASSES AND TYPES OF ADJUSTING ENTRIES

6. Adjusting entries can be grouped into these two broad classes.

   a. Deferred items requiring two types of adjusting entries: asset/expense adjustments and liability/revenue adjustments.

   b. Accrued items requiring two types of adjusting entries: asset/revenue adjustments and liability/expense adjustments.

ADJUSTMENTS FOR DEFERRED ITEMS

7. In the asset/expense group, adjusting entries for prepaid expenses and depreciation are recorded.
8. In the liability/revenue group, adjusting entries for unearned revenues are recorded.

ASSET/EXPENSE ADJUSTMENTS—PREPAID EXPENSES AND DEPRECIATION

9. A prepaid expense is an asset awaiting assignment to expense and includes prepaid insurance, prepaid rent, supplies on hand, and depreciable assets.

PREPAID INSURANCE

10. Prepaid Insurance (an asset) is recorded when the insurance policy premium is paid in advance.
    a. This asset expires with the passage of time and becomes an expense.
    b. Prepaid Insurance (an asset) is debited when the premium is paid, and Cash is credited.
    c. Insurance Expense is debited and Prepaid Insurance is credited at the end of the accounting period for the amount of insurance that has expired.

PREPAID RENT

11. Prepaid Rent (an asset) is recorded when rent is paid in advance to cover more than one accounting period.
    a. Because facilities are being rented continuously through time, the expense is incurred continuously as time elapses; but the entry is not usually made until financial statements are to be prepared.
    b. Prepaid Rent (an asset) is debited and Cash is credited when payment is made in advance.
    c. Rent Expense is debited and Prepaid Rent is credited at the end of the accounting period for the amount of rent that has expired.

SUPPLIES ON HAND

12. Supplies are often bought in large quantities and are assets until they are used.
    a. Supplies on Hand (an asset) is debited when the supplies are purchased, and Cash or Accounts Payable is credited.
    b. At the end of the period, the supplies on hand are counted, and an adjusting entry is made to reduce the account balance of Supplies on Hand to reflect the actual quantity on hand.
    c. Supplies Expense is debited and Supplies on Hand is credited for the amount of supplies used during the period.

DEPRECIATION

13. Depreciation is an expense associated with the gradual use of depreciable assets such as buildings and machines.
    a. Depreciaton expense is determined by dividing the asset cost less estimated salvage value by the asset's useful life.
    b. The useful life must be estimated in advance and represents the expected number of years the company plans to use the asset.
    c. Depreciation accounting is the process of recording depreciation expense.
    d. Straight-line depreciation assigns the same amount of expense to each period of use. The formula is:
    $$\frac{\text{Asset cost} - \text{Estimated salvage value}}{\text{Number of years of useful life}} = \text{Annual depreciation}$$
    e. The adjusting entry involves debiting Depreciation Expense and crediting Accumulated Depreciation (a contra asset account).
    f. Book value, which is an asset's cost less accumulated depreciation, is shown in the balance sheet along with the asset's original cost and accumulated depreciation.

LIABILITY/REVENUE ADJUSTMENTS—UNEARNED REVENUES

14. A liability called Unearned Revenue is recorded when assets are received before being earned.
    a. The liability account may be called Unearned Fees, Revenue Received in Advance, Advances by Customers, or Unearned Revenue.
    b. The seller is obligated to either refund the customer's money or provide the services.
    c. When cash is received in advance for future services, Cash is debited and Unearned Revenue is credited.
    d. After services are performed and revenue is earned, Unearned Revenue is debited and a revenue account is credited.

ADJUSTMENTS FOR ACCRUED ITEMS

15. Accrued items require two types of adjusting entries:
    a. Asset/revenue adjustments are one group involving accrued assets.
    b. Liability/expense adjustments are the other group involving accrued liabilities.

ASSET/REVENUE ADJUSTMENTS—ACCRUED ASSETS

16. Accrued assets are those assets that exist at the end of an accounting period but which have not yet been recorded.
    a. Accrued assets represent rights to receive payments that are not legally due at the balance sheet date.
    b. An adjusting entry recognizes these rights.
    c. Accrued assets adjustments may also be called accrued revenues adjustments.

INTEREST REVENUE

17. At the end of an accounting period, interest may have been earned that has not been received. To record this interest it is necessary to debit Interest Receivable and credit Interest Revenue.

UNBILLED DELIVERY FEES

18. A company may perform services at the end of the accounting period and bill the customer in the next accounting period. To record this activity in the period in which the services were performed, the adjusting entry debits Accounts Receivable and credits Service Revenue.

LIABILITY/EXPENSE ADJUSTMENTS—ACCRUED LIABILITIES

19. Accrued liabilities are those liabilities that exist at the end of an accounting period which have not yet been recorded, such as salaries earned by employees that have not been paid.
    a. Accrued liabilities represent obligations to make payments that are not legally due at the balance sheet date.
    b. Salaries Expense is debited and Salaries Payable is credited in an adjusting entry to record salaries that are owed but are unpaid.
    c. Accrued liabilities adjustments may also be called accrued expenses adjustments.

EFFECTS OF FAILING TO PREPARE ADJUSTING ENTRIES

20. The following diagram shows the effect on net income and balance sheet items of failing to record each of the major types of adjusting entries:

	Failure to recognize	*Effect on net income*	*Effect on balance sheet items*
a.	Consumption of the benefits of an asset (prepaid expense)	Overstates	Overstates assets Overstates retained earnings
b.	Earning of previously unearned revenues	Understates	Overstates liabilities Understates retained earnings
c.	Accrual of assets	Understates	Understates assets Understates retained earnings
d.	Accrual of liabilities	Overstates	Understates liabilities Overstates retained earnings

DEMONSTRATION PROBLEM

Using the following information, prepare the adjusting entries in general journal form for the Beason Company as of December 31, 1994.

The Beason Company adjusts its books annually on December 31. Following are some of the accounts that appeared in the trial balance on December 31, 1994, *before* adjusting entries were made:

Cash in bank	$ 10,000	
Buildings	200,000	
Accumulated depreciation—Buildings		$15,000
Office supplies on hand	605	
Prepaid advertising	400	
Prepaid insurance	1,600	
Utilities expense	60	
Prepaid rent	5,000	
Advertising expense	1,080	
Sales		20,400
Unearned service fees		1,200

The following additional information is available:

1. Beason Company deposited $10,000 in a local bank. The deposit earns 6% interest annually, and the bank pays interest on the last day of the following months: February, May, August, and November.
2. On December 31, Beason Company has just finished a bookkeeping service for a client. Beason Company will bill the client $1,000 in January for the bookkeeping service.
3. The Beason Company purchased a two-year flood hazard insurance policy on September 1, 1994, paying the full two-year premium of $570 in advance.
4. The Beason Company rented an office space on November 1, 1994, at a monthly rental of $1,000, paying five months rent in advance. The five months rent was debited to an asset account.
5. On December 1, 1994, the Beason Company purchased advertising in the Global Morning News for two months for $400 paying for the space in advance.
6. Since the last payday, employees have earned an additional $250.
7. Two-thirds of the unearned service fees have been earned by December 31.
8. The building was purchased for $200,000 in early 1991. It has an estimated useful life of 40 years with no salvage value. Straight-line depreciation is used.
9. Office supplies on hand amount to $300.

GENERAL JOURNAL

DATE	ACCOUNT TITLES AND EXPLANATION	POST. REF.	DEBIT	CREDIT

SOLUTION TO DEMONSTRATION PROBLEM

1.	Interest Receivable ($10,000 × .06 × 1/12)	50	
	Interest Revenue		50
2.	Account Receivable	1,000	
	Service Revenue		1,000
3.	Insurance Expense ($570 ÷ 24 months) × 4 months	95	
	Prepaid Insurance		95
4.	Rent Expense	2,000	
	Prepaid Rent		2,000
5.	Advertising Expense	200	
	Prepaid Advertising		200
	($400 × 1/2 = $200)		
6.	Salaries Expense	250	
	Salaries Payable		250
7.	Unearned Service Fees	800	
	Service Fees Revenue		800
	(1,200 × 2/3 = $800)		
8.	Depreciation Expense	5,000	
	Accumulated Depreciation—Building		5,000
9.	Office Supplies Expense ($605 − $300)	305	
	Office Supplies on Hand		305

MATCHING

Referring to the terms listed below, place the appropriate letter next to the corresponding description.

a.	Accounting period	f.	Book value	k.	Fiscal year
b.	Accrued asset	g.	Calendar year	l.	Prepaid expense
c.	Accrual basis of accounting	h.	Cash basis of accounting	m.	Salvage value
d.	Accumulated depreciation	i.	Depreciation	n.	Unearned revenue
e.	Adjusting entries	j.	Earned revenue	o.	Useful life

_____ 1. A plant asset's cost less its accumulated depreciation.

_____ 2. A period that begins on January 1 and ends on December 31.

_____ 3. Contra asset account.

_____ 4. An asset that will be assigned to expense at a later date.

_____ 5. A time period into which an entity's life is arbitrarily divided for financial reporting purposes.

_____ 6. Made at the end of an accounting period to reflect economic activity that has taken place but has not yet been recorded.

_____ 7. Recognizes revenues when cash is received and recognizes expenses when cash is paid out.

_____ 8. An asset that exists at the end of an accounting period but has not yet been recorded.

_____ 9. The expense resulting from a plant equipment's expiration of usefulness.

_____ 10. The estimated number of time periods that a company expects to make use of a plant asset.

_____ 11. A period of any twelve consecutive months used as an accounting period.

_____ 12. Cash received in advance for goods and services to be delivered at a later date.

COMPLETION AND EXERCISES

1. Entries made to update the accounts prior to the preparation of financial statements for economic activity that has taken place but has not yet been recorded are called _____ entries.

2. One expense that would probably be recognized in the same period under both the cash and accrual basis of accounting is _____.

3. Assume that a company received services from its employees in 1993 for which it had previously agreed it would pay $2,800. This sum was paid in 1994. The $2,800 would be treated as an expense of the year _____ under the cash basis accounting and of the year _____ under accrual basis accounting. Generally speaking, under cash basis accounting expenses are recognized in the accounting system when _____ _____.

4. Some small businesses, especially those rendering services, may employ _____ basis accounting. But most business firms use _____ basis accounting.

5. Assume that a consulting company rendered services for a client in 1993 and collected cash for those services in 1994. Under the cash basis of accounting, revenue would be recognized in _____, while under the accrual basis of accounting, revenue would be recognized in _____. Generally speaking, under the cash basis of accounting, revenue is recognized _____ _____.

6. The two major classes of adjusting entries and the types of adjusting entries included in each class are:

    1. _____
        _____

    Types of adjusting entries included in this class are: _____
    _____

    2. _____
        _____

    Types of adjusting entries included in this class are: _____
    _____

7. Every adjusting entry will involve one account that is reported in the _____ _____ and another account that is reported in the _____ _____.

8. When depreciation is recorded, it is credited to a contra account called _____ _____ and reported in the _____ _____ as a _____ from the depreciable asset to which it relates.

9. The process whereby the cost (less salvage value) of a long-lived asset used in a business is allocated to the periods in which it is used is called _____ _____. The amount of cost allocated to each period is called _____ _____.

10. _____ _____ is subtracted from a plant asset's cost to derive its _____ amount.

11. A liability that exists at the end of an accounting period, but which has not yet been recorded is a/an _____ _____.

12. The Martin Company has a monthly payroll of $300,000, and its employees are paid monthly on the first. The adjusting entry required on December 31 (the end of the company's fiscal year) would involve a debit of $_____ to the _____ _____ account and a credit of $_____ to the _____ _____ account.

13. The Folsom Company owns a warehouse that it leases to others for $1,000 per month, which is collected in advance in semiannual installments on March 31 and September 30. The entry required to record the receipt of the advance payment of rent on September 30 would involve a debit of $_____ to the _____ account and a credit of $_____ to the _____ _____ _____ account.

14. Refer to the data in Question 13. If monthly adjusting entries are made, the entry required on October 31 would consist of a debit to _____ _____ and a credit to _____ _____ in the amount of $_____.

15. Assume that the six basic elements in accounting consist of assets, liabilities, stockholders' equity, revenues, expenses, and net income. If the Martin Company in Question 12 failed to make the required adjusting entry, its financial statements for the period ending December 31 would show too much _____ _____ and _____ _____ and too little _____ and _____.

16. Refer to the data in Question 13. If financial statements are to be prepared for the period ending October 31 and if the Folsom Company failed to make the required adjusting entry, it would have overstated its _____ and understated its _____, _____ _____, and _____ _____.

17. James Call Company purchased $450 of store supplies during the quarter which were charged to an asset account. The beginning balance of store supplies on hand was $150. The end-of-quarter balance sheet showed store supplies on hand of $75. The amount charged to Store Supplies Expense and credited to Store Supplies on Hand is $_____.

18. A theater offered theater ticket books for use at future performances to its patrons at $50 per book for 5 tickets per book. During the year, 1,200 books were sold and this amount was erroneously credited to Theater Revenue. At the end of the period 2,400 tickets from the book sales had been turned in at the box office. The appropriate adjusting entry at the end of the period would be:

GENERAL JOURNAL

DATE	ACCOUNT TITLES AND EXPLANATION	POST. REF.	DEBIT	CREDIT

19. Standford Company started operations on December 1, 19___. Employees earn $85 per day and work a six-day week. There are twenty-seven workdays in December. By the last payday in December (December 27), the employees had been paid $1,955.

Required:

Prepare the adjustment needed on December 31.

GENERAL JOURNAL

DATE	ACCOUNT TITLES AND EXPLANATION	POST. REF.	DEBIT	CREDIT

20. State the effect that each of the following would have on the amount of net income reported for 1993, 1994, and 1995, and on assets and liabilities as of 12/31/94. The firm's accounting period ends on December 31.

   a. A collection in 1994 of $700 for services rendered in 1993 was credited to a revenue account instead of to Accounts Receivable in 1994.

   b. The collection of $400 for services not yet performed as of December 31, 1994, was credited to a revenue account and not adjusted. The services are to be performed next year in 1995.

   c. No adjustment was made for accrued salaries of $1,000 as of December 31, 1994.

_____

_____

_____

_____

_____

_____

_____

_____

_____

_____

_____

_____

_____

_____

_____

_____

_____

_____

_____

_____

_____

_____

21. Using the following information, prepare the adjusting entries in general journal form for the Brandon Company as of December 31, 1994.

The Brandon Company adjusts its books annually on December 31. Following are some of the accounts that appeared in the trial balance on December 31, 1994, *before* adjusting entries were made:

Buildings	$75,000	
Accumulated Depreciation—Buildings		$12,500
Office Supplies on Hand	445	
Prepaid Advertising	960	
Prepaid Insurance	1,600	
Utilities Expense	60	
Prepaid Rent	900	
Advertising Expense	1,080	
Sales		20,400
Unearned Service Fees		450

The following additional information is available:

1. The building has an estimated useful life of 15 years with no salvage value. Straight-line depreciation is used.
2. Office supplies on hand amount to $140.
3. The Brandon Company purchased a four-year fire insurance policy on July 1, 1994, paying the full four-year premium of $1,600 in advance.
4. The Brandon Company rented a warehouse on October 1, 1994, at a monthly rental of $300, paying three months rent in advance.
5. On December 1, 1994, the Brandon Company purchased advertising in the *Daily News* for three months for $960, paying for the space in advance.
6. Since the last payday, employees have earned an additional $600.
7. Two-thirds of the unearned service fees have been earned by December 31.

GENERAL JOURNAL

DATE		ACCOUNT TITLES AND EXPLANATION	POST. REF.	DEBIT	CREDIT

TRUE-FALSE QUESTIONS

Indicate whether each of the following statements is true or false by inserting a capital "T" or "F" in the blank space provided.

_____ 1. Transactions often overlap accounting periods.

_____ 2. Continuing transactions such as rent and utilities are usually only documented at the end of "billing periods."

_____ 3. Every adjusting entry affects both a balance sheet and an income statement account.

_____ 4. Some assets represent services that will be used up over many accounting periods.

_____ 5. Consumption of supplies used in the business results in an expense.

_____ 6. An accrued liability results from a transaction in which a cash payment has been made but the expense has not been incurred.

_____ 7. Adjusting entries usually must be prepared prior to the preparation of financial statements.

_____ 8. The balances of any unearned revenue accounts appear as debits in the trial balance statement.

_____ 9. An expense may only be recognized and recorded if cash has been paid.

_____ 10. The maximum length of an accounting period is usually one month.

_____ 11. Adjusting entries divide amounts in mixed accounts such as supplies and prepaid insurance into their proper balance sheet and income statement components.

_____ 12. Wages paid in advance to an employee would be classified by the employer as an accrued expense.

_____ 13. The Prepaid Insurance account shows a debit of $450, representing the cost of a three-year fire insurance policy dated September 1. The adjusting entry on December 31 of the first year of insurance coverage is a debit to Insurance Expense and a credit to Prepaid Insurance for $50.

_____ 14. The purpose of adjusting entries is to compile all elements required to compute income or loss in one ledger account.

_____ 15. The effect on the income statement if the adjusting entry for depreciation was omitted would be to understate net income.

_____ 16. Adjusting entries are needed when the cost, expense, or revenue components of a transaction relate to more than one accounting period.

_____ 17. Some adjusting entries anticipate expenses that are to be incurred, but adjusting entries never anticipate revenues that are to be earned.

_____ 18. The proper adjusting entry to recognize the expiration of rent paid in advance is to debit Rent Expense and credit Prepaid Rent.

_____ 19. To prepare the adjusting entry for an accrued liability, an expense account is debited and a liability account is credited.

_____ 20. Expenses for which cash expenditures have not yet been made are still reported as expenses on the income statement under the accrual basis of accounting.

_____ 21. Adjusting entries are first entered in the journal and then are posted to the general ledger.

_____ 22. The following are all examples of expenses recognized in adjusting entries: salaries expense, depreciation expense, insurance expense, and dividends.

_____ 23. An adjusting entry may be the result of an expenditure that occurred many years ago.

_____ 24. Economic activity occurs continuously.

_____ 25. Under the accrual basis of accounting, revenue is recognized when cash is received, and expenses are recognized when cash is paid.

MULTIPLE CHOICE QUESTIONS

For each of the following questions indicate the best answer by circling the appropriate letter.

1. Salaries incurred but unpaid at year-end would be classified on a financial statement as a(an):
   A. current asset.
   B. current liability.
   C. revenue.
   D. expense.
   E. other asset.

2. The Unearned Revenue account will normally have what type of balance?
   A. A negative balance
   B. A balance equal to salaries expense
   C. Credit balance
   D. Debit balance
   E. None of these.

3. The proper entry to recognize periodic depreciation of equipment is:
   A. Depreciation Expense—Equipment XXX
         Equipment XXX
   B. Accumulated Depreciation—Equipment XXX
         Depreciation Expense—Equipment XXX
   C. Accumulated Depreciation—Equipment XXX
         Equipment XXX
   D. Equipment XXX
         Depreciation Expense—Equipment XXX
   E. None of these.

4. No adjustment was made for accrued wages on December 31, 1993. The amount of wages earned but not payable until the second week in January 1994, was $600. If this omission is not discovered before financial statements are prepared:
   A. 1993 net income will be overstated by $600.
   B. 1993 net income will be understated by $600.
   C. assets will not be affected.
   D. liabilities will be understated.
   E. (A), and (C), and (D) are all true.

5. Which one of the following entries would be made to record rent expired during the current accounting period, but paid in the prior period?

A. Prepaid Rent XX
      Rent Expense XX

B. Rent Expense XX
      Prepaid Rent XX

C. Prepaid Rent XX
      Cash XX

D. Rent Expense XX
      Rent Accrued XX

E. None of the above.

6. On an income statement, which of the following groups of accounts would all be classified as expenses?

A. Depreciation Expense, Rent Expense, Accumulated Depreciation
B. Prepaid Insurance, Office Supplies Expense, Salaries Expense
C. Service Revenue, Sales, Salaries Expense
D. Office Supplies Expense, Rent Expense, Depreciation Expense

7. A company acquired supplies and, expecting to use them all in the current year, debited the full amount to the Office Supplies Expense account. At the end of the period, part of the supplies remained on hand. If no adjusting entry is made, the effect(s) on the balance sheet and the income statement is (are):

A. revenue of the company will be overstated.
B. net income and stockholders' equity will be overstated, while assets will be understated.
C. assets, net income, and stockholders' equity will all be understated.
D. net income and stockholders' equity will not be affected.
E. None of the above are correct.

8. A magazine company received cash for subscriptions in August for magazines to be mailed in August 1993 through September 1996. It originally recorded the amount as revenue. On December 31, 1993, the correct adjusting entry will be:

A. Unearned Advertising Revenue
      Subscriptions Revenue
B. Unearned Subscriptions Revenue
      Subscriptions Revenue
C. Subscriptions Revenue
      Unearned Subscriptions Revenue
D. Subscriptions Revenue
      Subscriptions Receivable
E. None of the above.

9. Make an adjusting entry to record the office supplies used when an asset account was originally debited for office supplies purchased.

A. Debit Retained Earnings; credit Office Supplies Expense.
B. Debit Office Supplies Expense; credit Retained Earnings.
C. Debit Office Supplies Expense; credit Office Supplies on Hand
D. Debit Office Supplies Expense; credit Cash

10. The accrual basis of accounting operates on which of the following assumption(s)?
    A. Expenses are recorded *only* when they are paid for.
    B. Revenues are recorded *only* when cash is received for them.
    C. Expenses are recorded when they are incurred, regardless of the time of payment.
    D. Revenues are recorded when they are earned, regardless of the time when payment is received.
    E. (C) and (D) are correct.

11. An advertising agency received an $800 check on December 2 for services that it was to perform during December, January, and February. The agency recorded the check as a liability. One-fourth of the services were performed in December. The adjusting entry required on December 31 for the advertising agency was:

    A. Advertising Expense 200
           Unearned Advertising Revenue   200
    B. Advertising Expense 600
           Advertising Revenue   600
    C. Unearned Advertising Revenue 200
           Advertising Revenue   200
    D. Unearned Advertising Revenue 600
           Advertising Revenue   600
    E. None of these.

12. Depreciation:
    A. represents expired utility of a plant asset.
    B. may be caused in part by wear and tear from use.
    C. may be caused in part by obsolescence due to technological change.
    D. is a fund of cash available for replacing the asset when it is no longer useful.
    E. Items (A), (B), and (C), above.

13. Prepaid Rent is classified as a(an):
    A. liability.
    B. part of stockholders' equity.
    C. asset.
    D. revenue.
    E. expense.

14. Insurance premiums received by an insurance company in advance of the coverage period would be classified by the insurance company as a(an):
    A. prepaid expense.
    B. unearned revenue.
    C. accrued asset.
    D. accrued liability.

15. An example of a contra account is:
    A. Insurance Expense.
    B. Accumulated Depreciation—Equipment.
    C. Store Supplies Expense.
    D. Prepaid Rent.
    E. None of these.

SOLUTIONS

Matching

1.	f	7.	h
2.	g	8.	b
3.	d	9.	i
4.	l	10.	o
5.	a	11.	k
6.	e	12.	n

Completion and Exercises

1. adjusting
2. depreciation expense
3. 1994; 1993; they are paid for in cash
4. cash; accrual
5. 1994; 1993; when cash is received
6. (Note order is not important)
   1. Entries that relate to data previously recorded in the accounts (deferred items).
      Prepaid expenses, depreciation, and unearned revenue.
   2. Entries relating to activity on which nothing has been previously recorded in the accounts (accrued items).
      Accrued assets and accrued liabilities.
7. balance sheet; income statement
8. Accumulated Depreciation; balance sheet; deduction
9. depreciation accounting; depreciation expense
10. Salvage value; depreciable
11. accrued liability
12. $300,000; Salaries Expense; $300,000; Salaries Payable
13. $6,000; Cash; $6,000; Unearned Rental Revenue
14. Unearned Rental Revenue; Rent Revenue; $1,000
15. stockholders' equity; net income; liabilities; expenses.
16. liabilities; revenues; net income; stockholders' equity.
17. $525; $150 + $450 purchases = $600 available for use − $75 ending inventory = $525.

18. Theater Revenue 36,000
       Unearned Theater Revenue 36,000
    1,200 × $50 = $60,000 credited to Theater Revenue
                   −24,000 Revenue earned
                   $36,000 Unearned Theater Revenue

19. Salaries Expense 340
       Salaries Payable 340
    $2,295 (27 days × $85)
    −1,955 paid to employees
    $ 340 adjustment

20. a. Net income is overstated in 1994 by $700. Accounts Receivable (an asset) would be overstated as of 12/31/94 by $700 because the claim against the customer was not credited at the time of collection in 1994. There is no effect on liabilities or on 1993 net income.

   b. Revenue for 1994 is overstated, causing net income to be overstated by $400. In the following year, 1995 revenue and net income will be understated by $400 assuming the services are performed in that year. Liabilities are understated by $400 as of 12/31/94. There is no effect on assets.

   c. Net income for 1994 would be overstated by $1,000 because salaries expense is understated. The following year, 1995, net income would be understated by $1,000 since salaries expense would be overstated assuming all other salaries incurred in 1995 are correctly recognized. Salaries Payable (a liability) would be understated by $1,000 as of 12/31/94. There is no effect on assets.

21. 1. Depreciation Expense—Buildings 5,000
       Accumulated Depreciation—Buildings 5,000
       ($75,000 ÷ 15 years)

    2. Office Supplies Expense 305
       Office Supplics on Hand 305
       ($445 − $140)

    3. Insurance Expense 200
       Prepaid Insurance 200
       [($1,600/4 years) = $400 × 1/2 year]

    4. Rent Expense 900
       Prepaid Rent 900

    5. Advertising Expense 320
       Prepaid Advertising 320
       ($960 × 1/3 = $320)

    6. Salaries Expense 600
       Salaries Payable 600

    7. Unearned Service Fees 300
       Service Revenue 300
       (2/3 × $450 = $300)

True-False Questions

1. T
2. T Rent and utilities are incurred continuously; however, they are recognized usually at stated periods often through adjusting entries.
3. T
4. T
5. T
6. F An accrued liability represents an obligation to make payments that are not legally due at the balance sheet date. No liability would result if cash has already been paid.
7. T
8. F Unearned revenue accounts are liabilities and normally have credit balances.
9. F Under the accrual basis of accounting, expenses only need be incurred (not paid) before they are recorded.
10. F Normally the maximum length of an accounting period is one year.
11. T This is the main purpose of adjusting entries.
12. F Wages paid in advance to an employee would be classified as a prepaid expense.
13. T $450/36 months = $12.50 insurance expense per month; $12.50 × 4 months = $50.
14. F Entries other than adjusting entries are needed to record expenses and revenues during a period.
15. F The adjusting entry to record depreciation recognizes an expense, which would decrease income. If this entry was omitted, income would be overstated.

16. T
17. F Adjusting entries never anticipate expenses because they merely record expenses that have occurred; it is true that adjusting entries never anticipate revenues that are to be earned.
18. T
19. T
20. T
21. T
22. F Dividends are not expenses.
23. T Depreciation may result from an expenditure made many years ago.
24. T Economic activity occurs continuously, which is why adjusting entries are needed before financial statements are prepared.
25. F This statement describes the cash basis of accounting.

Multiple Choice Questions

1. B Salaries payable is a current liability.
2. C Unearned Revenue is a liability and has a credit balance.
3. E The proper entry is to debit Depreciation Expense and credit Accumulated Depreciation.
4. E
5. B
6. D Accumulated Depreciation is a contra asset account; Prepaid Insurance is an asset, Service Revenue and Sales are revenue accounts.
7. C The asset account, Supplies on Hand, will be understated and Supplies Expense will be overstated, which will understate net income and stockholders' equity.
8. C The unearned subscription fees must be removed from the revenue account and placed in a liability account.
9. C
10. E Both (C) and (D) are correct.
11. C
12. E
13. C Prepaid Rent is an asset.
14. B To the insurance company, insurance premiums received in advance are unearned revenue until the period of coverage expires and the revenue is thereby earned.
15. B

COMPLETING THE ACCOUNTING CYCLE: WORK SHEET, CLOSING ENTRIES, AND CLASSIFIED BALANCE SHEET

Learning Objectives

1. *List the steps in the accounting cycle.*
2. *Prepare a work sheet for a service company.*
3. *Prepare an income statement, statement of retained earnings, and balance sheet using information contained in the work sheet.*
4. *Prepare adjusting and closing entries using information contained in the work sheet.*
5. *Prepare a post-closing trial balance.*
6. *Prepare a classified balance sheet.*
7. *Prepare reversing entries (Appendix 4-A).*
8. *Post adjusting and closing entries to three-column ledger accounts (Appendix 4-B).*

CHAPTER OUTLINE

THE ACCOUNTING CYCLE SUMMARIZED

1. The accounting cycle consists of a series of steps related to gathering, classifying, and reporting useful financial information. The steps in the accounting cycle and the chapter(s) in which they are discussed are given below along with when the steps are performed.

   Performed During Accounting Period

   a. Analyze transactions by examining source documents (Chapters 1 and 2).
   b. Journalize transactions in the journal (Chapter 2).
   c. Post journal entries to the accounts in the ledger (Chapter 2).

   Performed at End of Accounting Period

   d. Prepare a trial balance of the accounts (Chapter 2) and complete the work sheet (Chapter 4).
   e. Prepare financial statements (Chapter 4).
   f. Journalize and post adjusting entries (Chapters 3 and 4).
   g. Journalize and post closing entries (Chapter 4).
   h. Prepare a post-closing trial balance (Chapter 4).

THE WORK SHEET

2. A work sheet offers a convenient means for entering and summarizing information needed for making adjusting and closing entries and for preparing financial statements.

   a. A work sheet may be prepared each time financial statements are to be prepared.
   b. A work sheet is an internal statement and is not part of the formal accounting records.
   c. A work sheet may be prepared in various ways and is usually prepared in pencil.

THE TRIAL BALANCE COLUMNS

3. The work sheet usually contains Trial Balance columns; this avoids the preparation of a separate trial balance statement.

   a. The balances of the accounts are entered in the Trial Balance columns of the work sheet.
   b. The Trial Balance columns are totaled to check on equality of debit and credit totals.

THE ADJUSTMENTS COLUMNS

4. Adjustments needed to bring the accounts up to date are entered in the Adjustments columns of the work sheet.

   a. The following steps can assist the accountant in determining the adjusting entries needed.

      (1) Examine adjusting entries made at the end of the preceding accounting period.
      (2) Examine the account titles appearing in the trial balance.
      (3) Examine various business papers to discover other assets, liabilities, expenses, and revenues that have not yet been recorded.
      (4) Specific questions may be directed to the owner or other personnel.

THE ADJUSTED TRIAL BALANCE COLUMNS

5. All accounts having balances are extended to the Adjusted Trial Balance columns after entering adjustments on the work sheet.

THE INCOME STATEMENT COLUMNS

6. Revenue and expense accounts appearing in the Adjusted Trial Balance columns are extended to the Income Statement columns.
   a. After subtotaling the debit and credit columns, the net income or net loss for the period is determined.
      (1) If the debit subtotal exceeds the credit subtotal, a net loss has occurred.
      (2) If the credit subtotal exceeds the debit subtotal, net income has been earned.

THE STATEMENT OF RETAINED EARNINGS COLUMNS

7. The beginning balance in Retained Earnings, dividends, and net income (or loss) are extended to the Statement of Retained Earnings columns. The ending balance in Retained Earnings is equal to the difference between the column totals.

THE BALANCE SHEET COLUMNS

8. The amount for assets, liabilities, and capital stock listed in the Adjusted Trial Balance columns are extended to the Balance Sheet columns. The amount of retained earnings in the Statement of Retained Earnings column is extended to the Balance Sheet column.

LOCATING ERRORS

9. If the balance sheet column totals do not agree, work backward through the process used in preparing the work sheet.

PREPARING FINANCIAL STATEMENTS FROM THE WORK SHEET

10. After the work sheet is completed, the information is used to prepare the financial statements.

INCOME STATEMENT

11. The income statement can be prepared from data in the Income Statement columns in the work sheet.

STATEMENT OF RETAINED EARNINGS

12. The statement of retained earnings shows the addition of the net income to the beginning Retained Earnings balance and the deduction of dividends to arrive at the ending Retained Earnings balance.
    a. A net loss is deducted from the beginning Retained Earnings account balance.
    b. The ending Retained Earnings balance is then carried forward to the balance sheet.
    c. The statement of retained earnings relates the income statement information to the balance sheet.

BALANCE SHEET

13. The balance sheet is prepared from information contained in the Balance Sheet columns of the work sheet.

JOURNALIZING ADJUSTING ENTRIES

14. Adjusting entries that were entered on the work sheet must be entered in the general journal and posted to the appropriate ledger accounts.

THE CLOSING PROCESS

15. The closing process transfers the balances in the revenue and expense accounts to the Income Summary and then to Retained Earnings.
    a. Closing entries reduce revenue and expense account balances to zero.
    b. Closing entries are needed so that revenue and expense information for the current period will not be intermingled with information from all prior periods.

c. The balance in each revenue and expense account is transferred to an Income Summary account.

    (1) The Income Summary account is a clearing account used only at the end of the accounting period to summarize revenues and expenses for the period.

    (2) The Income Summary account does not appear on any financial statement.

    (3) The balance of the Income Summary account is transferred to the Retained Earnings account.

d. The Dividends account is closed to the Retained Earnings account.

    (1) The Dividends account is not closed to Income Summary.

    (2) Dividends have no effect on income and loss and are closed directly to Retained Earnings.

e. Asset, liability, and stockholders' equity accounts are not closed during the closing process.

CLOSING THE REVENUE ACCOUNT(S)

16. Because revenue accounts have credit balances, they must be debited to give them a zero balance.

    a. The revenue account is debited and Income Summary is credited in the closing process.

CLOSING THE EXPENSE ACCOUNT(S)

17. Because expense accounts have debit balances, they must be credited to give them a zero balance.

    a. The expense accounts are credited and the Income Summary account is debited in the closing process.

CLOSING THE INCOME SUMMARY ACCOUNT

18. After closing revenues and expenses to the Income Summary account, this account is closed to the Retained Earnings account.

    a. If revenues exceed expenses, income has been earned, and a closing entry debiting Income Summary and crediting the Retained Earnings account is needed.

    b. If instead, expenses exceed revenues, a loss has occurred, and a closing entry crediting Income Summary and debiting the Retained Earnings account is needed.

CLOSING THE DIVIDENDS ACCOUNT

19. The Dividends account is closed by crediting this account and debiting the Retained Earnings account.

CLOSING PROCESS SUMMARIZED

20. The closing process is summarized on pages 160 and 162 of the text.

POST-CLOSING TRIAL BALANCE

21. A post-closing trial balance is taken after revenue, expense, and Dividends accounts have been closed.

    a. Only asset, liability, and stockholders' equity accounts appear on the post-closing trial balance.

    b. The post-closing trial balance serves as a means of examining the accuracy of the closing process and ensures that the books are in balance at the start of the new accounting period.

THE CLASSIFIED BALANCE SHEET

22. A classified balance sheet divides the major categories of assets, liabilities, and stockholders' equity into more detailed classification.

    a. An unclassified balance sheet has only major categories labeled as assets, liabilities, and stockholders' equity.

    b. Balance sheets may be presented in a vertical format, with assets appearing above liabilities and stockholders' equity.

    c. A horizontal format of the balance sheet shows assets on the left and liabilities and stockholders' equity on the right.

CURRENT ASSETS

23. Current assets are cash and other assets that will be converted into cash or used up by the business in a relatively short time period, usually a year or less.

LONG-TERM ASSETS

24. Long-term assets are assets that a business will have on hand or use for a relatively long period of time.

LONG-TERM INVESTMENTS

25. Long-term investments are securities of another company held for long-term purposes.

PROPERTY, PLANT, AND EQUIPMENT

26. Property, plant, and equipment are assets acquired for use in a business rather than for resale.
    a. Property, plant, and equipment are also called plant assets or fixed assets.
    b. They are acquired for long-term use.
    c. Land, Buildings, Machinery, and Accumulated Depreciation are included in this classification.

INTANGIBLE ASSETS

27. Intangible assets consist of noncurrent, nonphysical assets of a business.

CURRENT LIABILITIES

28. Current liabilities are debts that are normally due within one year.
    a. The payment of current liabilities requires the use of current assets.
    b. Accounts Payable, Notes Payable, and Salaries Payable are included in this category.

LONG-TERM LIABILITIES

29. Long-term liabilities are not due for a relatively long period of time, usually more than a year.

STOCKHOLDERS' EQUITY

30. Stockholders' equity shows the owners' interest in the business.

APPENDIX 4-A REVERSING ENTRIES

31. Reversing entries reverse the effects of the adjusting entries to which they relate:
    a. The purpose of reversing entries is to simplify the accounting process.
    b. The adjusting entry and the closing entry are the same whether or not a reversing entry is made.
    c. The final result is the same whether or not a reversing entry is used.
    d. A general rule is that all adjusting journal entries that increase assets or liabilities may be reversed, but those that decrease assets or liabilities may not be reversed.

APPENDIX 4-B LEDGER ACCOUNTS AFTER CLOSING PROCESS COMPLETED

32. Expense and revenue accounts have zero balances after the closing entries have been posted.

DEMONSTRATION PROBLEM

The trial balance of the Charles Company at December 31, 1994, contains the following account balances (the accounts are listed in alphabetical order to increase your skill in sorting amounts to the proper work sheet columns.)

CHARLES COMPANY
Trial Balance Account Balances

Accounts Payable	$ 15,000
Accounts Receivable	55,000
Accumulated Depreciation—Building	20,000
Accumulated Depreciation—Equipment	3,500
Buildings	120,000
Capital Stock	58,200
Cash	16,000
Commissions Revenue	58,000
Dividends	10,000
Equipment	35,000
Land	90,000
Notes Payable	10,000
Salaries Expense	55,000
Prepaid Insurance	2,400
Retained Earnings, January 1, 1994	20,300
Supplies on Hand	3,500
Unearned Management Fees	204,000
Utilities Expense	2,100

a. Using the account balances given above and the additional information presented below, prepare a work sheet for the Charles Company. You do not need to include account numbers.

Part a. (work sheet) appears at the back of the book.

Additional data:

1. Store supplies on hand at December 31 have a cost of $500.
2. The balance in the Prepaid Insurance account represents the cost of a 12-month insurance policy beginning April 1, 1994. The company did not carry insurance from January through March 1994.
3. Depreciation for the building is $2,000 and for the equipment, $1,000.
4. The unearned management fees cover a 12-month management service of Charles Company from September 1, 1994, to August 31, 1995.

b. Prepare the adjusting and closing journal entries.

b.

GENERAL JOURNAL

DATE	ACCOUNT TITLES AND EXPLANATION	POST. REF.	DEBIT	CREDIT

SOLUTION TO DEMONSTRATION PROBLEM

CHARLES COMPANY
Work Sheet
For Year Ended December 31, 1994

Account Name	Trial Balance Debit	Trial Balance Credit	Adjustments Debit	Adjustments Credit	Adjusted Trial Balance Debit	Adjusted Trial Balance Credit	Income Statement Debit	Income Statement Credit	Statement of Retained Earnings Debit	Statement of Retained Earnings Credit	Balance Sheet Debit	Balance Sheet Credit
Cash	16,000				16,000						16,000	
Accounts Receivable	55,000				55,000						55,000	
Supplies on Hand	3,500			(1) 3,000	500						500	
Prepaid Insurance	2,400			(2) 1,800	600						600	
Buildings	120,000				120,000						120,000	
Accumulated Depr.—Buildings		20,000		(3) 2,000		22,000						22,000
Equipment	35,000				35,000						35,000	
Accumulated Depr.—Equipment		3,500		(3) 1,000		4,500						4,500
Land	90,000				90,000						90,000	
Accounts Payable		15,000				15,000						15,000
Notes Payable		10,000				10,000						10,000
Commissions Revenue		58,000				58,000		58,000				
Capital Stock		58,200				58,200						58,200
Retained Earnings, Jan. 1, 1994		20,300				20,300				20,300		
Dividends	10,000				10,000				10,000			
Unearned Management Fees		204,000	(4) 68,000			136,000						136,000
Salaries Expense	55,000				55,000		55,000					
Utilities Expense	2,100				2,100		2,100					
	389,000	389,000										
Management Fee Revenue				(4) 68,000		68,000		68,000				
Insurance Expense			(2) 1,800		1,800		1,800					
Depreciation Expense—Buildings			(3) 2,000		2,000		2,000					
Depreciation Expense—Equipment			(3) 1,000		1,000		1,000					
Supplies Expense			(1) 3,000		3,000		3,000					
			75,800	75,800	392,000	392,000	64,900	126,000				
Net Income							61,100			61,100		
							126,000	126,000	10,000	81,400		
Retained Earnings, Dec. 31, 1994									71,400			71,400
									81,400	81,400	317,100	317,100

a.

CHARLES COMPANY

b. *Adjusting Entries*

1994

(1) December 31 Supplies Expense 3,000
                Supplies on Hand 3,000
                To record supplies expense.

(2)   31 Insurance Expense 1,800
                Prepaid Insurance 1,800
                Insurance expense for year.

(3)   31 Depreciation Expense—Building 2,000
           Depreciation Expense—Equipment 1,000
                Accumulated Depreciation—Building 2,000
                Accumulated Depreciation—Equipment 1,000
                Depreciation expense for year.

(4)   31 Unearned Management Fees 68,000
                Management Fee Revenue 68,000

Closing Entries

1994

December 31 Management Fee Revenue 68,000
           Commissions Revenue 58,000
                Income Summary 126,000
                To close revenue accounts.

       31 Income Summary 64,900
                Salaries Expense 55,000
                Utilities Expense 2,100
                Supplies Expense 3,000
                Insurance Expense 1,800
                Depreciation Expense—Building 2,000
                Depreciation Expense—Equipment 1,000
                To close expense accounts.

       31 Income Summary 61,100
                Retained Earnings 61,100
                To close net income to Retained Earnings.

       31 Retained Earnings 10,000
                Dividends 10,000
                To close the Dividends account.

MATCHING

Referring to the terms listed below, place the appropriate letter next to the corresponding description.

a. Accrued assets
b. Accrued liabilities
c. Adjusting entries
d. Assets

e. Closing entries
f. Contra account
g. Income statement
h. Income Summary account

i. Prepaid expenses
j. Retained Earnings account
k. Statement of retained earnings
l. Work sheet

_____ 1. Accumulated depreciation.
_____ 2. Results from services that have been performed but have not yet been billed.
_____ 3. A statement showing changes in retained earnings.
_____ 4. Entries required at the end of the accounting period to clear out the temporary accounts.
_____ 5. Used to record the cost of office supplies used from inventory.
_____ 6. Classification(s) of accounts with debit balances remaining open after the accounting records are closed.
_____ 7. Is the account to which commissions earned is closed.
_____ 8. Assets that exist at the end of an accounting period but have not yet been recorded.
_____ 9. Amounts owed for expenses incurred but not yet billed or due to be paid.
_____ 10. Used to record the cost of prepaid insurance that has expired.
_____ 11. Account subtracted from plant and equipment to arrive at book value.
_____ 12. The Dividends account is closed to this account.
_____ 13. The account's balance is subtracted from the balance of an associated account to show the appropriate balance.
_____ 14. After these entries are posted, revenue and expense accounts have a zero balance.
_____ 15. A form that provides a convenient way for summarizing information needed for preparing financial statements.

COMPLETION AND EXERCISES

1. The financial accounting process has been shown to consist of eight steps, namely,

1. _____

2. _____

3. _____

4. _____

5. _____

6. _____

7. _____

8. _____

2. Depreciation expense is an _____ expense that is closed, at the end of the accounting year, to the _____ _____ account.

3. In the closing process or in closing the books, all revenue accounts are _____ and the _____ _____ account is _____. Similarly, all expense accounts are _____ and the _____ _____ account is _____.

4. After the closing entries have been prepared and posted, a _____ _____ _____ _____ is prepared as a means of checking upon the procedural accuracy of the process.

5. _____ entries may be used by the accountant, but they are not essential to the completion of the accounting cycle.

6. A _____ _____ is a large columnar sheet of paper used to summarize information needed to prepare the financial statements and the adjusting and closing entries.

7. Adjusting entries are entered in the _____ columns.

8. The Prepaid Insurance account has a debit balance of $2,500 in the Trial Balance columns. In the Adjustments columns, the account is credited for $1,200. The balance of the Prepaid Insurance account in the Adjusted Trial Balance column is a $ _____ _____ (debit or credit) balance.

9. Expense and revenue account balances in the Adjusted Trial Balance columns are extended to the _____ _____ columns; asset, liability, and capital stock account balances are extended to the _____ _____ columns. Retained Earnings and Dividends account balances are extended to the _____ _____ _____ _____ columns.

10. Net income appears in the _____ _____ debit column and the _____ _____ _____ _____ credit column; a net loss appears in the _____ _____ credit column and the _____ _____ _____ _____ debit column.

11. A statement of retained earnings summarizes changes in the _____ _____ account balance.

12. Use the information given below to complete the work sheet for B. B. Bean Company (on page 77). You do not need to show account numbers.
   a. Supplies on hand at December 31, 1994; $20.
   b. Rent expense for 1994; $60.
   c. Depreciation on equipment for 1994; $15.

12. (continued)

B. B. BEAN COMPANY
Work Sheet
For Year Ended December 31, 1994

Account Name	Trial Balance		Adjustments		Adjusted Trial Balance		Income Statement		Statement of Retained Earnings		Balance Sheet	
	Debit	Credit	Debit	Credit	Debit	Credit	Debit	Credit	Debit	Credit	Debit	Credit
Cash	100											
Accounts Receivable	200											
Supplies on Hand	60											
Prepaid Rent	80											
Equipment	150											
Accumulated Depr.— Equipment		60										
Accounts Payable		90										
Capital Stock		30										
Retained Earnings, Jan. 1, 1994		70										
Dividends	20											
Service Revenue		650										
Salaries Expense	200											
Insurance Expense	50											
Utilities Expense	30											
Miscellaneous Expense	10											
	900	900										

13. Refer to Question 12. Prepare the adjusting entries (omit explanations).

GENERAL JOURNAL

DATE		ACCOUNT TITLES AND EXPLANATION	POST. REF.	DEBIT	CREDIT

14. Refer to Question 12. Prepare the closing entries (omit explanations).

GENERAL JOURNAL

DATE		ACCOUNT TITLES AND EXPLANATION	POST. REF.	DEBIT	CREDIT

15. Refer to Question 12. Prepare an income statement.

16. Refer to Question 12. Prepare a statement of retained earnings.

17. Refer to Question 12. Prepare a balance sheet.

18. After adjustment, selected account balances of the Adelaide Company are:

	Debits	Credits
Interest revenue		$ 5,000
Service revenue		40,000
Service expense	$ 4,000	
Salaries expense	5,500	
Delivery expense	13,200	
Dividends	5,000	

In journal form, give the entries required to close the books for the period.

DATE	ACCOUNT TITLES AND EXPLANATION	POST. REF.	DEBIT	CREDIT

19. a. Illustrate how the Statement of Retained Earnings columns would be used. Assume a beginning balance in Retained Earnings of $15,000 and net income for the year of $10,000, and dividends declared of $4,900.

b. If there were a credit balance of $9,000 in the Retained Earnings account as of the beginning of the year and a net loss of $6,750 for the year, show how these items would be treated.

		Statement of Retained Earnings		Balance Sheet	
		Debit	Credit	Debit	Credit
a.					
b.					

20. You are given the following account balances. Prepare one entry to close the revenue accounts, prepare one entry to close the expense accounts, and prepare one entry to close out the balance in the Income Summary account.

Service Revenue	150,000	Rental Revenue	9,500
Utilities Expense	10,000	Advertising Expense	11,500
Accumulated Depreciation—Buildings	50,000	Delivery Expense	2,000
Salaries Expense	72,000	Salaries Payable	8,000
Depreciation Expense—Buildings	10,000	Retained Earnings	35,000

GENERAL JOURNAL

DATE	ACCOUNT TITLES AND EXPLANATION	POST. REF.	DEBIT	CREDIT

21. The accounts given in Question 20 suggest the need for at least one reversing entry, if such entries are made. Prepare this reversing entry.

DATE	ACCOUNT TITLES AND EXPLANATION	POST. REF.	DEBIT	CREDIT

22. The following account balances appeared in the Income Statement columns of the work sheet prepared for the Christabel Company for the year ended December 31, 19—.

	Income Statement	
	Debit	Credit
Interest Revenue		180,000
Painting Revenue		280,000
Advertising Expense	1,800	
Salaries Expense	200,000	
Utilities Expense	3,500	
Insurance Expense	2,000	
Rent Expense	8,800	
Supplies Expense	3,000	
Depreciation Expense—Buildings	7,000	
Interest Expense	1,500	
Rental Revenue		1,500
Gas and Oil Expense	700	
	228,300	461,500
Net Income	233,200	
	461,500	461,500

Prepare the closing journal entries. Assume the Dividends account has a balance of $50,000 on December 31, 19—.

GENERAL JOURNAL

DATE	ACCOUNT TITLES AND EXPLANATION	POST. REF.	DEBIT	CREDIT

23. Four of the major column headings on a work sheet are Adjusted Trial Balance, Income Statement, Statement of Retained Earnings, and Balance Sheet. For each of the following items, determine under which major column heading it would appear and whether it would be a debit or credit.

	Adjusted Trial Balance		Income Statement		Statement of Retained Earnings		Balance Sheet	
	Dr.	Cr.	Dr.	Cr.	Dr.	Cr.	Dr.	Cr.
a. Supplies Expense								
b. Accounts Receivable								
c. Accounts Payable								
d. Commissions Revenue								
e. Salaries Expense								
f. Retained Earnings (ending cr. bal.)								
g. Service Revenue								
h. Net Loss for the Year								

24. The Daphne Company reported net income of $25,750 for the current year. Examination of the work sheet and supporting data indicates that the following items were ignored.

1. A total of $750 of the Supplies on Hand represents supplies that were used.
2. Of the Prepaid Insurance, $1,200 has expired.
3. Depreciation on equipment acquired on July 1 amounts to $4,500.
4. Accrued salaries were $2,000 at December 31.
5. Delivery fees earned, $1,000. (Assume an Unearned Delivery Fees account was initially credited.)

   a. Based on the above information, what adjusting entries should have been made on December 31?
   b. What is the correct net income?

a.

GENERAL JOURNAL

DATE	ACCOUNT TITLES AND EXPLANATION	POST. REF.	DEBIT	CREDIT

b.

	DEBIT	CREDIT

TRUE-FALSE QUESTIONS

Indicate whether each of the following statements is true or false by inserting a capital "T" or "F" in the blank space provided.

_____ 1. The account "Accounts Receivable" is closed to Income Summary in the closing process.

_____ 2. The company has earned income for the period if a debit is needed to close the Income Summary account.

_____ 3. An adjusting entry is needed to transfer the information in the individual revenue and expense accounts to the Income Summary account.

_____ 4. The purpose of the Income Summary account is to summarize all expenses and revenues of the period in one account.

_____ 5. An expense account is normally closed by debiting it.

_____ 6. The important role of the work sheet is to aid the accountant by bringing together all the data needed for preparing the financial statements.

_____ 7. In a classified balance sheet, net income for the period would be included in the total of stockholders' equity.

_____ 8. The Income Summary account reveals that an operating loss of $800 has been incurred. Before closing entries are posted, the Dividends account shows a balance of $460. The entry to close the Income Summary is a debit of $340 to the Retained Earnings account and a credit of $340 to Income Summary.

_____ 9. The Income Summary account has a debit balance before it is closed if there was net income for the period.

_____ 10. It is necessary to adjust the accounts each time financial statements are to be prepared.

_____ 11. Dividends are an expense because they reduce retained earnings.

_____ 12. The post-closing trial balance is prepared immediately after all adjustments have been journalized and posted.

_____ 13. If a company's expenses are greater than its revenues, retained earnings is increased.

_____ 14. Income Summary is an account that will not appear on any financial statement.

_____ 15. If the balance in Income Summary is a credit balance, this means that the organization has earned net income of this amount.

_____ 16. Following the adjusting and closing process, the revenue and expense accounts are the only accounts remaining open.

_____ 17. If a company reports net income for the current year, this amount will be shown on the work sheet in the debit Income Statement column and credit Statement of Retained Earnings column.

_____ 18. One of the purposes of closing entries is to prepare revenue and expense accounts for the recording of the next period's revenue and expenses.

_____ 19. Work sheets furnish in a convenient form the information required for the periodic financial statements.

_____ 20. When a work sheet's Income Statement debit column total exceeds the Income Statement credit column total, a loss is indicated.

_____ 21. The post-closing trial balance contains asset, liability, and stockholders' equity accounts.

_____ 22. Entering the adjustments in the Adjustments columns of a work sheet makes it unnecessary to record and post adjusting entries.

_____ 23. The adjusted trial balance contains only revenue and expense accounts.

_____ 24. On a classified balance sheet, Wages Payable should be classified as a current liability.

_____ 25. A Note Payable due in eight years would be classified as part of current liabilities on a classified balance sheet.

MULTIPLE CHOICE QUESTIONS

For each of the following questions indicate the best answer by circling the appropriate letter.

1. The Trial Balance columns of the work sheet show store fixtures of $4,000. Estimated depreciation for the period is $400. The Store Fixtures amount in the Balance Sheet columns of the work sheet will be a:
   A. $3,600 debit.
   B. $3,600 credit.
   C. $4,400 debit.
   D. $4,000 debit.
   E. $4,000 credit.

2. Which of the following statements is incorrect?
   A. The work sheet eliminates the need for preparing and posting adjusting and closing journal entries.
   B. The work sheet serves as the basis for preparing the Income Statement.
   C. The work sheet serves as the basis for preparing the Balance Sheet.
   D. The work sheet serves as the basis for journalizing the adjusting entries.

3. If the debit subtotal of the Income Statement on the work sheet is $159,000 and the credit subtotal is $147,000, there is a:
   A. net income of $12,000.
   B. net loss of $12,000.
   C. net loss of $159,000.
   D. net income of $147,000.

4. The Trial Balance columns of a work sheet total $62,000. The Adjustments columns contain the following:
   1. Depreciation expense of $3,500.
   2. Rent expense of $500.
   3. Accrued salaries of $2,500.
   4. Insurance expense of $1,200.
   5. Supplies expense of $600.
   The total of the Adjusted Trial Balance columns is:
   A. $69,800
   B. $68,000
   C. $65,500
   D. $63,800
   E. $54,200

5. Supplies on Hand are shown as $315 in the Trial Balance columns of the work sheet. The Adjustments columns show that $290 of these supplies were used during the month. The amount shown as Supplies on Hand in the Balance Sheet columns is a:

   A. $25 debit.
   B. $315 debit.
   C. $290 debit.
   D. $25 credit.
   E. $290 credit.

6. The depreciation expense on office equipment was recorded by a debit to Depreciation Expense and a credit to Office Equipment. If statements are now prepared:

   A. net income and stockholders' equity are correct.
   B. the total dollar amount of total assets is correct but the details shown on the balance sheet are in error.
   C. total liabilities are correct.
   D. All of the above.
   E. (A) and (C), but not (B).

7. Salaries Expense before adjustment at September 30, the end of the fiscal year, has a balance of $140,000. The amount of accrued salaries is $3,100. The adjusting entry would be:

A.	Salaries Expense	3,100	
	Salaries Payable		3,100
B.	Salaries Payable	3,100	
	Salaries Expense		3,100
C.	Income Summary	3,100	
	Salaries Expense		3,100
D.	Income Summary	143,100	
	Salaries Expense		143,100
E.	None of these.		

8. The closing entry for Salaries Expense in the previous question would be:

A.	Salaries Expense	143,100	
	Salaries Payable		143,100
B.	Salaries Payable	3,100	
	Salaries Expense		3,100
C.	Income Summary	3,100	
	Salaries Expense		3,100
D.	Income Summary	143,100	
	Salaries Expense		143,100
E.	None of these.		

9. In adjusting and closing the books of Sally Smith Company at the end of the fiscal year, no provision was made for accrued sales salaries expense of $600. The effect of this omission was as follows:

   A. the assets on the balance sheet were the same regardless of the omission.
   B. stockholders' equity on the balance sheet is understated by $600.
   C. the liabilities reported on the balance sheet are overstated by $600.
   D. net income for the year was understated by $600.
   E. None of the preceding answers is correct.

10. Office Supplies on Hand shows up on the work sheet in the following columns, assuming office supplies expense must be deducted from the prepaid amount.

    A. Trial Balance, Adjustments, Adjusted Trial Balance, Balance Sheet
    B. Income Statement and Adjustments
    C. Balance Sheet and Adjustments
    D. Balance Sheet and Income Statement

11. Murray Sporting Goods began business on January 1, 1994, with capital stock of $15,000. At December 31, 1994, assets amounted to $25,000 and liabilities were $6,000. Revenue from services during the year amounted to $30,000 and dividends were $8,000. The expenses of Murray Sporting Goods for 1994 amounted to:

    A. $10,000
    B. $18,000
    C. $26,000
    D. $19,000
    E. some other amount

12. On a classified balance sheet, taxes payable should be classified as:

    A. Current asset.
    B. Property, plant, and equipment.
    C. Current liability.
    D. Long-term liability.
    E. Stockholders' equity.

13. If the subtotal of the income statement debit column is $250,000, the subtotal of the income statement credit column is $300,000, and the total of the Statement of Retained Earnings debit column is $475,000, what is the beginning balance in Retained Earnings?

    A. $425,000
    B. $250,000
    C. $525,000
    D. $300,000
    E. None of the above.

14. If at the end of a period there is a debit balance in the Income Summary account, this means that:

    A. total assets have decreased during the period.
    B. the business has suffered a net loss during the period.
    C. revenues have exceeded expenses.
    D. dividends were greater than the income for the period.

15. Which of the following is true regarding the work sheet?

    A. It is a form that the accountant uses for his/her own aid and convenience.
    B. It assists in the orderly preparation of the adjusting entries and financial statements at the end of accounting periods.
    C. It can substitute for journals and ledgers.
    D. All of the above are true.
    E. Only (A) and (B) are true.

SOLUTIONS

Matching

1.	f	9.	b
2.	a	10.	c
3.	k	11.	f
4.	e	12.	j
5.	c	13.	f
6.	d and i	14.	e
7.	h	15.	l
8.	a		

Completion and Exercises

1. The accounting cycle consists of the following steps:

    1. Analyze transactions by examining source documents.
    2. Journalize transactions in the journal.
    3. Post journal entries to the accounts in the ledger.
    4. Prepare a trial balance of the accounts and complete the work sheet.
    5. Prepare financial statements.
    6. Journalize and post adjusting entries.
    7. Journalize and post closing entries.
    8. Prepare a post-closing trial balance.

2. operating; Income Summary
3. debited; Income Summary; credited; credited; Income Summary; debited
4. post-closing trial balance
5. Reversing
6. work sheet
7. Adjustments
8. $1,300 debit
9. Income Statement; Balance Sheet; Statement of Retained Earnings
10. Income Statement; Statement of Retained Earnings; Income Statement; Statement of Retained Earnings
11. Retained Earnings
12. See page 92 for worksheet.
13. a. Supplies Expense 40
        Supplies on Hand 40
    b. Rent Expense 60
        Prepaid Rent 60
    c. Depreciation Expense—Equipment 15
        Accumulated Depreciation—Equipment 15

B. B. BEAN COMPANY
Work Sheet
For Year Ended December 31, 1994

12.

Account Name	Trial Balance Debit	Trial Balance Credit	Adjustments Debit	Adjustments Credit	Adjusted Trial Balance Debit	Adjusted Trial Balance Credit	Income Statement Debit	Income Statement Credit	Statement of Retained Earnings Debit	Statement of Retained Earnings Credit	Balance Sheet Debit	Balance Sheet Credit
Cash	100				100						100	
Accounts Receivable	200				200						200	
Supplies on Hand	60			(a) 40	20						20	
Prepaid Rent	80			(b) 60	20						20	
Equipment	150				150						150	
Accum. Depr.—Equip.		60		(c) 15		75						75
Accounts Payable		90				90						90
Capital Stock		30				30						30
Retained Earnings, Jan. 1, 1994		70				70				70		
Dividends	20				20				20			
Service Revenue		650				650		650				
Salaries Expense	200				200		200					
Insurance Expense	50				50		50					
Utilities Expense	30				30		30					
Miscellaneous Expense	10				10		10					
	900	900										
Supplies Expense			(a) 40		40		40					
Rent Expense			(b) 60		60		60					
Depr. Expense—Equip.			(c) 15		15		15					
			115	115	915	915	405	650				
Net Income							245			245		
							650	650	20	315		
Retained Earnings, Dec. 31, 1994									295			295
									315	315	490	490

Closing Entries

a. Service Revenue 650
   Income Summary 650
b. Income Summary 405
   Salaries Expense 200
   Insurance Expense 50
   Utilities Expense 30
   Miscellaneous Expense 10
   Supplies Expense 40
   Rent Expense 60
   Depreciation Expense—Equipment 15
c. Income Summary 245
   Retained Earnings 245
d. Retained Earnings 20
   Dividends 20

15.

B. B. BEAN COMPANY
Income Statement
For the Year Ended December 31, 1994

Revenues:
  Service revenue $650
Expenses:
  Salaries expense $200
  Insurance expense 50
  Utilities expense 30
  Miscellaneous expense 10
  Supplies expense 40
  Rent expense 60
  Depreciation expense—equipment 15   405
Net income $245

16.

B. B. BEAN COMPANY
Statement of Retained Earnings
For the Year Ended December 31, 1994

Retained earnings, January 1, 1994 .... $ 70
  Add: Net income 245
    Total $315
Less: Dividends 20
Retained earnings, December 31, 1994 .... $295

17.

B. B. BEAN COMPANY
Balance Sheet
December 31, 1994

Assets

Cash		$100
Accounts receivable		200
Supplies on hand		20
Prepaid rent		20
Equipment	$150	
Less: Accumulated depreciation—equipment	75	75
Total assets		$415

Liabilities and Stockholders' Equity

Liabilities:		
Accounts payable		$ 90
Stockholders' equity:		
Capital stock	$ 30	
Retained earnings, December 31, 1994	295	
Total stockholders' equity		325
Total liabilities and stockholders' equity		$415

Closing Entries

18.

Service Revenue	40,000	
Interest Revenue	5,000	
Income Summary		45,000
To close the revenue accounts.		
Income Summary	22,700	
Service Expense		4,000
Salaries Expense		5,500
Delivery Expense		13,200
To close the expense accounts.		
Income Summary	22,300	
Retained Earnings		22,300
To close the Income Summary account.		
Retained Earnings	5,000	
Dividends		5,000
To close the Dividends account.		

19. a.

	Statement of Retained Earnings		Balance Sheet	
	Dr.	Cr.	Dr.	Cr.
Retained Earnings, Jan. 1		15,000		
Net income for the year		10,000		
Dividends	4,900			
Retained Earnings, Dec. 31	20,100			20,100
	25,000	25,000		

b.

	Statement of Retained Earnings		Balance Sheet	
	Dr.	Cr.	Dr.	Cr.
Retained Earnings, Jan. 1		9,000		
Net loss for the year	6,750			
Retained Earnings (deficit), Dec. 31	2,250			2,250
	9,000	9,000		

Closing Entries

20.	Service Revenue	150,000	
	Rental Revenue	9,500	
	Income Summary		159,500
	To close revenue accounts.		
	Income Summary	105,500	
	Salaries Expense		72,000
	Depreciation Expense—Buildings		10,000
	Advertising Expense		11,500
	Utilities Expense		10,000
	Delivery Expense		2,000
	To close expense accounts.		
	Income Summary	54,000	
	Retained Earnings		54,000
	To close Income Summary account.		
21.	Salaries Payable	8,000	
	Salaries Expense		8,000
	To reverse accrued salaries.		

22.

CHRISTABEL COMPANY
Closing Entries

19—

December 31   Interest Revenue 180,000
                Painting Revenue 280,000
                Rental Revenue 1,500
                     Income Summary 461,500
                     To close the revenue accounts.

         31   Income Summary 228,300
                     Advertising Expense 1,800
                     Salaries Expense 200,000
                     Utilities Expense 3,500
                     Insurance Expense 2,000
                     Rent Expense 8,800
                     Supplies Expense 3,000
                     Depreciation Expense—Buildings 7,000
                     Interest Expense 1,500
                     Gas and Oil Expense 700
                     To close the expense accounts.

         31   Income Summary 233,200
                     Retained Earnings 233,200
                     To close net income to Retained Earnings.

         31   Retained Earnings 50,000
                     Dividends 50,000
                     To close the Dividends account.

23.

	Adjusted Trial Balance		Income Statement		Statement of Retained Earnings		Balance Sheet	
	Dr.	Cr.	Dr.	Cr.	Dr.	Cr.	Dr.	Cr.
a. Supplies Expense	X		X					
b. Accounts Receivable	X						X	
c. Accounts Payable		X						X
d. Commissions Revenue		X		X				
e. Salaries Expense	X		X					
f. Retained Earnings (ending cr. bal.)						X		X
g. Service Revenue		X		X				
h. Net Loss for the Year*				X	X			

*The net loss figure actually represents an excess of debits over credits in the Income Statement columns. It appears in the credit column only so that the debit and credit columns will balance. It is then transferred to the debit side of the Statement of Retained Earnings column.

24. a. The following adjusting journal entries should have been made at December 31.

      1. Supplies Expense 750
          Supplies on Hand 750
          To record supplies used.

      2. Insurance Expense 1,200
          Prepaid Insurance 1,200
          To record insurance expense.

      3. Depreciation Expense—Equipment 4,500
          Accumulated Depreciation—Equipment 4,500
          To record depreciation for half a year.

      4. Salaries Expense 2,000
          Salaries Payable 2,000
          To record accrued salaries.

      5. Unearned Delivery Fees 1,000
          Delivery Fees Revenue 1,000
          To record delivery fee earned.

   b. Correct net income is $18,300, computed as follows:

Reported net income	$25,750
Add: Total delivery fees earned	1,000
	$26,750

Less:

Supplies expense	$ 750	
Insurance expense	1,200	
Depreciation expense—equipment	4,500	
Salaries expense	2,000	8,450
Correct net income		$18,300

True-False Questions

1. F Accounts Receivable is a current asset, and assets are not closed.
2. T
3. F This statement describes a closing entry.
4. T
5. F Expenses are closed by debiting Income Summary and crediting the expense account.
6. T
7. T Net income would be included in total Retained Earnings, but would not be separately identified.
8. F The correct entry would be a debit to Retained Earnings and a credit to Income Summary in the amount of $800. The Dividends account would be closed directly to Retained Earnings.
9. F The Income Summary account would have a credit balance before closing.
10. T
11. F Dividends are a distribution of assets, not an expense of the company.
12. F The post-closing trial balance is prepared after the closing entries have been journalized and posted.
13. F
14. T
15. T Revenues are recorded on the credit side of the Income Summary and expenses are debits.
16. F Assets, liabilities, and stockholders' equity accounts remain open. Revenue and expense accounts are closed.
17. T
18. T
19. T
20. T

21. T
22. F Posting should not be made from the work sheet; journal entries are the source from which postings to the ledger are made.
23. F The adjusted trial balance contains assets, liabilities, stockholders' equity, and revenue and expense accounts.
24. T
25. F A note payable due in eight years would be classified as a long-term liability.

Multiple Choice Questions

1. D There will be an Accumulated Depreciation account showing the total depreciation taken on the store fixtures since their acquisition.
2. A Adjusting and closing entries must still be entered in the journal and posted to the ledger; postings cannot be made directly from the work sheet.
3. B $159,000 expenses − $147,000 revenues = $12,000 net loss.
4. B $62,000 + $3,500 depreciation expense + $2,500 salaries expense = $68,000.

   The other adjustments would result in a debit to an expense account and a credit to an asset account and there would be no new account involved as there would be for Salaries Payable and Accumulated Depreciation.
5. A $315 − $290 expense = $25 Supplies on Hand.
6. D
7. A
8. D
9. A The omitted journal entry would be a debit to Sales Salaries Expense and a credit to Sales Salaries Payable of $600; assets are not involved in this entry.
10. A
11. B $25,000 12-31 assets
    − 6,000 12-31 liabilities
    $19,000 12-31 stockholders' equity

    $30,000 revenues
    − 8,000 dividends
    − 4,000 increase in stockholders' equity during year
    $18,000 expenses
12. C
13. A $300,000 − $250,000 = $50,000 income; $475,000 − $50,000 income = $425,000.
14. B
15. E

5 MERCHANDISING TRANSACTIONS, INTRODUCTION TO INVENTORIES, AND CLASSIFIED INCOME STATEMENT

Learning Objectives

1. *Record journal entries for sales transactions involving merchandise.*
2. *Describe briefly cost of goods sold and the distinction between perpetual and periodic inventory procedures.*
3. *Record journal entries for purchase transactions involving merchandise.*
4. *Describe the freight terms and record transportation costs.*
5. *Determine cost of goods sold.*
6. *Prepare a classified income statement.*
7. *Prepare a work sheet and closing entries for a merchandising company.*

CHAPTER OUTLINE

TWO INCOME STATEMENTS COMPARED—SERVICE COMPANY AND MERCHANDISING COMPANY

1. A merchandising company's income statement is more involved than a service company's since inventories must be included on the merchandising company's statement.

SALES REVENUES

2. Sales revenues are earned from sales of merchandise to final consumers or to other companies.

RECORDING GROSS SALES

3. A sales transaction consists of the transfer of legal ownership, or passage of title, of goods from one party to another.
   a. The sales transaction is usually accompanied by physical delivery of goods.
   b. A revenue account entitled Sales is credited when a sale is made; Cash is debited if payment is received or Accounts Receivable is debited for sales on account.
   c. An invoice is prepared by the seller of merchandise and sent to the buyer. The invoice contains the details of a sale.
      (1) The invoice contains such items as the number of units sold, unit price, total price billed, terms of sale, and manner of shipment.
      (2) An invoice is called a sales invoice by the seller and a purchase invoice by the buyer.
   d. The following justification exists for recording revenue at the time of sale.
      (1) Legal title to the goods has passed and the goods are now the responsibility and property of the buyer.
      (2) The selling price of the goods has been established.
      (3) The seller's obligation has been completed.
      (4) The goods have been exchanged for another asset, such as cash or accounts receivable.
      (5) The costs incurred can be determined.

DETERMINING GROSS SALES PRICE WHEN COMPANIES OFFER TRADE DISCOUNTS

4. Trade discounts are deductions from the list or catalog price of merchandise to arrive at gross selling price.
   a. Trade discounts may be shown on the seller's invoice, but they are not recorded in the buyer's or seller's books.
   b. Trade discounts are used by various industries for a number of purposes.
      (1) Trade discounts are used to reduce the cost of catalog publications because separate discount lists can be distributed at less cost than reprinting a catalog.
      (2) Trade discounts can be used to grant quantity discounts.
      (3) Trade discounts facilitate the quotation of different prices to different types of customers, such as retailers and wholesalers.
   c. A chain discount occurs when a list price is subject to several trade discounts.

RECORDING DEDUCTIONS FROM GROSS SALES

5. Sales discounts and sales returns and allowances are two common deductions from gross sales that are recorded in contra accounts to the Sales account.

SALES DISCOUNTS

6. The terms of the cash discount vary between industries but all cash discounts are offered as an incentive for early payment and are a deduction from the gross selling price to arrive at actual cost of the purchase.
   a. To the seller, a cash discount is a sales discount.
   b. To the buyer, a cash discount is a purchase discount.
   c. Cash discount terms of 2/10, n/30 mean that a discount of 2% of the gross selling price of the merchandise may be taken if payment is made within ten days following the invoice date. Otherwise, the gross selling price is due 30 days from the invoice date.
   d. A 2/EOM, n/60 cash discount means a 2% discount may be deducted if the invoice is paid by the end of the month. The gross amount is due 60 days from the date of the invoice.
   e. A 2/10/EOM, n/60 cash discount means a 2% discount may be deducted if the invoice is paid by the 10th day of the month following the date of sale. The gross amount is due 60 days from the date of the invoice.
   f. The Sales Discount account is a contra revenue account to Sales and is shown as a deduction from gross sales in the income statement.

SALES RETURNS AND ALLOWANCES

7. Merchandise returned by the buyer is recorded in a Sales Returns and Allowances account, which is a contra revenue account to Sales.
   a. If cash has already been paid by the buyer for goods returned, the debit is to Sales Returns and Allowances and the credit is to Cash.
      (1) If the purchase was paid for in the discount period, only the net amount would be returned to the customer. The entry would be a debit to Sales Returns and Allowances and a credit to Sales Discounts (for the discount taken on the returned merchandise) and a credit to Cash.
      (2) The credit to Sales Discounts reduces the balance of that account.
   b. If the customer had not paid for the merchandise being returned, the debit is to Sales Returns and Allowances and the credit is to Accounts Receivable.

REPORTING NET SALES IN THE INCOME STATEMENT

8. Rather than report the details of the net sales computation with Sales Discounts and Sales Returns and Allowances deducted from Sales, the income statement may only indicate the net sales.

COST OF GOODS SOLD

9. Cost of goods sold indicates the cost to the seller of the goods sold to the buyer of the merchandise. This category is a section of the classified income statement.
   a. Merchandise inventory is the quantity of goods on hand and available for sale at any given time.
   b. Cost of goods sold is determined by computing the cost of beginning inventory plus the net cost of purchases less the ending inventory.

TWO PROCEDURES FOR ACCOUNTING FOR INVENTORIES—PERPETUAL AND PERIODIC

10. Perpetual inventory procedure and periodic inventory procedure comprise two procedures for accounting for inventory. Perpetual inventory procedure will be covered in a later chapter.
    a. Under periodic inventory procedure, the cost of goods sold and the ending inventory are determined *only* at the end of the accounting period.
    b. Periodic inventory procedure is more often used by companies selling low value items because there is less control under this approach.

PURCHASES OF MERCHANDISE

11. Under periodic inventory procedure, the Purchases account is used to record the cost of merchandise purchased during the period.

    a. Increases to the Purchases account are recorded as debits, and the credit is to Cash (if payment is made) or to Accounts Payable (if payment will be made later).

    b. The Purchases account is shown in the Income Statement debit column of the work sheet and as part of the Cost of Goods Sold section of the classified income statement.

DEDUCTIONS FROM PURCHASES

12. Deductions from purchases to arrive at net purchases include purchase discounts and purchase returns and allowances, which are recorded in contra accounts to the Purchases account.

PURCHASE DISCOUNTS

13. The buyer may be able to take a purchase discount on the merchandise bought when the credit terms specify that a discount can be deducted if the invoice is paid within a stated time period.

    a. The Purchase Discounts account is a contra account to Purchases that reduces the recorded gross invoice cost of the purchase to the price actually paid.

    b. The entry to record purchase discounts is to debit Accounts Payable and to credit Cash and Purchase Discounts.

NET PRICE METHOD

14. Instead of using the gross price method of recording purchases, the net price method can be used that emphasizes the importance of taking purchase discounts.

    a. Using the net price method, a purchase is recorded in Purchases and Accounts Payable net of the discount.

       (1) Using this approach, the discount is deducted before the transaction is entered in the journal.

       (2) The net price method has theoretical merit because the goods are recorded at their actual cash cost.

       (3) This approach does not show discounts taken.

       (4) Under this approach if the discount is missed, the lost discount is recorded as a nonoperating expense in an account called Discounts Lost.

PURCHASE RETURNS AND ALLOWANCES

15. Because the owners of the company may want to know the amounts of returns and allowances taken on goods purchased, a separate Purchase Returns and Allowances account is used.

    a. The Purchase Returns and Allowances account is a contra account to the Purchases account and is shown on the income statement as a deduction from purchases.

    b. The Purchase Returns and Allowances account normally has a credit balance.

TRANSPORTATION COSTS

16. There are various terms used to indicate whether the buyer or seller pays for the costs incurred to deliver the merchandise purchased to the buyer.

    a. The term "FOB shipping point" means free on board at shipping point, and the buyer incurs all transportation costs after the merchandise is loaded at the point of shipment.

    b. The term "FOB destination" means the seller incurs the transportation charges, and the goods are shipped to their destination without the buyer paying the freight charge.

    c. Passage of title is a legal term used to indicate transfer of legal ownership of goods.

    d. The term "freight prepaid" is used when the seller pays the freight at the time of shipment.

    e. The term "freight collect" is used when the buyer pays the freight bill upon arrival of the goods.

MERCHANDISE INVENTORIES

17. Merchandise inventory is the quantity of goods on hand that are available for sale.

   a. The beginning inventory cost is already known because it is the balance of the Merchandise Inventory account.

   b. The ending inventory cost is determined under the periodic inventory procedure by taking a physical count of goods on hand and costing them.

      (1) Goods delivered on consignment should not be recorded as sold because the owner has only shipped these goods to another party who is trying to sell them.

      (2) If passage of title has occurred, merchandise in transit must be recorded as a purchase by the buyer and included in inventory.

DETERMINING COST OF GOODS SOLD

18. The relationship between the items used in determining cost of goods sold is as follows:

   a. $\text{Beginning inventory} + \text{Net cost of purchases} = \text{Cost of goods available for sale}$

   b. $\text{Cost of goods available for sale} - \text{Ending inventory} = \text{Cost of goods sold}$

LACK OF CONTROL UNDER PERIODIC INVENTORY PROCEDURE

19. Periodic inventory procedure provides little control over inventory because this method assumes that any items not included in the physical count of inventory have been sold.

CLASSIFIED INCOME STATEMENT

20. Revenues and expenses are the only two categories on the unclassified income statement, while the classified income statement divides revenues and expenses into operating and nonoperating items.

   a. A classified income statement separates operating expenses into selling and administrative expenses.

   b. A classified income statement is also known as a multiple-step income statement.

   c. An income statement for a merchandising company usually has four sections.

      (1) Operating revenues—sales and sales contra accounts.

      (2) Cost of goods sold.

      (3) Operating expenses.

      (4) Nonoperating revenues and expenses—other revenues and other expenses.

   d. Gross margin is the excess of net sales over cost of goods sold.

IMPORTANT RELATIONSHIPS IN THE INCOME STATEMENT

21. The important relationships in the income statement of a merchandising firm can be summarized in the following equation forms.

   1. *Net sales* = Gross sales − Sales returns and allowances − Sales discounts.

   2. *Net purchases* = Purchases − Purchase returns and allowances − Purchase discounts.

   3. *Net cost of purchases* = Net purchases + Transportation-in.

   4. *Cost of goods sold* = Beginning inventory + Net cost of purchases − Ending inventory.

   5. *Gross margin* = Net sales − Cost of goods sold.

   6. *Net income from operations* = Gross margin − Operating (selling and administrative) expenses.

   7. *Net income* = Net income from operations + Nonoperating revenues − Nonoperating expenses.

THE WORK SHEET FOR A MERCHANDISING COMPANY

22. A merchandising company's completed work sheet is slightly different than a service company's work sheet.

COMPLETING THE WORK SHEET

23. The steps in completing the work sheet for a merchandising company are as follows:

    a. All revenue accounts and contra purchases accounts are carried to the Income Statement credit column.
    b. All expense accounts, contra revenue accounts, beginning inventory, purchases, and transportation-in are carried to the Income Statement debit column.
    c. The ending merchandise inventory is entered in the Income Statement credit column and the Balance Sheet debit column.

FINANCIAL STATEMENTS FOR A MERCHANDISING COMPANY

24. After the work sheet has been completed, the financial statements are prepared from data appearing in the Income Statement and Balance Sheet columns.

INCOME STATEMENT

25. The focus of a merchandising company's income statement is on the determination of cost of goods sold.

STATEMENT OF RETAINED EARNINGS

26. The statement of retained earnings summarizes the transactions affecting the Retained Earnings account balance.

BALANCE SHEET

27. A merchandising company's balance sheet differs from a service company's balance sheet only because of the addition of Merchandise Inventory as a current asset.

CLOSING ENTRIES

28. Closing entries may be prepared directly from the work sheet using information appearing in the Income Statement columns.

    a. Merchandise Inventory (ending balance), Sales, Purchase Discounts, and Purchase Returns and Allowances accounts are debited, and Income Summary is credited for the total.
    b. Merchandise Inventory (beginning balance), Sales Discounts, Sales Returns and Allowances, Purchases, Transportation-in, Selling Expense, and Administration Expense accounts are credited, and Income Summary is debited for the total.
    c. The balance of Income Summary is closed to the Retained Earnings account just as in a service company.
    d. The Dividends account is closed to the Retained Earnings account just as in a service company.

APPENDIX: ALTERNATIVE CLOSING PROCEDURE

29. An alternative closing procedure is to transfer the beginning inventory balance and balances in purchase-related accounts to the Cost of Goods Sold account in an adjusting entry. The ending inventory is established by debiting Merchandise Inventory and crediting Cost of Goods Sold. Finally the Cost of Goods Sold account is closed to Income Summary by debiting Income Summary and crediting Cost of Goods Sold.

The following trial balance was taken from the ledger of the Overlook Shop at the end of its annual accounting period:

THE OVERLOOK SHOP
Trial Balance
December 31, 1993

Cash	$ 4,000	
Merchandise Inventory	14,400	
Land	20,000	
Accounts Payable		$ 6,640
Notes Payable		7,000
Capital Stock		14,000
Retained Earnings, 1/1/93		20,000
Dividends	7,200	
Sales		90,000
Sales Returns and Allowances	1,000	
Purchases	72,000	
Purchase Returns and Allowances		1,440
Transportation-In	480	
Selling Expenses	12,000	
Administrative Expenses	8,000	
	$139,080	$139,080

Required:

a. Copy the trial balance onto a work sheet form and complete the work sheet under the assumption that there are no adjustments. The ending inventory is $19,200.

Part a. (Work sheet) Appears at the back of the book.

b. Prepare the income statement, statement of retained earnings and balance sheet.
c. Prepare closing entries.

b.

b. *(concluded)*

c.

DATE	ACCOUNT TITLES AND EXPLANATION	POST. REF.	DEBIT	CREDIT

Chapter 5

SOLUTION TO DEMONSTRATION PROBLEM

a.

THE OVERLOOK SHOP
Work Sheet
For Year Ended December 31, 1993

	Trial Balance		Adjustments		Adjusted Trial Balance		Income Statement		Statement of Retained Earnings		Balance Sheet	
	Debit	Credit	Debit	Credit	Debit	Credit	Debit	Credit	Debit	Credit	Debit	Credit
Cash	4,000	.....	.....	.....	4,000	.....	.....	.....	.....	.....	4,000	.....
Merchandise Inventory	14,400	.....	.....	.....	14,400	.....	14,400	19,200	.....	.....	19,200	.....
Land	20,000	.....	.....	.....	20,000	.....	.....	.....	.....	.....	20,000	.....
Accounts Payable	.....	6,640	.....	.....	.....	6,640	.....	.....	.....	.....	.....	6,640
Notes Payable	.....	7,000	.....	.....	.....	7,000	.....	.....	.....	.....	.....	7,000
Capital Stock	.....	14,000	.....	.....	.....	14,000	.....	.....	.....	.....	.....	14,000
Retained Earnings, 1/1/93	.....	20,000	.....	.....	.....	20,000	.....	.....	.....	20,000	.....	.....
Dividends	7,200	.....	.....	.....	7,200	.....	.....	.....	7,200	.....	.....	.....
Sales	.....	90,000	.....	.....	.....	90,000	.....	90,000	.....	.....	.....	.....
Sales Returns and Allowances	1,000	.....	.....	.....	1,000	.....	1,000	.....	.....	.....	.....	.....
Purchases	72,000	.....	.....	.....	72,000	.....	72,000	.....	.....	.....	.....	.....
Purchase Returns and Allowances	.....	1,440	.....	.....	.....	1,440	.....	1,440	.....	.....	.....	.....
Transportation-In	480	.....	.....	.....	480	.....	480	.....	.....	.....	.....	.....
Selling Expenses	12,000	.....	.....	.....	12,000	.....	12,000	.....	.....	.....	.....	.....
Administrative Expenses	8,000	.....	.....	.....	8,000	.....	8,000	.....	.....	.....	.....	.....
	139,080	139,080			139,080	139,080	107,880	110,640				
Net Income							2,760			2,760		
							110,640	110,640				
									7,200	22,760		
Retained Earnings									15,560			15,560
									22,760	22,760	43,200	43,200

b.

THE OVERLOOK SHOP
Income Statement
For the Year Ended December 31, 1993

Sales			$90,000
Less: Sales returns and allowances			1,000
Net sales			$89,000
Cost of goods sold:			
Merchandise inventory 1/1/93		$14,400	
Purchases	$72,000		
Less: Purchase returns and allowances	1,440		
Net purchases	$70,560		
Add: Transportation-in	480		
Net cost of purchases		71,040	
Cost of goods available for sale		$85,440	
Less: Merchandise inventory 12/31/93		19,200	
Cost of goods sold			66,240
Gross margin			$22,760
Operating expenses:			
Selling expenses		$12,000	
Administrative expenses		8,000	20,000
Net income			$ 2,760

THE OVERLOOK SHOP
Statement of Retained Earnings
For the Year Ended December 31, 1993

Retained earnings 1/1/93	$20,000
Add: Net income	2,760
Less: Dividends	(7,200)
Retained earnings 12/31/93	$15,560

THE OVERLOOK SHOP
Balance Sheet
December 31, 1993

Cash	$ 4,000	
Merchandise inventory	19,200	
Land	20,000	
Total assets		$43,200
Accounts payable	$ 6,640	
Notes payable	7,000	
Total liabilities		$13,640
Capital stock	$14,000	
Retained earnings	15,560	
Total stockholders' equity		29,560
Total liabilities and stockholders' equity		$43,200

c.

Closing Entries

Merchandise Inventory	19,200	
Sales	90,000	
Purchase Returns and Allowances	1,440	
Income Summary		110,640
Income Summary	107,880	
Merchandise Inventory		14,400
Sales Returns and Allowances		1,000
Purchases		72,000
Transportation-In		480
Selling Expenses		12,000
Administrative Expenses		8,000
Income Summary	2,760	
Retained Earnings		2,760
Retained Earnings	7,200	
Dividends		7,200

MATCHING

Referring to the terms listed below, place the appropriate letter next to the corresponding description. A term may be used more than once.

a.	Administrative expenses	f.	FOB destination	k.	Nonoperating revenues
b.	Chain discount	g.	FOB shipping point	l.	Operating revenues
c.	Cost of goods sold	h.	Freight collect	m.	Purchase discounts
d.	Credit	i.	Freight prepaid	n.	Sales discounts
e.	Debit	j.	Gross margin	o.	Selling expenses

_____ 1. Advertising Expense, Warehousing and Handling Expense, and Salaries Expense—Marketing Managers are grouped into this category.

_____ 2. Net sales − Cost of goods sold.

_____ 3. Expenses incurred in performing and facilitating the marketing effort.

_____ 4. Beginning inventory + Net cost of purchases − Ending inventory.

_____ 5. Operating expenses incurred in the overall management of a business.

_____ 6. Are deducted along with purchase returns and allowances from gross purchases to arrive at net purchases.

_____ 7. This term is used when the seller pays the freight at the time of shipment.

_____ 8. Revenues generated by the major activities of the business.

_____ 9. The term used when the seller incurs all the transportation charges.

_____ 10. The normal balance of the Purchase Discounts account.

_____ 11. This term is applied when a list price is subject to several trade discounts.

_____ 12. Cash discounts as recorded on the books of the buyer.

_____ 13. The term used when goods are shipped to their destination without charge to the buyer.

_____ 14. The term used when the buyer incurs all transportation costs after the merchandise is loaded at the point of shipment.

_____ 15. This term is used when the buyer pays the freight bill upon arrival of the goods.

1. When using periodic inventory procedure, how is the amount of the ending inventory determined?

   _____

   _____

   _____

2. Although cash discounts are offered to induce prompt payment of an account, they are theoretically viewed

   as _____ of revenue by the seller and of cost by the buyer.

3. The two basic inventory procedures are _____ and _____.

4. Suppose that **A** sold $2,000 of merchandise to **B** on July 26 under terms of 2/10, n/30. State exactly what is meant by these terms under these circumstances.

   _____

   _____

   _____

   _____

   _____

   _____

5. Use the data in Question 4 and assume that **B** returned $400 of the merchandise to **A** and then paid the balance of the invoice within the discount period. In the space below, give the necessary entries on **B**'s books for the purchase, the return, and the payment. (Assume **B** uses periodic inventory procedure and the gross method of recording purchases.)

DATE	ACCOUNT TITLES AND EXPLANATION	POST. REF.	DEBIT	CREDIT

6. Typically, _____ discounts are not recorded by either the buyer or the seller.

7. Smith purchased $4,000 of goods under terms 2/10, n/30, FOB destination, freight of $200 prepaid. Smith would pay the seller $_____ if Smith paid the invoice on these goods within the discount period.

8. Using the following information, prepare the necessary closing entries for the Salada Company.

Sales	$200,000
Merchandise inventory, 1/1	70,000
Merchandise inventory, 12/31	58,000
Purchases	140,000
Purchase discounts	2,400
Purchase returns and allowances	4,800
Transportation-in	7,000
Selling expenses	10,000
Administrative expenses	10,000

DATE	ACCOUNT TITLES AND EXPLANATION	POST. REF.	DEBIT	CREDIT

9. Use the information in Question 8 to prepare an income statement.

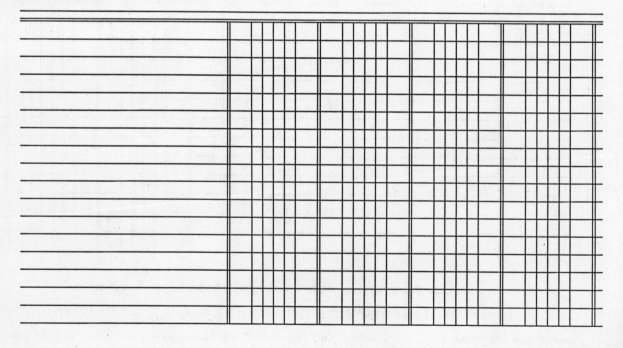

Chapter 5

10. A disadvantage of periodic inventory procedure is that losses from shrinkage, deterioration, and shoplifting are _____

    _____

    with the result that management can only estimate their amounts.

11. The following information is given:

Invoice Date	List Price	Trade Discounts	Credit Terms	Date Paid
May 21	$1,800	10%, 15%	2/10, n/30	June 17

    The amount to be recorded as the selling price is _____. The amount that was actually paid is

    _____.

12. In taking a physical inventory, care should be exercised to exclude _____ _____

    _____ and _____ _____.

13. Joe sold $2,000 of merchandise to Larry under terms 2/10, n/30, FOB destination, freight of $100 prepaid. The transportation company would receive payment from _____ who would charge (debit) the amount paid to _____.

14. If the terms in Question 13 had been FOB shipping point, freight collect, the transportation company would receive payment from _____ who would charge it to _____.

15. S sold merchandise to B, list price $20,000, less 50% and 20%, under terms of 2/10, n/30, FOB shipping point, freight of $200 collect. If B paid S within the discount period, B would send a check in the amount of $_____.

16. Marie Inc. purchased merchandise from Peggy Inc.; invoice price, $20,000; terms 2/10, n/30. The merchandise is FOB destination and the freight cost is $400. Marie returned $2,000 of the merchandise and then paid the balance due on the invoice before the discount period had expired. Give the entries required on Marie's books. Use the gross method.

DATE	ACCOUNT TITLES AND EXPLANATION	POST. REF.	DEBIT	CREDIT

17. The income statement of a merchandising company generally has four major sections, namely:

a. _____

b. _____

c. _____

d. _____

18. Distinguish between an operating expense and a nonoperating expense.

_____

_____

_____

_____

_____

_____

19. Accounts that appear on the work sheet of a merchandising company which do not appear on that of a service company are the following (in any order):

a. _____   e. _____

b. _____   f. _____

c. _____   g. _____

d. _____   h. _____

20. Determine the missing amounts in the following data. The individual cases are not related.

Sales	$ 80,000	$? (b)	$180,000	$ 80,000	$160,000
Gross margin	20,000	60,000	? (c)	20,000	20,000
Purchases	120,000	100,000	80,000	100,000	? (e)
Beginning inventory	? (a)	20,000	80,000	20,000	80,000
Ending inventory	100,000	40,000	20,000	? (d)	40,000
Answers	$_____	$_____	$_____	$_____	$_____

The subtotals of the income statement columns of a work sheet are $860,000 debit and $880,000 credit. What is the amount of the income or loss? (Indicate

whether income or loss.) .... $_____ (f)

21. Generally, a sale consists of transfer of _____ _____ to goods accompanied by actual _____ to the customer.

22. Net sales of a firm is usually equal to sales less _____ _____, _____

_____ and _____. The net sales amount is important because it represents an

approximate measure of the flow of _____ into a firm from its operations.

23. Give two reasons why the accountant finds recording revenue at the time of sale attractive.

1. _____

_____

2. _____

_____

24. Phenix Company purchased goods from City Company and received an invoice in the amount of $3,000. Phenix paid the $160 freight on the goods, which were sold under terms of 2/10, n/30, FOB shipping point. If Phenix uses the net price procedure in recording its purchases, it should record the account payable to

City in the amount of $_____.

25. The following data pertain to a particular purchase:

Date of invoice .... August 23
List price $4,000
Trade discount 40%
Prepaid freight $200
Terms .... 2/10, n/30; FOB shipping point

a. When the invoice is received from the vendor, the purchaser should expect the total of the invoice to be what amount? .... $ _____

b. What is the last day on which the purchaser may make payment and still be entitled to the cash discount? .... _____

c. What is the amount of cash discount that can be taken if the invoice is paid within the discount period? .... $ _____

26. Determine the amount to be paid in full settlement of each of the following invoices assuming that the credit memorandum was received prior to payment. The first invoice was paid within the discount period and the second invoice was paid after the discount period.

Purchase Invoice:	(a)	(b)
Merchandise	$6,000	$10,000
Transportation	$200 prepaid	
Terms	FOB shipping point 2/10, n/30	FOB destination 1/10, n/30
Credit memorandum:		
Merchandise returned	$200	$300

Amount to be paid in full settlement .... $_____ $_____

TRUE-FALSE QUESTIONS

Indicate whether each of the following statements is true or false by inserting a capital "T" or "F" in the blank space provided.

_____ 1. Sales Returns and Allowances is debited and Income Summary is credited in the closing entry.

_____ 2. Trade discounts are terms which allow deductions to customers if they pay their bills within a definite period of time.

_____ 3. The Purchase Returns and Allowances account normally has a credit balance.

_____ 4. Cash discounts taken on goods acquired for resale should be debited to a Sales Discounts account.

_____ 5. Periodic inventory procedure provides more control over inventory than does the perpetual inventory procedure.

_____ 6. A cash discount is synonymous with a trade discount.

_____ 7. Buyers determine their cash discount on the total amount of the invoice, including the freight charge under the terms FOB shipping point when the seller prepays the freight.

_____ 8. Under periodic inventory procedure, the cost of goods sold is reflected in the balance of the Purchases account.

_____ 9. An error that understates purchases will overstate net income in the year of the error.

_____ 10. Typically, neither a trade discount nor a cash discount is recorded by seller or buyer.

_____ 11. Assume that inventory was not counted and was omitted from the Merchandise Inventory account at year-end; this omission would cause inventory and retained earnings on the balance sheet to be understated because cost of goods sold would be understated.

_____ 12. The merchandise inventory amount in the Balance Sheet debit column of the work sheet is the ending inventory.

_____ 13. Cost of goods sold is the net cost of purchases of the period adjusted for any difference between beginning and ending inventories.

_____ 14. An income statement which separates revenues and expenses into operating and nonoperating items is called a classified or multiple-step income statement.

_____ 15. The work sheet of a merchandising company eliminates the need for preparing and posting adjusting and closing journal entries.

_____ 16. Using the credit terms 2/10, n/30 means that the buyer may deduct 10% of the amount of the invoice if payment is made by the 2nd of the following month.

_____ 17. Cash discounts are substantial reductions from the list price granted to retailers and wholesalers in differing amounts to reflect a variety of quantities purchased or services performed for the seller.

_____ 18. A company's cost of goods sold would be $106,000 for a period in which purchases were $70,000, beginning inventory was $36,000, and ending inventory was zero.

_____ 19. Sales would be $300,000 for a company based on the following data: Beginning inventory—$72,000; Ending inventory—$80,000; Cost of goods sold—$160,000; Gross margin—$100,000.

_____ 20. In a sale of merchandise, the buyer should receive an invoice from the seller.

_____ 21. With trade discounts of 20%, 10%, and 5% and a list price of $200, the sale should be recorded in the journal as $136.80.

_____ 22. If the accountant mistakenly places a revenue account balance in the Balance Sheet credit column of the work sheet, the work sheet columns will still balance.

_____ 23. Merchandise on consignment should not appear as inventory on the consignee's balance sheet.

_____ 24. The balances of the Purchase Returns and Allowances account and the Purchases Discount account are subtracted from Purchases on the Income Statement to show Cost of Goods Available for Sale.

_____ 25. Consigned goods should be included in the owner's inventory even though the owner may have delivered them to another party.

MULTIPLE CHOICE QUESTIONS

For each of the following questions indicate the best answer by circling the appropriate letter.

1. In the Income Statement:
   A. operating expenses are usually classified as either "Administrative Expenses" or "Selling Expenses."
   B. Ending Inventory is added to Purchases to determine Cost of Goods Available for Sale.
   C. "Net Income from Operations" and "Net Income" are synonymous.
   D. the amount shown as "Net Sales" includes all cash sales plus only those charge sales for which cash has been received.
   E. expenses are subtracted from revenues to determine the balance of the Retained Earnings account.

2. If the net cost of purchases was $50,000, what was the company's cost of goods sold if beginning inventory was $18,000 and ending inventory was $38,000?
   A. $70,000
   B. $106,000
   C. $30,000
   D. None of these.

3. Which of the following correctly describes the makeup of the cost of goods sold section of the income statement under periodic inventory procedure?
   A. Beginning inventory + Purchases – Purchase discounts – Purchase returns and allowances + Transportation-in + Ending inventory
   B. Beginning inventory – Purchases – Purchase discounts – Purchase returns and allowances + Transportation-in – Ending inventory
   C. Beginning inventory + Purchases – Purchase discounts – Purchase returns and allowances – Transportation-in + Ending inventory
   D. Beginning inventory + Purchases – Purchase discounts – Purchase returns and allowances – Transportation-in – Ending inventory
   E. None of the above.

4. Cost of goods sold is equal to:
   A. net cost of purchases plus beginning inventory.
   B. cost of goods available for sale less ending inventory.
   C. cost of the items that were sold during the period.
   D. net sales less gross margin.
   E. All of the above except (A).

5. The entry on the books of the seller to record the return of merchandise sold on account for which no payment has been received is:
   A. Sales
        Accounts Receivable
   B. Accounts Receivable
        Sales Returns and Allowances
   C. Sales Returns and Allowances
        Cash
   D. Sales Returns and Allowances
        Sales
   E. None of these.

6–7. In the following equations identify the item designated by X.

6. Merchandise inventory (beginning) + X = Cost of goods available for sale

    A. Purchase discounts
    B. Net cost of purchases
    C. Cost of goods sold
    D. Merchandise inventory (ending)
    E. None of these.

7. Net sales – X = Gross margin

    A. Net purchases
    B. Net profit
    C. Ending inventory
    D. Cost of goods sold
    E. None of these.

8. An account payable of $400 is subject to a 2% discount if paid within the 60-day discount period. Part of the entry to record this payment under the gross price method would be:

    A. a credit to Accounts Payable of $400.
    B. a credit to Accounts Payable of $392.
    C. a debit to Accounts Payable of $400.
    D. a credit to Cash of $400.
    E. a debit to Purchase Discounts of $8.

9. Determine the amount to be paid in full settlement of the invoice, assuming that credit for returns and allowances was received prior to payment and that the invoice was paid within the discount period. Merchandise $2,600, Transportation $100, Returns and allowances $200, and terms FOB shipping point, 1/10, n/30, freight prepaid.

    A. $2,475
    B. $2,476
    C. $2,260
    D. $2,450
    E. None of these.

10. Partial closing entries for Key Company are given below.

Commissions Revenue	10,000	
Merchandise Inventory	7,000	
Income Summary		17,000

    The debit item of $7,000 is:

    A. the cost of the ending inventory.
    B. the cost of the beginning inventory.
    C. the cost of purchases made during the period.
    D. the cost of goods available for sale during the period.
    E. None of the above.

11–13. Given the following information for Questions 11-13:

    Purchases—$88,000
    Operating Expenses—$28,000
    Ending Inventory—$24,000
    Net Income—$20,000
    Cost of Goods Sold—$108,000

11. What is beginning inventory?

    A. $132,000
    B. $44,000
    C. $112,000
    D. $24,000

12. What is the gross margin?

    A. $132,000
    B. $20,000
    C. $48,000
    D. $8,000

13. What are sales?

    A. $132,000
    B. $44,000
    C. $156,000
    D. $128,000

14. Merchandise on hand July 1 was $10,800; purchases during July were $56,400; transportation-out was $1,400; transportation-in was $3,000; purchase returns were $1,200; inventory, July 31, was found to be $12,400. The cost of goods sold for the month of July was:

    A. $56,600
    B. $69,000
    C. $55,200
    D. $81,400
    E. $58,000

15. In the income statement the inventory that was on hand at the beginning of the period is treated as a(an):

    A. asset item.
    B. addition in the computation of cost of goods sold.
    C. deduction from purchases.
    D. direct deduction from gross sales.

SOLUTIONS

Matching

1.	o	4.	c	7.	i	10.	d	13.	f
2.	j	5.	a	8.	l	11.	b	14.	g
3.	o	6.	m	9.	f	12.	m	15.	h

Completion and Exercises

1. Quantities (obtained by physical counts) are multiplied by prices obtained from vendor's invoices and the extensions summed to arrive at the total cost of the inventory.
2. deductions or reductions
3. perpetual and periodic
4. **B** can deduct $40 (0.02 × $2,000) from the $2,000 amount of the invoice for these goods if **B** pays on or before August 5. Otherwise, **B** must pay $2,000 by August 25.

5. Purchases 2,000
        Accounts Payable 2,000
        To record purchase on account.

    Accounts Payable 400
        Purchase Returns and Allowances 400
        To record return of merchandise to vendor.

    Accounts Payable 1,600
        Purchase Discounts 32
        Cash 1,568
        To record payment of invoice.

6. trade
7. $3,920 [$4,000 − ($4,000 × 0.02)]

8. Merchandise Inventory (ending) 58,000
    Purchase Discounts 2,400
    Purchase Returns and Allowances 4,800
    Sales 200,000
        Income Summary 265,200

    Income Summary 237,000
        Purchases 140,000
        Transportation-In 7,000
        Merchandise Inventory (beginning) 70,000
        Selling Expenses 10,000
        Administrative Expenses 10,000

    Income Summary 28,200
        Retained Earnings 28,200

9.
SALADA COMPANY
Income Statement
For the Year Ended December 31, 19___

Sales			$200,000
Cost of goods sold:			
Merchandise inventory, 1/1		$ 70,000	
Purchases	$140,000		
Less: Purchase discounts	$2,400		
Purchase returns and allowances	4,800	7,200	
Net purchases		$132,800	
Add: Transportation-in		7,000	
Net cost of purchases		139,800	
Cost of goods available for sale		$209,800	
Less: Merchandise inventory, 12/31		58,000	
Cost of goods sold			151,800
Gross margin			$ 48,200
Operating expenses:			
Selling expenses		$ 10,000	
Administrative expenses		10,000	20,000
Net income			$ 28,200

10. buried in cost of goods sold (when the cost of the ending inventory is deducted from total goods available for sale)

121

11. $1,377; $1,377
12. goods not owned; nonsalable goods
13. Joe; Delivery Expense
14. Larry; Transportation-In
15. $7,840 [$8,000 − ($8,000 × 0.02)]. $20,000 × .50 × .80 = $8,000. The transportation company would collect $200 from **B**.

16.
Purchases	20,000	
Accounts Payable		20,000

    To record invoice price of goods purchased.

Accounts Payable	2,000	
Purchase Returns and Allowances		2,000

    To record return of merchandise.

Accounts Payable	18,000	
Cash		17,640
Purchase Discounts		360

    To record payment of invoice before discount period has expired.

17. (a) operating revenues (sales); (b) cost of goods sold; (c) operating expenses; (d) nonoperating revenues and nonoperating expenses.
18. An operating expense is an expense incurred in carrying out a company's major activity, such as sales salaries. A nonoperating expense is an expense incurred that relates only remotely (or not at all) to a company's main line of activity, such as interest expense.
19. a. Merchandise Inventory
    b. Purchases
    c. Purchase Returns and Allowances
    d. Purchase Discounts
    e. Transportation-In
    f. Sales
    g. Sales Returns and Allowances
    h. Sales Discounts
20. (a) $40,000; (b) $140,000; (c) $40,000; (d) $60,000; (e) $100,000; (f) $20,000 income.
21. legal title; delivery
22. sales discounts, sales returns and allowances; assets
23. Any two of the following reasons could be given:
    1. Legal title to the goods has passed and the goods are now the responsibility and property of the buyer.
    2. The selling price of the goods has been established.
    3. The seller's part of the contract has been completed.
    4. The goods have been exchanged for another asset, such as cash or accounts receivable.
    5. The costs incurred can be determined.
24. $2,940 (Note that Phenix Company incurred the cost for freight.)
25. a. $2,600 [($4,000 × .60) + $200]
    b. September 2
    c. $48 ($2,400 × .02)

26.

	(a)	(b)
Purchase	$6,000	$10,000
Less return	200	300
	$5,800	$ 9,700
Less discount	116*	—
	$5,684	$ 9,700
Add transportation	200	—
	$5,884	$ 9,700

*(2% × $5,800)

True-False Questions

1. F Sales Returns and Allowances is a contra sales account and normally has a debit balance. To close this account requires a credit.
2. F This statement describes cash discounts.
3. T This account is a contra purchases account and will normally have a balance opposite to the Purchases account.
4. F Cash discounts taken on goods acquired for resale should be credited to a Purchase Discounts account.
5. F
6. F A cash discount is offered as an inducement to pay invoices early; whereas trade discounts are deductions from the list price.
7. F Cash discounts are not allowed on freight charges.
8. F The Purchases account balance shows the gross cost of merchandise acquired; cost of goods sold is determined by subtracting ending inventory from the total cost of goods available for sale.
9. T
10. F Cash discounts are usually recorded by both parties; but trade discounts are not recorded by either buyer or seller.
11. F It is true that inventory and retained earnings would be understated, but cost of goods sold would be overstated due to the omission.
12. T
13. T
14. T
15. F Postings cannot be made from the work sheet to the ledger.
16. F The buyer may deduct 2% from the invoice if payment is made within 10 days of the invoice date.
17. F This describes trade discounts.
18. T
19. F Sales would be $260,000; $160,000 cost of goods sold + $100,000 gross margin = $260,000 Sales.
20. T
21. T $200 × .8 × .9 × .95 = $136.80.
22. T
23. T The consignee does not have title to the goods because the consignor retains the title.
24. F This calculation would show Net Purchases.
25. T Consigned goods should be included in the owner's inventory because these are goods delivered to another party who will attempt to sell the goods for a commission. The consigned goods remain the property of the owner until sold by the consignee.

Multiple Choice Questions

1. A
2. C $50,000 Net cost of purchases + $18,000 Beginning inventory – $38,000 Ending inventory = $30,000 Cost of goods sold
3. E Under periodic inventory procedure, the cost of goods sold section is composed of: Beginning inventory + Purchases – Purchase discounts – Purchase returns and allowances + Transportation-in – Ending inventory.
4. E
5. E The correct entry is to debit Sales Returns and Allowances and to credit Accounts Receivable
6. B
7. D
8. C The credit would be to Cash, $392 and to Purchase Discounts, $8.
9. B $2,600 Merchandise – $200 Returns and allowances = $2,400; $2,400 – $24 Discount + $100 Transportation = $2,476
10. A
11. B $108,000 Cost of goods sold + $24,000 Ending inventory = $132,000; $132,000 – $88,000 Purchases = $44,000 Beginning inventory
12. C $20,000 Net income + $28,000 Operating expense = $48,000 Gross margin
13. C $48,000 Gross margin + $108,000 Cost of goods sold = $156,000
14. A $10,800 Beginning merchandise inventory + $56,400 Purchases + $3,000 Transportation-in – $1,200 Purchase returns = $69,000 Cost of goods available for sale; $69,000 – $12,400 Ending inventory = $56,600 Cost of goods sold
15. B

6 MEASURING AND REPORTING INVENTORIES

Learning Objectives

1. *Explain and calculate the effects of inventory errors on certain financial statement items.*
2. *Indicate which costs are properly included in inventory.*
3. *Calculate cost of ending inventory and cost of goods sold under the four major inventory costing methods using perpetual and periodic inventory procedures.*
4. *Explain the advantages and disadvantages of the four major inventory costing methods.*
5. *Record merchandise transactions under perpetual inventory procedure.*
6. *Apply net realizable value and the lower-of-cost-or-market method to inventory.*
7. *Estimate cost of ending inventory using the gross margin and retail inventory methods.*

CHAPTER OUTLINE

INVENTORIES AND COST OF GOODS SOLD

1. Inventory is one of the largest and most important assets owned by a merchandising or manufacturing business. An accurate valuation of ending inventory is necessary to reflect the proper net income for the period, since it is deducted from cost of goods available for sale to yield cost of goods sold.

2. The cost of inventory consists of all those outlays necessary to acquire the goods and place them in their desired condition and location for sale and includes:

    a. The net price of the goods.
    b. Insurance in transit.
    c. Transportation-in charges.
    d. Handling costs.

3. When purchase prices vary, alternative methods for valuing inventory and cost of goods sold will yield different amounts under each method.

4. The physical flow of inventory may differ from the cost flow used in any given situation.

DETERMINING INVENTORY COST

5. Comparison of perpetual and periodic inventory procedures

    a. Perpetual inventory procedure is often used to enhance internal control.

        1. Using perpetual inventory procedure, there are no purchases or purchase-related accounts.
        2. The Merchandise Inventory account is used to record purchases for resale.
        3. At the time of sale, Merchandise Inventory is credited, leaving a balance showing the cost of inventory on hand.
        4. The Cost of Goods Sold account is debited every time a sale is made.

    b. Under periodic inventory procedure, the Purchases, Purchase Discounts, and Purchase Returns and Allowances accounts are used to record purchases and subsequent adjustments.

        1. The Merchandise Inventory account is not adjusted until the end of the period.
        2. Goods not in ending inventory are assumed to have been sold.
        3. The cost of goods sold under periodic procedure is determined only at the end of the period after a physical inventory has been taken.

6. Four methods can be used to determine the cost of inventory.

    a. Specific identification calls for the assignment to the units on hand of their specific costs.

        1. Identification is usually made through means of a serial number or identification tag.
        2. Income may be manipulated if different units of a given product have different costs.
        3. Relatively homogeneous units are included in inventory at different prices.
        4. In many cases the method is too costly to apply.

    b. First-in, first-out (FIFO) method assumes that the oldest units acquired are the first sold; ending inventory is valued at the most recent purchase prices.

        1. Perpetual Procedure—When merchandise is sold, the cost of goods sold consists of the oldest units on hand. Thus, the Merchandise Inventory account will reflect the most recent purchases at any given time.

2. Periodic Procedure—At the end of the year, a physical count is taken and then costed by starting with the most recent purchase and going back through the year until all of the ending inventory has been costed. Cost of goods sold = Cost of goods available − Cost of ending inventory.
3. Under the FIFO method, the use of perpetual and periodic inventory procedures will result in the same total cost for ending inventory and the same total cost of goods sold.
4. Income exists if sales revenues are sufficient to cover the historical cost of the units sold and other expenses.

c. Last-in, first-out (LIFO) method assumes that the newly acquired units are the first ones sold; cost of goods sold is the cost of the latest goods acquired.
1. The method can only be used for tax purposes if it is used for financial reporting purposes.
2. Perpetual Procedure—The inventory composition and balance are updated with each purchase and sale.
3. Periodic Procedure—To compute the cost of ending inventory, begin with the beginning inventory cost and continue listing purchases until enough units have been listed to equal the number of units in the ending inventory. Cost of goods sold = Cost of goods available for sale − Cost of ending inventory.
4. Income exists only if sales revenues are sufficient to cover all expenses and the cost of replacing the units sold, provided replacement occurs before the end of the period.
5. In a period of rising prices, inventory is often understated.
6. Income can be manipulated by delaying or advancing replacement purchases.

d. Weighted-average inventory procedure also uses actual costs; units sold and in ending inventory are all costed at the weighted-average figure.
1. Perpetual Procedure—The weighted-average unit cost (often called the moving weighted-average) is computed after each purchase or before each sale. Weighted-average unit cost = Total cost of goods available for sale ÷ Total units available for sale.
2. Periodic Procedure—The weighted-average unit cost is computed at the end of the period. Weighted-average unit cost = [(Cost of Beginning Inventory + Total Cost of Purchases) ÷ (Units in Beginning Inventory + Units Purchased)].
3. Averaging tends to slow the rise of the unit cost as the purchase price increases.
4. Income can be manipulated by delaying or advancing replacement purchases.

e. Under conditions of varying prices, each of the above methods will produce a different inventory valuation and net income.
f. Each method has its advantages and disadvantages.
1. LIFO matches current costs with current revenues and reduces current taxes.
2. Critics often claim that LIFO charges revenues with the cost of goods still on hand. It also allows manipulation of net income through the timing of purchases.
3. FIFO and specific identification more precisely match historical cost with revenue.
4. LIFO supporters argue that FIFO can result in the reporting of "paper profits."

DEPARTURES FROM COST BASIS OF INVENTORY MEASUREMENT

7. *Accounting Research Bulletin No. 43* requires a departure from cost when the utility of the goods is less than their cost.
a. Damaged, worn, or obsolete goods should be carried at net realizable value, if lower than cost.
1. Net realizable value = Estimated selling price − Estimated disposal and selling costs.
b. Under the lower-of-cost-or-market method, cost is modified for downward market value fluctuations.
1. The method is based on the assumption that if purchase prices fall, sales prices will also fall.
2. Cost must still be determined by means of one of the methods outlined above.

3. "Market" is "replacement cost" in terms of the quantity usually purchased.
4. The method may be applied to each item in inventory, to each class of inventory, or to total inventory.

8. A company using periodic inventory procedure may wish to estimate its inventory for several reasons: to obtain an inventory cost to be used in monthly or quarterly statements, to test the reasonableness of a previously determined ending inventory amount, or to estimate the cost of goods destroyed or stolen.

   a. Sometimes the value of the ending inventory and cost of goods sold are estimated by the gross margin method.

      1. This method assumes that the gross margin rate is highly stable from period to period.
      2. Estimated gross margin is computed by applying the gross margin rate to the net sales figure.
      3. Net sales − Estimated gross margin = Estimated cost of goods sold.
      4. (Beginning inventory + Net purchases) − Estimated cost of goods sold = Estimated ending inventory.

   b. The retail inventory method can also be used to estimate ending inventory.

      1. Ending inventory is determined first at retail price by subtracting sales from goods available for sale at retail.
      2. A cost/retail price ratio is determined by relating the cost of goods available for sale to the retail price of goods available for sale.
      3. Cost of ending inventory = Cost/retail price ratio × Ending inventory at retail.

DEMONSTRATION PROBLEM

Lark Company had 3,000 units of Article AX 25 in its end-of-the-year inventory. Its beginning inventory, year's purchases, and year's sales of Article AX 25 were as follows:

Jan.	1 Beg. inv.	1,000 units @ $14.20	May 3 Sale	2,800 units
Apr.	14 Purchase	3,000 units @ $14.80	June 25 Sale	3,200 units
June	2 Purchase	5,000 units @ $15.58	July 15 Sale	2,000 units
Oct.	28 Purchase	4,000 units @ $15.60	Nov. 5 Sale	4,000 units
Dec.	15 Purchase	2,000 units @ $15.92		

Required:

a. Using the information given above, compute the ending inventory and the cost of goods sold under each of the following methods using perpetual procedure.

   1. FIFO
   2. LIFO
   3. Weighted-average

b. Compute the ending inventory and the cost of goods sold under each of the following methods using periodic procedure:

   1. FIFO
   2. LIFO
   3. Weighted-average

c. In analyzing your answers for a. and b., explain the effect of price inflation on the inventory costing method used.

a. The ending inventory consists of:

	Units
Beginning inventory	1,000
Purchases	14,000
Goods available for sale	15,000
Sales	12,000
Ending inventory	3,000

1. Ending inventory and cost of goods sold under FIFO using perpetual procedure:

Date	Purchased			Sold			Balance		
	Units	Unit Cost	Total Cost	Units	Unit Cost	Total Cost	Units	Unit Cost	Total Cost
Beg. Inv.							1,000	$14.20	$14,200
Apr. 14	3,000	$14.80	$44,400				1,000	14.20	14,200
							3,000	14.80	44,400
May 3				1,000	$14.20	$14,200			
				1,800	14.80	26,640	1,200	14.80	17,760
June 2	5,000	15.58	77,900				1,200	14.80	17,760
							5,000	15.58	77,900
June 25				1,200	14.80	17,760			
				2,000	15.58	31,160	3,000	15.58	46,740
July 15				2,000	15.58	31,160	1,000	15.58	15,580
Oct. 28	4,000	15.60	62,400				1,000	15.58	15,580
							4,000	15.60	62,400
Nov. 5				1,000	15.58	15,580			
				3,000	15.60	46,800	1,000	15.60	15,600
Dec. 15	2,000	15.92	31,840				1,000	15.60	15,600
							2,000	15.92	31,840
Cost of goods sold				12,000		$183,300			

Ending inventory = (1,000 × $15.60) + (2,000 × $15.92) = $47,440

2. Ending inventory and cost of goods sold under LIFO using perpetual procedure:

	Purchased			Sold			Balance		
Date	Units	Unit Cost	Total Cost	Units	Unit Cost	Total Cost	Units	Unit Cost	Total Cost
Beg. Inv.							1,000	$14.20	$14,200
Apr. 14	3,000	$14.80	$44,400				1,000	14.20	14,200
							3,000	14.80	44,400
May 3				2,800	$14.80	$41,440	1,000	14.20	14,200
							200	14.80	2,960
June 2	5,000	15.58	77,900				1,000	14.20	14,200
							200	14.80	2,960
							5,000	15.58	77,900
June 25				3,200	15.58	49,856	1,000	14.20	14,200
							200	14.80	2,960
							1,800	15.58	28,044
July 15				1,800	15.58	28,044			
				200	14.80	2,960	1,000	14.20	14,200
Oct. 28	4,000	15.60	62,400				1,000	14.20	14,200
							4,000	15.60	62,400
Nov. 5				4,000	15.60	62,400	1,000	14.20	14,200
Dec. 15	2,000	15.92	31,840				1,000	14.20	14,200
							2,000	15.92	31,840
Cost of goods sold				12,000		$184,700			

Ending inventory = (1,000 × $14.20) + (2,000 × $15.92) = $46,040

3. Ending inventory and cost of goods sold under weighted-average using perpetual procedure:

	Purchased			Sold			Balance		
Date	Units	Unit Cost	Total Cost	Units	Unit Cost	Total Cost	Units	Unit Cost	Total Cost
Beg. Inv.							1,000	$14.20	$14,200
Apr. 14	3,000	$14.80	$44,400				4,000	14.65[a]	58,600
May 3				2,800	$14.65	$41,020	1,200	14.65	17,580
June 2	5,000	15.58	77,900				6,200	15.40[b]	95,480
June 25				3,200	15.40	49,280	3,000	15.40	46,200
July 15				2,000	15.40	30,800	1,000	15.40	15,400
Oct. 28	4,000	15.60	62,400				5,000	15.56[c]	77,800
Nov. 5				4,000	15.56	62,240	1,000	15.56	15,560
Dec. 15	2,000	15.92	31,840				3,000	15.80[d]	47,400
Cost of goods sold				12,000		$183,340			

Ending inventory = (3,000 × $15.80) = $47,400

[a] $\frac{\$58,600}{4,000 \text{ units}} = \$14.65$ [b] $\frac{\$95,480}{6,200 \text{ units}} = \$15.40$ [c] $\frac{\$77,800}{5,000 \text{ units}} = \$15.56$ [d] $\frac{\$47,400}{3,000 \text{ units}} = \$15.80$

b. 1. Ending inventory and cost of goods sold under FIFO using periodic procedure:

Ending inventory:

Date	Units	Unit Cost	Total Cost
Dec. 15 purchase	2,000	$15.92	$31,840
Oct. 28 purchase	1,000	15.60	15,600
Ending inventory	3,000		$47,440

Cost of goods sold:

Beginning inventory	$ 14,200
Purchases	216,540
Cost of goods available for sale	$230,740
Ending inventory	47,440
Cost of goods sold	$183,300

2. Ending inventory and cost of goods sold under LIFO using periodic procedure:

Ending inventory:

Date	Units	Unit Cost	Total Cost
Beg. Inv.	1,000	$14.20	$14,200
Apr. 14 purchase	2,000	14.80	29,600
Ending inventory	3,000		$43,800

Cost of goods sold:

Cost of goods available for sale (from b.1.)	$230,740
Ending inventory	43,800
Cost of goods sold	$186,940

3. Ending inventory and cost of goods sold under weighted-average using periodic procedure:

Date	Units	Unit Cost	Total Cost
Beg. Inv.	1,000	$14.20	$14,200
Apr. 14 purchase	3,000	14.80	44,400
June 2 purchase	5,000	15.58	77,900
Oct. 28 purchase	4,000	15.60	62,400
Dec. 15 purchase	2,000	15.92	31,840
	15,000		$230,740

Weighted-average unit cost = $230,740 ÷ 15,000 = $15.3827

Ending inventory = $15.3827 × 3,000 = $46,148

Cost of goods sold = $230,740 − $46,148 = $184,592

c. In a period of rising prices, as experienced by Mark Company, LIFO gives a higher cost of goods sold and a lower ending inventory than FIFO. Weighted-average costing tends to average out the effects of price increases and decreases.

MATCHING

Referring to the terms listed below, place the appropriate letter next to the corresponding description.

a. FIFO
b. Gross margin method
c. LIFO

d. Lower-of-cost-or-market
e. Market value
f. Net realizable value

g. Retail inventory method
h. Specific identification
i. Weighted-average

_____ 1. An inventory costing method that involves the assignment of a known actual cost to a particular identifiable unit of product.

_____ 2. Estimated selling price of merchandise less estimated cost of completion and disposition.

_____ 3. A method for estimating inventory. Gross margin percentages from previous periods are applied to sales of the current period to arrive at an estimated amount of gross margin and cost of goods sold. Cost of goods sold is deducted from cost of goods available for sale to arrive at estimated ending inventory.

_____ 4. A method of costing inventory under which the costs of the last goods acquired are the first costs charged to cost of goods sold when goods are actually sold.

_____ 5. A method of costing inventory under which the number of units in the beginning inventory plus the total of those purchased is divided into the total cost of goods available for sale to arrive at an average unit cost. Ending inventory is carried at this cost per unit.

_____ 6. A procedure for estimating the cost of the ending inventory by applying the ratio of cost to retail price to the ending inventory at retail.

_____ 7. Replacement cost in terms of the quantity usually purchased.

_____ 8. A method of costing inventory under which the costs of the first goods acquired are the first costs charged to cost of goods sold when goods are actually sold.

_____ 9. A method of costing inventory under which cost or market, whichever is lower, is selected for each item, each group, or for the whole inventory.

COMPLETION AND EXERCISES

1. Inventory can be defined as the sum of:

   a. _____

   b. _____

   _____

   c. _____

   _____

2. Assuming periodic inventory procedure, what effect would an understatement of ending inventory have on the following different sections of the financial statements?

Balance Sheet	*Income Statement*
Current assets _____	Cost of goods sold _____
Total assets _____	Gross margin _____
Stockholders' equity _____	Net income _____
Total liabilities and stockholders' equity _____	

3. What is included in the cost of inventory?

   _____

   _____

   _____

   _____

   _____

   _____

4. When perpetual inventory procedure is being used, the accountant debits _____ _____ and credits accounts payable when goods are purchased and debits cost of goods sold and credits

   _____ _____ when goods are sold, along with the proper sales entry.

5. When is the specific identification method of inventory valuation most applicable?

   _____

   _____

   _____

6. Both _____-_____, _____-_____ and _____-

   _____, _____-_____ methods of inventory valuation are assumptions as to the flow of costs.

7. Following are data related to Cozy Company's beginning inventory, purchases, and sales of a given item for the year 1994:

Purchases	Units	Cost	Sales	
Beginning inventory	1,000	@ $10.00	February 4	500
Purchases:			March 16	1,500
January 7	1,000	@ $10.10	July 5	1,000
March 6	2,000	@ $ 9.60	October 24	2,000
July 4	1,500	@ $ 9.80		
November 1	500	@ $10.40		
	6,000			5,000

Compute the ending inventory using FIFO under perpetual and periodic procedures.

8. Using the information in Question 7, compute the ending inventory using LIFO under perpetual and periodic procedures.

9. Under FIFO, net income exists if revenues are sufficient to cover the _____ cost of the units of inventory sold (assuming the physical flow of goods is FIFO).

10. Under LIFO, net income exists if revenues are sufficient to cover the _____ cost of the units of inventory sold, provided new units are acquired before the end of the accounting period.

11. The principal argument for _____ is that it more precisely matches current costs with current revenues.

12. During a period of rising prices, _____ will give a higher net income figure.

13. Below is a record of beginning inventory and purchases. Compute the ending inventory under the weighted-average method, assuming periodic inventory procedure, if a physical count showed 150 units on hand at the end of the month.

Inventory on January 1	140 units at $12.00 =	$ 1,680
Purchases:		
April 1	500 units at $12.30 =	6,150
July 4	800 units at $12.00 =	9,600
December 5	1,000 units at $11.00 =	11,000
	2,440	$28,430

14. What is the cost of goods sold in the example in Question 13?

15. The lower-of-cost-or-market method uses market values only to the extent that these values are

_____ than cost.

16. The Earnest Company has three different products in its inventory at December 31, 1993, which have costs and current market values as follows:

Item	Cost	Market
1	$14,000	$14,100
2	2,280	2,000
3	4,200	4,390

If each product is priced at the lower of cost or market, the inventory is $_____.

If the total is priced at the lower of cost or market, the inventory is $_____.

17. Concerning the gross margin method of estimating inventory, what assumption must be correct for this method to be satisfactory?

_____

_____

18. To apply the gross margin method, the rate of gross margin on sales is multiplied by _____ _____ to arrive at gross margin. The gross margin is then subtracted from net sales to arrive at _____

_____ _____ _____ _____. This figure is then subtracted from

_____ _____ _____ _____ _____ _____ to arrive at ending inventory.

19. Use the following information and the retail inventory method to estimate the ending inventory at cost:

	Cost	Retail
Beginning inventory	$ 48,000	$ 96,000
Purchases, net	585,600	960,000
Sales		1,000,000

20. Under perpetual inventory procedure, Michael Company sold 100 computers to Tino Inc. for $140,000 that cost Michael Company $100,000. What journal entries are required to record this sale?

_____

_____

_____

_____

TRUE-FALSE QUESTIONS

Indicate whether each of the following statements is true or false by inserting a capital "T" or "F" in the blank space provided.

____ 1. In a period of rising prices, LIFO will result in a lower net income figure than that resulting from the FIFO method.

____ 2. If the utility or value of inventory items is less than the cost of those items, departures from cost are justified.

____ 3. The two bases of inventory costing most widely used are cost and lower-of-cost-or-market.

____ 4. An understatement of the beginning inventory will result in an understatement of the net income for the period.

____ 5. Income can be manipulated by the timing of purchases if the FIFO method is used.

____ 6. Inventory costing methods should not be changed at will in order to control reported net income.

____ 7. Inventory costs include only the seller's net price less any purchase discounts.

____ 8. In a period of rising prices, FIFO yields the greatest cost of goods sold.

____ 9. In a period of constant prices, FIFO and LIFO will give identical results.

____ 10. The gross margin method of calculating an inventory amount produces accurate results.

____ 11. An understated ending inventory leads to understated net income.

____ 12. If prices are steadily rising or falling, the use of the weighted-average method will yield a cost for inventory between those yielded by FIFO and LIFO.

____ 13. An error in the determination of the cost of the ending inventory of a period generally results in misstated income for three periods.

____ 14. The gross margin method uses the gross margin rates experienced in prior periods to estimate the cost of inventory.

____ 15. When changing inventory costing methods, a company must fully disclose the change and the reasons for the change in a footnote to the financial statements.

____ 16. The retail inventory method can be used at the end of any period except the end of the fiscal year.

____ 17. Inventory costing errors lead to a balance sheet that does not balance and are thus readily observed.

____ 18. The net realizable value of an inventory item can be greater than its expected selling price.

____ 19. An advantage of using LIFO is that the balance sheet valuation for inventory is based on an up-to-date cost.

____ 20. In a period of rising prices, higher income will be reported using FIFO as compared with using LIFO.

____ 21. When using periodic inventory procedure, it is necessary to count merchandise on hand at year-end.

____ 22. Purchases are recorded in the Merchandise Inventory account when using periodic inventory procedure.

____ 23. The closing entries necessary under perpetual and periodical inventory procedure do not differ because all expense and revenue accounts must be closed.

____ 24. If the beginning inventory exceeds the ending inventory, net income is overstated.

____ 25. Because of the importance of consistency, a company cannot change inventory costing methods unless the prior method is one that is unacceptable to the accounting profession.

MULTIPLE CHOICE QUESTIONS

For each of the following questions indicate the best answer by circling the appropriate letter.

Use the following information for the first six questions.

On January 1, 1994, John Company's inventory of Item X consisted of 2,200 units that cost $17.60 each. During 1994 the company purchased 5,500 units of Item X at $22 each, and it sold 4,950 units.

1. Cost of ending inventory using FIFO is:
   A. $90,900
   B. $60,500
   C. $82,820
   D. None of the above.

2. Cost of goods sold using FIFO is:

    A. $60,500
    B. $181,500
    C. $99,220
    D. None of the above.

3. Cost of goods sold using LIFO is:

    A. $48,400
    B. $87,120
    C. $108,900
    D. $121,000
    E. None of the above.

4. Cost of ending inventory using LIFO is:

    A. $108,900
    B. $72,600
    C. $38,720
    D. $50,820
    E. None of the above.

5. Cost of goods sold using weighted-average cost is (round to nearest cent in computing average unit cost):

    A. $108,900
    B. $102,663
    C. $98,011
    D. $121,000
    E. None of the above.

6. Cost of ending inventory using weighted-average cost is (round to nearest cent in computing average unit cost):

    A. $50,820
    B. $61,711
    C. $38,720
    D. $57,057
    E. None of the above.

7. If the ending inventory is understated by $450 the cost of goods sold is:

    A. overstated by $900.
    B. overstated by $750.
    C. overstated by $450.
    D. understated by $750.
    E. understated by $450.

8. If the ending inventory is overstated by $200 the net income is:

    A. understated by $200.
    B. understated by $100.
    C. overstated by $200.
    D. overstated by $100.
    E. None of the above.

9. The following principle requires companies to show in its statements by means of a footnote or other manner, the inventory costing method used:

A. conservation principle.
B. full-disclosure principle.
C. consistency principle.
D. business entity principle.
E. stable monetary concept.

10. Aiken & Sons Company for several years has maintained a 35% average gross margin on sales. Given the following data for 1994, what is the approximate inventory on December 31, 1994, computed by the gross margin method of estimating inventory?

	Cost
Inventory, January 1	$ 60,000
Net cost of purchases	272,000
Total	$332,000

Net sales at retail in 1994 were $372,000.

A. $140,400
B. $56,000
C. $90,200
D. $60,000
E. $108,000

11–13. The following inventory data are obtained:

	Purchased		Sold
	Units	Unit Cost	Units
Beg. Inv.	300	$100	
Jan. 13	180	105	
Jan. 29			200
Mar. 4	160	110	
Apr. 20			200
June 8	200	112	
Aug. 19			100
Nov. 5	120	115	
Dec. 23			140
	960		640

The units of ending inventory consist of:

	Units
Beg. Inv.	300
Purchases	660
Goods available for sale	960
Sales	640
	320

Assuming that perpetual procedure is used, answer the following questions:

11. If the weighted-average method is used, what is the cost of ending inventory? (Carry unit cost to two decimal places and round total cost to nearest dollar.)

    A. $34,233
    B. $35,250
    C. $68,466
    D. $35,165
    E. None of the above.

12. Using the FIFO method, what is the cost of ending inventory?

    A. $32,100
    B. $36,200
    C. $32,000
    D. $30,720
    E. None of the above.

13. Using the LIFO method, what is the cost of ending inventory?

    A. $36,200
    B. $32,100
    C. $32,960
    D. $33,200
    E. None of the above.

14. The system that continuously provides the cost of the inventory on hand is called:

    A. perpetual.
    B. average cost.
    C. periodic.
    D. physical.
    E. gross profit.

15. During a period of rising prices, which inventory costing method might be expected to give the lowest valuation for inventory on the balance sheet?

    A. LIFO
    B. FIFO
    C. Weighted-average cost
    D. Specific identification

SOLUTIONS

Matching

1.	h	6.	g
2.	f	7.	e
3.	b	8.	a
4.	c	9.	d
5.	i		

Completion and Exercises

1. (a) goods held for sale in the ordinary course of business (finished goods); (b) goods in the process of production for such sale (work in process); (c) goods to be currently consumed in the production of goods or services to be available for sale (materials)

2.
Balance Sheet

Current assets—understated
Total assets—understated
Stockholders' equity—understated
Total liabilities and stockholders' equity—understated

Income Statement

Cost of goods sold—overstated
Gross margin—understated
Net income—understated

3. The cost of inventory includes all outlays necessary to acquire the goods, including the net price, insurance in transit, transportation charges, and handling costs. In theory, all costs incurred to acquire the goods and get them to their existing condition and location should be included in inventory.

4. Merchandise inventory;
   Merchandise inventory.

5. The specific identification method is most applicable when the products bought and sold are large, readily identifiable, and of high unit value.

6. first-in, first-out; last-in, first-out

7. The units of ending inventory consist of:

	Units
Beginning inventory	1,000
Purchases	5,000
Goods available for sale	6,000
Sales	5,000
Ending inventory	1,000

a. Ending inventory using FIFO under perpetual procedure:

Date	Purchased Units	Purchased Unit Cost	Sold Units	Sold Unit Cost	Balance Units	Balance Unit Cost	Balance Total Cost
Beg. Inv.					1,000	$10.00	$10,000
Jan. 7	1,000	$10.10			1,000	10.00	10,000
					1,000	10.10	10,100
Feb. 4			500	$10.00	500	10.00	5,000
					1,000	10.10	10,100
Mar. 6	2,000	9.60			500	10.00	5,000
					1,000	10.10	10,100
					2,000	9.60	19,200
Mar. 16			500	10.00			
			1,000	10.10	2,000	9.60	19,200
July 4	1,500	9.80			2,000	9.60	19,200
					1,500	9.80	14,700
July 5			1,000	9.60	1,000	9.60	9,600
					1,500	9.80	14,700
Oct. 24			1,000	9.60			
			1,000	9.80	500	9.80	4,900
Nov. 1	500	10.40			500	9.80	4,900
					500	10.40	5,200

Ending inventory = (500 × $9.80) + (500 × $10.40) = $10,100

b. Ending inventory using FIFO under periodic procedure:

Purchased	Units	Unit Cost	Total Cost
November 1	500	$10.40	$ 5,200
July 4	500	9.80	4,900
	1,000		$10,100

8. a. Ending inventory using LIFO under perpetual procedure:

	Purchased		Sold		Balance		
Date	Units	Unit Cost	Units	Unit Cost	Units	Unit Cost	Total Cost
Beg. Inv.					1,000	$10.00	$10,000
Jan. 7	1,000	$10.10			1,000	10.00	10,000
					1,000	10.10	10,100
Feb. 4			500	$10.10	1,000	10.00	10,000
					500	10.10	5,050
Mar. 6	2,000	9.60			1,000	10.00	10,000
					500	10.10	5,050
					2,000	9.60	19,200
Mar. 16			1,500	9.60	1,000	10.00	10,000
					500	10.10	5,050
					500	9.60	4,800
July 4	1,500	9.80			1,000	10.00	10,000
					500	10.10	5,050
					500	9.60	4,800
					1,500	9.80	14,700
July 5			1,000	9.80	1,000	10.00	10,000
					500	10.10	5,050
					500	9.60	4,800
					500	9.80	4,900
Oct. 24			500	9.80			
			500	9.60			
			500	10.10			
			500	10.00	500	10.00	5,000
Nov. 1	500	10.40			500	10.00	5,000
					500	10.40	5,200

Ending inventory = (500 × $10.00) + (500 × $10.40) = $10,200

b. Ending inventory using LIFO under periodic procedure:

	Units	Unit Cost	Total Cost
Beginning inventory	1,000	$10.00	$10,000
	1,000		$10,000

9. historical
10. current
11. LIFO
12. FIFO
13. Weighted-average unit cost is $28,430 \div 2,440$, or $11.6516
    Ending inventory is $150 \times \$11.6516 = \$1,748.00$

14. Cost of goods available for sale $28,430.00
    Less: Ending inventory 1,748.00
    Cost of goods sold $26,682.00

15. less
16. $20,200; $20,480
17. The assumption that the rate of gross margin realized is highly stable from period to period.
18. net sales; estimated cost of goods sold; cost of goods available for sale

19.

	Cost	Retail
Beginning inventory	$ 48,000	$ 96,000
Purchases, net	585,600	960,000
Goods available for sale	$633,600	$1,056,000
Cost/retail price ratio: $633,600/$1,056,000 = 60\%$		
Sales		1,000,000
Ending inventory at retail prices		$ 56,000
Times cost/retail price ratio		× 60%
Ending inventory at cost	33,600	
Cost of goods sold	$600,000	

20. Accounts Receivable 140,000
       Sales 140,000

    Cost of Goods Sold 100,000
       Merchandise Inventory 100,000

True-False Questions

1. T LIFO results in a higher amount of cost of goods sold, which is applied against revenue in calculating net income.
2. T
3. T
4. F Income will be overstated.
5. F
6. T
7. F Examples of other includable items are insurance, transportation charges and handling costs.
8. F
9. T
10. F The gross margin method is only an estimation procedure.
11. T
12. T
13. F Results in misstated income for two periods.

14. T
15. T
16. T   At the end of a fiscal year, the inventory must be based on a physical count.
17. F   The balance sheet will still balance. If ending inventory is understated, for instance, Retained Earnings will be understated by the same amount.
18. F
19. F   The inventory amount will contain very old costs.
20. T
21. T   Inventory must even be counted at year-end using perpetual procedure.
22. F
23. F   The closing entries do differ.
24. F
25. F   A company is allowed to change to the better of two acceptable methods. However, the principle of consistency prevents a company from changing inventory methods more than a very few times.

Multiple Choice Questions

1. B   ($22 × 2,750 = $60,500)
2. C   ($17.60 × 2,200) + ($22 × 2,750) = $99,220
3. C   ($22 × 4,950 = $108,900)
4. D   ($17.60 × 2,200) + ($22 × 550) = $50,820
5. B   ($20.74 × 4,950 = $102,663.00)
6. D   ($159,720.00 − 102,663.00 = $57,057.00)
7. C
8. C
9. B
10. C   (Cost of goods sold = $372,000 × .65 = $241,800; $332,000 − $241,800 = $90,200
11. D   Ending inventory using weighted-average method::

	Purchased		Sold		Balance		
Date	Units	Unit Cost	Units	Unit Cost	Units	Unit Cost	Total Cost
Beg. Inv.					300	$100.00	$30,000
Jan. 13	180	$105			480	101.88[a]	48,900
Jan. 29			200	$101.88	280	101.88	28,526
Mar. 4	160	110			440	104.83[b]	46,126
Apr. 20			200	104.83	240	104.83	25,159
June 8	200	112			440	108.09[c]	47,559
Aug. 19			100	108.09	340	108.09	36,751
Nov. 5	120	115			460	109.89[d]	50,551
Dec. 23			140	109.89	320	109.89	35,165

$$^{a}\frac{\$48,900}{480} = \$101.88 \qquad ^{b}\frac{\$46,126}{440} = \$104.83 \qquad ^{c}\frac{\$47,559}{440} = \$108.09 \qquad ^{d}\frac{\$50,551}{460} = \$109.89$$

Ending inventory = 320 × $109.89 = $35,165

12. B Ending inventory using FIFO:

Date	Purchased Units	Unit Cost	Sold Units	Unit Cost	Balance Units	Unit Cost	Total Cost
Beg. Inv.					300	$100	$30,000
Jan. 13	180	$105			300	100	30,000
					180	105	18,900
Jan. 29			200	$100	100	100	10,000
					180	105	18,900
Mar. 4	160	110			100	100	10,000
					180	105	18,900
					160	110	17,600
Apr. 20			100	100			
			100	105	80	105	8,400
					160	110	17,600
June 8	200	112			80	105	8,400
					160	110	17,600
					200	112	22,400
Aug. 19			80	105			
			20	110	140	110	15,400
					200	112	22,400
Nov. 5	120	115			140	110	15,400
					200	112	22,400
					120	115	13,800
Dec. 23			140	110	200	112	22,400
					120	115	13,800

Ending inventory = (200 × $112) + (120 × $115) = $36,200

13. C Ending inventory using LIFO:

Date	Purchased Units	Purchased Unit Cost	Sold Units	Sold Unit Cost	Balance Units	Balance Unit Cost	Balance Total Cost
Beg. Inv.					300	$100	$30,000
Jan. 13	180	$105			300	100	30,000
					180	105	18,900
Jan. 29			180	$105			
			20	100	280	100	28,000
Mar. 4	160	110			280	100	28,000
					160	110	17,600
Apr. 20			160	110			
			40	100	240	100	24,000
June 8	200	112			240	100	24,000
					200	112	22,400
Aug. 19			100	112	240	100	24,000
					100	112	11,200
Nov. 5	120	115			240	100	24,000
					100	112	11,200
					120	115	13,800
Dec. 23			120	115			
			20	112	240	100	24,000
					80	112	8,960

Ending inventory = $(240 \times \$100) + (80 \times \$112) = \underline{\$32,960}$

14. A
15. A

7 ACCOUNTING SYSTEMS AND SPECIAL JOURNALS

Learning Objectives

1. *Describe the relationship between subsidiary accounts in subsidiary ledgers and control accounts in the general ledger.*
2. *Describe the relationship between special journals and the general journal.*
3. *Record transactions in special journals.*
4. *Post special journals.*
5. *Describe alternative methods of processing data.*
6. *Describe microcomputer applications in accounting (Appendix 7-A).*
7. *Describe basic computer concepts (Appendix 7-B).*

CHAPTER OUTLINE

THE PROCESSING OF DATA—MANUAL SYSTEM

1. An accounting system can be defined as a set of records, such as journals, ledgers, work sheets, trial balances, and reports, plus the procedures and equipment regularly used to process business transactions.
2. For accounting systems to be effective, they should:

    a. Provide for the efficient processing of data at the least cost. The cost of the system should be equal to or less than the benefits received.

    b. Ensure a high degree of accuracy.

    c. Provide for internal control to prevent theft or fraud.

    d. Provide for the growth of a business.

CONTROL ACCOUNTS AND SUBSIDIARY LEDGERS

3. The method of initially recording and summarizing transaction data is influenced by the nature of the transactions, the materiality of the amounts, the means available for processing the data, and the reports desired.

    a. Sometimes a company needs general information and at other times it needs specific information.

    b. In order to provide for both types of information, control accounts are maintained to provide balance sheet data, and subsidiary accounts are maintained to provide specific information relating to customers and creditors.

CONTROL ACCOUNT

4. A control account is an account in the general ledger that shows the total balance of all the subsidiary accounts related to it.

SUBSIDIARY LEDGER ACCOUNTS

5. Subsidiary ledger accounts show the details supporting the related general ledger control account balance.

SUBSIDIARY LEDGER

6. A subsidiary ledger is a group of related accounts showing the details of the balance of the general ledger control account.

    a. A subsidiary ledger relieves the general ledger of a mass of detail and shortens the general ledger trial balance.

    b. A subsidiary ledger promotes a division of labor.

SPECIAL JOURNALS

7. Special journals have been designed to systematize the original recording of major recurring transactions.

    a. The general journal is used for all transactions that cannot be entered readily in one of the special journals.

    b. Each of the special journals is a record of original entry that contains the data that will be posted to ledger accounts.

ADVANTAGES OF SPECIAL JOURNALS

8. Several advantages are obtained from the use of special journals.
   a. Time is saved in journalizing.
   b. Time is saved in posting.
   c. Detail is eliminated from the general journal.
   d. Division of labor is promoted.
   e. Management analysis is aided.

SALES JOURNAL

9. The sales journal should be used to record all sales of merchandise on account.
   a. The simplest form has only one money column entitled Accounts Receivable Dr. and Sales Cr.
   b. Columns are included for the date, name of the customer, and invoice number.
   c. A Sales Cr. column can be provided for each department, if needed.
   d. The posting of sales involves entering the total of the Sales Cr. column as a credit to the general ledger Sales account.
   e. The total of the Accounts Receivable Dr. column is posted as a debit to the Accounts Receivable account in the general ledger.
   f. The individual amounts in the Accounts Receivable Dr. column are posted to each individual customer's account in the subsidiary ledger.

CASH RECEIPTS JOURNAL

10. The cash receipts journal is used to record all receipts of cash, including cash sales.
    a. Typically, the following columns will be provided: Cash Dr., Sales Discounts Dr., Date, Description, Sales Cr., Accounts Receivable Cr., Other Accounts Cr.
    b. The Cash Dr., Sales Discounts Dr., Sales Cr., and Accounts Receivable Cr. column totals are posted to those accounts in the general ledger.
    c. The individual amounts in the Accounts Receivable Cr. column are posted to each individual customer's account in the subsidiary ledger.
    d. The amounts appearing in the Other Accounts Cr. column are posted in the general ledger to the accounts indicated; the column total is not posted.

PURCHASES JOURNAL

11. The purchases journal is used to record all purchases made on account.
    a. The simplest form has only one money column entitled Purchases Dr., Accounts Payable, Cr.
    b. Columns are included for the date, terms of sale, invoice number, and name of creditor.
    c. A Purchases Dr. column can be provided for each department if needed.
    d. The total of the Purchases Dr. Column is posted as a debit to the general ledger Purchases account.
    e. The total of the Accounts Payable Cr. column is posted as a credit to the general ledger Accounts Payable account.
    f. The individual amounts in the Accounts Payable Cr. column are posted to each individual creditor's account in the subsidiary ledger.

CASH DISBURSEMENTS JOURNAL

12. The cash disbursements journal is used to record all disbursements of cash.
    a. Typically, the following columns will be provided: Accounts Payable Dr., Supplies Expense Dr., Other Accounts Dr., Date, Description, Check Number, Cash Cr., Purchase Discounts Cr.
    b. The Accounts Payable Dr., Supplies Expense Dr., Purchase Discounts Cr., and Cash Cr. column totals are posted to those accounts in the general ledger.
    c. The individual accounts in the Accounts Payable Dr. column are posted to each individual creditor's account in the subsidiary ledger.
    d. The amounts appearing in the Other Accounts Dr. column are posted in the general ledger to the accounts indicated; the column total is not posted.

Chapter 7

GENERAL JOURNAL

13. Transactions that do not belong in a special journal are entered in the general journal.

ALTERNATIVE METHODS OF PROCESSING DATA

14. Accountants have a wide range of equipment that can be used in accounting systems to process data, including the following:
    a. Manual system
    b. Microcomputers and minicomputers
    c. Service bureaus
    d. Time-sharing terminals
    e. Mainframe in-house-computer

MANUAL SYSTEM

15. Small businesses often use a hand-posted system in which the accounting function is handled by the accountant and possibly one or two clerks.

MINICOMPUTERS AND MICROCOMPUTERS

16. With the lowering of computer prices, many small and medium-sized businesses are replacing their manual systems with microcomputers and minicomputers.
    a. Microcomputers are smaller than minicomputers.
    b. Cost is often the distinction between a microcomputer and a minicomputer.

SERVICE BUREAUS

17. Some companies have their business transactions processed by a local service bureau that rents out computer time on its large computer.

TIME-SHARING TERMINALS

18. Time sharing occurs when several users utilize the same host computer to process data by using remote terminals.

MAINFRAME IN-HOUSE COMPUTER

19. The purchase of an in-house computer is often justified if the volume of transactions is very large.

APPENDIX 7-A: THE USE OF THE MICROCOMPUTER IN ACCOUNTING

20. Several accounting system packages for microcomputers are currently available.
21. Electronic spreadsheets have numerous applications in accounting.
22. Database management systems on microcomputers are prominently used in accounting.
23. Microcomputers are used in tax, auditing, and management consulting services.

APPENDIX 7-B: THE COMPUTER—BASIC CONCEPTS

24. The computer has the distinguishing features of having to accept instructions for the processing of transaction data, store those instructions, and execute them any number of times precisely in the desired sequence.
25. A storage unit, an arithmetic unit, and a control unit comprise the three components of a computer.
26. Almost all applications of data processing to accounting involve the use of files, which are groupings of similar data arranged in an identifiable order.

DEMONSTRATION PROBLEM

The following column headings do not state whether the columns are debit or credit columns:

Purchases Journal		Sales Journal	
Account	*Amount*	*Account*	*Amount*
ABC Company	1,500	Nancy Blair	1,800
LMN Company	2,250	Frank Harris	2,100
XYZ Company	3,000	Teresa Long	2,400
Total	6,750	Total	6,300

General Journal

Sales Returns and Allowances	600	
Accounts Receivable—Frank Harris		600
Customer returned merchandise.		
Accounts Payable—XYZ Company	300	
Purchase Returns and Allowances		300
Returned defective merchandise.		

Cash Receipts Journal

Account	Other Accounts	Accounts Receivable	Sales	Sales Discounts	Cash
Nancy Blair		1,800		36	1,764
Frank Harris		750		15	735
Sales			1,875		1,875
Notes Payable	7,500				7,500
Teresa Long		1,200		24	1,176
Sales			1,725		1,725
Totals	7,500	3,750	3,600	75	14,775

Cash Disbursements Journal

Account	Other Accounts	Accounts Payable	Purchase Discounts	Cash
LMN Company		1,125	22.50	1,102.50
Salaries Expense	975			975.00
XYZ Company		1,500	30.00	1,470.00
Salaries Expense	975			975.00
Totals	1,950	2,625	52.50	4,522.50

Required:

a. Prepare T-accounts for the following general ledger and subsidiary ledger accounts.

General Ledger Accounts	Accounts Receivable Subsidiary Ledger Accounts
Cash	Nancy Blair
Accounts Receivable	Frank Harris
Notes Payable	Teresa Long
Accounts Payable	
Sales	
Sales Returns and Allowances	Accounts Payable Subsidiary Ledger Accounts
Sales Discounts	ABC Company
Purchases	LMN Company
Purchase Returns and Allowances	XYZ Company
Purchase Discounts	
Salaries Expense	

b.   Post the journal amounts to the proper T-Accounts.

a. and b.   Accounts Receivable Subsidiary Ledger

Nancy Blair	Frank Harris	Teresa Long

                             Accounts Payable Subsidiary Ledger

ABC Company	LMN Company	XYZ Company

                             General Ledger

Cash	Sales	Purchase Returns and Allowances

Accounts Receivable	Sales Returns and Allowances	Purchase Discounts

Notes Payable	Sales Discounts	Salaries Expense

Accounts Payable	Purchases	

SOLUTION TO DEMONSTRATION PROBLEM

a. and b.   Accounts Receivable Subsidiary Ledger

Nancy Blair		Frank Harris		Teresa Long	
1,800	1,800	2,100	600	2,400	1,200
			750		

                             Accounts Payable Subsidiary Ledger

ABC Company		LMN Company		XYZ Company	
	1,500	1,125	2,250	300	3,000
				1,500	

General Ledger

Cash	
14,775.00	4,522.50

Sales	
	6,300
	3,600

Purchase Returns and Allowances	
	300

Accounts Receivable	
6,300	600
	3,750

Sales Returns and Allowances	
600	

Purchase Discounts	
	52.50

Notes Payable	
	7,500

Sales Discounts	
75	

Salaries Expense	
975	
975	

Accounts Payable	
300	6,750
2,625	

Purchases	
6,750	

The Sales account must have a $3,600 column-total posting from the Cash Receipts Journal, and the Salaries Expense account must have two individual $975 debits and not a $1,950 column-total posting from the Cash Disbursements Journal.

MATCHING

Referring to the terms listed below, place the appropriate letter next to the corresponding description. A term may be used more than once.

a. Cash disbursements journal
b. Cash receipts journal
c. Control accounts

d. General journal
e. Management accounting
f. Service bureaus

g. Special journals
h. Subsidiary accounts
i. Time-sharing terminals

_____ 1. Used when several companies utilize the same host computer which they own jointly to process data.
_____ 2. This book of original entry would contain such columns as: Cash Dr., Sales Discounts Dr., Sales Cr., and Accounts Receivable Cr.
_____ 3. A special journal used only to record all payments of cash.
_____ 4. A special journal used only to record all inflows of cash.
_____ 5. Are maintained to provide specific information relating to customers and creditors.
_____ 6. Companies that take data from a client, perform data processing services, and then return the output to the client.
_____ 7. This book of original entry would contain such columns as: Accounts Payable Dr., Supplies Expense Dr., Cash Cr., and Purchase Discounts Cr.
_____ 8. Are maintained to provide balance sheet data.
_____ 9. Used to record one particular type of transaction.
_____ 10. Book of original entry for adjusting and closing entries.
_____ 11. Accounts typical of this classification are: Joe Smith, Brown Brooks, Mary Jones, Carter Supply Company and Star Equipment Company.
_____ 12. Accounts Payable and Accounts Receivable accounts in the general ledger.

1. Name four features of an effective accounting system:

    a. _____

    b. _____

    c. _____

    d. _____

2. All transactions that cannot be entered readily in one of the special journals are entered in the

    _____ _____.

3. Sales on account are recorded in the _____ _____, while cash sales are recorded in

    the _____ _____ _____.

4. The information contained in _____ _____ serves as the input for recording
    transactions.

5. Distinguish between a service bureau and a time-sharing system.

    _____

    _____

    _____

    _____

    _____

    _____

6. A _____ account is an account in the general ledger that is supported by a detailed
    classification of accounting information in a subsidiary record or ledger.

7. List three things the orderly and efficient processing of accounting data accomplishes.

    a. _____

    _____

    b. _____

    _____

    c. _____

    _____

8. Claxton Company's Accounts Receivable control account beginning balance was $37,500. If the
    following column totals in the special journals exist, what is the Accounts Receivable account ending
    balance?

Cash receipts journal—Accounts Receivable column	=	$172,500
Sales journal	=	150,000
Purchases journal	=	80,000
Sales returns and allowances recorded in the general journal	=	1,000
Purchase returns and allowances recorded in the general journal	=	4,300

9. A comparison of the _____ account balance with the sum of the individual _____ account balances aids in determining that all amounts have been posted to the subsidiary accounts.

10. Indicate where each of the following transactions would be posted by checking the proper column or columns for a clothing store.

	Sales Journal	Purchases Journal	Cash Receipts Journal	Cash Disbursements Journal	General Journal
Made cash sales					
Made sales on account					
Sold delivery equipment for cash					
Recorded depreciation					
Purchased merchandise on account					
Wrote checks for accounts payable					
Paid salaries					
Obtained loan from bank					
Bought equipment on account					
Paid for the new equipment					
Collected accounts receivable					

11. How are accounts receivable posted from the sales journal?

_____

_____

_____

_____

12. Where is the information contained in a single column purchases journal posted?

_____

_____

_____

_____

_____

13. List four advantages of using special journals.

a. _____

b. _____

c. _____

d. _____

_____

14.

	Cash	Accounts Receivable	Sales Discounts	Sales	Sundry	
Date	Dr.	Cr.	Dr.	Cr.	Dr.	Cr.
19-1						
April						
1 Jay Parker	200	204	4			
2 Greg James	294	300	6			
3 Ben Baines	350	350				
4 Cash Sales	1,200			1,200		
5 Equipment Sale	600					
Cost						5,000
Accumulated Depreciation					4,000	
Loss					400	
6 Merchandise sale for cash	800			800		
	3,444	854	10	2,000	4,400	5,000

Answer the following questions about the above journal?

a. How many different amounts will be posted to the Accounts Receivable (control) account? _____

b. How many different amounts will be posted to the subsidiary ledger accounts for Accounts Receivable? _____

c. How many different amounts will be posted to general ledger accounts? _____

d. How many different amounts will be posted to the Cash account? _____

15. The following data relating to credit sales have been taken from Harrison Company records at the end of August.

From General Journal

August 20   Sales Returns and Allowances   40
                  Accounts Receivable—Alan Dailey   40

Sales from Sales Journal

August 1	Chris Aldridge	$ 675
9	Jan Hart	320
12	Alan Dailey	175
24	Chris Aldridge	55
31	Total	$1,225

Required:

a. Post the sales journal entries to the customer accounts in the accounts receivable subsidiary ledger. Post the portion of the general journal entry that affects a customer's account. Indicate the accounting record to which you are posting.

b. Set up a general ledger having an Accounts Receivable control account, a Sales account, and a Sales Returns and Allowances account. Post the sales journal entries that affect these accounts.

c. Using a schedule of accounts receivable, prove that the accounts receivable subsidiary ledger account balances are equal to the control account balance.

a. Accounts Receivable Ledger

Chris Aldridge	Jan Hart	Alan Dailey

b. General Ledger

Accounts Receivable	Sales	Sales Returns and Allowances

c. _____
   _____
   _____

_____
_____
_____
_____
_____

The following questions are based on Appendix 7A.

16. The modules generally included in accounting system packages are: _____ _____, _____ _____, _____ _____, _____ _____, _____ and _____.

17. _____ _____ are used to play "what if" games.

18. _____ management systems store data together independent of any specific application.

19. Microcomputers are used to draw _____ _____ for statistical sampling purposes.

20. In the area of taxes, microcomputers are used to prepare _____ _____ and for _____ _____.

21. Consultants advise clients on _____ and _____ acquisition.

22. Software programs designed to duplicate the decision of an expert are called _____ _____.

23. _____ _____ is devoted to making the computer think like a human being.

The following questions are based on Appendix 7B.

24. What are the three basic components of a computer? (a) _____ _____, (b) _____ _____, and (c) _____ _____.

25. A _____ is a detailed set of instructions in coded form dictating how certain input should be processed.

26. A _____ is any grouping of similar items of data arranged in some identifiable order.

27. The development of a _____ _____ _____ has limited human participation in the preparation of input data and the program.

28. The computer _____ allows the operator to exercise control over the computer when necessary.

29. _____ equipment is used mainly to feed unprocessed information into and receive processed information from the computer.

30. The internal memory system of a computer is called the _____ _____ .

31. _____ and _____ factors must be considered in determining the optimum size of internal core storage.

32. Problems that require more storage space than originally provided in the computer can be solved by utilizing _____ devices such as _____ , _____ , or _____ storage units.

33. The _____ unit of the computer is the unit that interprets the set of instructions submitted to the computer specifying the operations to be performed and the correct sequence.

TRUE-FALSE QUESTIONS

Indicate whether each of the following statements is true or false by inserting a capital "T" or "F" in the blank space provided.

_____ 1. Control accounts reduce the number of postings from journals.

_____ 2. The total of the Accounts Payable column in the cash disbursements journal is posted as a debit to Accounts Payable in the general ledger.

_____ 3. Control accounts reduce the number of columns in special journals and the number of accounts in subsidiary ledgers.

_____ 4. When special journals are used, only transactions that cannot be recorded in the special journals are recorded in the general journal.

_____ 5. Assume that a company has the following special journals: sales journal, cash disbursements journal, purchases journal, and cash receipts journal with Cash Dr., Sales Discounts Dr., Sales Cr., and Accounts Receivable Cr. columns. Using these journals, a transaction involving borrowing money from a creditor by giving him a noninterest bearing note would be recorded in the cash receipts journal.

_____ 6. Using the cash receipts journal and sales journal described in #5 above, a cash sale would be recorded in the sales journal.

_____ 7. There will be no change in the transactions that had previously been recorded in the general journal after special journals are adopted.

_____ 8. The preparation, processing, and storage of business papers are very expensive for businesses.

_____ 9. Company A's purchases journal may differ from the purchases journal of Company B because of differences in the types of routine transactions.

_____ 10. The total of the Other Accounts column of the cash receipts journal is posted as a credit to the general ledger.

_____ 11. When an accounting system is put on the computer, the format of the financial statements is not affected materially.

_____ 12. The journal used for recording miscellaneous transactions is known as a general journal.

_____ 13. When special journals are designed and used correctly, there is no need for the general journal.

_____ 14. Individual amounts in the Purchases/Accounts Payable column in the purchases journal are not posted because the total is posted.

_____ 15. Individual amounts in the Accounts Receivable Cr. column of the cash receipts journal are posted infrequently in order to save processing cost.

_____ 16. Division of work and specialization are enhanced by the use of subsidiary ledgers.

_____ 17. Source documents for use in accounting systems are prepared only by accountants and bookkeepers.

_____ 18. All sales journals have a single column that is posted as a debit to Accounts Receivable and as a credit to Sales.

_____ 19. Since manual accounting systems are used less and less frequently, not much can be learned by studying them.

_____ 20. Two different accounting systems can be used to achieve the same result.

_____ 21. If special journals are designed for unique transactions, the accountant minimizes postings when these transactions are recorded.

_____ 22. Control accounts reduce the number of accounts in the general ledger.

_____ 23. The customary practice in medium-size and large businesses is to employ a number of special journals, each of which is designed to record a particular type of transaction.

_____ 24. A check mark in parentheses is placed immediately below the column total for Other Accounts Cr. in the Other Accounts Cr. column when the column total is posted to the general ledger.

_____ 25. All purchases, regardless of whether cash is paid at the time goods are bought or not, are recorded in the same special journal.

MULTIPLE CHOICE QUESTIONS

For each of the following questions indicate the best answer by circling the appropriate letter.

1. An important advantage of control accounts is that their use makes it possible to:
   A. reduce the number of postings from journals.
   B. reduce the number of columns in special purpose journals.
   C. reduce the number of accounts in subsidiary ledgers.
   D. reduce the number of accounts in the general ledger.
   E. None of the above is true.

2. After preparing the 1994 trial balance, the accountant of the Aiken Co. discovered that the Accounts Receivable control account had a debit balance of $150,200, whereas the schedule of accounts receivable indicated a total of $151,100. A possible reason for this discrepancy is:

A. the Accounts Receivable column in the cash receipts journal was overstated $900 as a result of an error in addition.

B. the amount column in the sales journal was overstated $900 as a result of an error in addition.

C. A remittance of $900 by J. Henry, a customer, was erroneously credited to the account of T. Honey, a customer.

D. a cash sale of $900 to J. Henry was recorded as a $900 credit sale in the sales journal.

3. The total of the balances in the Accounts Receivable subsidiary ledger is larger than the balance in the control account. This difference may be caused by:

A. a failure to post to a subsidiary account from the sales journal.

B. a failure to post to a subsidiary account from the cash receipts journal.

C. a failure to post a sales return to the control account.

D. overstating the debit side total of the control account.

E. None of the above could cause the discrepancy.

4. A customer's account showed the following entries: items of $25, $40, and $15 posted from the cash receipts journal; items of $50 and $100 posted from the sales journal; an item of $10, relating to the return of defective goods, posted from the general journal. This account should have a balance of:

A. $70
B. $230
C. $60
D. $240
E. something else.

5. A book of similar accounts represented in the general ledger by a control account is known as a:

A. special journal.
B. summarizing journal.
C. general journal.
D. subsidiary ledger.
E. None of these.

6. Control accounts:

A. are used only for Accounts Receivable.
B. reduce the number of accounts in the general ledger.
C. reflect the total dollar amount of accounts in a "subsidiary ledger."
D. aid the accountant in preparing a trial balance, since fewer accounts need be listed on the trial balance of general ledger accounts.
E. All but (A) above.

7. The bookkeeper of the X Corp. made an error in addition when totaling the dollar amount column in the purchases journal. This error would be discovered:

A. in the preparation of the trial balance.
B. by comparing the Accounts Payable control account with the schedule of accounts payable.
C. by comparing the Accounts Receivable control account with the schedule of accounts receivable.
D. by any of the above methods.

8. The column total of the Other Accounts column of the cash disbursements journal is:

   A. not posted.
   B. posted as a debit to the general ledger.
   C. posted as a credit to the general ledger.
   D. posted as a debit to a subsidiary ledger.
   E. posted as a credit to a subsidiary ledger.

9. In posting from the sales journal to the accounts receivable subsidiary ledger, the bookkeeper posts a charge sale of $283 (per sales journal) as $238. This error will be discovered:

   A. when the sales journal is footed.
   B. when the subsidiary ledger is reconciled with the control account.
   C. when a general ledger trial balance is prepared.
   D. when the control account is posted.
   E. None of the above would disclose the error.

10. Indicate the journal in which cash received from the owner as an additional investment can be recorded most conveniently.

    A. General journal
    B. Purchases journal
    C. Sales journal
    D. Cash receipts journal
    E. Cash disbursements journal

11. Indicate the journal in which office supplies sold at cost on account can be recorded most conveniently.

    A. General journal
    B. Purchases journal
    C. Sales journal
    D. Cash receipts journal
    E. Cash disbursements journal

12. Indicate the journal in which merchandise sold for cash can be recorded most conveniently.

    A. General journal
    B. Purchases journal
    C. Sales journal
    D. Cash receipts journal
    E. Cash disbursements journal

The following questions are based on Appendix 7-A.

13. Which one of the following is *not* usually included as one of the modules in accounting system packages?

    A. Accounts receivable
    B. Inventory management
    C. Sales
    D. Invoicing

14. The software package that allows the user to play "what if" games by changing numbers or formulas is called a(an):

    A. electronic spreadsheet.
    B. database management system.
    C. expert system.
    D. artificial intelligence application.

15. Which statement is false? In auditing, the microcomputer is used to:

    A. draw random samples.
    B. prepare trial balances
    C. perform analytical review.
    D. perform financial modeling tasks.

The following questions are based on the Appendix 7-B.

16. The three basic components of electronic computers are:

    A. storage unit, memory unit, and control unit.
    B. program, arithmetic unit, collator.
    C. storage unit, arithmetic unit, and control unit.
    D. sorter, reproducer, collator.

17. A set of instructions for guiding the operations of an electronic computer is called:

    A. a compiler.
    B. a program.
    C. an operating manual.
    D. a flow chart.
    E. Cobol.

18. Peripheral equipment:

    A. consists of a storage unit, an arithmetic unit and a processing unit.
    B. can be attached to the computer's basic components.
    C. includes tape drives, card readers, and printers.
    D. All of the above.
    E. (B) and (C) above.

SOLUTIONS

Matching

1.	i	7.	a
2.	b	8.	c
3.	a	9.	g
4.	b	10.	d
5.	h	11.	h
6.	f	12.	c

Completion and Exercises

1. Features of an effective accounting system include the following:

    a. Provide for the efficient processing of data at the least possible cost. (The cost of the system should be less than the value of the benefits received.)
    b. Ensure a high degree of accuracy.
    c. Provide for internal control to prevent theft or fraud.
    d. Provide for the growth of a business.

2. general journal
3. sales journal; cash receipts journal
4. source documents

5. A service bureau is an organization that operates a computer system to which a client must bring his or her data to be processed. A time-sharing system is similar, but allows the user to communicate with the computer through a terminal located in the user's office.

6. control

7. Any three of the following are the result of orderly and efficient processing of accounting data.

   a. Results of operations and financial position of the company can be determined and reported on a timely basis.
   b. Bills can be paid when due.
   c. The proper quantities and items of inventory can be sent to customers.
   d. Other aspects of business can be conducted in an orderly and purposeful manner.
   e. Reports required by the government or regulatory agencies can be prepared efficiently.

8.

Accounts receivable, beginning		$ 37,500
Add: Sales		150,000
		$187,500
Less: Cash receipts	$172,500	
Sales returns and allowances	1,000	173,500
Accounts receivable, ending		$ 14,000

9. control; subsidiary

10.

	Sales Journal	Purchases Journal	Cash Receipts Journal	Cash Disbursements Journal	General Journal
Made cash sales			X		
Made sales on account	X				
Sold delivery equipment for cash			X		
Recorded depreciation					X
Purchased merchandise on account		X			
Wrote checks for accounts payable				X	
Paid salaries				X	
Obtained loan from bank			X		
Bought equipment on account					X
Paid for the new equipment				X	
Collected accounts receivable			X		

11. The total of the money column is debited to the Accounts Receivable control account in the general ledger, and each individual amount in the money column is posted to the appropriate customer's account in the Accounts Receivable subsidiary ledger.

12. The total of the column is debited to the Purchases account and credited to the Accounts Payable control account. The individual items are posted to the individual accounts in the Accounts Payable subsidiary ledger.

13. Any four of the following advantages are correct.

   a. Time is saved in journalizing.
   b. Time is saved in posting.
   c. Detail is eliminated from the general ledger.
   d. Division of labor is promoted.
   e. Management analysis is aided.

14. a. 1 ($854)
    b. 3 ($204, $300, and $350)
    c. 7 ($3,444, $854, $10, $2,000, $5,000, $4,000, and $400)
    d. 1 ($3,444)

15. a. Accounts Receivable Ledger

Chris Aldridge		Jan Hart		Alan Dailey	
Aug. 1 675		Aug. 9 320		Aug. 12 175	Aug. 20 40
24 55					

   b. General Ledger

Accounts Receivable		Sales		Sales Returns and Allowances	
Aug. 31 1,225	Aug. 20 40		Aug. 31 1,225	Aug. 20 40	

   c.

HARRISON COMPANY
Schedule of Accounts Receivable
August 31, 19—

Chris Aldridge	$ 730
Jan Hart	320
Alan Dailey	135
Total Accounts Receivable	$1,185

16. general ledger; accounts receivable; accounts payable; inventory management; payroll; invoicing
17. Electronic spreadsheets
18. Database
19. random samples
20. tax returns; tax planning
21. computer; software
22. expert systems
23. Artificial intelligence
24. (a) storage unit; (b) arithmetic unit; (c) control unit
25. program
26. file
27. computerized accounting system
28. console
29. Peripheral
30. storage unit
31. Speed; cost
32. peripheral, disks, drums, tape
33. control

True-False Questions

1. T
2. T
3. F
4. T   This is one of the advantages of special journals as it saves posting and recording time.

5. F   This transaction would be recorded in the general journal because there is no column in the cash receipts journal described to credit Notes Payable. There is a Cash Dr. column in the cash receipts journal described but no Other Accounts Cr. column. Note that special journals vary in the columns contained.

6. F   Cash sales are recorded in the cash receipts journal.

7. F

8. T

9. T

10. F   The total is not posted because the amounts are posted individually to the accounts recorded in the Other Accounts column.

11. T

12. T

13. F   Transactions that cannot fit into the special journals must be recorded in the general journal.

14. F   Individual amounts are posted to the Accounts Payable subsidiary ledger.

15. F   The individual customer amounts are posted daily to keep the customer balances current.

16. T

17. F   Source documents may be prepared by persons other than accountants and bookkeepers, and these documents come from a variety of sources.

18. F   Variations can be made in sales journals to accommodate the company depending on the number of departments.

19. F   Since computerized systems accomplish the same tasks as manual systems, the study of manual systems is still useful.

20. T   For instance, either a manual or electronic accounting system can be used to produce financial statements for a company.

21. F   Special journals should be designed for routine transactions rather than unique transactions.

22. T

23. T

24. F   The column total entitled Other Accounts Cr. in the cash receipts journal is not posted; instead the individual amounts are posted to the separate ledger accounts.

25. F   A cash purchase is recorded in the cash disbursements journal, while a purchase on account is recorded in a purchases journal.

Multiple-Choice Questions

1. D

2. A   The Accounts Receivable control account would have been credited for $900 too much.

3. B   The subsidiary account should have been credited (reduced).

4. C $50 + $100 − $25 − $40 − $15 − $10 = $60.

5. D   Subsidiary ledgers include the Accounts Receivable and Accounts Payable ledgers (and possibly others).

6. E

7. B

8. A   Postings are made to the individual accounts recorded in the Other Accounts column.

9. B   The Accounts Receivable subsidiary ledger would total $45 (or $283 − $238) less than the correct balance in the Accounts Receivable control account in the general ledger.

10. D

11. A

12. D

13. C

14. A

15. D   Financial modeling tasks are performed by consultants rather than auditors.

16. C

17. B   The control unit of a computer interprets the program.
18. E

8 CONTROL OF CASH

Learning Objectives

1. *Describe the necessity for and features of internal control.*
2. *Define cash and list the objectives sought by management in handling a company's cash.*
3. *Identify procedures for controlling cash receipts and disbursements.*
4. *Prepare a bank reconciliation and make necessary journal entries based on that schedule.*
5. *Explain why a petty cash fund is used, describe its operations, and make the necessary journal entries.*
6. *Describe the operation of the voucher system and make entries in its special journals—the voucher register and the check register.*

CHAPTER OUTLINE

INTERNAL CONTROL

1. An effective internal control structure includes an entity's plan of organization and all the procedures and actions taken by an entity to (a) protect its assets against theft and waste, (b) ensure compliance with company policies and Federal law, (c) evaluate the performance of all personnel in the company so as to promote efficiency of operations, and (d) ensure accurate and reliable operating data and accounting reports.

    a. Assets can be protected by (1) segregation of employee duties, (2) separation of employee functions, (3) rotation of employee job assignments, and (4) use of mechanical devices.

    b. Internal control policies must be followed by employees, and those policies must satisfy the requirements of the Foreign Corrupt Practices Act.

    c. Internal auditing can assist in evaluating how well company employees are doing their jobs.

    d. Since source documents serve as documentation of business transactions, the validity of these documents should be checked from time to time.

    e. For added protection, a company should carry both casualty insurance on assets and fidelity bonds on employees.

    f. The use of computers can present special internal control problems.

CONTROLLING CASH

2. Many business transactions involve cash utilizing a checking account.

    a. By definition, cash includes currency, coins, amounts in checking and savings accounts, and money orders.

    b. Cash also includes certificates of deposit, which are interest-bearing deposits at a bank that can be withdrawn at will.

    c. Cash does not include IOUs, notes receivable, or postage stamps.

    d. Petty Cash and Cash are the typical cash accounts.

    e. Management has the following objectives in regard to cash.

        1. Account for all cash transactions accurately, so that correct information will be available regarding cash flows and balances.

        2. Make certain enough cash is available to pay bills as they come due.

        3. Avoid holding too much idle cash because excess cash could be invested to generate income, such as interest.

        4. Prevent loss of cash due to theft or fraud.

CONTROLLING CASH RECEIPTS

3. All assets owned by the company must be protected from theft or mishandling, but cash requires additional care.

    a. Cash is more likely to be the object of theft because it is easily concealed.

    b. Cash is not readily identifiable, which makes it a likely target for thieves.

    c. Cash may be more desirable than other company assets because it can be quickly spent to acquire other things of value.

4. Several basic principles for controlling cash receipts exist, though these principles may vary with each business.

    a. Records of all cash receipts should be prepared soon after cash is received.

    b. All cash receipts should be deposited intact on the day received or the next business day.

        1. Cash disbursements should not be made from cash receipts but only by check or from petty cash funds.

        2. If refunds for returned merchandise are made from the cash register, refund tickets should be prepared and approved by a supervisor.

    c. The person who handles cash receipts should not record them in the accounting system.

    d. The person receiving cash should not also disburse cash.

CONTROLLING CASH DISBURSEMENTS

5. Basic control procedures are established for cash disbursements because most of the firm's cash is spent by check.

    a. All disbursements should be made by check or from petty cash.

    b. All checks should be serially numbered, and access to checks should be limited.

    c. Preferably, two signatures should be required on each check.

    d. If possible, the person who authorizes payment of a bill should not be allowed to sign checks.

    e. Approved invoices or vouchers should be required to support checks issued.

    f. The person authorizing disbursements should be certain that payment is legitimate and is made to the proper payee.

    g. When invoices and vouchers are paid, they should be stamped "paid," with the date and number of the check issued indicated.

    h. The person(s) who signed the checks should not have access to cancelled checks and should not prepare the bank reconciliation.

    i. A bank reconciliation should be prepared each month, preferably by a person who has no other cash duties.

    j. All voided and spoiled checks should be retained and defaced to prevent their unauthorized use.

    k. A voucher system may be needed in large firms to provide close cash control.

    l. Use of the net price method of recording purchases helps avoid loss of purchase discounts by calling attention to cash discounts lost.

THE BANK CHECKING ACCOUNT

6. One of the services provided by a bank is a checking account, which is a balance maintained in a bank that is subject to withdrawal by the depositor on demand.

THE SIGNATURE CARD

7. A new depositor completes a signature card, which has spaces for the signatures of persons authorized to sign checks drawn on an account.

DEPOSIT TICKET

8. In making a bank deposit, the depositor prepares a deposit ticket, which is a form showing the date and the items comprising the deposit; in addition, the depositor's name, address, and bank account number are shown.

CHECK

9. A check is a written order on a bank to pay a specific sum of money to the party designated as the payee by the party issuing the check.

    a. There are three parties to every bank check transaction:

        1. The party issuing the check.

        2. The bank on which the check is drawn.

        3. The party to whose order the check is made payable.

b. A remittance advice may be attached to a check informing the payee why the drawer of the check is making this payment.

BANK STATEMENT

10. A bank statement is used by a bank to describe the deposits and checks cleared during the period and any other increases or decreases in the bank account.

    a. Cancelled checks and original deposit tickets generally are returned with the bank statement.
    b. Debit memos and credit memos may also be returned with the bank statement.
        1. Debit memos are forms used by banks to explain a deduction from the depositor's account. The company's Cash account is a liability to the bank and a debit memo is used to reduce the liability.
        2. Credit memos explain additions to the account. Increases to the bank's liability accounts require credits.
    c. The balance shown in the bank statement usually differs from the balance in the depositor's Cash in Bank ledger account.
        1. Outstanding checks have not yet been deducted from the bank balance.
        2. Deposits in transit have not yet been added to the bank balance.
        3. Bank errors can occur in a depositor's account caused by scanners misreading the account number printed in magnetic ink or bank employees encoding the wrong amount on the check.
        4. Service charges have not yet been recognized by the depositor and deducted from the Cash account balance.
        5. "Not sufficient funds" checks have not yet been deducted from the depositor's Cash account balance.
        6. The bank may have collected a customer's note or received a wire transfer of funds, which is an inter-bank transfer of funds by telephone.
        7. The depositor may have made errors by recording a check in the accounting records for a different amount than the actual figure.

BANK RECONCILIATION

11. A bank reconciliation is prepared to account for the difference between the two balances.

    a. Both the balance per the bank statement and the balance per the ledger account are adjusted to the true balance of expendable cash.
    b. The documents used are the bank statement and any accompanying debit and credit memoranda, returned checks, a list of checks issued, and a record of deposits made.
    c. After the reconciliation has been prepared, an adjusting entry is prepared to record the previously unrecorded items.

CERTIFIED AND CASHIER'S CHECKS

12. A certified check is a check drawn by a depositor and taken to his or her bank for certification, which indicates that the depositor's balance is large enough to cover the check.

    a. The amount of the certified check is deducted immediately after certification from the depositor's checking account.
    b. The certified check now becomes a liability of the bank rather than the depositor.

13. A cashier's check is a check drawn by a bank made out to either the depositor or a third party after deducting the amount of the check from the depositor's account or receiving cash from the depositor.

PETTY CASH FUNDS

14. Petty cash funds are usually established so that small disbursements can be made without writing a check.

ESTABLISHING THE FUND

15. Petty cash funds are established by writing a check on the general ledger Cash account.
    a. The entry to establish a petty cash fund is a debit to Petty Cash and a credit to Cash for the amount drawn.
    b. A petty cash cashier is responsible for operation of the fund so that adequate control is maintained over cash disbursements.

OPERATING THE FUND

16. A petty cash voucher is a form that indicates the amount and reason for the petty cash disbursement.
    a. A voucher should be prepared for each disbursement from the fund.
    b. Invoices for the expenditure should be stapled to the petty cash voucher.
    c. The person responsible for petty cash is accountable for having cash and petty cash vouchers equal to the total amount of the fund.

REPLENISHING THE FUND

17. To replenish petty cash, a check is drawn for the amount that will restore the fund to its original amount.
    a. The journal entry is to debit expenses and assets for the amount disbursed and to credit Cash.
    b. Replenishments are made when the petty cash fund becomes low in currency and may also be made at the end of the accounting period.
    c. If the petty cash fund is found to be larger than needed, excess petty cash can be transferred back to the Cash account. This transaction is recorded by debiting Cash and crediting Petty Cash.
    d. Increases in the petty cash fund can be made by transferring cash over to the individual responsible for the petty cash fund. This transaction is recorded by debiting Petty Cash and crediting Cash.

CASH SHORT AND OVER

18. The petty cash fund must always be restored to its set amount, therefore the credit to Cash will always be for the difference between the set amount and the actual cash in the fund.
    a. Debits will be made for all items vouchered.
    b. Any discrepancy will be debited or credited to an account called Cash Short and Over.
        1. The Cash Short and Over account is an expense or a revenue depending on whether it has a debit or credit balance.
        2. Entries in the Cash Short and Over account may be entered from other change-making funds, such as those in the cash register.

THE VOUCHER SYSTEM

19. A voucher system is a set of procedures, special journals, and authorization forms designed to provide control over cash payments.

PROCEDURES FOR PREPARING A VOUCHER

20. The procedures are as follows:
    a. Basic data are entered on a voucher from an invoice.
    b. The invoice, voucher, and receiving report undergo careful examination before the voucher receives approval or disapproval for payment.
    c. The accounting department notes on the voucher the proper debits and credits.
    d. Proper entries are made in the voucher register, and the voucher is filed in the unpaid voucher file.

SPECIAL JOURNALS USED

21. A voucher register is a multicolumn special journal having a special debit column for accounts most frequently debited when a liability is incurred.
    a. The credit for all entries in the voucher register is to Vouchers Payable.
    b. After the voucher is entered in the voucher register, it is filed in the unpaid vouchers file.

c. When the voucher is paid, it is filed in the paid vouchers file and the payment date and check number are inserted in the proper columns in the voucher register.

22. A check register is a special journal showing all checks issued, listed by date and check number.

a. If vouchers are entered at the gross amount before discount deductions in the voucher register, a Purchase Discounts Cr. column should be included in the check register.

b. Separate columns would be needed for the debit to Vouchers Payable and the credit to Cash since the dollar amounts posted to these two accounts would differ by the amount of the discount taken.

c. An alternative system is to enter the invoices net of discount in the vouchers register. Then only one dollar amount column is needed for the debit to Vouchers Payable and credit to Cash.

PROCEDURES FOR PAYING A VOUCHER

23. When a voucher is due for payment, it is removed from the unpaid voucher file and a check is prepared for the amount payable.

a. The treasurer usually receives the prepared check, voucher, and supporting documents.

b. If the treasurer approves the payment, the check is signed and mailed.

c. The voucher is then returned to the accounting department.

FILES MAINTAINED IN A VOUCHER SYSTEM

24. An unpaid voucher file and a paid voucher file are maintained in a voucher system.

a. Unpaid vouchers are filed according to their due dates; if the credit terms run from the end of the month, the invoices of each creditor are included in one voucher and then filed by due date.

b. The paid voucher file is filed by voucher number in numerical order and contains all vouchers that have been paid.

DEMONSTRATION PROBLEM

Lamonica Company uses a voucher system. It records all purchases net of the discount offered and prepares a second voucher when a discount is lost.

Record the following transactions in the proper register:

May 1 Prepared Voucher No. 235 payable to Locke and Reed, Inc., for advertising expense, $96.

4 Prepared Voucher No. 236 payable to Keefer Co. for merchandise, $320, terms 2/10, n/30.

5 Issued Check No. 192 in payment of Voucher No. 235.

9 Prepared Voucher No. 237 payable to Wolfe, Inc., for merchandise, $400, plus transportation-in of $40. Credit terms are 2/10, n/30.

10 Prepared Voucher No. 238 payable to Maddox Office Supply Co. for office equipment, $1,080, terms n/60.

11 Prepared Voucher No. 239 payable to Havens Co. for merchandise, $760, terms 2/10, n/30.

14 Issued Check No. 193 in payment of Voucher No. 236.

18 Prepared Voucher No. 240 payable to Leland, Inc., for transportation of merchandise purchased, $48.

18 Issued Check No. 194 in payment of Voucher No. 240.

19 Issued Check No. 195 in payment of Voucher No. 237.

24 Prepared Voucher No. 241 payable to Stroud Co. for merchandise, $800, terms 2/10, n/30.

31 Issued Check No. 196 in payment of Voucher No. 239, plus the discount lost.

LAMONICA
Check Register

Date	Payee	Voucher No.	Check No.	Vouchers Payable Dr., Cash Cr.
1 May				
2				
3				
4				
5				
6				
7				
8				
9				

LAMONICA COMPANY
Voucher Register

Date	Vchr. No.	Payee	Date Paid	Check No.	Vouchers Payable Cr.	Merchandise Purchases Dr.	Transportation-in Dr.	Discounts Lost Dr.	Other Accounts Debit		
									Account Name	No.	Amount
1 May											
2											
3											
4											
5											
6											
7											
8											
9											

SOLUTION TO DEMONSTRATION PROBLEM

LAMONICA
Check Register

	Date	Payee	Voucher No.	Check No.	Vouchers Payable Dr., Cash Cr.
1	May 5	Locke and Reed, Inc.	235	192	96.00
2	14	Keefer Co.	236	193	313.60
3	18	Leland, Inc.	240	194	48.00
4	19	Wolfe, Inc.	237	195	432.00
5	31	Havens Co.	239 & 242	196	760.00
6					1,649.60
7					
8					
9					

LAMONICA COMPANY
Voucher Register

	Date	Vchr. No.	Payee	Check No.	Date Paid	Vouchers Payable Cr.	Merchandise Purchases Dr.	Transportation-in Dr.	Discounts Lost Dr.	Other Accounts Debit — Account Name	No.	Amount
1	May 1	235	Locke and Reed, Inc.	192	May 5	96.00				Advertising Expense		96.00
2	4	236	Keefer Co.	193	May 14	313.60	313.60					
3	9	237	Wolfe, Inc.	195	May 19	392.00	392.00	40.00				
4	10	238	Maddox Office Supply Co.			1,080.00				Office Equipment		1,080.00
5	11	239	Havens Co.	196	May 31	744.80	744.80					
6	18	240	Leland, Inc.	194	May 18	48.00		48.00				
7	24	241	Stroud Co.			784.00	784.00					
8	31	242	Havens Co.	196	May 31	15.20			15.20			
9						3,513.60	2,234.40	88.00	15.20			1,176.00

MATCHING

Referring to the terms listed below, place the appropriate letter next to the corresponding description.

a. Bank reconciliation
b. Bank statement
c. Cancelled checks
d. Cash short and over
e. Credit memo
f. Certificate of deposit

g. Debit memo
h. Deposits in transit
i. Discounts lost
j. NSF check
k. Outstanding checks
l. Paid voucher file

m. Petty cash fund
n. Petty cash voucher
o. Remittance advice
p. Unpaid voucher file
q. Voucher register

_____ 1. An interest-bearing deposit at a bank that can be withdrawn at will or at a fixed maturity date.
_____ 2. Form used by bank to explain a deduction from the depositor's account.
_____ 3. Form used by bank to explain an addition to the depositor's account.
_____ 4. This account may be either a revenue or an expense account, depending on its balance.
_____ 5. A form explaining a payment made from a petty cash fund.
_____ 6. When a voucher system is used, this file serves as a subsidiary Accounts Payable ledger.
_____ 7. Checks issued by the depositor that have not yet cleared the bank for payment.
_____ 8. A special journal used instead of a purchases journal when a voucher system is used.
_____ 9. A fixed amount of cash advanced to a custodian who will be reimbursed after making payments with the cash.
_____ 10. A statement issued by a bank describing activities in a depositor's account.
_____ 11. A form attached to a check informing the payee why the drawer of the check is making payment.
_____ 12. A check that the bank has refused to pay because the writer of the check does not have enough money in his or her account to cover the check.
_____ 13. Cash receipts entered in the depositor's accounts and placed in the bank's night depository box. The bank will show the deposit on next month's statement.

COMPLETION AND EXERCISES

1. What purposes are served through use of an effective internal control structure?

   a. _____

   b. _____

   c. _____

   d. _____

2. Give three objectives that management has in regard to cash.

   a. _____

   _____

   b. _____

   _____

   c. _____

   _____

3. Why do most firms exercise special care in safeguarding cash?

_____

_____

_____

_____

_____

4. What is the composition of cash?

_____

_____

_____

_____

_____

5. Give at least five reasons why the bank statement balance usually differs from the balance in the depositor's ledger account for cash. Categorize them as to which require entries on the depositor's books and which do not.

    a. Items that cause the bank statement to differ from the Cash ledger account that *do not* require an entry on the depositor's books.

        1. _____

        2. _____

        3. _____

    b. Items that cause the bank statement to differ from the Cash ledger account that *do* require an entry on the depositor's books.

        1. _____

        2. _____

        3. _____

        4. _____

6. List five basic control procedures for cash disbursements.

    1. _____

        _____

    2. _____

        _____

    3. _____

        _____

    4. _____

        _____

    5. _____

        _____

7. What is the purpose of the bank reconciliation? _____

_____

_____

_____

_____

8. From the following information prepare a bank reconciliation for the Sentra Company:

Balance of Cash account on March 31, 1993	$30,373.08
Balance on March 31, 1993, bank statement	34,314.32
Deposits in transit	2,021.44
Outstanding checks	4,774.68

The bank statement also contained the following information which had not been recorded on the books of Sentra Company:

The bank had collected a note for Sentra Company for $1,200.
The bank had charged Sentra Company $12 for servicing the account.

9. The Cash Short and Over Account is a(n) _____ if it has a debit balance and a(an) _____ if it has a credit balance.

10. A _____ _____ _____ should be prepared for each disbursement from the petty cash fund.

11. A _____ _____ _____ _____ is an inter-bank transfer of funds by telephone.

12. At the time of replenishing, the $200 petty cash fund had $24 remaining and the following petty cash vouchers:

Stamps	$ 60
Transportation-in	100
Stationery	14

What entry would be made to record the replenishment of the fund?

13. A method of achieving close control over cash disbursements is called a _____ system.

14. Two special journals used in a voucher system are the _____ _____ and _____ _____.

15. The _____ _____ _____ serves as an Accounts Payable subsidiary ledger.

16. When a voucher is paid it is placed in the _____ _____ _____.

17. The Accounts Receivable clerk in the Davis Corporation is in charge of the petty cash fund. This procedure is an example of poor _____ _____.

18. An overdraft in a bank account should be shown in the balance sheet as a _____.

19. Outstanding checks should be _____ _____ (deducted from or added to) the _____ _____ (Cash ledger account or bank account) balance when a bank reconciliation is prepared.

20. A NSF check of your customer (returned by your bank) would be _____ _____ (added to or deducted from) the Cash in Bank account during the preparation of a bank reconciliation.

21. On January 1, the Lynx Company has a petty cash fund, which was established at $220. When the fund is found to contain only $16, it is replenished. Petty cash receipts are found for the following:

Delivery Expense	$ 50
Transportation-In	20
Office Supplies	100
Miscellaneous Office Expense	40

Record the replenishment of the fund in journal form.

DATE	ACCOUNT TITLES AND EXPLANATION	POST. REF.	DEBIT	CREDIT

22. Hassán Company records purchases at net invoice price. It also has a petty cash fund. For each transaction, state the name of the journal in which the transaction should be recorded and give the entry required in general journal form.

a. Prepared Voucher No. 123 for merchandise purchased, $10,000; terms 2/10, n/30.
b. Prepared Voucher No. 124 to replenish petty cash fund for expenditures of $100 for postage and $200 for office supplies.
c. Issued Check No. 1101 to pay Voucher No. 123 within the discount period.
d. Issued Check No. 1102 to pay Voucher No. 124.

DATE	ACCOUNT TITLES AND EXPLANATION	POST. REF.	DEBIT	CREDIT

23. Two weeks ago Aaron Company established a $200 petty cash fund. On December 15, the contents in the petty cash box included $6 in cash and the following paid petty cash receipts: postage, $60; transportation-in, $40; and delivery fee on merchandise sent to a customer, $90. In the space below give the entry to reimburse the fund.

DATE	ACCOUNT TITLES AND EXPLANATION	POST. REF.	DEBIT	CREDIT

24. Data for Games Company are given below:

(1) A deposit placed in the bank's night depository after banking hours on May 31 appeared on the June bank statement; (2) but one placed there after hours on June 30 did not. Two checks, (3) No. 1010 and (4) 1013, were outstanding on May 31. Check No. 1010 was returned with the June bank statement but Check No. 1013 was not. (5) Check No. 1100 for $138 was incorrectly entered in cash disbursements journal and posted as though it were for $183. (6) Enclosed with the June bank statement was a debit memorandum for a bank service charge. (7) Also enclosed was a check received from a customer and deposited on June 23 but returned by the bank marked "Not sufficient funds." (8) Check No. 1841, written on June 27, was not returned with the cancelled checks.

Required:

a. If an item in the foregoing list should not appear on the June bank reconciliation, ignore it. However, if an item should appear, enter its number in a set of parentheses below to show where it should be added or subtracted in preparing the reconciliation.

GAMES COMPANY
Bank Reconciliation, June 30, 19—

Balance per ledger .... $X,XXX	Bank statement balance .... $X,XXX
Add:	Add:
( )	( )
( )	( )
Deduct:	Deduct:
( )	( )
( )	( )
Adjusted balance .... $X,XXX	Adjusted balance .... $X,XXX

b. Certain of the reconciliation items require entries on the company's books. Place the numbers of these items within the following parentheses.

( ), ( ), ( ), ( ), ( ), ( ), ( ), ( ).

25. At August 31 of the current year, the Cash account of Ramsey Company reflected a balance of $19,370.80. At the same date, the bank statement indicated a balance of $19,775.34. The following items were revealed in the comparison of the bank statement and the analysis of cancelled checks and bank notices:

1. Bank service charges for August totaled $17.10.
2. A check for $168 in payment of a voucher was erroneously recorded in the check register as $186.
3. A deposit of $8,793.62, representing receipts of August 31, had been made too late to appear on the bank statement.
4. Checks outstanding totaled $8,199.26.
5. A check drawn for $40 had been erroneously charged by the bank as $400.
6. The bank had collected for Ramsey Company $1,358 on a note left for collection.

Required:

a. Prepare a bank reconciliation.
b. Journalize the necessary entries assuming the accounts have not been closed and a voucher system is used.

				DEBIT	CREDIT

DATE		ACCOUNT TITLES AND EXPLANATION	POST. REF.	DEBIT	CREDIT

26. Data for Magic Company are given below:

(1) A $2,000 deposit placed in the bank's night depository after banking hours on May 31 appeared on the June bank statement; (2) but a $3,000 deposit placed there after hours on June 30 did not. Two checks (3) No. 1010 for $500 and (4) No. 1013 for $250 were outstanding on May 31. Check No. 1010 was returned with the June bank statement but Check No. 1013 was not. (5) Check No. 1100 for $128 to a creditor was incorrectly entered in the cash disbursements journal and posted as though it were $182. (6) Enclosed with the June bank statement was a debit memorandum for a bank service charge of $200. (7) Also enclosed was a check for $500 received from a customer and deposited on June 23 but returned by the bank marked "Not sufficient funds." (8) Check No. 1841, for $2,000 written on June 27, was not returned with the cancelled checks.

Required:

a. Prepare a bank reconciliation for Magic Company. Assume the balance of the Cash account is $40,000 and the balance on the bank statement is $38,604. If an item in the foregoing list should not appear on the June bank reconciliation, ignore it.

b. Journalize the necessary entries assuming the accounts have not been closed.

a.

b.

DATE	ACCOUNT TITLES AND EXPLANATION	POST. REF.	DEBIT	CREDIT

27. On December 31, 1993, the Cash in Bank account of Auto Co. reflected a balance of $24,242. This balance was determined after the cash receipts journal had been posted. At the same date, the bank statement indicated a balance of $20,300. The following items were revealed in the comparison of the bank statement and the analysis of cancelled checks and bank notices:

1. Bank service charges for December totaled $30.
2. A check for $268 in payment of a voucher was erroneously recorded in the check register as $286.
3. A deposit of $10,000, representing receipts of December had been made too late to appear on the bank statement.
4. Checks outstanding totaled $5,000.
5. A check drawn for $40 had been erroneously charged by the bank as $400.
6. The bank had collected for Auto Co. $1,430 on a note left for collection.

Required:

a. Prepare a bank reconciliation.
b. Journalize the necessary entries assuming the accounts have not been closed and a voucher system is used.

a.

b.

DATE	ACCOUNT TITLES AND EXPLANATION	POST. REF.	DEBIT	CREDIT

TRUE-FALSE QUESTIONS

Indicate whether each of the following statements is true or false by inserting a capital "T" or "F" in the blank space provided.

_____ 1. Cash includes certain negotiable instruments and demand certificates of deposit, among other items.

_____ 2. While a company must make sure enough cash is available to pay bills, no problem exists from holding excess cash.

_____ 3. All disbursements should be by check or from a petty cash fund.

_____ 4. The cash balance shown on the bank statement usually is not equal to the amount in the depositor's Cash account before reconciliation.

_____ 5. Outstanding checks will require an entry in the depositor's books after the bank reconciliation is prepared.

_____ 6. When certified, a check is a liability of the bank on which it is drawn.

_____ 7. If the Cash Short and Over account has a debit balance at the end of the accounting period, it will be included in "other expenses" on the income statement.

_____ 8. Petty Cash is credited when the petty cash fund is reimbursed.

_____ 9. If a voucher register contains a column for discounts lost, the company is using the net price procedure for handling purchase discounts.

_____ 10. Vouchers in the unpaid voucher file should be filed in the order of the voucher numbers.

_____ 11. The person who authorizes the disbursements should also be the person who signs the checks.

_____ 12. Misappropriations of cash can occur just as easily before or after a record is made of the receipt.

_____ 13. All cash receipts should be deposited intact in the bank.

_____ 14. Cash disbursements should not be made from cash receipts.

_____ 15. The person who receives the cash should also record cash transactions in the accounting records.

_____ 16. Cash receipts and cash disbursements should be the function of one person to facilitate record keeping for cash.

_____ 17. Cash includes coin, currency, postdated checks, money orders, and money on deposit with banks.

_____ 18. In reconciling the bank account, the deposits in transit are deducted from the balance per ledger to determine the correct amount of cash owned by the depositor.

_____ 19. The Petty Cash account is debited for the establishment of the fund but is not credited for expenditures from the fund.

_____ 20. In preparing a bank reconciliation, the total amount of outstanding checks is deducted from the balance per ledger amount.

_____ 21. Outstanding checks are ascertained by comparing the amounts in the Deposits column on the bank statement with a record of deposits in the cash receipts book.

_____ 22. After preparing a bank reconciliation, the items found immediately below the 'Balance per bank statement' caption necessitate journal entries.

_____ 23. NSF checks should be deducted from the Balance per ledger when preparing a bank reconciliation.

_____ 24. In the bank reconciliation, deposits in transit are added to the Balance per ledger.

_____ 25. Postage stamps should be included in the Cash balance.

MULTIPLE CHOICE QUESTIONS

For each of the following questions indicate the best answer by circling the appropriate letter.

1. The June 30 bank statement shows a balance of $1,297.72. A comparison with the check register shows that two checks, for $136.00 and $73.40 respectively, have not been paid by the bank. The receipts of June 30, amounting to $832.64, were not recorded by the bank as deposited until July 1. The correct checkbook balance for June 30 is:

    A. $674.48
    B. $2,339.76
    C. $1,920.96
    D. $1,665.28
    E. $418.80

2. The Cash account contained a balance of $1,120 on January 1. The totals of the Cash columns in the special journals at the end of January were as follows: cash receipts journal, $2,980; cash disbursements journal, $3,260. Checks written and entered in the cash disbursements journal, but outstanding at the end of the month, amount to $400. The January 31st balance of Cash will be:

    A. $1,120
    B. $1,400
    C. $840
    D. $4,100
    E. None of the above.

3. Which of the following items would be least likely to be paid from petty cash?

    A. Postage
    B. Office supplies
    C. Office furniture addition
    D. Post office box rental

4. A petty cash fund has been established at $500. The petty cash cashier in balancing the records on June 30 lists the following items:

(1)	Cash on hand	$196.40
(2)	Vouchers for merchandise purchased	121.60
(3)	Vouchers for office supplies purchased	100.00
(4)	Vouchers for miscellaneous expenses	82.00
	Total	$500.00

    The entry to replenish the petty cash fund on June 30 would include a:

    A. debit to Petty Cash for $303.60.
    B. credit to Petty Cash for $303.60.
    C. credit to Cash for $303.60.
    D. credit to Purchases for $121.60.
    E. None of these.

5. The voucher is prepared and filed in the unpaid voucher file:
   A. by the department manager desiring the item to be purchased.
   B. after the purchase order is sent out.
   C. by the receiving department after goods are requested.
   D. when payment is made.
   E. after receipt of the goods has been verified by the receiving department and the prices and extensions on the invoice have been verified.
   F. at the time the check number and date paid are entered in the voucher register.

6. A voucher system:
   A. is an internal control system for cash receipts.
   B. is not needed in some concerns.
   C. is a desirable addition to the accounting system of any concern.
   D. eliminates the need for cash disbursement records.
   E. makes no distinction in the handling of cash and credit transactions.

7. When a company installs a voucher system, it no longer has need for a(an):
   A. purchases journal.
   B. cash disbursements journal.
   C. sales journal.
   D. accounts payable subsidiary ledger.
   E. (A), (B), and (D).

8. In reference to a check, the payee is:
   A. the one to whose order the check is drawn.
   B. the bank on which the check is drawn.
   C. the one who signs the check.
   D. None of the above.

9. If a customer's check is returned by the bank for lack of sufficient funds (NSF), the accountant should:
   A. debit Bad Checks and credit Cash.
   B. debit Accounts Receivable and credit Cash.
   C. file the check with Notes Receivable.
   D. debit Miscellaneous Expense and credit Cash.

10. A company prepared a voucher to reimburse the petty cash fund for disbursements made for store supplies. The required entry is:
   A. Vouchers Payable
          Cash
   B. Store Supplies Expense
          Vouchers Payable
   C. Store Supplies Expense
          Cash
   D. Store Supplies Expense
          Petty Cash

11. As of March 1 of the current year, the Capstone Company had outstanding checks of $30,000. During March the company issued an additional $114,000 in checks. As of March 31, the bank statement indicated that $102,000 of the checks had cleared the bank during the month. The amount of outstanding checks as of March 31 is:

    A. $18,000
    B. $12,000
    C. $42,000
    D. None of these.

12. In reference to a check, the drawer is:

    A. the one to whose order the check is drawn.
    B. the bank on which the check is drawn.
    C. the one who signs the check.
    D. None of the above.

Questions 13–15. assume the following:

Cash per bank statement $8,351.96
Outstanding checks 3,089.98
Cash balance per books 5,285.98
Bank service charge 24.00

13. The adjusted cash balance is:

    A. $5,237.98
    B. $11,441.94
    C. $5,285.98
    D. $5,261.98

14. In reconciling the bank statement, checks outstanding should be:

    A. deducted from balance per ledger.
    B. deducted from balance per bank statement.
    C. disregarded, as they have been entered in the cash disbursements journal.
    D. added to the balance per bank statement.

15. To record a bank service charge, which of the following accounts should be credited?

    A. Cash Short and Over
    B. Cash
    C. Petty cash
    D. None of these.

SOLUTIONS

Matching

1.	f	8.	q
2.	g	9.	m
3.	e	10.	b
4.	d	11.	o
5.	n	12.	j
6.	p	13.	h
7.	k		

Completion and Exercises

1. a. Protect cash against fraud and waste.
   b. Ensure compliance with company policies and federal law.
   c. Evaluate the performance of all personnel in the company so as to promote efficiency of operations.
   d. Ensure accurate and reliable operating data and accounting reports.

2. Any three of the following are objectives that management has in regard to cash.

   a. Account for all cash transactions accurately, so that correct information will be available regarding cash flows and balances.
   b. Make certain there is enough cash available to pay bills as they come due.
   c. Avoid holding too much idle cash because excess cash could be invested to generate income, such as interest.
   d. Prevent loss of cash due to theft or fraud.

3. Cash can easily be misappropriated because it can be concealed and is not readily identifiable. It can also be used to acquire anything else.

4. Cash is composed of those items commonly acceptable as a medium of exchange and also immediately convertible into money at face value. Cash includes the following: currency, coins, negotiable instruments, checking accounts, savings accounts, and demand certificates of deposit.

5. a. Items requiring no entry on the depositor's books would include:
      1. outstanding checks.
      2. deposits in transit.
      3. bank errors in depositor's account.

   b. Items requiring an entry on the depositor's books would include:
      1. service charges.
      2. deductions for not sufficient funds (NSF) checks.
      3. nonroutine deposits such as collection of a customer's note by the bank or a wire-transfer of funds.
      4. errors made by the depositor.

6. Any five of the following are basic control procedures for cash disbursements.

   1. All disbursements should be made by check or from petty cash.
   2. All checks should be serially numbered, and access to checks should be limited.
   3. Preferably, two signatures should be required on each check.
   4. If possible, the person who authorizes payment of a bill should not be allowed to sign checks.
   5. Approved invoices or vouchers should be required to support checks issued.
   6. The person authorizing disbursements should be certain that payment is legitimate and is made to the proper payee.
   7. When invoices and vouchers are paid, they should be stamped "paid," with the date and number of the check issued indicated.
   8. The person(s) who signed the checks should not have access to cancelled checks and should not prepare the bank reconciliation.
   9. A bank reconciliation should be prepared each month, preferably by a person who has no other cash duties.
   10. All voided and spoiled checks should be retained and defaced to prevent their unauthorized use.
   11. A voucher system may be needed in large firms to provide close cash control.
   12. Use of the net price method of recording purchases helps avoid loss of purchase discounts by focusing attention on purchase discounts lost.

7. The purpose of a bank reconciliation is to account for the difference between the cash balance on the books and the depositor's balance at the bank as shown on the bank statement. Such a statement concludes with the properly adjusted Cash account balance.

8.

SENTRA COMPANY
Bank Reconciliation
March 31, 1993

Balance per bank statement,		Balance per ledger,	
March 31, 1993	$34,314.32	March 31, 1993	$30,373.08
Add: Deposits in transit	2,021.44	Add: Note collected by bank	1,200.00
	$36,335.76		$31,573.08
Less: Outstanding checks	4,774.68	Less: Bank charges	12.00
Adjusted Balance, March 31, 1993	$31,561.08	Adjusted Balance, March 31, 1993	$31,561.08

9. expense; revenue
10. petty cash voucher
11. wire transfer of funds

12.

Stamps and Stationery	74.00	
Transportation-In	100.00	
Cash Short and Over	2.00	
Cash		176.00

To record check drawn to replenish petty cash fund.

13. voucher
14. voucher register; check register
15. unpaid voucher file
16. paid voucher file
17. internal control
18. liability
19. deducted from; bank account
20. deducted from

21.

Delivery Expense	50	
Transportation-In	20	
Office Supplies	100	
Miscellaneous Office Expense	40	
Cash Short and Over		6
Cash		204

22.

a.	Voucher Register: Purchases	9,800	
	Vouchers Payable		9,800
b.	Voucher Register: Postage Expense	100	
	Office Supplies	200	
	Vouchers Payable		300
c.	Check Register: Vouchers Payable	9,800	
	Cash		9,800
d.	Check Register: Vouchers Payable	300	
	Cash		300

23.

Postage Expense	60	
Transportation-In	40	
Delivery Expense	90	
Cash Short and Over	4	
Cash		194

24. a.

GAMES COMPANY
Bank Reconciliation, June 30, 19—

Balance per ledger .... $X,XXX	Bank statement balance .... $X,XXX
Add:	Add:
(5)	(2)
( )	( )
Deduct:	Deduct:
(6)	(4)
(7)	(8)
Adjusted balance .... $X,XXX	Adjusted balance .... $X,XXX

b. (5), (6), (7).

25. a.

RAMSEY COMPANY
Bank Reconciliation
August 31, 19—

Balance per bank statement		$19,775.34
Add: Deposit of August 31 not recorded by bank	$8,793.62	
Bank error in charging check for $400 instead of $40	360.00	9,153.62
		$28,928.96
Deduct: Outstanding checks		8,199.26
Adjusted cash balance		$20,729.70
Balance per ledger		$19,370.80
Add: Proceeds of note collected by bank	$1,358.00	
Error in recording check	18.00	1,376.00
		$20,746.80
Deduct: Bank service charges		17.10
Adjusted cash balance		$20,729.70

b.

Cash	1,376.00	
Notes Receivable		1,358.00
Vouchers Payable		18.00
Bank Service Charge	17.10	
Cash		17.10

26. a.

MAGIC COMPANY
Bank Reconciliation
June 30, 19—

Balance per ledger			Bank statement balance		
June 30, 19—		$40,000	June 30, 19— ....—...		$38,604
Add: Error correction		54	Add: Deposit in transit		3,000
		$40,054			$41,604
			Deduct: Outstanding checks:		
Deduct: Bank service charge	$200		No. 1013	$ 250	
NSF check	500	700	No. 1841	2,000	2,250
Adjusted balance		$39,354	Adjusted balance		$39,354

b.

Cash	54	
Accounts Payable		54
To record additions to Cash account.		
Bank Service Charge	200	
Accounts Receivable	500	
Cash		700
To record deductions from Cash account.		

27. a.

AUTO CO.
Bank Reconciliation
August 31, 1993

Balance per bank statement		$20,300.00
Add: Deposit of December 31 not recorded by bank	$10,000.00	
Bank error in charging check for $400 instead of $40	360.00	10,360.00
		$30,660.00
Deduct: Outstanding checks		5,000.00
Adjusted balance, August 31, 1993		$25,660.00
Balance per ledger		$24,242.00
Add: Proceeds of note collected by bank	$ 1,430.00	
Error in recording check	18.00	1,448.00
		$25,690.00
Deduct: Bank service charges		30.00
Adjusted balance, August 31, 1993		$25,660.00

b.

Cash	1,448.00	
Notes Receivable		1,430.00
Vouchers Payable		18.00
Bank Service Charge	30.00	
Cash		30.00

True-False Questions

1. T
2. F Proper management of cash is important, and management does not wish to have idle cash on which no return is being earned.
3. T
4. T Checks may have been written and deducted from the company's Cash ledger account but may not have cleared the bank (these are outstanding checks), and some deposits may have been recorded as debits to the Cash account but are in transit to the bank.
5. F Outstanding checks are ones that have been correctly recorded as credits to the Cash account but have not yet cleared the bank.

6. T
7. T
8. F   Cash is credited and the related expenses and assets debited when the petty cash fund is reimbursed.
9. T
10. F   Unpaid vouchers are usually filed by the date the voucher is due.
11. F   These responsibilities should be assigned to different persons.
12. F   Misappropriations of cash can more easily occur before a record is made of the receipt.
13. T
14. T
15. F
16. F   This procedure violates good internal control features of an accounting system.
17. F   Postdated checks are not included as cash.
18. F
19. T   Expenditures from the fund are debited to the related expense or asset account and credited to Cash when the fund is reimbursed.
20. F   These amounts have already been deducted from the Cash account.
21. F.   Outstanding checks are ascertained by comparing the checks written per the Cash ledger account with the checks that have cleared the bank account as shown on the bank statement.
22. F
23. F
24. F   These deposits have already been debited to Cash.
25. F

Multiple Choice Questions

1. C $1,297.72 - $136.00 - $73.40 + $832.64 = $1,920.96
2. C   Debits to the Cash account include $1,120 + $2,980. Credits are $3,260 (which includes the $400). This leaves a balance of $840.
3. C
4. C
5. E
6. B   When the owner of a small company is directly involved with paying bills, a voucher system is unnecessary.
7. E   The voucher register replaces the purchases journal, the check register replaces the cash disbursements journal, and the unpaid voucher file serves as an accounts payable subsidiary ledger.
8. A
9. B   The claim against the customer is established again.
10. B
11. C $30,000 + $114,000 - $102,000 = $42,000
12. C
13. D $5,285.98 - $24.00 = $5,261.98 or $8,351.96 - $3,089.98 = $5,261.98
14. B
15. B   The company has not recorded the bank service charge and must debit an expense and credit Cash.

9 RECEIVABLES AND PAYABLES

Learning Objectives

1. *Account for uncollectible accounts receivable under the allowance method.*
2. *Account for uncollectible accounts receivable under the direct write-off method.*
3. *Record credit card sales and collections.*
4. *Define liabilities, current liabilities, and long-term liabilities.*
5. *Define clearly determinable, estimated, and contingent liabilities.*
6. *Account for clearly determinable, estimated, and contingent liabilities.*
7. *Account for notes receivable and payable, including calculation of interest.*
8. *Record the discounting of notes receivable.*
9. *Account for borrowing money using an interest-bearing note versus a noninterest-bearing note.*

CHAPTER OUTLINE

ACCOUNTS RECEIVABLE

1. Accounts receivable (or trade receivables) are amounts due from customers for goods sold and services performed on account.

   a. The Accounts Receivable account should contain only amounts due from customers.

   b. Loans to officers, claims for tax refunds, and interest receivable are not included in accounts receivable.

THE ALLOWANCE METHOD FOR RECORDING UNCOLLECTIBLE ACCOUNTS

2. Losses from customers' accounts that prove uncollectible are an operating (selling) expense and are referred to as Uncollectible Accounts Expense.

   a. The matching principle requires that the expense be matched against the revenue it generates.

   b. Estimates of uncollectible accounts are made through an adjusting entry by debiting Uncollectible Accounts Expense and crediting Allowance for Uncollectible Accounts.

   c. Net realizable value is the amount expected to be collected from accounts receivable, and is equal to recorded Accounts Receivable less the Allowance for Uncollectible Accounts.

ESTIMATING UNCOLLECTIBLE ACCOUNTS

3. The percentage-of-sales method and the percentage-of-receivables method are two methods of estimating periodic uncollectible accounts.

   a. The percentage-of-sales method focuses attention on the income statement and the relationship of uncollectible accounts expense to current sales revenue.

   b. The percentage-of-receivables method focuses attention on the balance sheet and the relationship of the Allowance for Uncollectible Accounts to Accounts Receivable.

PERCENTAGE-OF-SALES METHOD

4. The percentage-of-sales method is based on a ratio of prior years' actual uncollectible account losses to prior years' credit sales (or to total sales).

   a. The percentage is reviewed annually to see if it is still valid.

   b. Any existing balance in the Allowance for Uncollectible Accounts is ignored in calculating the amount of the year-end adjustment.

PERCENTAGE-OF-RECEIVABLES METHOD

5. The percentage-of-receivables method estimates the percentage of period-end accounts receivable that might be uncollectible. The goal "or target" is to make the credit balance in the allowance account after adjustment equal to a certain percentage of accounts receivable.

   a. Any existing balance in the Allowance for Uncollectible Accounts before adjustment must be considered when adjusting for uncollectible accounts.

   b. One overall rate may be used or a different rate may be used for each age category of receivables.

c. An aging schedule may be used under the percentage-of-receivables method to classify accounts receivable according to their age. An aging schedule reflects that, the older a receivable is, the more likely it will not be collected. On an aging schedule, accounts receivable are placed in categories of number of days past due.

WRITE-OFF OF RECEIVABLES

6. To write off a customer's account, the Allowance for Uncollectible Accounts is debited and Accounts Receivable is credited. The credit is also posted to the specific customer's account in the subsidiary ledger.

UNCOLLECTIBLE ACCOUNTS RECOVERED

7. If a customer pays the account and the company had previously written off the account under the assumption that it was uncollectible, the accounts receivable must be reinstated by reversing the original write-off entry.

   a. The entry to reinstate the account is to debit Accounts Receivable and credit Allowance for Uncollectible Accounts.
   b. The receipt of cash requires a debit to Cash and a credit to Accounts Receivable.
   c. Each debit or credit to Accounts Receivable is also posted to the customer's account in the subsidiary ledger.

DIRECT WRITE-OFF METHOD

8. Using the direct write-off method, specific accounts which are considered uncollectible are debited directly to Uncollectible Accounts Expense and credited to Accounts Receivable.

   a. If it becomes necessary to reinstate a customer's account using this method, Accounts Receivable is debited and Uncollectible Accounts Expense is credited.
   b. Cash is then debited for the receipt and Accounts Receivable is credited.
   c. Each debit or credit to Accounts Receivable is also posted to the customer's account in the subsidiary ledger.

CREDIT CARDS

9. Credit cards that are used by customers to charge their purchases of goods and services enable companies to pass losses from uncollectible accounts on to banks or other credit card agencies.

   a. A fee ranging from 2% to 8% of sales price is charged for the credit card agency to absorb the bad debts.
   b. At the same time the card sale is made using a nonbank credit card, the seller debits Accounts Receivable—Credit Card Agency and Credit Card Expense and credits Sales. If a bank credit card is used, the debit is to Cash instead of Accounts Receivable.
   c. When payment for nonbank credit card receipts is received from the credit card agency, Cash is debited, and Accounts Receivable—Credit Card Agency is credited.

CURRENT VERSUS LONG-TERM LIABILITIES

10. Current liabilities are obligations that are:

    a. payable within one year or one operating cycle, whichever is longer.
    b. debts that will be paid out of current assets or result in the creation of other current liabilities.

11. Long-term liabilities are obligations that do not qualify as current liabilities.

12. An operating cycle is the time it takes to begin with cash and end with cash in producing revenues.

TYPES OF CURRENT LIABILITIES

13. The three groups of current liabilities are: clearly determinable liabilities, estimated liabilities, and contingent liabilities.

CLEARLY DETERMINABLE LIABILITIES

14. Clearly determinable liabilities, such as accounts payable, notes payable, and wages payable, are set up in journal entries.

ESTIMATED LIABILITIES

15. Estimated liabilities, such as estimated product warranty payable, have an existence that is certain but an amount of liability that can only be estimated.

CONTINGENT LIABILITIES

16. Contingent liabilities have both an existence and an amount of liability that are uncertain.

NOTES RECEIVABLE AND NOTES PAYABLE

17. A promissory note is a written promise by a maker to pay a certain sum of money to the lender or payee on demand or on a specific date.

INTEREST CALCULATION

18. Notes may be noninterest bearing or may bear interest at a rate specified on the face of the note.
    a. Interest may be computed using the formula $I = P \times R \times T$, where I is the interest, P is the principal or face amount of the note, R is the specified interest rate, and T is the period of the note, or
    b. Interest may be computed by means of the 6% method under which the interest at 6% for 60 days is 1% of the principal amount. Other rates or time intervals are multiples or fractions of this basic equation.

DETERMINATION OF MATURITY DATE

19. The maturity date is specified in the note as one of the following:
    a. On demand.
    b. On a stated date.
    c. At the end of a stated period.

20. The maturity value is the amount that the maker must pay on a note on its maturity date, and maturity value includes principal and accrued interest.

ACCOUNTING FOR NOTES IN NORMAL BUSINESS TRANSACTIONS

21. A note may be received when high-priced merchandise is sold or from the conversion of an overdue account receivable.

DISHONORED NOTES

22. A note is dishonored if the maker fails to pay it at maturity.
    a. The payee may establish an account receivable and credit Notes Receivable.
    b. The note loses its negotiability when the maturity date has passed.
    c. If a firm has many notes receivable transactions, it may set up an allowance for uncollectible notes against which can be charged dishonored notes that are deemed uncollectible.
    d. If only part of a note is paid at maturity, the dishonored portion is treated as above.

RENEWAL OF NOTES

23. Notes are frequently renewed rather than paid at their maturity date.

ACCRUING INTEREST

24. Even though interest is usually recorded only at the maturity date, interest accrues on an interest-bearing note on a day-to-day basis.
    a. The adjusting entry needed to accrue interest on a note receivable is a debit to Interest Receivable and a credit to Interest Revenue.
    b. Interest Receivable is a current asset showing the asset for interest revenue earned but not yet collected.
    c. The adjusting entry needed to accrue interest on a note payable is a debit to Interest Expense and a credit to Interest Payable.
    d. Interest Payable is a current liability showing the liability for interest expense incurred but not yet paid.

DISCOUNTING (SELLING) NOTES RECEIVABLE

25. A company may discount notes receivable that it holds, as a means of borrowing money.

    a. The maturity value must be calculated.

        1. For noninterest-bearing notes receivable or payable, the maturity value is the face amount.
        2. For interest-bearing notes receivable, the maturity value is the face amount of the note plus the interest for the life of the note.

    b. The discount period must be calculated; this is the number of days from the date of discounting to the date of maturity. A convenient way of calculating the discount period is: Life of the note minus the time the company held the note.

    c. The discount on the maturity value is then computed, using the rate of discount charged by the bank.

    d. The amount of the cash proceeds to the borrower is the maturity value minus the discount charged by the bank.

    e. For discounted notes receivable, Cash is debited for the proceeds and Notes Receivable is credited for the face amount of the note.

    f. On discounted notes receivable, the difference between the face value of the note and the cash proceeds is either charged to Interest Expense or credited to Interest Revenue.

26. Notes receivable that have been discounted should be mentioned in a note to the financial statements. The notes receivable amount in the body of the statement should not include the notes that have been discounted.

DISCOUNTED NOTES RECEIVABLE PAID BY MAKER

27. When discounted notes receivable are paid by the maker, the payee makes no entry. The contingent liability is removed.

DISCOUNTED NOTES RECEIVABLE NOT PAID BY MAKER

28. When a discounted note is dishonored, the contingent liability of the payee becomes a real liability and the payee must pay the maturity value to the bank.

    a. Accounts Receivable is debited and Cash is credited for the amount paid to the bank.

    b. The payee will then look to the maker for reimbursement of the amount paid to the bank.

SHORT-TERM FINANCING THROUGH NOTES PAYABLE

29. Funds may be borrowed by signing either an interest-bearing note or a noninterest-bearing note.

INTEREST-BEARING NOTES

30. An interest-bearing note carries a stated interest rate and will mature on a specific date.

NONINTEREST-BEARING NOTES

31. A noninterest-bearing note does not have a stated interest rate that is applied to face value to calculate interest.

    a. The note is drawn for the maturity value and a bank discount is deducted.

    b. The proceeds are the amount received by the maker and are equal to the difference between the maturity value and the discount.

    c. Cash and Discount on Notes Payable are debited and Notes Payable is credited.

    d. Discount on Notes Payable is a contra account used to reduce Notes Payable from face value to book value.

        1. Discount on Notes Payable is reported on the balance sheet as a deduction from the Notes Payable account.
        2. Over time, this discount becomes interest expense.

DEMONSTRATION PROBLEM

Analysis of Green Company's ledger reveals that the January 1 credit balance in Allowance for Uncollectible Accounts was $1,800. During the month $2,025 of accounts receivable were written off as uncollectible; credit sales during the month totaled $300,000.

Required:

a. Prepare the adjusting entry to record the estimated uncollectible accounts for the month *and* give the January 31 balance in the Allowance for Uncollectible Accounts, after adjustment, assuming:

   (1) Analysis of the accounts receivable subsidiary ledger indicates a desired balance in Allowance for Uncollectible Accounts of $1,500.

   (2) Instead of (1), uncollectible accounts are estimated at one percent of credit sales.

b. Follow the same requirements as above except assume that on January 1 the Allowance for Uncollectible Accounts account had a credit balance of $2,790 and that January credit sales were $375,000.

	DATE	ACCOUNT TITLES AND EXPLANATION	POST. REF.	DEBIT	CREDIT
a. (1)					
(2)					
b. (1)					
(2)					

a. (1) Percentage-of-receivables method:

Uncollectible Accounts Expense 1,725
    Allowance for Uncollectible Accounts 1,725

    $1,500   Desired credit balance
      225   Present debit balance ($2,025 − $1,800)
    $1,725   Required adjustment

    $1,500   Allowance for Uncollectible Accounts balance as of January 31.

   (2) Percentage-of-sales method:

Uncollectible Accounts Expense (1% × $300,000) 3,000
    Allowance for Uncollectible Accounts 3,000

    $2,775   Allowance for Uncollectible Accounts balance as of January 31
               ($3,000 credit − $225 debit balance)

b. (1) Uncollectible Accounts Expense 735
    Allowance for Uncollectible Accounts 735

    $1,500   Desired credit balance
      765   Present credit balance ($2,790 − $2,025)
    $ 735   Required adjustment

    $1,500   Allowance for Uncollectible Accounts balance as of January 31

   (2) Uncollectible Accounts Expense (1% × $375,000) 3,750
    Allowance for Uncollectible Accounts 3,750

    $4,515   Allowance for Uncollectible Accounts balance as of January 31 ($765 + $3,750)

MATCHING

Referring to the terms listed below, place the appropriate letter next to the corresponding description.

a. Accounts Receivable
b. Aging
c. Allowance for Uncollectible Accounts
d. Credit cards
e. Direct write-off method
f. Discounting notes receivable
g. Discount on Notes Payable

h. Maker
i. Maturity value
j. Mortgage
k. Payables
l. Payee
m. Percentage-of-accounts-receivable method
n. Percentage-of-sales method

o. Promissory note
p. Receivables
q. Uncollectible Accounts Expense
r. Uncollectible Accounts Recovered
s. Contingent liabilities
t. Estimated liabilities

_____ 1. A legal document that gives a lender possession of pledged property if the borrower does not pay the obligation as required.

_____ 2. The principal of a note plus interest accrued to maturity date.

_____ 3. Sometimes erroneously called Prepaid Interest.

_____ 4. An unconditional written promise made by one person to another, signed by the maker, agreeing to pay on demand or at a definite time a sum certain in money to order or to bearer.

_____ 5. A method of estimating the expected amount of uncollectible accounts from a given period's credit sales.

_____ 6. Virtually the same as the sale of a customer's note to a bank, usually with the agreement to pay the note at maturity if its maker does not.

_____ 7. Plastic cards issued by certain banks and other credit agencies that permit their holders to charge purchases of goods or services.

_____ 8. The account that is debited when a dishonored note is recorded.

_____ 9. A method of accounting for uncollectible accounts in which they are charged directly to expense.

_____ 10. The person or party to whose order payment is promised or ordered on a note.

_____ 11. A contra account to Accounts Receivable designed to reduce gross accounts receivable to its net realizable value.

_____ 12. An operating expense a business incurs when it sells on credit and that results from nonpayment of accounts receivable.

_____ 13. Sums of money due to be received for any reason resulting from past transactions.

_____ 14. A method of determining the desired size of the allowance for uncollectible accounts and, indirectly, the uncollectible accounts expense for the period.

_____ 15. The person or party preparing and signing a note.

_____ 16. Sums of money due to be paid to other parties for any reason resulting from a past transaction.

_____ 17. A process of classifying accounts receivable according to their age in appraising the accounts for purposes of adjusting the balance in the Allowance for Uncollectible Accounts.

_____ 18. Have an existence that is certain but an amount of liability that can only be estimated.

_____ 19. Have both an existence and an amount of liability that are uncertain.

COMPLETION AND EXERCISES

1. The Allowance for Uncollectible Accounts is a _____ account to _____ and shows _____ _____.

2. The following information was taken from a trial balance:

$$\text{Accounts Receivable} \dots\dots\dots\dots\dots\dots\dots \$25,500$$
$$\text{Allowance for Uncollectible Accounts} \dots\dots\dots \quad 0$$

If the company's experience shows that 3% of its outstanding receivables (at year-end) will prove uncollectible, uncollectible accounts expense is $ _____ .

3. Give the two methods of estimating the amount of uncollectible accounts under the allowance method.

   a. _____

   b. _____

4. Assume that 3% of the $75,000 of accounts receivable is estimated to be uncollectible. A credit balance of $1,200 already exists in Allowance for Uncollectible Accounts. The _____ _____ _____ account should be debited, and the _____ _____ _____ _____ account should be credited for $ _____ in the end-of-period adjusting entry.

5. If an account for $450 is deemed to be uncollectible, the _____ _____ _____ _____ account should be debited and the _____ _____ account should be credited for $ _____ .

6. If $300 of the amount written off in Question 5 is collected (with no prospect of collecting the remainder) what entry(ies) would be made?

DATE	ACCOUNT TITLES AND EXPLANATION	POST. REF.	DEBIT	CREDIT

7. Of the $135,000 total credit sales for the year, $54,000 were made using a national nonbank credit card. Assume that an estimated 1 1/2% of non-credit-card sales are considered uncollectible. The end-of-period adjusting entry would include a debit to _____ _____ _____ of $ _____ .

8. Delta Company submitted sales invoices of $7,000 to the credit granting agency. The company received a check for $6,574 and the invoice for one sale of $80 made using a credit card, which the company had been notified was stolen. The company's only credit sales are made using credit cards. Give the journal entry for the above receipt of the check and return of the $80 invoice.

DATE	ACCOUNT TITLES AND EXPLANATION	POST. REF.	DEBIT	CREDIT

9. Scott Company sold a customer jewelry that is subject to a 5.5% sales tax and a 10% federal excise tax. The customer agreed to pay for the jewelry within 30 days. Record the sale of the jewelry, which has an invoice price of $5,000.

10. When sales taxes are remitted to the appropriate government agency, a retail store debits _____ _____ _____ account and credits _____.

11. If a 90-day note is dated August 7, what is the due date?

12. In a commercial transaction, interest is commonly calculated on the basis of _____ days per year.

13. What is the interest on $300,000 for 60 days at 12%? _____

14. What is a dishonored note? _____

_____

_____

15. Assume that on December 1, 1993, Power Company discounted its own $75,000 noninterest-bearing 90-day note at the bank. The discount rate is 10%. Give the entries required on December 1, December 31 (the end of the accounting period), and on the maturity date.

DATE		ACCOUNT TITLES AND EXPLANATION	POST. REF.	DEBIT	CREDIT	

16. Watson received from PT Shop a 12%, 60-day, $1,500,000 note.
   a. What entry would Watson make if on the same day he discounts the note at the bank at 14%? (Show all calculations.)
   b. What entry would Watson make if he had held the note for 25 days before discounting it?
   c. What entries would Watson make if the PT Shop defaulted the note payment on the maturity day?
   d. What entry would Watson make if he then decided to write off the note? Use the direct write-off method.

DATE	ACCOUNT TITLES AND EXPLANATION	POST. REF.	DEBIT	CREDIT
a.				
b.				
c.				
d.				

17. On June 1, Bounty Company discounted a 60-day, noninterest-bearing note payable for $18,000 at Gotham Bank. The discount rate was 9%. Record in general journal form (a) the entry needed on June 1; (b) the entry needed on the due date.

DATE		ACCOUNT TITLES AND EXPLANATION	POST. REF.	DEBIT	CREDIT
a.					
b.					

18. A customer gave Horace Company a $300,000, 6-month, 6% note on September 1. Prepare the adjusting entry required on December 31.

DATE		ACCOUNT TITLES AND EXPLANATION	POST. REF.	DEBIT	CREDIT

19. Zeus Company sold a $150,000, 5-year, 9% bond to the public. If the semiannual interest is paid on April 1 and October 1, what is the adjusting entry required on December 31 to record the interest expense?

DATE		ACCOUNT TITLES AND EXPLANATION	POST. REF.	DEBIT	CREDIT

20. When a note has been discounted, the _____ usually presents the note to the maker for payment.

21. The term _____ is often used to include any sum of money due to be received as a result of a past transaction.

22. The term _____ is used to describe any amount of money due to be paid to any party resulting from a past transaction.

23. A customer gave a note in payment of an account. If the semiannual interest amounts to $1,800 and is paid on March 1 and September 1, what is the adjusting entry required on December 31 to record the interest revenue earned?

DATE		ACCOUNT TITLES AND EXPLANATION	POST. REF.	DEBIT	CREDIT

24. A company borrowed $37,500 on October 1 for 120 days with interest payable at the maturity of the loan at the rate of 12% per annum. Prepare the adjusting entry required on December 31.

DATE		ACCOUNT TITLES AND EXPLANATION	POST. REF.	DEBIT	CREDIT

25. On October 3 a company discounted its own 30-day, noninterest-bearing note payable for $12,000 at First National Bank. The discount rate was 12%. Record in general journal form (a) the entry needed on October 3; (b) the entry needed on the due date.

DATE	ACCOUNT TITLES AND EXPLANATION	POST. REF.	DEBIT	CREDIT	
a.					
b.					

26. Analysis of Oxford Company's ledger reveals that the July 1 credit balance in Allowance for Uncollectible Accounts was $750; credit sales during the month totaled $60,000.

Required:

a. Prepare the adjusting entry to record the estimated uncollectible accounts for the month and give the July 31 balance in the Allowance for Uncollectible Accounts. Based on last year's sales, uncollectible accounts are estimated at 1.5% of credit sales.

b. On August 1, Oxford Company decided that Dale's $1,500 account is uncollectible. What is the correct entry if Dale's account is written off?

c. On August 29, a $1,350 check is received from Dale. What are the correct entries in Oxford's book to record the payment? (No further payments from Dale are anticipated.)

DATE		ACCOUNT TITLES AND EXPLANATION	POST. REF.	DEBIT	CREDIT

27. West Co. received a $1,020,000, 12%, 120-day note dated March 20 on account from Marshall Co. On June 10, West Co. discounted the note at the bank at 10%. Determine the items below and insert answers in spaces provided.

    a. Due date of note _____

    b. Maturity value of note $ _____

    c. Discount period _____

    d. Discount amount $ _____

    e. Proceeds from discounting note $ _____

    f. Interest _____ $ _____
              (Insert "Revenue" or "Expense")

28. 1. Interest on $270,000 for 16 days at 8% is $ _____

    2. The due date of a 90-day note dated April 2 is _____

    3. The discount period for a 120-day note dated May 5 and discounted on July 15 is _____ days

    4. The amount of cash that would be received from discounting a 60-day, 5% $2,100,000 note at 6% 12 days before maturity is $ _____

TRUE-FALSE QUESTIONS

Indicate whether each of the following statements is true or false by inserting a capital "T" or "F" in the blank space provided.

_____ 1. Allowance for Uncollectible Accounts is shown in the Current Assets section of the balance sheet.

_____ 2. A control account is one account in the subsidiary ledger that agrees with the total of the detailed accounts in the general ledger.

_____ 3. If the control account is out of agreement with the subsidiary ledger accounts, the control account must be wrong.

_____ 4. If a control account agrees with the total of its subsidiary ledger accounts, no errors exist in the subsidiary ledger.

_____ 5. Every promissory note is an asset from the standpoint of the maker because the maker has a legal right to receive money.

_____ 6. Accounts receivable from officers should be shown separately in the balance sheet unless the receivables arose from sales and are collectible in accordance with the company's regular terms.

_____ 7. The entry providing for uncollectible accounts is an adjusting entry, but the entry writing off an uncollectible account may be made at any time that an account proves to be uncollectible.

_____ 8. The maker of a note is the party that has the legal obligation to pay money.

_____ 9. Under the allowance method, when an outstanding account receivable is written off, Allowance for Uncollectible Accounts is debited and Accounts Receivable is credited for the amount of the write-off.

_____ 10. Estimating uncollectible accounts is subject to errors, but the effects involved in not estimating are likely to be larger in most years and certainly larger in some years.

_____ 11. The Allowance for Uncollectible Accounts may at times have a debit balance.

_____ 12. When properly adjusted, the Allowance for Uncollectible Accounts will always have a credit balance.

_____ 13. Recoveries of accounts previously written off are, when an Allowance for Uncollectible Accounts is used, credited to Uncollectible Accounts Recovered.

_____ 14. One of the objectives sought through use of an allowance for uncollectible accounts is a proper matching of expense and revenue.

_____ 15. Under the direct write-off method, an uncollectible account is debited to the Allowance for Uncollectible Accounts.

_____ 16. When a company discounts a customer's note, Cash is debited and Notes Receivable is credited. Interest Expense or Interest Revenue is used to account for the difference.

_____ 17. The sale of goods to a customer who charged them using a credit card usually leads to the recording of a credit card expense on the seller's books.

_____ 18. Clearly determinable liabilities have an existence that is certain but an amount that is uncertain.

_____ 19. Estimated product warrant payable is a contingent liability.

_____ 20. If Ron Hall gives Sue Jones a note for some merchandise he purchased from her, Ron is called the payee of the note.

_____ 21. Because it normally has a debit balance, the Discount on Notes Payable account should be reported in the balance sheet among the assets.

_____ 22. If the proceeds received from discounting a customer's note are greater than the face value of the note this difference is credited to Interest Revenue.

_____ 23. The due date of a 90-day note dated May 8 which Loan Company received from Bank Company on account is August 4.

_____ 24. After the year-end closing entries have been posted, the Allowance for Uncollectible Accounts will have no balance.

_____ 25. An excessive provision for uncollectible accounts will understate assets, net income, and stockholders' equity.

_____ 26. The direct write-off method of accounting for uncollectible accounts violates the accounting principle of consistency.

_____ 27. By observing the account Allowance for Uncollectible Accounts on the balance sheet, one would know that the firm uses the direct write-off method.

MULTIPLE CHOICE QUESTIONS

For each of the following questions indicate the best answer by circling the appropriate letter.

1. In the balance sheet, the Allowance for Uncollectible Accounts account should be presented as a(an):
    A. part of stockholders' equity.
    B. liability.
    C. deduction from an asset.
    D. asset.
    E. None of these.

2. Which of the entries given below, made at the end of the accounting period, properly records the expense arising from estimated uncollectible accounts?
    A. Allowance for Uncollectible Accounts
            Uncollectible Accounts Expense
    B. Allowance for Uncollectible Accounts
            Accounts Receivable
    C. Uncollectible Accounts Expense
            Allowance for Uncollectible Accounts
    D. Accounts Receivable
            Allowance for Uncollectible Accounts
    E. None of these.

3. Unpaid interest on a note given the bank would be classified by the maker of the note as:
    A. prepaid expense.
    B. unearned revenue.
    C. an accrued asset.
    D. an accrued liability.

4. Interest deducted by a bank on a company's discounted noninterest bearing note payable would be classified by the company as:

   A. prepaid expense.
   B. a contra liability.
   C. an accrued asset.
   D. an accrued liability.

5. A credit to Notes Receivable is proper when:

   A. we discount a note received from one of our customers.
   B. irrespective of whether it was paid or dishonored by the maker, a note previously discounted has matured and settlement has been made with the purchaser of the note.
   C. a correction is made in the accounts because it was our own note instead of a customer's note that was discounted.
   D. we have turned a dishonored note over to an attorney for collection.

6. When the direct write-off method is used to write off an uncollectible account the:

   A. Accounts Receivable account should be debited.
   B. Uncollectible Accounts Expense account should be credited.
   C. Uncollectible Accounts Expense account should be debited.
   D. combination of (A) and (B).
   E. None of these.

7. What are contingent liabilities?

   A. Liabilities that are due and payable within a year.
   B. Liabilities that are classified as long term on the balance sheet.
   C. Liabilities that are to be liquidated in periodic installments.
   D. Possible obligations that occur only if certain events occur in the future.
   E. All of the above.

8–12. Kilo Company received a $740,000, 6%, 90-day note dated March 8 on account from Swan Company. On May 22, Kilo Company discounted the note at the bank at 5%.

8. The due date of the note is:

   A. June 7.
   B. June 6.
   C. June 5.
   D. June 1.

9. The maturity value of the above note is:

   A. $751,100
   B. $740,000
   C. $759,500
   D. $784,400

10. The discount period of the note described above is:

   A. 15 days.
   B. 16 days.
   C. 20 days.
   D. None of these.

11. The discount amount of the note described above is:

    A. $1,460
    B. $1,565
    C. $1,669
    D. None of these.

12. The proceeds from discounting the note above are:

    A. $769,350
    B. $749,535
    C. $627,989
    D. None of the above.

13. The process of analyzing the trade receivable accounts according to their age is sometimes called:

    A. aging the receivables.
    B. reduction of receivables.
    C. the determination of which receivables to write off.
    D. extending the credit terms on your receivables.
    E. All of the above.

14. At year-end the accounts of the Stable Company show Accounts Receivable, $270,000; Allowance for Uncollectible Accounts (Cr.), $900; Sales, $1,590,000; and Sales Discounts, $20,250. At this time, the company decides to write off the account of the Shakey Corporation, $2,250. The Allowance for Uncollectible Accounts account is then to be adjusted to 4% of the outstanding receivables. The amount of uncollectible accounts expense recognized for the year is:

    A. $12,060
    B. $10,710
    C. $6,060
    D. $9,360
    E. $10,800

15. Which of the following methods of determining uncollectible accounts expense most closely matches expenses and revenues?

    A. Using a percentage of accounts receivable to estimate the allowance for uncollectible accounts.
    B. Estimating the allowance for uncollectible accounts by aging the accounts receivable.
    C. Debiting Uncollectible Accounts Expense with a percentage of credit sales for that period.
    D. Debiting Uncollectible Accounts Expense only as accounts are written off as uncollectible.

SOLUTIONS

Matching

1.	j	11.	c
2.	i	12.	q
3.	g	13.	p
4.	o	14.	m
5.	n	15.	h
6.	f	16.	k
7.	d	17.	b
8.	a	18.	t
9.	e	19.	s
10.	1		

1. contra; Accounts Receivable; the amount of outstanding accounts receivable that the company does not expect to collect in cash
2. $765
3. (a) percentage-of-sales; (b) percentage-of-accounts-receivable.
4. Uncollectible Accounts Expense; Allowance for Uncollectible Accounts; $1,050 [which is (0.03 × $75,000) − $1,200]
5. Allowance for Uncollectible Accounts; Accounts Receivable; $450
6. Accounts Receivable 300
       Allowance for Uncollectible Accounts 300
       To reverse part of original entry to write off an account receivable.

   Cash 300
       Accounts Receivable 300
       To record collection of $300 on account.
7. Uncollectible Accounts Expense; $1,215, [($135,000 − $54,000) × 0.015]
8. Delta Company

   Cash 6,574
   Credit Card Expense 346
   Loss on Acceptance of Stolen Credit Card 80
       Accounts Receivable (Credit Card Company) 7,000
       To record collection of credit card invoices, less discount, and return of one invoice for which stolen credit card was used.
9. Accounts Receivable 5,775
       Sales 5,000
       Sales Tax Payable 275
       Federal Excise Tax Payable 500
10. Sales Tax Payable, Cash
11. Total note days 90
        August—days 31
        Date of note 7
                                                       24
        September—days 30
        October—days 31   85
        Date due, November 5
12. 360
13. $6,000. $\left[\$300,000 \times .12 \times \dfrac{60}{360} \right]$
14. A note is dishonored if the maker fails to pay at maturity.

15. Power Company

Dec. 1   Cash 73,125.00
             Discount on Notes Payable ($75,000 × .10 × 90/360) 1,875.00
             Notes Payable 75,000.00
             To record discounting of own note at the bank.

Dec. 31   Interest Expense 625.00
             Discount on Notes Payable 625.00
             To record interest incurred on note.

$$\left(\$75,000 \times .10 \times \frac{30}{360} \right)$$

Mar. 1   Interest Expense 1,250.00
             Discount on Notes Payable 1,250.00
             To record interest on note to maturity date.

            Notes Payable 75,000.00
             Cash 75,000.00
             To record payment of note payable.

16. Watson

a. Face value of note $1,500,000
     Add: Interest at 12% for 60 days 30,000
    Maturity value $1,530,000
    Bank discount for 60 days at 14% 35,700
    Cash proceeds $1,494,300

    Cash 1,494,300
    Interest Expense 5,700
        Notes Receivable 1,500,000

b. Maturity value of note $1,530,000
     Less: Bank discount for 35 days at 14% 20,825
    Cash proceeds $1,509,175

    Cash 1,509,175
        Notes Receivable 1,500,000
        Interest Revenue 9,175
        To record discounting of note at the bank at 14%.

c. Accounts Receivable 1,530,000
        Cash 1,530,000
        To record payment to the bank of note that was discounted at the bank
        and dishonored when due.

d. Uncollectible Accounts Expense 1,530,000
        Accounts Receivable 1,530,000
        To record write off of PT Shop account receivable.

17. a. June 1
    Cash 17,730
    Discount on Notes Payable 270
        Notes Payable 18,000

b. July 31
    Notes Payable 18,000
    Interest Expense 270
        Cash 18,000
        Discount on Notes Payable 270

18. Horace Company
    Interest Receivable 6,000
        Interest Revenue 6,000
    To record interest earned from September 1 to December 31.

$$\left(\$300{,}000 \times .06 \times \frac{4}{12} \right)$$

19. Interest Expense 3,375
        Interest Payable 3,375
    To record accrued interest from October 1 to December 31.

$$\left(\$150{,}000 \times .09 \times \frac{3}{12} = \$3{,}375 \right)$$

20. holder
21. receivables
22. payables
23. Interest Receivable 1,200
        Interest Revenue 1,200
    To record interest earned from September 1 to December 31.

$$\left(\$1{,}800 \times \frac{4}{6} = \$1{,}200 \right)$$

24. Interest Expense 1,125
        Interest Payable 1,125
    To record accrued interest for 91 days (October, 30 days; November,
    30 days; December, 31 days).

$$\$37{,}500 \times .12 \times \frac{91}{360} = \$1{,}137.50$$

25. a. Oct. 3   Cash 11,880
                 Discount on Notes Payable 120
                     Notes Payable 12,000
    b. Nov. 2   Notes Payable 12,000
                     Cash 12,000

26. a. Uncollectible Accounts Expense 900
            Allowance for Uncollectible Accounts 900
        To record estimated uncollectible accounts.

        Balance at July 31 of Allowance for Uncollectible Accounts: $1,650

    b. August 1
        Allowance for Uncollectible Accounts 1,500
            Accounts Receivable—Dale 1,500
        To write Dale's account off as uncollectible.

c. August 29

Accounts Receivable—Dale	1,350	
Allowance for Uncollectible Accounts		1,350
To reverse original write-off of Dale's account.		
Cash	1,350	
Accounts Receivable—Dale		1,350
To record collection of account.		

27. a. Due date of note (March, 11 days; April, 30 days; May, 31 days; June, 30 days; July, 18 days)   July 18

    b. Maturity value of note $1,060,800

    c. Discount period (120 days − 82 days)   38 days

    d. Discount amount ($1,060,800 × .10 × 38/360) $11,197

    e. Proceeds from discounting note $1,049,603

    f. Interest   Revenue (recorded on 6/10) $29,603

28. 1. Interest on $270,000 for 16 days at 8% is $960

    2. The due date of a 90-day note dated April 2 is   July 1

    3. The discount period for a 120-day note dated May 5 and discounted on July 15 is (120 days − 71 days)   49 days

    4. The amount of cash that would be received from discounting a 60-day, 5% $2,100,000 note at 6% 12 days before maturity is $2,117,500 − ($2,117,500 × .06 × 12/360) $2,113,265

True-False Questions

1. T   This account is a contra asset to Accounts Receivable.
2. F   A control account is an account in the general ledger that summarizes the accounts in the subsidiary ledger.
3. F
4. F
5. F   A promissory note is a liability to the maker because he or she has the legal obligation to pay money.
6. T   Accounts receivable from officers other than from normal sales are shown as other receivables.
7. T
8. T
9. T
10. T
11. T   A debit balance could occur when there have been more write-offs of specific accounts receivable than the estimate for uncollectibles credited to the Allowance for Uncollectible Accounts.
12. T
13. F   The credit is to Allowance for Uncollectible Accounts, and Accounts Receivable is debited.
14. T
15. F   The debit is to Uncollectible Accounts expense when the direct write-off method is used.
16. T
17. T
18. F   Both their existence and amount are uncertain.
19. F   Estimated product warranty payable is an estimated liability.
20. F   Ron is called the maker of the note, and Sue Jones is the payee as she will receive cash.
21. F.   This account is reported on the balance sheet as a deduction from the Notes Payable account.

22.	T	
23.	F	The due day is August 6. (May, 23 days; June, 30 days; July, 31 days; August, 6 days)
24.	F	This account will have a credit balance as it is a contra asset and is not closed at the end of the period.
25.	T	
26.	F	The principle of matching revenues and expenses is violated.
27.	F	Under the direct write-off method, no Allowance for Uncollectible Accounts exists.

Multiple Choice Questions

1.	C	Allowance for Uncollectible Accounts is a deduction from Accounts Receivable.
2.	C	
3.	D	
4.	B	Discount on Notes Payable becomes Interest Expense as time passes.
5.	A	
6.	C	
7.	D	
8.	B	(March, 23 days; April, 30 days; May, 31 days; June, 6 days)
9.	A	$740,000 + ($740,000 \times .06 \times 90/360) = $751,100.
10.	A	(90 days − 75 days)
11.	B	($751,100 \times .05 \times 15/360) = $1,565.
12.	B	$751,100 − $1,565 = $749,535.
13.	A	
14.	A	$270,000 Accounts Receivable − $2,250 write-off = $267,750. $267,750 × 4% = $10,710. $900 (cr. balance) Allowance for Uncollectible Accounts balance − $2,250 write-off = $1,350 debit balance. $10,710 + $1,350 debit balance = $12,060 needed credit to Allowance for Uncollectible Accounts.
15.	C	

10 PROPERTY, PLANT, AND EQUIPMENT

Learning Objectives

1. *List the characteristics of plant assets and identify the costs of acquiring plant assets.*
2. *List the four major factors affecting depreciation expense.*
3. *Describe the various methods of calculating depreciation expense.*
4. *Distinguish between capital and revenue expenditures for plant assets.*
5. *Describe the subsidiary records used to control plant assets.*

CHAPTER OUTLINE

NATURE OF PLANT ASSETS

1. Property, plant, and equipment consist of land and depreciable property such as buildings, machinery, delivery equipment, and office equipment.

   a. The category, property, plant, and equipment, is often referred to as plant assets.

   b. Proper recording of plant assets is important because of the effect on net income.

2. To be classified as a plant asset, an item must possess the following three attributes:

   a. It must be tangible (must be capable of being seen and touched).

   b. It must have a useful service life of more than one year.

   c. It must be used in business operations rather than held for resale to a customer.

3. Plant asset costs are an extreme form of prepaid expenses because the cost of these services must be allocated to the periods benefited.

INITIAL RECORDING OF PLANT ASSETS

4. Plant assets usually are recorded initially at cost, which includes all normal, reasonable, and necessary expenditures made to place the asset in its intended operating condition and location for use.

   a. The initial plant asset cost includes repair and reconditioning costs for assets that were acquired in used or damaged condition.

   b. Unnecessary costs, such as traffic fines that result from hauling machinery to a new plant, are not part of the asset cost.

LAND AND LAND IMPROVEMENTS

5. The cost of land includes the purchase price and costs such as attorney fees, cost of a title search, and assessments for streets and sewers.

   a. Because land purchased as a building site is considered to have an unlimited life, it is not depreciable.

   b. Land improvements, such as landscaping, driveways, parking lots, fences, and lighting and sprinkler systems, have limited lives and are depreciable.

BUILDINGS

6. The cost of a purchased building includes the price of items such as remodeling costs, real estate broker commissions, and legal costs.

7. Land and buildings might be purchased together.

   a. If land and buildings are purchased for a lump-sum amount, the total cost should be apportioned among the individual assets based on their appraised values.

   b. Separation of land and buildings is needed to record proper depreciation on the buildings.

MACHINERY AND OTHER EQUIPMENT

8. The cost of machinery includes the net price and items such as transportation charges, insurance in transit, and cost of installation.

   a. Discounts not taken are best viewed as losses and are not capitalized as part of an asset's cost.

   b. The cost of various types of equipment includes all costs necessary to place the equipment in a condition and location for its intended use.

   c. Machinery cost does not include costs of removing and disposing of a replaced old machine that has been used in operations.

SELF-CONSTRUCTED ASSETS

9. When a company builds a plant asset for its own use, the cost would include the cost of material and labor directly traceable to construction.

    a. Cost would also include extra heat, light, power, and other indirect services related to construction.

NONCASH ACQUISITIONS

10. Assets acquired in noncash exchanges are generally recorded at the fair market value of the securities or assets given up or the fair market value of the asset acquired, whichever is more clearly evident; but there are several asset valuation bases available.

FAIR MARKET VALUE

    a. The plant asset may be recorded at its fair market value or the fair market value of what was given up, whichever is more clearly evident.

APPRAISED VALUE

    b. If neither the plant asset acquired nor the noncash asset given up has a fair market value, the exchange may be recorded at appraised value.

        1. Appraised value is an expert's opinion as to what an item's market price would be if the item were sold.
        2. Appraisals are often used to value works of art, rare books, and antiques.

BOOK VALUE

    c. Book value of an asset is its recorded cost less accumulated depreciation.

        1. Book value is an acceptable basis only if there is no better basis available.
        2. Book value of an old asset is usually not a valid indicator of the new asset's economic value.

GIFTS OF PLANT ASSETS

11. Gifts of plant assets are generally recorded at their fair market value at the time of the donation or at an appraised value if a market value cannot be ascertained.
12. A city may give land to a company to build a factory that will provide jobs for local residents.
13. Gifts of plant assets are debited to an asset account at fair market value and credited to a Paid-In Capital— Donations account.

DEPRECIATION OF PLANT ASSETS

14. Depreciation is the amount of plant asset cost allocated to each period benefiting from the asset's use.

    a. Depreciation is recorded on all plant assets except land, because these assets will eventually wear out or become so inadequate or outmoded that they will be sold or discarded.
    b. Depreciation is the allocation in a reasonable and systematic manner of the cost (or other basic value) of a plant asset to the periods comprising its useful life.
    c. The major causes of depreciation are:

        1. Physical deterioration resulting from the use of the asset.
        2. Inadequacy of the asset resulting from its inability to produce enough products or provide enough services to meet current demand.
        3. Obsolescence, which is its decline in usefulness brought on by invention and technological progress.

FACTORS AFFECTING DEPRECIATION

15. The following factors must be considered in determining depreciation:

    a. Cost of asset.
    b. Estimated salvage value of asset.
    c. Estimated useful life of asset.
    d. Depreciation method to use in depreciating the asset.

COST OF ASSET

16. Cost is the amount of cash and/or cash equivalent given up to acquire the asset and place it in its intended operating condition at its proper location.

ESTIMATED SALVAGE VALUE

17. Salvage value is the amount of money expected to be recoverable, less disposal costs on the date a plant asset is scrapped, sold, or traded-in.

    a. Depreciable cost is acquisition cost less estimated salvage value.
    b. The accuracy of estimating salvage value varies among plant assets.

ESTIMATED USEFUL LIFE

18. Useful life is the period of time over which an asset is expected to provide services to the company.

    a. Useful or economic life of an asset may differ from its physical life.
    b. Estimates of useful life are influenced by three factors: physical deterioration, inadequacy, and obsolescence.
       1. Physical deterioration results from use, wear and tear, and the actions of the elements.
       2. Inadequacy is the inability of a plant asset to produce enough products or provide enough services to meet current demands.
       3. Obsolescence is the decline in usefulness of an asset brought about by invention and technological progress.

DEPRECIATION METHODS

19. Four common methods of depreciation exist, leaving a company normally free to adopt the method it believes most appropriate for its operations.

STRAIGHT-LINE METHOD

20. Straight-line depreciation is one of the methods commonly used and allocates the same dollar amount of depreciation to each period: Depreciation per period = (Cost − Estimated salvage value) ÷ Number of accounting periods in the estimated useful life.

UNITS-OF-PRODUCTION (OUTPUT) METHOD

21. The units-of-production method is often used if usage is the dominant factor causing expiration of an asset: Depreciation per unit = (Cost − Estimated salvage value) ÷ Estimated total output over asset's life; Depreciation per period = Depreciation per unit × Output for period in units.

ACCELERATED DEPRECIATION METHODS

22. Accelerated depreciation methods record higher amounts of depreciation in the early years of an asset's life and lower amounts in the asset's later years.

    a. A company may choose one of these methods because the value of the benefits received from an asset declines with age.
    b. Accelerated depreciation methods may also be used if the asset is of the high-technology type that is subject to rapid obsolescence.
    c. Accelerated depreciation methods may also be used if repairs increase substantially in later years and the amount of depreciation and repairs together remain fairly constant over the asset's life.

SUM-OF-THE-YEARS'-DIGITS METHOD

23. The sum-of-the-years'-digits method results in larger charges in the early years: Depreciation per period = (Cost − Estimated salvage value) × Ratio. The numerator of the ratio is the number of years of life remaining from the beginning of the year in question and the denominator is the sum of the numbers from one through the estimated total life of the asset.

DOUBLE-DECLINING-BALANCE METHOD

24. The double-declining-balance method results in larger amounts of depreciation being recorded in the early years of the asset's life: Depreciation per period = Net book value of asset at beginning of period × Double the straight-line rate of depreciation.

    a. Salvage value is ignored in making annual calculations.
    b. At the point where book value is equal to the salvage value, no more depreciation is taken.

PARTIAL-YEAR DEPRECIATION

25. When plant assets are acquired sometime during an accounting period, depreciation is usually computed to the nearest full month.

CHANGES IN ESTIMATES

26. If original estimates of asset lives are proven incorrect, the revised annual depreciation will be based on the depreciable net book value remaining when the error is discovered.

DEPRECIATION FOR TAX PURPOSES

27. Tax depreciation is different from depreciation used for accounting purposes in that the depreciable period used for tax purposes is based on tax laws.

DEPRECIATION AND FINANCIAL REPORTING

28. *APB Opinion No. 12* requires that the amount of depreciation expense for the period be separately disclosed in the body of the income statement or in the footnotes.

A MISCONCEPTION

29. The amount of accumulated depreciation does not represent funds available for replacing old plant assets with new assets.

COSTS OR MARKET VALUES IN THE BALANCE SHEET

30. Under the going-concern concept, the assumption is made that the firm will remain in business and will use its plant assets in operations rather than sell them.

    a. This concept is the reason that market values are not considered relevant.
    b. The going-concern concept is the justification for reporting remaining undepreciated costs rather than market values.

CAPITAL AND REVENUE EXPENDITURES

31. Expenditures that are directly related to plant assets are often made during the period of ownership at times after the date of acquisition.

EXPENDITURES CAPITALIZED IN ASSET ACCOUNTS

32. Betterments or improvements to existing plant assets are capital expenditures because they increase the quality of services obtained from the asset.

    a. Betterments add to the total service-rendering ability of the assets and are properly capitalizable as additions to asset accounts.

EXPENDITURES CAPITALIZED AS CHARGES TO ACCUMULATED DEPRECIATION

33. Expenditures that merely extend the life of the asset beyond the original estimate are capitalized as charges to the accumulated depreciation accounts. The remaining depreciable net book value is depreciated over the extended life remaining.

34. Sometimes expenditures for major repairs that do not extend the asset's life are charged to the accumulated depreciation account to avoid distorting the net income of the year in which the major repair occurs.

EXPENDITURES CHARGED TO EXPENSE

35. Expenditures for ordinary repairs and part replacements are treated as periodic expenses.
36. The distinction between capital and revenue expenditures is primarily the length of the period of time benefited.

SUBSIDIARY RECORDS USED TO CONTROL PLANT ASSETS

37. General ledger accounts are maintained for each major class of plant assets, and some of these accounts may be supported by a subsidiary ledger.

DEMONSTRATION PROBLEM

On January 2, 1992, Craft Company purchased a machine for $75,000 with an estimated life of five years and an expected salvage value of $7,500. The machine was expected to produce 135,000 units. Production was 30,000 units in 1992, 22,500 units in 1993, and 36,000 units in 1994.

Complete the table using the four given methods to compute depreciation.

Method	Annual Depreciation Expense			Accumulated Depreciation at the End of 1994	Book Value at the End of 1994
	1992	1993	1994		
Straight-Line					
Units-of-Production					
Sum-of-the-Years'-Digits ...					
Double-Declining-Balance ...					

SOLUTION TO DEMONSTRATION PROBLEM

Method	Annual Depreciation Expense			Accumulated Depreciation at the End of 1994	Book Value at the End of 1994
	1992	1993	1994		
Straight-Line	$13,500	$13,500	$13,500	$40,500	$34,500
Units-of-Production	15,000	11,250	18,000	44,250	30,750
Sum-of-the-Years'-Digits ...	22,500	18,000	13,500	54,000	21,000
Double-Declining-Balance ...	30,000	18,000	10,800	58,800	16,200

MATCHING

Referring to the terms listed below, place the appropriate letter next to the corresponding description. An answer may be used more than once.

a. Accelerated depreciation
b. Betterment (improvement)
c. Book value
d. Capital expenditure
e. Depreciable amount
f. Depreciation

g. Depreciation accounting
h. Extraordinary repairs
i. Inadequacy
j. Land improvements
k. Property, plant, and equipment
l. Plant assets

m. Physical deterioration
n. Revenue expenditure
o. Salvage value
p. Obsolescence
q. Modified Accelerated Cost Recovery Act

_____ 1. Cost less salvage value.
_____ 2. The process of allocating a portion of the cost of a depreciable plant asset to the periods in which it provides benefits.
_____ 3. Cost less accumulated depreciation.
_____ 4. An alteration, addition to, or structural change in a depreciable asset that makes the asset more durable, productive, or efficient.
_____ 5. Improvements to real estate that have a limited life.
_____ 6. Tangible long-lived assets used in a business.
_____ 7. The amount expected to be recovered for a plant asset at the end of its useful life.
_____ 8. An estimate of the amount (cost) of service potential of a plant asset that expired during a period.
_____ 9. An accounting procedure under which the amounts of depreciation recorded in the early years of an asset's life are greater than those recorded in later years.
_____ 10. Inability of a plant asset to produce enough product to meet current demands.
_____ 11. Another term for plant and equipment.
_____ 12. An expenditure made on plant assets that is properly added to a plant asset account.
_____ 13. The decline in usefulness of a plant asset brought about by invention and technological progress.
_____ 14. A normal recurring expenditure made on a plant asset to keep it operating and that is believed to benefit only the current period.
_____ 15. The cost of overhauling or reconditioning a plant asset that increases its expected life.
_____ 16. The decline in usefulness of a plant asset resulting from wear and tear and the action of the elements.
_____ 17. The tax law governing depreciation for tax purposes.

COMPLETION AND EXERCISES

1. From the following information, what is the yearly depreciation charge under the straight-line method?

    Cost of asset $65,000
    Estimated salvage value 5,000
    Estimated useful life .... 12 years

2. From the following information, compute the depreciation for the current year under the units-of-production method.

Cost of asset	$72,000
Estimated salvage value	0
Estimated production for entire life	360,000 units
Current year's production	62,000 units

3. What is the *general* rule for determining the valuation to be placed on an exchange of noncash assets?

_____

_____

_____

_____

4. The major causes of deprecation are _____ _____, _____,

and _____.

5. Is the following statement true or false? _____ Why? Accountants depreciate assets so that the assets will be reported on the balance sheet at their current market values.

_____

_____

_____

_____

_____

6. The _____-_____ method of depreciation allocates the same dollar amount of depreciation to each period in the estimated useful life of the asset.

7. The Gilbert Company purchased a machine for $35,000 plus a 5% sales tax. Gilbert paid for the machine in time to take advantage of a 2% discount. Transportation charges were $200, and installation and testing costs totaled $2,300. While being unloaded, the machine was dropped and damaged. It cost $250 to repair the damage. What is the cost of the machine? (Work space is provided below.)

8. The sum-of-the-years'-digits method of depreciation is suitable for those assets that have the greatest use

_____ (early or late) in their lives. If used indiscriminately, this method would tend to

_____ (overstate or understate) the asset values on the balance sheet.

9. If you assume that straight-line depreciation is correct, the sum-of-the-years'-digits method of depreciation is incorrect and will cause the net income during the early years of life to be

_____ (understated or overstated), and during the later years of life to be

_____ (understated or overstated).

10. To what are accountants referring when they use the term "plant assets"?

_____

_____

_____

_____

11. Plant assets can be broadly classified as _____ and _____

_____.

12. What is included in the cost of plant assets?

_____

_____

_____

_____

_____

13. The Howard Company acquired land and a building at a lump-sum price of $450,000. The building is to be renovated and used by the company. According to competent appraisers, the land and the building have

values of $200,000 and $300,000, respectively, on the acquisition date. A cost of _____ should

be assigned to the land, and a cost of _____ should be assigned to the building.

14. Compute depreciation for each of the first two years of the asset's life under the double-declining-balance method.

    Cost of asset $75,000
    Estimated salvage value   5,000
    Estimated useful life ....   10 years

15. Compute depreciation for the first year of the asset's life under the sum-of-the-years'-digits method.

Cost of asset	$25,500
Estimated salvage value	3,000
Estimated useful life	8 years

16. A machine was acquired on September 1, 1992, at a cost of $60,000. It has an estimated salvage value of $4,500, and an estimated useful life of five years. The double-declining-balance method of depreciation is to be used. Compute depreciation for 1992 and 1993 assuming the accounting period ends on December 31.

17. A machine that cost $29,000 has an estimated salvage value of $3,000 and an estimated useful life of five years. The machine is being depreciated on a straight-line basis. At the beginning of the fourth year, it is estimated that the machine will last five more years with the same estimated salvage value. The revised annual depreciation charge is $_____.

18. Expenditures for additions to existing assets, such as betterments or improvements, should be charged to

_____.

230   Chapter 10

19. If $750 is spent overhauling the engine in a machine, and, as a result, the machine will be used an additional two years beyond its original estimated life, what entry is necessary?

DATE		ACCOUNT TITLES AND EXPLANATION	POST. REF.	DEBIT	CREDIT

20. What effect will the engine overhaul in Question 19 have on periodic depreciation of the machine if the overhaul is accounted for as a debit to the accumulated depreciation account, but the original estimated useful life stays the same?

_____

_____

_____

_____

21. Assume the machine in Question 19 at acquisition had an estimated useful life of eight years, a cost of $4,640, and an estimated salvage value of $160. If the overhaul increased the machine's estimated useful life by one year and was made at the beginning of the eighth year, what will be the charge to depreciation expense for each of the last two years of the machine's useful life on a straight-line basis?

22. The main distinction between capital and revenue expenditure is _____

_____

_____.

23. Chip Co., on April 1, 1992, debited to expense the $4,500 cost of installing a new machine. The machine had a cost (exclusive of installation costs) of $10,000 and an estimated useful life of 6 years. The company uses the straight-line method of depreciation. No salvage value is expected from the machine. State whether net income (ignoring income taxes) is overstated or understated for 1992. Compute the amount of the error.

24. Honor Co. bought a lot for $67,000 cash on which it intended to construct a new building. The company paid legal fees of $950 to cover costs of transfer of title and $5,750 to remove an old building. Prepare the journal entry to record the total cost of the land.

DATE		ACCOUNT TITLES AND EXPLANATION	POST. REF.	DEBIT	CREDIT

25. Equipment was acquired on January 1, 1989, at a cost of $52,600. It has an estimated life of five years, an estimated salvage value of $600, and an estimated total of 40,000 service hours. Compute the depreciation for 1993 using each of the four methods.

a. Straight-line method .... _____

b. Sum-of-the-years'-digits .... _____

c. Double-declining-balance .... _____

d. Service-hours method (assume it was used 6,000 hours) .... _____
   (known as units-of-production method)

TRUE-FALSE QUESTIONS

Indicate whether each of the following statements is true or false by inserting a capital "T" or "F" in the blank space provided.

_____ 1. One of the reasons for recording depreciation is to achieve a proper matching of revenues and expenses.

_____ 2. The periodic expense associated with the use of land is called depreciation expense.

_____ 3. The basis of valuation or measurement of a plant asset is called historical cost.

_____ 4. The price paid for a plant asset is actually a prepayment of an expense.

_____ 5. In general, plant assets should be recorded initially at their cash or cash equivalent price.

_____ 6. A company that constructs a machine for its own use for $40,000 should record this machine at $45,000, the price that it would have to pay to purchase it.

_____ 7. In some situations, the depreciation recorded on one plant asset may be added to the cost of another asset.

_____ 8. Depreciation must be recorded on limited life plant assets simply because the asset will not last indefinitely no matter how well it is maintained.

_____ 9. The cost of changing the oil and lubricating an auto is a revenue expenditure.

_____ 10. Treating a capital expenditure as an expense will overstate net income in the years after this action was taken.

_____ 11. Plant assets with a nominal cost may be charged to expense when acquired.

_____ 12. Failure to record depreciation will not affect the final determination of net income.

_____ 13. Freight paid on a new machine should be included in the cost of the machine.

_____ 14. The sum-of-the-years'-digits method results in larger total depreciation than does the straight-line method.

_____ 15. Expenditures incurred on plant assets that extend the quantity of services beyond the original estimate but do not improve the quality of service are debited to the Accumulated Depreciation account.

_____ 16. When depreciation is computed individually on a substantial number of assets comprising a functional group, it is advisable to maintain a subsidiary ledger.

_____ 17. The purchase price of a fixed asset is a capital expenditure.

_____ 18. Depreciation is the process of periodically writing down an asset to arrive at its fair market value.

_____ 19. Depreciation Expense for the period must be separately disclosed in the body of the income statement or in the footnotes according to _APB Opinion No. 12_.

_____ 20. Depreciation accounting automatically provides the cash required to replace plant assets as they wear out.

_____ 21. Depreciation expense does not require an equivalent outlay of cash in the period in which the expense is recorded.

_____ 22. The purpose of depreciation accounting is to provide funds for replacing fixed assets.

_____ 23. Depreciation is an estimate that reflects the cost of using up an asset.

_____ 24. The cost of the original installation of a machine should be credited to the Machinery account.

_____ 25. Land improvements should never be depreciated, since they are attached to land.

MULTIPLE CHOICE QUESTIONS

For each of the following questions indicate the best answer by circling the appropriate letter.

1. A betterment represents a(an):
    A. ordinary repair.
    B. revenue expenditure.
    C. capital expenditure.
    D. None of the above.

2. The effect of recording a capital expenditure as a revenue expenditure is an:
    A. understatement of current year's expense.
    B. overstatement of current year's net income.
    C. understatement of subsequent year's net income.
    D. understatement of current year's net income.
    ·E. None of the above.

3. The credit balance in an Accumulated Depreciation account represents:
    A. a fund accumulated for the purpose of buying new assets.
    B. the amount of cost of plant assets expensed in the past.
    C. a long-term liability.
    D. None of the above.

4. The depreciation expense for a company at the close of its first fiscal year, as determined by three different methods, is as follows: straight-line, $32,500; units-of-production, $24,050; and sum-of-the-years'-digits, $52,000. If the straight-line method is employed, the net income reported will be $71,500.

    What will be the amount of reported net income if the sum-of-the-years'-digits method is used?
    A. $104,000
    B. $95,550
    C. $52,000
    D. $76,050
    E. $43,550

5. Which of the following methods would be considered accelerated depreciation methods?
    A. Double-declining-balance method
    B. Sum-of-the-years'-digits method
    C. Straight-line method
    D. (A) and (B)
    E. All of the above.

6. An expenditure that is to be capitalized because of the benefit it will render in subsequent periods could be any of the following except a(an):
    A. capital expenditure.
    B. improvement.
    C. land improvement.
    D. revenue expenditure.

7. In the financial statements prepared at the end of the accounting period, the item "accumulated depreciation" should appear on the:

   A. income statement as an expense.
   B. statement of retained earnings as a subtraction from net income.
   C. balance sheet as a liability.
   D. balance sheet as a deduction from the related asset.
   E. None of these.

8. An expenditure that should appear on the current income statement as an expense and a deduction from revenue is called a(an):

   A. operating revenue.
   B. revenue expenditure.
   C. capital expenditure.
   D. None of the above.

9. Hughes Company acquired a delivery truck for $25,500 on September 1, 1992. The truck has an estimated salvage value of $1,600 and an estimated useful life of eight years. The company operates on a calendar-year accounting period and uses double-declining-balance depreciation. What amounts of depreciation should be recorded for years 1992 and 1993 respectively?

   A. $1,018.22 and $4,072.86
   B. $2,125 and $6,375
   C. $2,125 and $5,843.75
   D. $1,062.50 and $3,187.50

10. The book value of an asset equals:

    A. fair market value.
    B. cost plus accumulated depreciation.
    C. cost minus estimated salvage value.
    D. fair market value less accumulated depreciation and estimated salvage value.
    E. None of the above.

Questions 11–14.

Watch Company purchased for $3,000 a new machine having a $300 trade-in value. It is estimated that the machine will have a four-year life and can produce 6,000 units of finished product during its service life. The machine produced 3,000 units during its first year of operation and 2,000 units during its second year of operation.

11. Straight-line depreciation per year is:

    A. $810
    B. $900
    C. $675
    D. $750
    E. None of these.

12. Sum-of-the-years'-digits depreciation for the second year is:

    A. $810
    B. $1,080
    C. $600
    D. $540
    E. None of the above.

13. Double-declining-balance depreciation for the second year is:
    A. $675
    B. $562.50
    C. $750
    D. $900
    E. None of these.

14. Units-of-production depreciation for the second year is:
    A. $1,000
    B. $675
    C. $750
    D. $900
    E. None of these.

15. Depreciation accounting is primarily for the purpose of:
    A. providing a fund to replace depreciable assets.
    B. showing conservative figures on the financial statements.
    C. providing a deduction for income tax purposes.
    D. revaluing assets whose fair market values have declined.
    E. systematically allocating the cost of depreciable assets against the revenues produced by those assets.

SOLUTIONS

Matching

1.	e	7.	o	13.	p
2.	g	8.	f	14.	n
3.	c	9.	a	15.	h
4.	b	10.	i	16.	m
5.	j	11.	l	17.	q
6.	k,l	12.	d		

Completion and Exercises

1. Depreciation per year = ($65,000 − $5,000) ÷ 12 = $5,000
2. Depreciation per unit = $72,000/360,000 = $0.20 per unit; $62,000 × $0.20 per unit = $12,400 depreciation for current year
3. The *general* rule is that the fair market value of the assets received or of the assets surrendered or securities issued, whichever is the more clearly evident, should be used.
4. physical deterioration; inadequacy; obsolescence
5. False. Accountants attempt to distribute in a systematic and rational manner the cost less salvage value of the plant asset over the estimated useful life of the asset to match the cost of the asset with the revenue produced by the asset.
6. straight-line
7.

Invoice price including 5% sales tax	$36,750
Less: 2% cash discount (on $35,000)	700
	$36,050
Transportation charges	200
Installation and testing costs	2,300
Cost of machine	$38,550

8. early; understate
9. understated; overstated.
10. Plant assets are the relatively long-lived tangible assets acquired for use in the operations of a business rather than for resale.
11. land; depreciable property
12. The cost of a plant asset consists of all the normal and reasonable expenditures necessary to place the asset in its intended location in a usable condition. Cost is usually measured by the amount of cash and/or cash equivalent given up.
13. $180,000 \left(\$450,000 \times \dfrac{\$200,000}{\$500,000} \right)$

    $270,000 \left(\$450,000 \times \dfrac{\$300,000}{\$500,000} \right)$

14. First year: Depreciation = $\$75,000 \times 0.20 = \$15,000$
    Second year: Depreciation = $(\$75,000 - \$15,000) \times 0.20 = \$12,000$
15. Sum-of-the-years'-digits = $8 + 7 + 6 + 5 + 4 + 3 + 2 + 1 = 36$
    Depreciation for first year = $8/36 \times \$22,500 = \$5,000$
16. 1992: Depreciation = $\$60,000 \times 0.40 \times 4/12 = \$8,000$
    1993: Depreciation = $(\$60,000 - \$8,000) \times .40 = \$20,800$
17. $2,080. ($29,000 - $3,000)/5 = $5,200; $29,000 - ($5,200 \times 3) = $13,400; ($13,400 - $3,000)/5 = $2,080
18. the asset accounts

19. Accumulated Depreciation—Machinery 750
       Cash 750
       Cost of overhauling machine engine.

20. The machine will still be depreciated over the same number of years, but the yearly charge to depreciation expense will be greater for the remaining years.

21. At the beginning of eighth year:
    Cost of machine $4,640
       Less: Estimated salvage value 160
                                                                          $4,480
       Less: Accumulated depreciation [($4,480/8) \times 7] 3,920
    Net depreciable book value before overhaul .... $ 560
    Cost of engine overhaul 750
    Net depreciable book value after overhaul $1,310
       $1,310 \div 2 remaining years of useful life = $655 depreciation per year.

22. the length of time that the expenditure will be beneficial.

23. Expenses are overstated for the year 1992 .... $4,500.00
    Depreciation that should have been recorded on the installation costs ($4,500/6) \times 9/12 year   562.50
    Net income for 1992 is understated $3,937.50

24. Land 73,700
       Cash 73,700

25. a. Straight-line method .... $10,400 ($52,000 ÷ 5)
    b. Sum-of-the-years'-digits .... 3,467 (1/15 × $52,000)
    c. Double-declining-balance .... 2,727 * (or $6,217—see below)
    d. Service-hours method .... 7,800 **

    *Declining-balance depreciation:
       1989 (40% × $52,600) $21,040
       1990 (40% × $31,560) 12,624
       1991 (40% × $18,936)   7,574
       1992 (40% × $11,362)   4,545
       1993 (40% × $ 6,817)   2,727 (or $6,217 if the asset is to be depreciated down to the $600 salvage value)

$$**\frac{\$52,000}{40,000} = \$1.30 \text{ per service hour}$$

    $1.30 × 6,000 = $7,800

True-False Questions

1. T
2. F Land is not a depreciable asset.
3. T
4. T The expense associated with the use of a plant asset is called depreciation, and it is recorded over the life of the plant asset.
5. T
6. F The machine should be recorded at its cost of $40,000; the $5,000 savings will be recognized over the life of the machine due to less depreciation expense being recorded.
7. T An example is when a truck is used to construct a building.
8. T
9. T
10. T In the year the capital expenditure is expensed, net income will be understated; then in later years, there will be no depreciation expense.
11. T The principle of materiality allows immaterial costs to be treated as revenue expenditures rather than capital expenditures.
12. F Depreciation is an expense and will be closed to Income Summary in the same manner as other expenses.
13. T
14. F The total depreciation over the life of the asset will be the same whether the straight-line method or the sum-of-the-years'-digits method is used.
15. T
16. T
17. T Revenue expenditures are charged off in the period in which they are incurred.
18. F Fair market value is determined by such factors as supply and demand in the marketplace, however, it is not the purpose of depreciation to arrive at this figure.
19. T
20. F
21. T
22. F
23. T
24. F This is a proper debit to the Machinery account.
25. F Land improvements are attached to land, but since they have limited lives they are subject to depreciation.

Multiple Choice Questions

1. C
2. D Revenue expenditures are improperly charged off in the current period; thus understating the current year's net income.
3. B
4. C $52,000 sum-of-the-years'-digits depreciation − $32,500 straight-line depreciation = $19,500 difference. $71,500 income using straight-line depreciation − $19,500 difference = $52,000 income using sum-of-the-years'-digits depreciation.
5. D
6. D
7. D
8. B
9. C 1992: 25% × $25,500 × 4/12 months = $2,125
      1993: 25% × ($25,500 − $2,125) = $5,843.75
10. E Book value is the cost of the asset less the balance in the related accumulated depreciation account.

11. C $\dfrac{\$3,000 - \$300}{4 \text{ years}} = \$675$

12. A 3/10 × $2,700 = $810
13. C 1st year depreciation: 50% × $3,000 = $1,500
       2nd year depreciation: 50% × ($3,000 − $1,500) = $750
14. D $2,700/6,000 units = $.45 per unit; $.45 × 2,000 units = $900
15. E

11 PLANT ASSET DISPOSALS, NATURAL RESOURCES, AND INTANGIBLE ASSETS

Learning Objectives

1. *Calculate and prepare entries for the sale, retirement, and destruction of plant assets.*
2. *Describe and record exchanges of dissimilar and similar plant assets.*
3. *Discuss the differences between accounting principles and tax rules in the treatment of gains and losses from the exchange of plant assets.*
4. *Determine the periodic depletion cost of a natural resource and calculate depreciation of plant assets located on extractive industry property.*
5. *Prepare entries for the acquisition and amortization of intangible assets.*

CHAPTER OUTLINE

DISPOSAL OF PLANT ASSETS

1. When a plant asset is disposed of, the balances in the asset and related accumulated depreciation accounts must be removed.

SALE OF PLANT ASSETS

2. When a plant asset is sold, the difference between the book value of the asset and the amount received represents the gain or loss on the sale.
   a. To record the sale, Cash and Accumulated Depreciation are debited and the plant asset account is credited.
   b. The difference is either a gain or a loss on disposal of plant assets.

RETIREMENT OF PLANT ASSETS WITHOUT SALE

3. If an asset is retired without sale, it must be removed from the accounts. If it has any salvage value, this value should be set up in a Salvaged Materials account.

DESTRUCTION OF PLANT ASSETS

4. The loss resulting from any assets destroyed is reduced by any insurance proceeds received.
5. Nonmonetary assets are inventories, property, plant, and equipment and other assets whose price may change over time.
   a. When nonmonetary assets are exchanged, the recorded amount should be based on the fair value of the asset given up or the fair value of the asset received, whichever is clearly more evident.
   b. A loss resulting from the exchange is always recognized.
   c. Recognition of any gain resulting from the exchange depends on whether the assets exchanged are similar or dissimilar in nature.

EXCHANGES OF DISSIMILAR PLANT ASSETS

6. When dissimilar plant assets are exchanged, both gains and losses are recognized. The new asset is recorded at its cash price, which is equal to the fair cash value of the old asset at the time of the exchange plus the amount of cash paid.
   a. If the cash price is not stated, the fair market value of the old asset plus any cash paid is used to record the new asset.
   b. The book value of the old asset is removed from the accounts by debiting Accumulated Depreciation and crediting the old asset.

EXCHANGES OF SIMILAR PLANT ASSETS

7. When similar plant assets are exchanged, losses are recognized, but gains are not recognized.
   a. If a loss is indicated on an exchange of similar plant assets, the loss is recognized and the new asset is recorded at its cash price.
   b. If a gain is indicated on an exchange of similar plant assets, the gain is not recognized and the new asset is recorded at the sum of the cash paid and the book value of the old asset.
8. The Internal Revenue Code does not allow either gains or losses to be recognized when similar productive assets are exchanged. For tax purposes, the new asset must be recorded at the book value of the old asset plus any additional cash paid.

REMOVAL COSTS

9. Removal costs are incurred to dismantle and remove an old asset that has been used by the company.
   a. Removal costs are deducted from salvage proceeds to determine net salvage value.

b. If removal costs exceed salvage proceeds, they increase the loss or reduce the gain recognized on disposal of a plant asset.

c. Removal costs are not a cost of benefits expected from the new asset because they are costs of benefits already received.

NATURAL RESOURCES

10. Mines, quarries, oil reserves, gas deposits, and timber stands are known as natural resources or wasting assets.

11. Natural resources should be recorded in the accounts at the cost of acquisition plus the cost of development. In addition, natural resources should be reported on the balance sheet at total cost less accumulated depletion.

12. If land and the natural resource are acquired together, the cost of acquisition of the natural resources is equal to the purchase price less the residual value of the land.

DEPLETION

13. The amount of depletion recognized in a period is an estimate of the cost of the amount of resource removed during the period. Depletion is recorded by debiting the depletion account and crediting either the natural resource account directly or an accumulated depletion account.

INTANGIBLE ASSETS

14. Intangible assets are nonphysical and noncurrent assets that arise from exclusive privileges granted by governmental authority or by legal contract and superior entrepreneurial capacity or management know-how. Intangible assets include patents, copyrights, franchises, trademarks, leaseholds, leasehold improvements, and goodwill.

ACQUISITION OF INTANGIBLE ASSETS

15. Intangible assets are initially recorded at their cost of acquisition.

a. They should be amortized over the shortest of their economic useful life, their legal life, or 40 years.

b. Only purchased intangibles are recorded in the accounting records.

AMORTIZATION OF INTANGIBLE ASSETS

16. Amortization is the systematic write-off to expense of the cost of an intangible asset.

a. All intangible assets are subject to amortization.

b. Amortization is recorded by debiting Amortization Expense and crediting the intangible asset account. An Accumulated Amortization account could be used, but in most cases the information gained would be insignificant.

c. Straight-line amortization must be used unless another method of amortization can be shown to be more appropriate.

PATENTS

17. A patent is a right granted by a government that gives the owner of the patent an exclusive right to manufacture, sell, lease, or benefit from an invention.

a. The legal life of a patent is 17 years.

b. Patents are recorded at cost if purchased.

c. The Patent account should be debited for the cost of the first successful defense if an outside law firm is hired and for the cost of any competing patents that were purchased to ensure the revenue-generating capability of the purchased patent.

COPYRIGHTS

18. A copyright gives exclusive right protection for writings, designs, and literary productions against being reproduced illegally.

    a. A copyright has a legal life equal to the life of the creator plus 50 years.
    b. Generally the cost of the copyright is expensed over the life of the first edition published.

FRANCHISES

19. A franchise is a contract between two parties that grants the franchisee certain rights and privileges ranging from name identification to exclusive right to operate in a given geographical area.

    a. A franchise also places certain restrictions on the company that purchased the franchise, such as the prices charged.
    b. If the franchise agreement specifies periodic payments to the grantor of the franchise, the Franchise Expense account should be debited.
    c. If, instead, the franchise agreement specifies a lump-sum payment be made to acquire the franchise, the cost should be recorded in an asset account entitled Franchise and amortized over the shorter of the useful life of the franchise or 40 years.

TRADEMARKS; TRADE NAMES

20. Trademarks and trade names may be acquired that are used in conjunction with a particular product or company.

    a. A trademark is a symbol, design, or logo that is used in conjunction with a particular product or company.
    b. A trade name is a brand name under which a product is sold or a company does business.

LEASEHOLDS

21. A lease is a contract made with the owner of property to rent that property. The lessee obtains the right to possess and use property.

    a. Rights granted under the lease are called a leasehold.
    b. Accounting for a lease depends on whether it is a capital lease or an operating lease.
        1. A capital lease transfers to the lessee virtually all rewards and risks that accompany ownership of property.
            (a) A lease is a capital lease if it transfers ownership of the leased property to the lessee at the end of the lease term or contains a bargain purchase option that permits the lessee to buy the property at a price significantly below fair value at the end of the lease term.
            (b) A capital lease is a means of financing property acquisitions and has the same economic impact as an installment purchase.
        2. Operating leases are those leases that do not qualify as capital leases.
            (a) An operating lease does not transfer any of the rewards and risks of ownership to the lessee.
            (b) If the operating lease requires an immediate cash payment for a future year's occupancy or that does not cover a specific year's rent, a Leasehold account is debited. This Leasehold account is a long-term Prepaid Rent account and is amortized when the services are received.

LEASEHOLD IMPROVEMENTS

22. Leasehold improvements should be written off over the life of the lease or the life of the improvements, whichever is shorter.

    a. Leasehold improvements are physical alterations made by the lessee to the leased property. These improvements are expected to yield benefits beyond the current accounting period.
    b. Leasehold improvements made by a lessee usually become the property of the lessor after the lease has expired.
    c. To amortize a leasehold improvement, Rent Expense or Leasehold Improvement Expense is debited and Leasehold Improvements is credited.

SOLUTION TO DEMONSTRATION PROBLEM

a.	Cash	800	
	Accumulated Depreciation	9,800	
	Machine		10,600

b.	Cash	3,400	
	Accumulated Depreciation	9,800	
	Machine		10,600
	Gain on Disposal of Plant Assets		2,600

c.	Cash	600	
	Accumulated Depreciation	9,800	
	Loss on Disposal of Plant Assets	200	
	Machine		10,600

d.	Machine (New)	12,400	
	Accumulated Depreciation	9,800	
	Machine (Old)		10,600
	Cash		11,600

e.	Machine (New)	12,400	
	Accumulated Depreciation	9,800	
	Machine (Old)		10,600
	Cash		11,600

MATCHING

Referring to the terms listed below, place the appropriate letter next to the corresponding description.

a.	Amortization	h.	Goodwill	n.	Materiality concept
b.	Copyright	i.	Patent	o.	Natural resources
c.	Boot	j.	Wasting asset	p.	Intangible asset
d.	Depletion	k.	Lease	q.	Leasehold
e.	Leasehold improvement	l.	Operating lease	r.	Research and development
f.	Trademark	m.	Franchise		costs
g.	Capital lease				

_____ 1. A noncurrent asset classification, having no physical existence, that is valued because of the advantages or exclusive rights it provides its owner.

_____ 2. A symbol, design, brand name, or any other indicator of easy and ready recognition attributed to the product.

_____ 3. The amount of cash or other assets paid in addition to the asset surrendered to acquire another asset.

_____ 4. An estimate, usually expressed in terms of cost, of the service potential of an intangible asset that expired in a period.

_____ 5. The intangible value attached to a firm resulting from the ability of its management to produce above-average earnings.

_____ 6. An exclusive privilege conferred on the owner that protects his or her writings, designs, and literary productions from unauthorized reproduction.

_____ 7. The amount of cost assigned to a natural resource extracted, mined, or harvested in a period.

_____ 8. A contract in which a lessor grants a lessee the right to operate or use property for a stated period of time in exchange for stipulated payments.

_____ 9. Allows the accountant to deal with unimportant items in a theoretically incorrect manner.

_____ 10. A privilege granted by the federal government to an inventor giving the exclusive right to manufacture, lease, sell, or otherwise benefit from an invention.

_____ 11. The agreement that allows the owner (operator) of a local fast-food restaurant to use the McDonald's name.

_____ 12. Examples are ore bodies, mineral deposits, oil reserves, and timber stands.

_____ 13. A lease that is, in effect, an installment purchase of an asset.

_____ 14. Another name for a depletible natural resource.

_____ 15. All leases that do not meet the criteria for a capital lease.

_____ 16. The account to which the down payment, other than the first period's rent, on a long-term operating lease is debited.

_____ 17. Costs incurred in a planned search for new knowledge and in translating such knowledge to produce a new product or process.

_____ 18. Any physical alteration to leased property from which benefits are expected beyond the current accounting period.

COMPLETION AND EXERCISES

---

1. A truck is purchased by the Lem Company on April 1, 1993, for $7,500, with an estimated useful life of five years and an estimated salvage value of $1,500. The company uses the double-declining-balance method of depreciation. If the truck is sold on December 31, 1994, for $4,000, what is the amount of gain or loss on the sale?

2. A machine is purchased on August 1, 1993, for $6,200 with an estimated useful life of six years and an estimated salvage value of $460. The company uses the sum-of-the-years'-digits method of depreciation. If the machine is exchanged for a similar machine with a cash price of $10,000 on December 31, 1994, and the company received a trade-in allowance of $3,000, what is the depreciable basis of the new machine for tax purposes?

3. A gain or loss on the sale of a plant asset is determined by comparing the asset's _____ _____ with its _____ _____.

4. A machine that cost $60,000 and has an Accumulated Depreciation account balance of $22,500 is sold for $20,500. There is a (gain/loss) _____ on the sale of $ _____.

5. Prepare the journal entry if the plant asset described below is sold for $23,400 and depreciation has been recorded to the date of sale. (Omit explanation.)

Cost of asset $45,000
Accumulated depreciation 21,020

DATE	ACCOUNT TITLES AND EXPLANATION	POST. REF.	DEBIT	CREDIT

6. What entry is required to record the retirement of the machine described below? (Omit explanation.)

Cost $26,500
Accumulated depreciation 25,000
Estimated value of salvaged materials .. 1,500

DATE	ACCOUNT TITLES AND EXPLANATION	POST. REF.	DEBIT	CREDIT

7. Assume that a building costing $180,000 is completely destroyed by fire. Depreciation accumulated to the date of destruction amounts to $78,000. What journal entry is required to record the destruction if $48,000 is expected to be recovered from an insurance company? (Omit explanation.)

DATE	ACCOUNT TITLES AND EXPLANATION	POST. REF.	DEBIT	CREDIT

Chapter 11

8. Assume that factory equipment costing $32,000 and having an Accumulated Depreciation account balance of $26,000 is exchanged for an automobile. In addition to the factory equipment, cash of $11,000 is given in exchange for an automobile. The automobile has a cash price of $12,000. What journal entry is required to record the exchange? (Omit explanation.)

DATE	ACCOUNT TITLES AND EXPLANATION	POST. REF.	DEBIT	CREDIT

9. Assume that $426,000 cash and an old machine that cost $334,000 and has an Accumulated Depreciation account balance of $200,000 are exchanged for a similar new machine that has a cash price of $600,000. What entry is required to record this exchange? (Omit explanation.)

DATE	ACCOUNT TITLES AND EXPLANATION	POST. REF.	DEBIT	CREDIT

10. Assume that $38,400 cash and an old delivery truck that cost $23,200 and has an Accumulated Depreciation account balance of $20,500 are exchanged for a new delivery truck that has a cash price of $40,000. What entry is required to record this exchange in accordance with generally accepted accounting principles? (Omit explanation.)

DATE	ACCOUNT TITLES AND EXPLANATION	POST. REF.	DEBIT	CREDIT

11. Assume that Machine No. 1, which cost $105,000 and on which $70,000 of depreciation has been recorded, is exchanged for Machine No. 2, which has a cash price of $120,000. Machine No. 1 and $80,000 are given in exchange. What entry is needed to record this exchange for income tax purposes? (Omit explanation.)

DATE	ACCOUNT TITLES AND EXPLANATION	POST. REF.	DEBIT	CREDIT

12. _____ is caused by the physical removal of a quantity of natural resources.

13. What are the forms of the two different possible entries for recording periodic depletion?

DATE	ACCOUNT TITLES AND EXPLANATION	POST. REF.	DEBIT	CREDIT

14. Turner Company paid $1,015,000 for the mineral rights, estimated at 7,000,000 tons, in a certain tract of land. In its first year of operations, Turner Company extracted 320,000 tons of minerals and sold 310,000 tons. The depletion cost per ton is _____, and the depletion cost to be charged to expense in the first year of operations is _____.

15. Specialized machinery was installed at the site of an oil reserve. The machinery has an estimated physical life of 25 years. The oil reserve is expected to be productive for 30 more years. The machinery should be depreciated over _____ years.

16. What are intangible assets?

_____

_____

_____

_____

17. _____ is an estimate, usually expressed in terms of cost, of the services received from an intangible asset in a period.

18. Over what period of time should patents be amortized?

_____

_____

_____

_____

19. _____ is an intangible value attached to a business because its management is able to produce above-average earnings per dollar of investment.

20. Research and development costs should be _____ as incurred.

21. On July 1, 1993, the first day of its fiscal year, Darcy Co. leased a warehouse for five years at an annual rental of $10,000. The warehouse has an estimated life of 30 years. Darcy Co. paid the first and fifth years' rent on July 1. This is a(an) _____ lease. The first year's rent of $10,000 should be debited to _____ _____; the fifth year's rent should be debited to _____.

22. Eno Co. leased a computer-controlled photoengraving machine on December 31, 1993. The lease runs for four years, which is the estimated useful life of the machine, and calls for four annual payments on December 31 of $10,000. The estimated salvage value of the machine is zero. The lease is a(n) _____ lease. The leased property is recorded as an _____ and the lease obligation as a _____. The property is depreciated over _____.

23. On January 1, 1993, Brown bought an oil well for $650,000. He has no right to any land value after the oil is pumped. It is estimated that there are 880,000 barrels of oil in the ground. In 1993, he pumped and sold oil for $30 per barrel showing total credit sales of $3,000,000. Journalize entries for 1993 relating to the oil well.

24. Make the necessary general journal entries required in the following transactions for Belcher Company.

   a. Purchased a patent for $75,000.

   b. Amortized the above patent for one full year. Belcher Company received exclusive rights to the patent for 12 years, but the patent is expected to have economic value for only ten years.

25. Georgia Co. acquired Machine 1 on July 1, 1993, for $16,800. Machine I was traded in on Machine II on December 31, 1994. For depreciation purposes, machines of this type are expected to have useful lives of five years and no salvage value. Use straight-line depreciation for Machine I. Data regarding the trade-in is shown below: (Assume depreciation has already been recorded to December 31, 1994.)

	Cash Price	Cash paid
Machine II	$18,900	$8,400

   a. Journalize in the space below the entry required on December 31, 1994, recording the trade-in assuming the income tax method is followed.

b. Journalize in the space below the entry required on December 31, 1994, recording the trade-in assuming the accounting method is used.

TRUE-FALSE QUESTIONS

Indicate whether each of the following statements is true or false by inserting a capital "T" or "F" in the blank space provided.

_____ 1. A loss generally will be recorded on the sale of a plant asset if the sales price is less than the asset's book value.

_____ 2. The total depreciation recorded on a plant asset before its retirement can never exceed the asset's cost.

_____ 3. Neither generally accepted accounting principles nor income tax regulations permits the recording of a gain on an exchange of similar assets by a party paying cash and an old asset for a new asset.

_____ 4. Natural resources are generally recorded at cost, including the cost of exploration and development.

_____ 5. In calculating depletion for a period, the residual value of acquired land containing an ore deposit should be deducted from the total purchase price.

_____ 6. All recorded intangible assets are subject to amortization.

_____ 7. Goodwill is recorded by accountants only if it is purchased.

_____ 8. A patent should be amortized over 40 years.

_____ 9. Because it has an indefinite life, a trademark need not be amortized.

_____ 10. A capital lease has no effect on the balance sheet.

_____ 11. Intangible assets should be amortized over the longer of their economic life or legal life.

_____ 12. The Patent account should be debited for the cost of the first successfully defended patent infringement suit if an outside law firm was retained.

_____ 13. If a fully depreciated asset continues to be used, management can continue to take depreciation.

_____ 14. An operating lease is a lease that transfers to the lessee virtually all advantages and risks of ownership of property.

_____ 15. Trademarks and trade names should be recorded at their fair market value and amortized over their legal life.

_____ 16. If a franchise is purchased for a lump sum, the amount is recorded as an asset and amortized over 40 years or its useful life, whichever is shorter.

_____ 17. A copyright's legal life is 50 years, and it gives its owner protection against writings and literary productions from being reproduced without authorization.

_____ 18. When plant assets are disposed of in a sale, no gain or loss can be recognized for tax purposes.

_____ 19. Before disposing of a plant asset, depreciation to the date of sale or disposition must be recorded in the journal.

_____ 20. If a company purchases a competing patent to ensure revenue-generating capability of an existing patent, the cost of the purchased patent should be expensed in the period of purchase.

_____ 21. When dissimilar plant assets are exchanged, the asset received would normally be recorded at the fair value of the new asset or the fair value of the asset given up plus cash paid.

_____ 22. According to generally accepted accounting principles, when similar assets are exchanged, the new asset will be recorded at the book value of the old asset plus the cash paid or the cash price of the asset received, whichever is lower.

_____ 23. Generally accepted accounting principles and income tax laws differ in their recognition of gains on the exchange of similar assets.

_____ 24. If removal costs exceed the proceeds from salvage, such removal costs increase the loss or reduce the gain recognized on disposal of a plant asset.

_____ 25. Accumulated Depletion is a contra account to an asset reported in the natural resources section of the balance sheet.

MULTIPLE CHOICE QUESTIONS

For each of the following questions indicate the best answer by circling the appropriate letter.

1. On August 15, 1993, Fowler, Inc. traded in a word processor for a newer model. The cost of the old machine was $2,600 and its book value (adjusted to Aug. 15, 1993), was $780. The new machine had a cash price of $6,500 but was acquired for $5,200 plus the old machine. The new asset should be recorded at:
   A. $5,200
   B. $5,980
   C. $6,240
   D. $6,500
   E. None of these (must know fair value of the old machine at date of trade-in).

2. Which of the following accounts is not a plant asset?
   A. Delivery Equipment
   B. Shop Supplies on Hand
   C. Buildings
   D. Furniture & Fixtures
   E. Automobiles

3. Natural resources such as timberlands, mineral deposits, and oil reserves, which are known as wasting assets, are carried in the accounts at cost less accumulated:

   A. depreciation.
   B. depletion.
   C. usage.
   D. deterioration.
   E. None of these.

4. Company Q received exclusive rights to a patent for 15 years, but it is expected to have value for only five years. The patent cost is $69,000. The entry to record the amortization for one full year is:

   A. Patent Amortization Expense 13,800
         Patents 13,800
   B. Patent Amortization Expense 4,600
         Patents 4,600
   C. Patents 69,000
         Cash 69,000
   D. Patents written off 69,000
         Patents 69,000
   E   None of the above.

The following information relates to Questions 5 and 6. On August 1 of the current fiscal year Dan Grubbs traded an old bookkeeping machine for a new one with a cash price of $1,500. He received a trade-in allowance of $250 and paid the balance in cash. The following information about the old equipment is obtained from the account in the office equipment ledger: cost, $800; accumulated depreciation at December 31, the close of the previous fiscal period, $640; monthly depreciation, $8.

5. The valuation of the new machine will be:

   A. $1,410
   B. $1,250
   C. $1,354
   D. $1,500
   E. None of the above.

6. Using the accounting method, the gain or loss on the exchange recorded in a ledger account will be:

   A. Gain, $90
   B. Loss, $110
   C. Gain, $146
   D. Gain, $150
   E. None of the above.

7. The Price Company bought a truck on July 1, 1993, for $4,600. The company uses the straight-line method of depreciation. It is estimated that this truck will have a salvage value of $920 at the end of its estimated useful life of 8 years. The book value of this truck on the December 31, 1994, balance sheet is:

   A. $4,600
   B. $4,370
   C. $2,300
   D. $3,910
   E. $3,680

8. A mine having an estimated 500,000 tons of economically extractible ore is purchased for $100,000. If 25,000 tons of ore are mined and sold during the first year, the amount of depletion included as expense for the year is:

  A. $100,000
  B. $10,000
  C. $5,000
  D. $2,000
  E. None of the above.

9. On January 2, 1990, Ling's Cameras purchased office equipment at a cost of $3,480 that had an estimated life of six years with no salvage value. On March 1, 1994, the equipment was sold for $870 cash. At the close of the annual accounting period on December 31, 1993, the accounts showed the following:

Office Equipment $3,480
Accumulated Depreciation—Office Equipment 2,320

The proper entries (to the nearest dollar) to be made on March 1, 1994, assuming the straight-line method, are:

  A. Cash 870
     Accumulated Depreciation—Office Equipment 2,320
     Loss on Disposal of Plant Assets 290
       Office Equipment 3,480
  B. Depreciation Expense 97
       Accumulated Depreciation—Office Equipment 97
     Cash 870
     Accumulated Depreciation—Office Equipment 2,417
     Loss on Disposal of Plant Assets 193
       Office Equipment 3,480
  C. Depreciation Expense 97
       Accumulated Depreciation—Office Equipment 97
     Cash 870
     Accumulated Depreciation—Office Equipment 2,320
     Loss on Disposal of Plant Assets 290
       Office Equipment 3,480
  D. Depreciation Expense 580
       Accumulated Depreciation—Office Equipment 580
     Cash 870
     Accumulated Depreciation—Office Equipment 2,900
       Office Equipment 3,480
       Gain on Disposal of Plant Assets 290
  E. None of these.

10. Equipment costing $12,000 and having an original life of five years and an estimated salvage value of $1,500 is exchanged for new equipment. The old equipment has been depreciated under double-declining-balance for two years. The cash price of the new equipment is $19,500 and a trade-in allowance of $5,400 is allowed. The entry to record the exchange, assuming the income tax method is used, is:

A.
Equipment	23,460	
Accumulated Depreciation	4,800	
Loss on Disposal of Plant Assets	3,240	
Equipment		12,000
Cash		19,500

B.
Equipment	18,420	
Accumulated Depreciation	7,680	
Cash		14,100
Equipment		12,000

C.
Equipment	19,500	
Accumulated Depreciation	3,360	
Loss on Disposal of Plant Assets	3,240	
Equipment		12,000
Cash		14,100

D.
Equipment	19,500	
Loss on Disposal of Plant Assets	6,600	
Equipment		12,000
Cash		14,100

E. None of these.

11. Under the depletion method, if a mine having an estimated 2,000,000 tons of available ore is purchased for $750,000, the depletion charge per ton of ore mined is:

A. $6.00
B. $0.75
C. $0.375
D. $15.00

12. If a fully depreciated asset is still in use:

A. the cost should be adjusted to market value.
B. prior years' depreciation should be adjusted.
C. the cost and accumulated depreciation should remain in the ledger and no more depreciation should be taken.
D. part of the depreciation should be reversed.
E. it should be written off the books.

13. How is the book value of a plant asset determined?

A. By deducting the accumulated depreciation from the balance of the asset account
B. By deducting the current depreciation expense from the amount in the asset account
C. By adding the accumulated depreciation to the balance of the asset account
D. By deducting the accumulated depreciation from the sales value of the asset
E. None of these.

14. Accumulated depreciation is debited for:

A. loss of cash.
B. the write-off of a fully depreciated asset.
C. the yearly depreciation expense.
D. None of these.

15. At the beginning of its fiscal year on July 1, 1990, a company purchased office equipment costing $9,000. On September 1, 1994, the equipment was sold for $1,875 cash. Depreciation expense was recorded to fiscal year-end on June 30, 1994, using a six-year life and straight-line depreciation with no expected salvage value. The correct entry to record the sale on September 1, 1994 is:

A. Depreciation Expense 250
       Accumulated Depreciation—Office Equipment 250
    Cash 1,875
    Accumulated Depreciation—Office Equipment 6,250
    Loss on Sale of Plant Assets 875
       Office Equipment 9,000
B. Depreciation Expense 375
       Accumulated Depreciation—Office Equipment 375
    Cash 1,875
    Accumulated Depreciation—Office Equipment 6,250
    Loss on Sale of Plant Assets 750
       Office Equipment 9,000
C. Depreciation Expense 250
       Accumulated Depreciation—Office Equipment 250
    Loss on Sale of Plant Assets 1,125
    Cash 1,875
    Accumulated Depreciation—Office Equipment 6,000
       Office Equipment 9,000
D. Cash 18,750
    Accumulated Depreciation—Office Equipment 6,000
       Gain on Sale of Plant Assets 15,750
       Accumulated Depreciation—Office Equipment 9,000
E. None of these.

SOLUTIONS

Matching

1.	p	10.	i
2.	f	11.	m
3.	c	12.	o (or j)
4.	a	13.	g
5.	h	14.	j
6.	b	15.	l
7.	d	16.	q
8.	k	17.	r
9.	n	18.	e

Completion and Exercises

1. Gain of $850
   Depreciation taken:
   1993 40% × $7,500 × 9/12 = $2,250
   1994 40% × ($7,500 − 2,250) = 2,100
   $4,350

   $7,500 $4,000 Sales price
   −4,350   −3,150
   $3,150 Book value $ 850 Gain

2. $10,991

   Depreciation taken:
   8/1/93–8/1/94: 6/21 × ($6,200 − $460)   = $1,640
   8/1/94–12/31/94: 5/21 × 5/12 × ($6,200 − $460) =   569
   $2,209

   Book value:
   Cost .... $ 6,200
   Less: Accumulated Depreciation 2,209
   Book value .... $ 3,991
   Cash paid ($10,000 − $3,000) 7,000
   Basis for tax purposes $10,991

3. book value (cost less accumulated depreciation); sales price
4. loss; $17,000, calculated as [($60,000 − $22,500) − $20,500]

5. Cash 23,400
   Accumulated Depreciation—Plant Assets 21,020
   Loss on Disposal of Plant Assets 580
       Plant Assets 45,000

6. Salvaged Materials 1,500
   Accumulated Depreciation—Machinery 25,000
       Machinery 26,500

7. Receivable from Insurance Company 48,000
   Fire Loss 54,000
   Accumulated Depreciation—Building 78,000
       Building 180,000

8. Automobiles 12,000
   Accumulated Depreciation—Factory Equipment 26,000
   Loss on Disposal of Plant Assets 5,000
       Factory Equipment 32,000
       Cash 11,000
   [Loss on disposal is difference between book value of $6,000 ($32,000 − $26,000), and trade-in allowance of $1,000 (12,000 − 11,000).]

9. Machinery (new) 560,000
   Accumulated Depreciation—Machinery 200,000
       Machinery (old) 334,000
       Cash 426,000

10. Delivery Trucks (new) 40,000
    Accumulated Depreciation—Delivery Trucks 20,500
    Loss on Disposal of Plant Assets 1,100
        Delivery Trucks (old) 23,200
        Cash 38,400
        [Loss on disposal is difference between book value of $2,700 ($23,200 − $20,500), and trade-in allowance of $1,600 ($40,000 − $38,400).]

11. Machinery (No. 2) 115,000
    Accumulated Depreciation—Machinery 70,000
        Machinery (No. 1) 105,000
        Cash 80,000

12. Depletion

13. Depletion xxx
        Natural Resource xxx
    Depletion xxx
        Accumulated Depletion xxx

14. $0.145 ($1,015,000 ÷ 7,000,000 tons); $44,950 ($0.145 × 310,000 tons sold).

15. 25 (because useful life of the machinery is shorter than life of the oil reserve)

16. Intangible assets are noncurrent, nonphysical assets acquired for use in business operations rather than for resale. They provide business advantages and exclusive rights or privileges to their owners.

17. Amortization

18. Patents should be amortized over the shorter of their legal life of 17 years or their estimated useful life.

19. Goodwill

20. expensed

21. operating; Prepaid Rent (or Rent Expense); Leasehold

22. capital; asset; liability; the useful life to the lessee

23.   Oil Deposits 650,000
        Cash 650,000
    Accounts Receivable 3,000,000
        Sales 3,000,000
    Depletion Expense* 74,000
        Accumulated Depletion—Mineral Deposits 74,000

    * $\dfrac{\$650,000}{880,000 \text{ barrels}} = \$.74 \text{ per barrel}$

    $3,000,000 ÷ $30 = 100,000 barrels

    ($.74 × 100,000 = $74,000 depletion)

24. a. Patents 75,000
        Cash 75,000
   b. Patent Amortization Expense 7,500
        Patents 7,500

25. a. Machine II 20,160
    Accumulated Depreciation 5,040
        Machine I 16,800
        Cash 8,400

b.	Machine II	18,900	
	Accumulated Depreciation	5,040	
	Loss on Disposal of Plant Assets	1,260	
	Machine I		16,800
	Cash		8,400

Book value = $16,800 − $5,040 = $11,760
Trade-in   = $18,900 − $8,400 = 10,500
            Loss $ 1,260

True-False Questions

1. T
2. T
3. T Losses are recognized for accounting purposes, but not for tax purposes.
4. T Depletion is recorded so that the cost is allocated over the time periods benefited.
5. T
6. T (but not for tax purposes)
7. T
8. F Patents should be amortized over the shorter of their economic or legal life.
9. F Trademark should be amortized over its economic life or 40 years, whichever is shorter.
10. F A capital lease is a lease that transfers to the lessee virtually all rewards and risks that accompany ownership of property. The lessee must record the leased property as an asset and the lease obligation as a liability.
11. F It is the shorter of their economic or legal life rather than the longer.
12. T
13. F No more depreciation can be taken on a fully depreciated plant asset.
14. F This statement describes a capital lease.
15. F Trademarks and trade names should be recorded at cost and amortized over their economic life or 40 years, whichever is shorter.
16. T
17. F A copyright's legal life is equal to the life of the creator plus 50 years.
18. F For tax purposes, no gain or loss is recognized on an exchange of similar plant assets, not a sale of plant assets.
19. T
20. F The cost of a purchased patent used for protection of an existing patent should be debited to the Patents account.
21. T
22. T This prevents a gain from being recorded.
23. F Gains are not recognized by either, but losses are recognized by generally accepted accounting principles on the exchange of similar assets. Income tax regulations do not recognize these losses.
24. T
25. T

Multiple Choice Questions

1. B $780 book value + $5,200 cash paid = $5,980
2. B Shop supplies on hand is a current asset.
3. B
4. A
5. C $800 − $696 = $104 Book value; $250 trade-in − $104 = $146 gain; $1,500 − $146 = $1,354 valuation of the new machine
6. E No gain is recorded on exchanges of similar assets.

7. D $\dfrac{\$4,600 - \$920 \text{ salvage value}}{8 \text{ years}} = \$460 \text{ per yr.}$

$\$460 \times 1\ 1/2$ years = \$690 accumulated depreciation balance

\$4,600 cost − \$690 accumulated depreciation = \$3,910 book value

8. C ($100,000 ÷ 500,000 = $.20; $.20 × 25,000 = $5,000)

9. B

10. B $12,000 × 40% = $4,800 first year depreciation

($12,000 − $4,800) × 40% = $2,880 second year depreciation

$12,000 − $4,800 − $2,880 = $4,320 book value

$19,500 − $5,400 trade-in = $14,100 cash paid

$14,100 cash + $4,320 book value = $18,420 tax basis cost of new equipment

11. C $750,000/2,000,000 tons = $0.375

12. C

13. A

14. B

15. A $9,000 ÷ 6 = $1,500 per yr.; $1,500 × 4 = $6,000 (depr. to 6/30/94). $1,500 × 1/6 = $250 (depr. for July and August). $6,000 + $250 = $6,250 (accumulated depreciation).

12 ACCOUNTING THEORY AND INTERNATIONAL ACCOUNTING

Learning Objectives

1. *Identify and discuss the underlying assumptions or concepts of accounting.*
2. *Identify and discuss the major principles of accounting.*
3. *Identify and discuss the modifying conventions (or constraints) of accounting.*
4. *Describe the Conceptual Framework Project of the Financial Accounting Standards Board.*
5. *Discuss the differences in international accounting among nations (Appendix).*

CHAPTER OUTLINE

UNDERLYING ASSUMPTIONS OR CONCEPTS

1. Accounting theory is a set of basic concepts or assumptions and related principles or standards that explain and guide the accountant's actions in identifying, measuring, and communicating economic information.

BUSINESS ENTITY

2. An entity is a specific unit for which accounting information is gathered. An entity has an existence apart from its owners, creditors, employees, and other parties.

GOING CONCERN (CONTINUITY)

3. The going-concern (continuity) assumption is that the entity will continue to operate indefinitely unless there is evidence that the entity will terminate.

   a. If liquidation (the process of termination) appears likely, the going-concern assumption is no longer used.

   b. The going-concern assumption is used to justify the use of costs rather than market values in measuring assets because market value has limited value to an entity that intends to use rather than sell its assets.

MONEY MEASUREMENT

4. Instead of quantification of business transactions in terms of other measurements, money terms are used. Money measurement provides accountants with a common unit of measure in reporting on economic activity.

STABLE DOLLAR

5. The stable dollar assumption is that fluctuations in the value of the dollar may be ignored because they are insignificant.

PERIODICITY (TIME PERIODS)

6. According to the periodicity assumption, an entity's life can be subdivided into time periods for purposes of reporting on the entity's economic activities.

   a. The periodicity assumption requires the use of the accrual basis of accounting and leads to approximations requiring the exercise of judgment.

   b. Estimates must often be made of such things as expected uncollectible accounts and useful lives of depreciable assets.

GENERAL-PURPOSE FINANCIAL STATEMENTS

7. General-purpose financial statements are presented to external parties and top-level internal managers. The statements try to meet the common needs of these and other users by showing the results of the financial accounting process.

SUBSTANCE OVER FORM

8. Accountants should always record the economic substance of a transaction rather than be guided by the legal form of the transaction.

CONSISTENCY

9. Consistency requires a company to use the same accounting principles and reporting practices through time.

   a. The consistency concept bars indiscriminate switching of principles or methods every year.

   b. The consistency concept does not bar a change in principles if the information needs of users are better served by the change.

DOUBLE ENTRY

10. Every transaction has a two-sided effect on each company or party engaging in the transaction.

ARTICULATION

11. Financial statements are fundamentally related and articulate with each other.

MEASUREMENT IN ACCOUNTING

12. Accounting is defined as a measurement process because the accountant measures the assets, liabilities, and stockholders' equity of an accounting entity.

MEASURING ASSETS AND LIABILITIES

13. Cash is measured at its specified amount. Notes and accounts receivable are measured at expected cash inflows, allowing for possible uncollectibles. Inventories, prepaid expenses, plant assets, and intangibles are measured at acquisition cost.

14. Liabilities are measured in terms of the cash that will be paid or the value of services that will be performed to satisfy the liabilities.

MEASURING CHANGES IN ASSETS AND LIABILITIES

15. While some changes in assets and liabilities are easily measured, the accountant must rely on the matching principle and other principles in other exchanges.

THE MAJOR PRINCIPLES

16. The accounting profession relies upon generally accepted accounting principles (GAAP) in recording changes in assets, liabilities, and stockholders' equity.

EXCHANGE PRICE (OR COST) PRINCIPLE

17. According to the exchange price principle, transfers of resources are recorded at prices agreed on by the parties at the time of exchange. This principle determines the following three issues:
    a. What goes into the accounting systems—transaction data.
    b. When it is recorded at the time of exchange.
    c. The amounts—exchange prices at which assets, liabilities, stockholders' equity, revenues, and expenses are recorded.

MATCHING PRINCIPLE

18. Under the matching principle net income of a period is determined by associating or relating revenues earned in a period with the expenses incurred to generate the revenues.

REVENUE RECOGNITION PRINCIPLE

19. According to the revenue recognition principle, revenue should be earned and realized before it is recognized and recorded.
    a. Under the realization principle, revenue is recognized only after the seller acquires the right to receive payment from the buyer.
    b. There are several advantages to recognizing revenue at time of sale including the following:
       (1) Delivery of goods is an observable event.
       (2) Revenue is measurable.
       (3) Risk of loss due to price decline or destruction of the goods has passed to the buyer.
       (4) Revenue has been earned or substantially earned.
       (5) Expenses and net income can be determined because the revenue has been earned.
    c. The disadvantage of recognizing revenue at time of sale is that the revenue might not be recorded in the period in which most of the activity creating it occurred.

EXCEPTIONS TO THE REALIZATION PRINCIPLE

20. Practical considerations may cause accountants to vary the point of revenue recognition from the point of sale.

RECEIPT OF CASH

    a. Cash collection as point of revenue recognition is known as the cash basis of accounting; the cash basis is acceptable primarily in service organizations.

INSTALLMENT BASIS

b. The installment basis may be used when the selling price of goods sold is to be collected in installments and considerable doubt exists as to collectibility.

    (1) Gross margin on an installment sale is recognized in proportion to the cash collected on the receivable.

    (2) The installment basis of revenue recognition may be used for tax purposes only in very limited circumstances.

REVENUE RECOGNITION ON LONG-TERM CONSTRUCTION PROJECTS

c. Revenue from a long-term construction project can be recognized under either the completed-contract method or the percentage-of-completion method.

    (1) The completed-contract method recognizes revenue on long-term projects in the period in which the project is completed.

        (a) Costs incurred on the project are carried forward in an inventory account called Construction in Process and are charged to expense in the period in which revenue is recognized.

        (b) It can be argued that it is unreasonable to wait in recognizing revenue because revenue-producing activities have been performed during each year of construction.

    (2) Under the percentage-of-completion method, revenue is recognized based on the estimated stage of completion of a long-term project.

REVENUE RECOGNITION AT COMPLETION OF PRODUCTION

d. Recognizing revenue at the time of product completion is referred to as the production basis and it is considered acceptable for certain precious metals and for many farm products.

    (1) Arguments in support of the production basis for revenue recognition include the following:

        (a) Homogeneous nature of the products.

        (b) Products can usually be sold at their market prices.

        (c) Difficulties sometimes are encountered in determining unit production costs.

    (2) Inventory is debited and a revenue account is credited for the expected selling price of the goods at the time of production or extraction.

EXPENSE RECOGNITION

21. Expenses are incurred voluntarily to produce revenue.

    a. Most assets used in operating a business are measured in terms of historical cost.

    b. The matching principle implies that a relationship exists between expenses and revenues and this timing of expense recognition is guided by the concepts of product costs and period costs.

    c. Product costs are incurred in the acquisition or manufacture of goods and are carried forward in inventory accounts as long as the goods are on hand; product costs become expenses when the goods are sold.

    d. Period costs are expensed in the period in which incurred because they cannot be traced to specific revenues.

GAIN AND LOSS RECOGNITION PRINCIPLE

22. Gains may be recorded only when realized, but losses should be recorded when they first become evident. Losses are usually involuntary.

FULL DISCLOSURE PRINCIPLE

23. Information that is important enough to influence the decisions of an informed user of the statements should be disclosed.

MODIFYING CONVENTIONS

24. Modifying conventions are customs emerging from accounting practice that alter results that would be obtained from a strict application of accounting principles. These conventions include cost-benefit, materiality, and conservatism.

    a. The materiality convention allows the accountant to deal with unimportant items in a theoretically incorrect manner simply because it is more convenient and less expensive to handle them this way.

    b. The conservatism convention means being cautious or prudent and making certain that any errors in estimates tend to understate rather than overstate net assets and net income.

CONCEPTUAL FRAMEWORK PROJECT OF THE FINANCIAL ACCOUNTING STANDARDS BOARD

25. The debate over the exact nature of the basic concepts and related principles comprising accounting theory has surfaced with the Financial Accounting Standards Board (FASB) issuing concepts statements.

OBJECTIVES OF FINANCIAL REPORTING

26. According to the FASB, the three overriding objectives of financial reporting are:

    a. To provide information that is useful to present and potential investors and creditors and other users in making rational investment, credit, and similar decisions.

    b. To provide information to help present and potential investors and creditors and other users in assessing the amounts, timing, and uncertainty of prospective cash receipts.

    c. To provide information about the economic resources of an enterprise, the claims to those resources, and the effects of transactions, events, and circumstances that change its resources and claims to those resources.

QUALITATIVE CHARACTERISTICS

27. Qualitative characteristics are those characteristics which accounting information should possess to be useful; included in these characteristics are relevance, reliability, and comparability.

    ### RELEVANCE

    a. Information has relevance if it is pertinent to a decision and makes a difference to someone who does not already have the information.

    ### RELIABILITY

    b. Information has reliability when it faithfully depicts for users what it purports to represent; reliability of information depends upon its representational faithfulness, verifiability, and neutrality.

    c. Information has verifiability when it can be substantially duplicated by independent measures using the same measurement methods.

    d. Neutrality in accounting information means that the information should be free of measurement method bias.

    ### COMPARABILITY AND CONSISTENCY

    e. In order for comparability in financial information to exist, differences and similarities that are real are noted.

        (1) Consistency leads to comparability of financial information for a single company through time.

        (2) Comparability between companies is harder to achieve because the same activities may be accounted for in different ways.

    ### PERVASIVE CONSTRAINTS

    f. The two pervasive constraints faced in providing useful information are the cost/benefit analysis and materiality.

THE BASIC ELEMENTS OF FINANCIAL STATEMENTS

28. The FASB has defined several technical terms that are likely to have a major impact upon financial accounting.

APPENDIX: INTERNATIONAL ACCOUNTING

WHY ACCOUTING PRINCIPLES AND PRACTICES DIFFER AMONG NATIONS

29. Accounting reflects the national economic and social environment.

   a. Each country's environment differs, which causes an effect on accounting principles and practices.
   b. Accounting for inventories and natural resources, cost accounting techniques, and methods of foreign currency translation have a different orientation and refinement in different economies.

30. The legal and political systems vary among nations and this has an impact on accounting principles.

31. The degree of development of the accounting profession and the general level of education of a country influence accounting practices and procedures.

ATTEMPTED HARMONIZATION OF ACCOUNTING PRACTICES

32. Several organizations are working to achieve greater understanding and harmonization of different accounting practices.

   a. These organizations include the Organization for Economic Cooperation and Development (OECD), the European Community (EC), the International Accounting Standards Committee (IASC), and the International Federation of Accountants (IFAC).
   b. The IASC is making a significant contribution to the development of international accounting standards, but has the problem of obtaining compliance with these standards.

FOREIGN CURRENCY TRANSLATION

33. Foreign currency translation is probably the most common problem in an international business environment. Foreign currency translation has two main components: Accounting for transactions in a foreign currency and translating the financial statements of foreign enterprises into a different, common currency.

ACCOUNTING FOR TRANSACTIONS IN A FOREIGN CURRENCY

34. Deciding what exchange rate should be used to record purchases is an issue—the rate in effect on the purchase date or on the payment date?

TRANSLATING FINANCIAL STATEMENTS

35. Financial statements of foreign subsidiaries are translated into a single common unit of measurement, such as the dollar. The methods used to translate financial statements are of two basic groups.

   a. The current- or closing-rate approach translates all assets and liabilities at the exchange rate in effect on the balance sheet date.
   b. The current/historical-rates approach views the parent company and its foreign subsidiaries as a single business undertaking. Three translation methods are commonly used under this approach.

      (1) The current-noncurrent method translates current assets and current liabilities at the current rate—the rate in effect on the balance sheet date and noncurrent items are translated at their respective historical rates.
      (2) The monetary-nonmonetary method uses the current rate for monetary assets and liabilities and historical rates for nonmonetary items.
      (3) The temporal method is a variation of the monetary-nonmonetary method.

         (a) Cash receivables and payables and other assets and liabilities carried at current prices are translated at the current rate of exchange.
         (b) All other assets and liabilities are translated at historical rates.

INVENTORIES

36. Variations in accounting for inventories relate principally to the basis for determining cost and whether cost once determined should be increased or decreased to reflect the market value of the inventories.

DETERMINATION OF COST

37. FIFO and average cost are frequently used methods.

MARKET VALUE OF INVENTORIES

38. Lower of cost or market in valuing inventory is a common practice.

ACCOUNTING FOR THE EFFECTS OF CHANGING PRICES

39. Appendix A at the end of the text presents two approaches to accounting for the effects of changing prices on business enterprises—general price-level accounting and current-cost accounting.

   a. *FASB Statement 33* required both methods.
   b. *FASB Statement 82* eliminates the requirement to use the general price-level accounting approach.

DEMONSTRATION PROBLEM

Give the letter of the item that indicates the accounting concept or principle that is applied for each item below of Watson, Inc. An item may be used more than once.

A. Stable monetary unit (money measurement)
B. Quantifiability—objective evidence
C. Consistency
D. Periodicity
E. Historical cost
F. Business entity
G. Continuity of life—going concern

_____ 1. The balance sheet shows an investment in an art painting at its cost of $50,000; however, an art dealer has indicated he could find a museum that would pay $75,000 since the price index has shown a rapid rise during the five years since the purchase of the painting.

_____ 2. Sum-of-the-years'-digits depreciation is recorded at the end of each accounting period.

_____ 3. This concept assumes that a business enterprise is separate and distinct from the persons who supply its assets.

_____ 4. Store equipment costing $500 at the time of purchase is shown at its book value of $300 even though its market value is only $250.

_____ 5. Equipment purchases costing $50,000 are not charged to expense in the period purchased.

_____ 6. Inventories are reported at FIFO each period rather than changing from FIFO to LIFO.

_____ 7. A liability is established at the end of each year for the estimated number of cents-off coupons issued as part of the current year's advertising campaign that will be redeemed next year.

_____ 8. Periodic payments of $2,250 per month for services of J. Reed, who owns all the stock of the company, are reported as salary; additional amounts are reported as dividends.

_____ 9. Cash received for magazine subscriptions to be delivered for the next two years is reported as a liability.

_____ 10. The accounting equation is an expression of this concept.

_____ 11. Prepaid insurance of $600 is shown on the balance sheet as an asset even though the chance of obtaining a premium refund is slim.

_____ 12. A memorandum entry indicating the additional shares received is made when a stock split is declared by a company in which Watson, Inc. holds 100 shares of stock acquired at a cost of $80. The total current market value of the stock is $95.

_____ 13. Physical counts of merchandise on hand, bank statements indicating the amount of cash in bank, and invoices for purchases support accounting transactions.

_____ 14. The declining value of the unit of measurement due to inflation is not recognized in the ledger accounts.

_____ 15. Application of this concept involves the revenue recognized during the period and the expired costs to be allocated to the period.

SOLUTION TO DEMONSTRATION PROBLEM

1. E	6. C	11. G	
2. D	7. D	12. E	
3. F	8. F	13. B	
4. G,E	9. D	14. A	
5. D	10. F	15. D	

MATCHING

Referring to the terms listed below, place the appropriate letter next to the corresponding description.

a. Cash basis   e. Liquidation   h. Period costs
b. Entity   f. Loss   i. Product costs
c. Expense   g. Modifying conventions j. Revenue
d. Installment sales

_____ 1. Procedure of accounting when revenues and expenses are recorded at the time of cash collection and payment.
_____ 2. Selling and administrative costs comprise this cost classification because these costs cannot be traced to specific revenues.
_____ 3. Conservatism is an example of this.
_____ 4. Inventory costs, freight, and other costs incurred in the acquisition or manufacture of goods.
_____ 5. Asset expiration that is incurred voluntarily to produce revenue.
_____ 6. Sales of merchandise under terms that allow the buyer to make equal periodic payments over an extended period of time.
_____ 7. Asset expiration that is incurred involuntarily and does not create revenue.
_____ 8. The process of termination of an entity.
_____ 9. A specific unit for which accounting information is gathered.
_____ 10. The inflow of assets from the sale of goods and services to customers.

COMPLETION AND EXERCISES

1. Give three advantages of recognizing revenue at the time of sale.

   a. _____

   _____

   b. _____

   _____

   c. _____

   _____

2. A disadvantage of recognizing revenue at the time of sale is that _____
_____
_____

3. Give two arguments in support of the use of the production basis for recognizing revenue.

    a. _____
    _____

    b. _____
    _____

4. In financial accounting, substance is to be emphasized over form. This concept means that _____
_____
_____

5. An item is to be considered material if _____
_____

6. The basic ideas that make the accounting practices followed by different accountants fairly similar are
called _____ _____ _____ _____.

7. An underlying assumption of accounting that has not been true in recent years is the assumption that the
_____ _____ _____ _____ unit of measure.

8. Accounting measurements are characterized by approximation and judgment from application of the
_____ basis of accounting which is required if the activities of an enterprise are to be reflected in
_____ _____ _____.

9. The primary data entered in the accounting system are _____
_____.

10. In general, in accounting, net income is determined through a process of _____
revenues and expenses by _____ _____.

11. In general, revenue must be _____ and _____ before it is
recorded in the accounts. Revenue is considered realized at the _____ _____
_____ for merchandise transactions and when _____ _____
_____ for service transactions.

12. In specified, limited circumstances, it is considered acceptable to recognize revenue

    a. _____
    b. _____
    c. _____

13. In accounting for expenses, a line of distinction is usually drawn between _____ costs and _____ costs. The former are expensed when the _____ _____ _____; the latter are expensed in the _____ _____ _____ _____.

14. Neutrality essentially means that accounting information should not be _____.

15. Financial reporting is, according to the FASB, intended primarily for informed _____ and _____ to aid them in making _____ and _____ _____. It also seeks to help these parties assess the prospects of receiving _____ from their investments or loans to an enterprise. Because they affect cash inflows and outflows, financial statements should provide information about the _____ _____, _____ _____, and _____ of an enterprise.

16. Relevance and verifiability are examples of _____ _____ which accounting information should possess to be useful.

17. The president of Finance Company asks you to determine the amount of revenue earned by his company for 1994. The following statements relate to 1994 data:

    1. Cash sales were $140,000.
    2. Credit sales were $250,000 of which $180,000 was collected. Included in the $250,000 was a sale to John Smith in the amount of $15,000; John Smith has since declared bankruptcy and Finance Company has written off his account. Also included in the $250,000 is a sale to Control Company in the amount of $10,000; it appears now that $6,000 of the $10,000 must be written off as uncollectible.
    3. Cash of $66,000 was collected in 1994 on sales made in 1993.
    4. Machinery with an original cost of $9,000 and accumulated depreciation of $5,600 was sold for $4,000. Cash of $1,800 was collected with an 8% note of $2,200 signed also.

    Required: Determine the revenue earned in 1994.

18. Kramer Company had reported net income amounts for 1993 of $180,000 and 1994 of $95,000. No adjusting entries were made at either year-end for any of the transactions given below:

    1. On January 1, 1993, a machine costing $65,000 and having an estimated useful life of 10 years and a salvage value of $5,000 was put into service. The machine was debited to the Machinery account.
    2. The Service Supplies on Hand account balance on December 31, 1993, is $4,600. A count of the supplies on December 31, 1993, showed that only $2,800 of supplies were actually on hand. No purchases of supplies were made during 1994. A count of the supplies showed that $700 of supplies were on hand at December 31, 1994.

3. Painting services performed in December 1993 in the amount of $22,000, were not billed until January 1994. A debit to Cash and a credit to Service Revenue when payment was received in January is the only transaction that was recorded.

4. A truck was rented on April 1, 1993. Prepaid Rent was debited when cash of $12,000 was paid on that date to cover a two-year period.

Required: Compute the correct net income for 1993 and 1994, beginning with the net income amounts as reported. Show the effects of each correction (adjustment) for each year using a plus or a minus to indicate whether reported income should be increased or decreased as a result of the correction. Your final net income for each year should be the correct amount after adding or deducting the adjustments.

_____

_____

_____

_____

_____

_____

_____

_____

_____

_____

_____

_____

_____

_____

_____

_____

_____

_____

_____

_____

TRUE-FALSE QUESTIONS

Indicate whether each of the following statements is true or false by inserting a capital "T" or "F" in the blank space provided.

_____ 1. The cash basis of accounting is acceptable primarily in enterprises which do not have substantial credit transactions or inventories.

_____ 2. The completed-contract method recognizes revenues at the point of sale.

_____ 3. Period costs are carried in inventory accounts as long as the goods are on hand.

_____ 4. The consistency principle implies that a relationship exists between expenses and revenues.

_____ 5. The historical cost approach to recording accounting data has been severely criticized in periods of high inflation because often the income statement reports income when the economic value of the owner's investment has declined.

_____ 6. The completed-contract method is a method of recognizing revenue on long-term projects in which no revenue is recognized until the period in which the project is completed.

_____ 7. Period costs are costs incurred in the acquisition or manufacture of goods.

_____ 8. Materiality is a modifying convention which allows the accountant to deal with immaterial items in a theoretically incorrect but expedient manner.

_____ 9. The percentage-of-completion method recognizes revenue at the point of sale.

_____ 10. Losses are asset expirations which are incurred voluntarily to produce revenue.

_____ 11. The matching principle provides that net income of a period can be determined by associating the revenues earned in a period with the expenses incurred to generate the revenues.

_____ 12. One of the reasons for recognizing revenue at the time of sale is that the risk of loss due to price decline or destruction of the goods is passed to the buyer.

_____ 13. The installment basis of revenue recognition is acceptable only when a high degree of certainty exists as to the collectibility of the installments.

_____ 14. The cash basis of accounting recognizes revenues when cash is collected.

_____ 15. Recognizing revenue at the time of completion of production is called the installment basis of accounting.

_____ 16. Most assets used in operating a business are measured in terms of current cost.

_____ 17. The practice of conservatism tends to understate rather than overstate net assets and net income.

_____ 18. The stable dollar assumption is that fluctuations in the value of the dollar are significant and may not be ignored.

_____ 19. Many accounting measurements are estimates and involve approximation and judgment.

_____ 20. Under the transactions approach used in financial accounting, every transaction has a single effect upon each party engaging in it.

MULTIPLE CHOICE QUESTIONS

For each of the following questions indicate the best answer by circling the appropriate letter.

1. In a period of inflation, which of the following inventory valuation methods will give the highest gross profit?
   A. First-in, first-out (FIFO)
   B. Last-in, first-out (LIFO)
   C. Lower of cost or market
   D. Average costing
   E. There is no difference in the profit determined under (A) and (D).

2. This convention is used as a response to the uncertainty faced in the environment in which accounting is practiced.

    A. Matching
    B. Conservatism
    C. Materiality
    D. Neutrality
    E. Relevance

3. A company uses the straight-line method of depreciation in 1993. In 1994, the company decides to change to the double-declining-balance method of depreciation. This procedure violates the rule of:

    A. the matching principle.
    B. consistency.
    C. the cost principle.
    D. periodicity.

4. Qualitative characteristics include:

    A. relevance.
    B. timeliness.
    C. predictive value.
    D. All of the above.
    E. None of the above.

5. The required disclosures to financial statements may be in all of the following except:

    A. notes to the financial statements.
    B. special communications or reports.
    C. a special letter to the Board of Directors.
    D. the body of the financial statements.

6. When information is free of measurement method bias, it is said to be:

    A. neutral.
    B. verifiable.
    C. reliable.
    D. None of the above.

7. Some of the advantages of recognizing revenue at the time of sale are that:

    A. delivery of goods is an observable event.
    B. revenue is measurable.
    C. risk of loss due to price decline or destruction of the goods has passed to the buyer.
    D. All of the above.

8. Which of the following is a generally accepted accounting principle?

    A. The exchange price (or cost) principle
    B. The matching principle
    C. The realization principle
    D. All of the above.
    E. Only (B) and (C).

9. Which of the following accounts requires a substantial amount of judgment by the accountant?

    A. Cash
    B. Accounts Receivable
    C. Depreciation
    D. Notes Payable

10. In classifying the following items as monetary or nonmonetary, your answer would be:
    1. Cash
    2. Copyrights
    3. Store Equipment
    4. Stock Subscriptions Receivable
    5. Common Stock
    6. Merchandise Inventory
    7. Unearned Rent Revenue
    8. Wages Payable

    A. All items listed above are monetary.
    B. Items 1, 4, and 8 are monetary.
    C. Items 1, 2, 4, and 7 are monetary.
    D. Items 1, 3, 5, and 6 are monetary.

11. Under the accrual basis of accounting, revenues are recorded when:

    A. received and expenses are recorded when incurred.
    B. received and expenses are recorded when paid.
    C. services are rendered or products sold, and expenses are recorded when incurred.
    D. services are rendered or products sold, and expenses are recorded when paid.

12. Consistency generally:

    A. requires a company to use the same accounting principles as other companies in the same industry.
    B. requires a company to use the same accounting principles and reporting practices through time.
    C. bars indiscriminate switching of principles or methods.
    D. (B) and (C) above.

13. Under the realization principle:

    A. revenue is recognized after the seller acquires the right to receive payment from the buyer.
    B. revenue is not recognized until after payment is received from the buyer.
    C. (A) and (B) above.
    D. None of the above.

14. The percentage-of-completion method is a:

    A. revenue recognition procedure in which the gross margin on an installment sale is recognized in proportion to the cash collected on the receivable.
    B. method of recognizing revenue based on the estimated stage of completion of a long-term project.
    C. means of allowing greater comparability of the financial statements of a single company through time since the effects of price-level changes are removed.
    D. means of reflecting the purchasing power of the dollar relative to that of the base year by using the reciprocal of the price index.
    E. None of the above.

15. Historical cost accounting:

    A. measures accounting transactions in terms of the actual dollars expended or received.
    B. is a set of basic concepts and assumptions and related principles that explain and guide the accountant's actions in identifying, measuring, and communicating economic information.
    C. is supported by the stable dollar assumption which uses the current cost accounting approach.
    D. uses a general price index such as the Consumer Price Index in its valuation of assets.
    E. None of the above.

16. Under the production basis of revenue recognition, at the time of completion of production or extraction, the following journal entry is made:
    A. Debit-Expenses of Production or Extraction; Credit-Revenue account.
    B. Debit-Accounts Receivable; Credit-Revenue account.
    C. Debit-Cost of Gold or Farm Products Sold; Credit-Revenue account.
    D. Debit-Inventory account; Credit-Revenue account.
    E. None of the above.

SOLUTIONS

Matching

1.	a	5.	c	8.	e
2.	h	6.	d	9.	b
3.	g	7.	f	10.	j
4.	i				

Completion and Exercises

1. The following are advantages of recognizing revenue at the time of sale.
   a. Delivery of goods is an observable event.
   b. Revenue is measurable.
   c. Risk of loss due to price decline or destruction of goods has passed to the buyer.
   d. Revenue has been earned or substantially earned.
   e. Expenses and net income can be determined because the revenue has been earned.

2. revenue might not be recorded in the period in which most of the activity creating it occurred.
3. Arguments for the production basis could include the following:
   a. homogeneous nature of the products
   b. products can usually be sold at their market prices
   c. difficulties sometimes encountered in determining unit production costs

4. where economic substance and legal form conflict, economic substance is to be entered in the accounting system and reported.
5. knowledge of it would make a difference in the decision of an informed investor or creditor.
6. generally accepted accounting principles
7. dollar is a stable
8. accrual; periodic financial statements
9. exchange prices
10. matching; time periods
11. earned; realized; time of sale; services are rendered
12. (a) at completion of production; (b) when cash is received (installment method); (c) as production progresses
13. product; period; product is sold; period in which incurred
14. biased
15. investors; creditors; investment; credit decisions; cash; economic resources; economic obligations; earnings
16. qualitative characteristics

17. $140,000
    + 250,000
    +   600
    $390,600 Revenue earned in 1994

The cash collected from 1993 sales is not included in 1994 revenues.

18.

Explanation of Corrections		1993	1994
Reported net income		$180,000	$95,000

To correct error in accounting for:

1. Depreciation:

$$\frac{\$65,000 - \$5,000}{10 \text{ years}} = \$6,000$$

		1993	1994
For 1993		−6,000	
For 1994			−6,000

2. Service Supplies:

		1993	1994
Correct expense for 1993 ($4,600 − $2,800)		−1,800	
Correct expense for 1994 ($2,800 − $700)			−2,100

3. Service revenue:

For 1993:

	1993	1994	
Reported	$ 0		
Correct amount	22,000		
Necessary correction		+22,000	

For 1994:

	1993	1994	
Reported	$22,000		
Correct amount	0		
Necessary correction			−22,000

4. Truck rental:

		1993	1994
Correct expense for 1993 ($12,000 ÷ 2 × 3/4 year)		−4,500	
Correct expense for 1994 ($12,000 ÷ 2)			−6,000
Correct Net Income		$189,700	$58,900

True-False Questions

1. T
2. T The sale occurs when the project is completed and delivered.
3. F This statement describes product costs.
4. F The matching principle implies that a relationship exists between expenses and revenues.
5. T
6. T
7. F Product costs are incurred in the acquisition or manufacture of goods.
8. T
9. F Revenue is recognized as work is completed.
10. F Losses are usually incurred involuntarily; this statement describes expenses.
11. T
12. T
13. F A high degree of uncertainty must exist.
14. T
15. F Under the installment basis, revenue is recognized as cash is collected.
16. F Most assets are measured in terms of historical costs.
17. T
18. F The stable dollar assumption is that fluctuations in the value of the dollar are insignificant and may be ignored.
19. T
20. F Transactions have a dual effect.

1. A
2. B
3. B
4. D
5. C
6. A
7. D
8. D   The exchange price, matching, and realization principles are all GAAP.
9. C   The accountant must make a decision regarding the following: depreciation method, useful life, amount to capitalize including freight, installation costs, cash discount deductions available, and estimated salvage value.
10. B
11. C
12. D
13. A
14. B
15. A
16. D

CHAPTER

13

CORPORATIONS: FORMATION, ADMINISTRATION, AND CLASSES OF CAPITAL STOCK

Learning Objectives

1. State the advantages and disadvantages of the corporate form of business.
2. List the values commonly associated with capital stock and give their definitions.
3. List the various kinds of stock and describe the differences between them.
4. Present in proper form the stockholders' equity section of a balance sheet.
5. Account for the issuances of stock for cash, by subscription, and for other assets.
6. Determine book values of both preferred and common stock.

CHAPTER OUTLINE

THE CORPORATION

1. A corporation is an entity recognized by law as possessing an existence separate and distinct from its owners, the stockholders.

ADVANTAGES OF THE CORPORATE FORM OF BUSINESS

2. The advantages offered to investors by the corporate form of business include the following:
   a. easy transferability of shares.
   b. limited liability to the shareholders.
   c. perpetual life.
   d. easy capital generation.
   e. opportunity to employ professional management.
   f. separation of owners and entity.

DISADVANTAGES OF THE CORPORATE FORM OF BUSINESS

3. The disadvantages of the corporate form of business include:
   a. taxation of income to the corporation and of distributed income to stockholders.
   b. greater government regulation than other forms of business.
   c. possibility of management becoming entrenched and looking out only for its own interests.
   d. limited ability to raise creditor capital.

INCORPORATING

4. The precise requirements that must be met by the incorporators are enumerated in the various states' laws.
   a. A charter is the contract between the state and the incorporators and their successors which permits them to operate as a corporation.

ARTICLES OF INCORPORATION

   a. Articles of incorporation comprise the application for the charter and include information regarding the types and amounts of stock to be issued.

5. The charter specifies the number of shares the corporation is authorized to issue and the par value, if any, to be attached to each share.

   a. All authorized shares need not be issued immediately.

   b. Outstanding stock is stock that has been authorized, subsequently issued, and is currently held by stockholders.

ORGANIZATION COSTS

6. Costs of organizing a corporation should be debited to the Organization Costs account and reported on the balance sheet as an intangible asset.

7. The basic rights of stockholders include the right to:

   a. dispose of their shares of stock.

   b. subscribe for additional shares from new issues of stock of the class owned in proportion to their holdings at the new issue date. (This is the preemptive right.)

   c. share in income when declared as dividends.

   d. receive a proportionate share of undistributed assets in excess of creditors' claims at the time of liquidation.

   e. share in management by voting at stockholders' meetings. This right may be signed over to a designated person in a proxy.

DIRECTING THE CORPORATION

8. The board of directors is elected by the stockholders.

   a. It, in turn, appoints administrative officers and delegates authority to them.

   b. It declares dividends when deemed appropriate.

   c. It establishes executive salaries.

   d. At its first meeting it adopts the bylaws which specify the power of the directors, method of selecting officers, and manner of calling stockholders' meetings.

DOCUMENTS, BOOKS, AND RECORDS RELATING TO CAPITAL STOCK

9. A stockholders' ledger contains an account for each stockholder and shows the number of shares held, the certificate numbers, and the dates of acquisition and sale. The minutes book is a written record of the actions taken at board of directors' and stockholders' meetings.

PAR VALUE AND NO-PAR CAPITAL STOCK

10. Each share of stock may or may not have a par or stated value attached to it.

    a. Par value is an arbitrary amount specified in the charter and assigned to each share. It is the amount credited to the Capital Stock account for each share issued.

    b. Stated value is a value assigned to no-par stock by the board of directors and is the amount credited to the Capital Stock account for each share issued.

    c. Shares may be without par or stated value, in which case the entire amount received is credited to the Capital Stock account.

    d. Other values commonly associated with capital stock include market value, book value, liquidation value, and redemption value.

CAPITAL STOCK AUTHORIZED AND OUTSTANDING

11. Capital stock authorized is the number of shares of stock the corporation is authorized to issue. Outstanding stock is stock that has been authorized and issued and is currently held by stockholders.

CLASSES OF CAPITAL STOCK

12. The two ordinary classes of stock which may be issued are common and preferred. Common represents the residual equity in the corporation; all other claims must be settled before the claims of the common stockholders.

TYPES OF PREFERRED STOCK

13. Preferred may be preferred as to dividends and consequently may be:
    1. cumulative—all dividends in arrears must be paid before dividends can be paid on common.
    2. noncumulative—a dividend passed need not be paid in any future year.
    3. participating—under certain circumstances it may receive a dividend greater than its stated basic dividend.
    4. nonparticipating—it is entitled to its basic dividend only.

14. Preferred may also be:
    1. preferred as to assets in the event of liquidation. A liquidation value may be stated in the stock contract.
    2. convertible into specified numbers of shares of common stock at the stockholders' option.
    3. nonconvertible.
    4. callable if the issuing corporation can request the stockholders to surrender their shares, often at a call price.

BALANCE SHEET PRESENTATION OF STOCK

15. The stockholders' equity section of a corporation's balance sheet contains two main elements, paid-in capital and retained earnings.
    a. Paid-in capital results from cash or other assets invested by owners and shows classes of capital stock.
    b. Retained earnings result from income earned but not distributed as dividends.

STOCK ISSUANCES FOR CASH

16. Stock may be issued for cash. The Cash account is debited for the proceeds received, the appropriate stock account is credited for the par or stated value, and any proceeds received in excess of par or stated value are credited to a Paid-in Capital in Excess of Par (or Stated) Value account. The Paid-In Capital in Excess of Par (or Stated) Value account should be shown separately in the stockholders' equity section of the balance sheet for each class of stock issued.

RECORDING CAPITAL STOCK ISSUED BY SUBSCRIPTION

17. The issuance of stock through subscriptions involves several steps.
    a. When stock subscriptions are accepted, a Subscriptions Receivable account is debited and a Stock Subscribed account credited.
    b. When the subscriptions are collected, an appropriate asset account is debited and the Subscriptions Receivable account is credited.
    c. When the stock is finally issued, the Stock Subscribed account is debited and the stock account is credited.
    d. If the price received for the shares is greater than the par or stated value, the Stock Subscribed account is credited for the par or stated value and a Paid-In Capital in Excess of Par (or Stated) Value account is credited for the difference.
    e. The Stock Subscribed account is shown in the stockholders' equity section of the balance sheet if the stock remains unissued at the end of the period.

18. If a subscriber defaults on a subscription contract, the action taken by the corporation depends upon the applicable state laws.
    a. The subscriber may receive as many shares as the subscriber has paid for in full and the balance of the contract may be canceled.
    b. The amount paid in may be refunded, often less expenses to resell the shares and any loss incurred.
    c. The amount paid in may be forfeited to the corporation, in which case the amount retained is credited to Paid-In Capital from Defaulted Subscriptions.

BOOK VALUE

19. Book value is the stockholders' equity per share.

    a. Book value of preferred stock is equal to the liquidation value plus any dividends in arrears and/or currently payable. These dividends in arrears are expressed in per share terms.

    b. Book value of common stock is what remains after all amounts assignable to preferred stock issues are deducted from total stockholders' equity.

CAPITAL STOCK ISSUED FOR PROPERTY OR SERVICES

20. When stock is issued for property or services, it is recorded at either the fair value of the property or services received, or of the shares issued, whichever is more clearly evident.

BALANCE SHEET PRESENTATION OF PAID-IN CAPITAL IN EXCESS OF PAR (OR STATED) VALUE—COMMON OR PREFERRED

21. The amounts received in excess of par or stated value are carried in a separate owners' equity account as Paid-In Capital in Excess of Par (or Stated) Value—Common or Preferred.

DEMONSTRATION PROBLEM

On January 4 of this year, Helen Corporation was organized with an authorization of 30,000 shares of 8% cumulative preferred stock, $200 par and 100,000 shares of $2 par common stock.

The following selected transactions occurred during the first year of operations:

Jan 30: Issued 175 shares of preferred stock to an attorney in payment of a bill for $40,000 of legal fees for the organization of the corporation.

Jan. 31: Issued 20,000 shares of common stock at $40 per share for cash.

Feb. 8: Issued 60,000 shares of common stock in exchange for land, buildings, equipment, and patents with fair market values of $800,000, $1,800,000, $600,000, and $101,000 respectively.

July 16: Received subscription for 10,000 shares of preferred stock at par value; received 60% of subscription price in cash; remainder due in three months.

Oct. 10: Received the remaining 40% preferred stock subscription payment; stock certificates are issued.

Required:

a. Record journal entries for the above transactions.

b. Prepare the stockholders' equity section of the balance sheet as of December 31, the end of the current year. A loss of $1,000,000 is incurred for the year.

DATE		ACCOUNT TITLES AND EXPLANATION	POST. REF.	DEBIT	CREDIT
a.					

b.

SOLUTION TO DEMONSTRATION PROBLEM

a.

Jan. 30 Organization Costs 40,000
        Preferred Stock 35,000
        Paid-in Capital in Excess of Par Value—Preferred 5,000
        To record the receipt of legal services for captial stock.

Jan. 31 Cash 800,000
        Common Stock 40,000
        Paid-in Capital in Excess of Par Value—Common 760,000
        To record the issuance of common stock. (20,000 shares @ $40)

Feb. 8 Land 800,000
      Buildings 1,800,000
      Equipment 600,000
      Patents 101,000
        Common Stock 120,000
        Paid-In Capital in Excess of Par Value—Common 3,181,000
        To record the receipt of assets for capital stock.

July 16 Subscriptions Receivable—Preferred 2,000,000
        Preferred Stock Subscribed 2,000,000
        Subscriptions received for 10,000 shares of preferred stock.

        Cash 1,200,000
        Subscriptions Receivable—Preferred 1,200,000
        Received 60% on each of the subscriptions.

Oct. 10 Cash 800,000
        Subscriptions Receivable—Preferred 800,000
        To record collection of the remaining subscriptions.

        Preferred Stock Subscribed 2,000,000
        Preferred Stock 2,000,000
        Certificate issued for 10,000 shares paid in full.

b.   Stockholders' Equity

Paid-in Capital:

Preferred stock, $200 par value, 8% cumulative (30,000 shares authorized, 10,175 shares issued and outstanding)	$2,035,000	
Paid-in capital in excess of par value—Preferred stock	5,000	$2,040,000
Common stock, $2 par (100,000 shares authorized, 80,000 shares issued and outstanding)	$ 160,000	
Paid-in capital in excess of par value—Common stock	3,941,000	4,101,000
Total paid-in capital		$6,141,000
Retained earnings		(1,000,000)
Total stockholders' equity		$5,141,000

MATCHING

Referring to the terms listed below, place the appropriate letter next to the corresponding description.

a. Call premium (on preferred stock)
b. Liquidation value
c. Cumulative preferred stock
d. Organization costs
e. Participating preferred stock
f. Common stock
g. Code of regulations (bylaws)
h. Minutes book
i. Capital stock authorized
j. Preemptive right
k. Par value
l. Subscription

_____ 1. The stock that a corporation is entitled to issue as designated in its charter.

_____ 2. An intangible asset consisting of the various costs incurred in bringing a corporation into existence.

_____ 3. The record book in which actions taken at stockholders' and board of directors' meetings are recorded.

_____ 4. The right to receive a basic dividend each year accumulates if not paid.

_____ 5. A contract to acquire a certain number of shares of stock, at a specified price, with payment to be made at a specified date or dates.

_____ 6. The right of stockholders to subscribe to additional shares of the same class of stock they hold in any subsequent issuance of new shares.

_____ 7. Shares of stock representing the residual equity in the corporation.

_____ 8. The difference between the amount at which a corporation may call its preferred stock for redemption and the par value of the stock.

_____ 9. A set of rules or regulations adopted by the board of directors of a corporation to govern the conduct of corporate affairs within the general laws of the state and the policies and purposes stated or implied in the corporate charter.

_____ 10. The amount to be paid per share of preferred stock upon liquidation of the corporation.

_____ 11. An arbitrary amount assigned to each share of a given class of stock and printed on the stock certificate.

_____ 12. A preferred stock that is entitled to receive dividends above the stated preference rate under certain conditions that are stated in the preferred stock contract.

COMPLETION AND EXERCISES

1. How can a corporation determine the number of shares of stock outstanding? _____

_____

_____

2. A corporation may issue preferred stock for the following reasons:

    a. _____

    b. _____

    c. _____

3. The evidence of ownership issued to a stockholder is called a _____ _____.

4. Give the entries if a corporation received subscriptions for 1,000 shares at $15 per share of $5 par value common stock on May 1 and received payment in full on May 27.

DATE		ACCOUNT TITLES AND EXPLANATION	POST. REF.	DEBIT	CREDIT
May	1				
May	27				

5. What are three possible ways of handling defaulted stock subscriptions? (a) _____ _____ , (b) _____ _____ , or (c) _____ _____

6. Most state corporation laws require a minimum of _____ incorporators.

7. The law of each state views a corporation in that state as a _____ corporation and a corporation organized in any other state as a _____ corporation.

8. The _____ is the contract between the state and the incorporators and their successors.

9. The application for a charter is known as the _____ _____ _____ .

10. When does a corporation come into existence?

_____

_____

11. Organization costs are classified on the balance sheet as a(an) _____ asset.

12. What is the source of the authority of the board of directors?

_____

13. A _____ is a document of authority, signed by the stockholder, giving another person the authority to vote the stockholders' shares.

14. From whom do the officers of a corporation derive their authority?

_____

15. What is another name for the code of regulations of a corporation?

_____

16. What is meant by capital stock authorized?

_____

_____

_____

17. What is meant by capital stock outstanding?

_____

_____

18. What are the two ordinary classes of capital stock that may be issued by a corporation?

a. _____

b. _____

19. What is meant when common stock is referred to as the residual equity in a corporation?

_____

_____

20. What is the meaning of par value?

_____

_____

_____

21. What are the advantages of the corporate form of business?

a. _____

b. _____

c. _____

d. _____

e. _____

22. A corporation is an artificial, invisible, intangible being or person created by _____.

23. The balance sheet of May 31 of the Battle Corporation is as follows (no dividends are in arrears or are currently payable):

Total assets		$316,226
Liabilities		$100,226
Preferred stock (500 shares outstanding, 10% noncumulative, nonparticipating $100 par value, $100 liquidation value)	$ 50,000	
Common stock (10,000 shares outstanding, no-par value)	125,000	
Retained earnings	41,000	216,000
Total liabilities and stockholders' equity		$316,226

a. The book value of the preferred stock is $ _____.

b. The book value of the common stock is $ _____.

24. A company issued 100 shares of $100 par value common stock for a parcel of land. No cash price was fixed for the land, but similar parcels in the vicinity had recently sold for $12,500. Prepare the entry for this stock issuance.

			DEBIT	CREDIT

25. If a corporation is obligated to pay arrearages for prior years on preferred stock before paying dividends to the common stockholders, the preferred stock would be called _____ preferred stock.

26. On May 4, a corporation issued for cash 200,000 shares of its no-par common stock at $1.75 per share. Prepare the entry for the sale under each of the unrelated assumptions:
   a. The common stock has no stated or legal value assigned to it.
   b. The board voted to place a one dollar per share stated value on the no-par stock.

DATE	ACCOUNT TITLES AND EXPLANATION	POST. REF.	DEBIT	CREDIT
a.				
b.				

27. What is the amount of the credit to the capital stock account for a corporation issuing capital stock without par or stated value?

_____

28. Give the entries if a corporation issued 2,000 shares of $30 par value common stock for $35 a share and if it issued on the same date 1,000 shares of stock in exchange for land.

29. When property or services are received for capital stock, what value is placed on the exchange?

_____

_____

30. The _____ _____ contains supporting detail for the stock accounts contained in the general ledger.

31. The _____ _____ is a written record of the action taken at official meetings of the board of directors and at stockholders' meetings.

32. What is meant by liquidation value of stock?

_____

_____

_____

_____

33. When only common stock is outstanding, how is book value per share calculated?

_____

_____

34. From the following information, compute the book value per share of both preferred and common stock.

Preferred stock, 6% cumulative, par value $50; liquidation value $50
    1,000 shares authorized, issued and outstanding .... $ 50,000
Common stock, without par or stated value; 20,000 shares authorized,
    18,000 shares issued and outstanding 126,000
Retained earnings 94,000
Total stockholders' equity $270,000

Note: Two years dividends are in arrears on the preferred stock, including those for the current year.

TRUE-FALSE QUESTIONS

Indicate whether each of the following statements is true or false by inserting a capital "T" or "F" in the blank space provided.

_____ 1. The major advantages of a corporation over a single proprietorship are sharing of responsibilities and risks, and broadening the base of investment and talent.

_____ 2. The corporate form of business organization is superior to the partnership form for businesses that are long-lived.

_____ 3. Through the use of a proxy, a stockholder gives another person authority to vote his or her shares at a stockholders' meeting.

_____ 4. The par value of a share of common stock must be $100.

_____ 5. The par value of a share of capital stock is an indicator of the market value or book value of a share of stock.

_____ 6. The laws of each state view a corporation organized within the United States as a domestic corporation and a corporation organized in any other state as a foreign corporation.

_____ 7. The stockholders' ledger contains a group of subsidiary accounts for each stockholder that show the number of shares owned, their certificate numbers, and the dates on which shares are acquired or sold.

_____ 8. The corporate book is a record book in which actions taken at stockholders' and board of directors' meetings are recorded.

_____ 9. The total ownership of a corporation rests with the holders of the outstanding shares of stock.

_____ 10. Dividends in arrears on cumulative preferred stock must be paid before any dividends can be paid on common stock.

_____ 11. The rights of stockholders include the power to bind the corporation to contracts.

_____ 12. The receipt of subscriptions to preferred stock without par or stated value is recorded by a debit to Subscriptions Receivable—Preferred and a credit to Preferred Stock Subscribed.

_____ 13. When shares of stock are issued for property other than cash, the exchange may be recorded at the fair market value of the shares issued.

_____ 14. Items that may influence the selection of the state of incorporation include the powers granted a corporation, the taxes levied against it, the reports required of it, and defenses permitted against hostile takeovers.

_____ 15. The issuance of par value stock at a discount may create a contingent liability on stockholders to creditors of the corporation.

MULTIPLE CHOICE QUESTIONS

For each of the following questions indicate the best answer by circling the appropriate letter.

1. The amount per share that a corporation agrees to pay if it elects to call its stock for retirement is known as:
   A. redemption price.
   B. market price.
   C. subscription price.
   D. par value.

2. All of the following are advantages of the corporate form of organization except:

   A. continuity of life.
   B. government supervision
   C. separate legal entity.
   D. no mutual agency.

Questions 3–5. Slate Corporation accepted subscriptions for 2,000 shares of its $200 par value preferred stock at $196 per share.

3. The entry to record the subscription is:

   A. Subscriptions Receivable 392,000
      Discount on Preferred Stock 8,000
         Preferred Stock Subscribed 400,000
   B. Subscriptions Receivable 400,000
         Preferred Stock Subscribed 400,000
   C. Cash 392,000
         Preferred Stock Subscribed 392,000
   D. Subscriptions Receivable 392,000
      Discount on Preferred Stock 8,000
         Preferred Stock 400,000

4. Received 20% down payment from the preferred stock subscribers:

   A. Subscriptions Receivable 78,400
         Cash 78,400
   B. Cash 78,400
         Subscriptions Receivable 78,400
   C. Cash 78,400
         Preferred Stock 78,400
   D. Cash 78,400
      Discount on Preferred Stock 1,600
         Subscriptions Receivable 80,000

5. Received the balance due on stock subscriptions and issued the shares:

   A. Preferred Stock 400,000
         Preferred Stock Subscribed 400,000
   B. Cash 313,600
         Preferred Stock 313,600
   C. Cash 313,600
         Subscriptions Receivable 313,600
      Preferred Stock Subscribed 400,000
         Preferred Stock 400,000
   D. Cash 313,600
      Discount on Stock 86,400
         Preferred Stock 400,000

Questions 6–8. The Tiger Corporation had the following two classes of capital stock outstanding as of December 31, 1994.

6% preferred, $200 par, 1,500 shares outstanding .... $ 300,000
Common stock, $200 par, 7,500 shares outstanding 1,500,000

On December 31, 1994, the Board of Directors declared $180,000 in cash dividends for 1994. Indicate the total dollar amount of the $180,000 that would go to preferred stockholders under each of the following independent cases:

6. If the preferred stock is noncumulative, but fully participating per share of stock, the total dividend to preferred is:
   A. $180,000
   B. $18,000
   C. $21,000
   D. $30,000

7. If the preferred stock is noncumulative and nonparticipating, the total dividend to preferred is:
   A. $180,000
   B. $18,000
   C. $30,000
   D. $36,000
   E. None of the above.

8. If the preferred stock is cumulative but nonparticipating and dividends are in arrears from 1992, the total to preferred is:
   A. $90,000
   B. $36,000
   C. $54,000
   D. $18,000

9. Given the following information: Capital Stock $60,000 ($20 par), Premium on Capital Stock $150,000, Retained Earnings $300,000. Assuming only one class of stock, the book value per share is:
   A. $170
   B. $20
   C. $70
   D. $100
   E. None of the above.

SOLUTIONS

Matching

1.	i	7.	f
2.	d	8.	a
3.	h	9.	g
4.	c	10.	b
5.	l	11.	k
6.	j	12.	e

Completion and Exercises

1. A corporation can determine the number of shares outstanding by summing the shares shown on the open stubs or stubs without certificates attached in the stock certificate book.

2. A company may issue preferred stock for the following reasons:

   a. To avoid the use of bonds that have fixed interest charges that must be paid regardless of the company's profitability.

   b. To avoid issuing so many additional shares of common stock that earnings per share will be less in the current year than in prior years'.

   c. To avoid diluting the common stockholders' control of the corporation, since preferred stockholders have no voting rights.

3. stock certificate

4.

May 1	Subscriptions Receivable—Common	15,000	
	Common Stock Subscribed		5,000
	Paid-in Capital in Excess of Par Value—Common		10,000
	To record receipt of common stock subscriptions at $15.		
May 27	Cash	15,000	
	Subscriptions Receivable—Common		15,000
	To record collection of the common stock subscribed on May 1.		
	Common Stock Subscribed	5,000	
	Common Stock		5,000
	Stock certificates issued for 1,000 shares paid in full.		

5. (a) The subscriber may receive as many shares as are equal to the amount paid in divided by the per share subscription price, with the balance of the contract canceled; (b) the amount paid in for the defaulted shares less costs of selling and any loss incurred may be refunded; or (c) the amount paid in may be declared forfeited to the corporation. The specific method used depends on applicable state laws.

6. three

7. domestic; foreign

8. charter

9. articles of incorporation

10. when the articles of incorporation are approved and the charter is granted

11. intangible

12. the stockholders

13. proxy

14. the board of directors

15. the bylaws

16. the number of shares and par value, if any, per share of each class of stock that the corporate charter will permit to be issued.

17. the shares authorized, issued, and currently held by stockholders

18. (a) preferred stock; (b) common stock

19. This reference means that all claims rank ahead of the claims of the common stockholders.

20. Par value is an arbitrarily assigned dollar amount appearing on stock certificates that serves as the basis for the credit to the capital stock account.

21. (a) transferable shares; (b) limited liability; (c) continuous existence; (d) opportunity to employ professional management; (e) separation of owners and entity

22. law

23. a. Preferred stock

   $50,000 \div 500$ shares $= $100

   b. Common stock

   $216,000

   $- 50,000

   $166,000 \div 10,000$ shares $= $16.60

24. Land 12,500
      Common Stock 10,000
      Paid-in Capital in Excess of Par Value—Common Stock 2,500
25. cumulative
26. a. Cash 350,000
      Common Stock 350,000
  b. Cash 350,000
      Common Stock 200,000
      Paid-in Capital in Excess of Stated Value—Common Stock 150,000
27. The entire amount received for the stock.
28. Cash 70,000
      Common Stock 60,000
      Paid-in Capital in Excess of Par—Common 10,000
    To record issuance of common stock.
    Land 35,000
      Common Stock 30,000
      Paid-In Capital in Excess of Par—Common 5,000
    To record issuance of common stock for land.
29. The fair market value of the property or services received or of the stock issued, whichever is more clearly evident.
30. stockholders' ledger
31. minutes book
32. The liquidation value is the amount a stockholder would receive if a corporation were to discontinue operations and liquidate by selling its assets, paying its liabilities, and distributing the remaining cash among the stockholders.
33. Book value per share is calculated by dividing stockholders' equity by the number of shares outstanding.
34.

	Total	Per share
Total stockholders' equity	$270,000	
Book value of preferred stock (1,000 shares):		
Liquidation value	$50,000	
Dividends (two years at $3,000)	6,000	56,000 $56.00
Book value of common stock (18,000 shares)		$214,000 11.89

True-False Questions

1. T
2. T The business continues to exist even when the ownership changes.
3. T
4. F The par value may be any amount.
5. F
6. F
7. T
8. F The minutes book retains these records.
9. T
10. T
11. F Stockholders are not agents of the corporation.
12. T
13. T The fair market value of what was given up or what was received is used, whichever is more clearly determinable.

14. T
15. T

1. A
2. B
3. A
4. B
5. C
6. D   Basic dividend to preferred, $18,000 (or $12 per share); Common gets $12 × 7,500 shares = $90,000; of the remaining $72,000 of dividends, each share of stock receives $8 (or $72,000 ÷ 9,000 shares). Thus, preferred stockholders receive $18,000 + ($8 × 1,500) = $30,000.
7. B   ($300,000 × .06) = $18,000.
8. C   (3 × $18,000) = $54,000.
9. A $60,000 ÷ $20 = 3,000 shares; ($60,000 + $150,000 + $300,000) ÷ 3,000 shares = $170.

CHAPTER

14

CORPORATIONS: PAID-IN CAPITAL, RETAINED EARNINGS, DIVIDENDS, AND TREASURY STOCK

Learning Objectives

1. *Identify the different sources of paid-in capital and describe how they would be presented on a balance sheet.*
2. *Account for a cash dividend, a stock dividend, a stock split, and a retained earnings appropriation.*
3. *Account for the acquisition and reissuance of treasury stock.*
4. *Describe the proper accounting treatment of discontinued operations, extraordinary items, and changes in accounting principles.*
5. *Define prior period adjustments and show their proper presentation in the financial statements.*
6. *Compute earnings per share.*

CHAPTER OUTLINE

PAID-IN CAPITAL OR CONTRIBUTED CAPITAL

1. Capital contributed by stockholders includes:

   a. The par or stated value or amount received for shares without par or stated value.

   b. Amounts in excess of par or stated value, including capital from recapitalization and capital from treasury stock transactions.

   c. Capital donated in the form of assets.

RETAINED EARNINGS

2. Stockholders' equity generally consists of two elements: Paid-In Capital and Retained Earnings.

3. Total retained earnings generally results from the difference between a corporation's net income earned from the date of incorporation to the present and the dividends declared during the same period.

   a. Net income increases retained earnings.

   b. Dividends reduce retained earnings.

   c. A debit balance in Retained Earnings represents a deficit.

4. A retained earnings appropriation represents a segregation of retained earnings.

   a. An appropriation is created:

      (1) to restrict the distribution of retained earnings as dividends because of the need to reinvest earnings or the need to fulfill an expected obligation.

      (2) by debiting Retained Earnings and crediting an appropriately titled appropriation account.

   b. The appropriation is shown in the balance sheet in the stockholders' equity section as a part of total retained earnings.

CASH DIVIDENDS

5. Dividends are distributions made by a corporation to its stockholders.

   a. Cash is normally distributed, but other types of assets may be distributed.

   b. The declaration date is the date on which the board of directors declares the dividend payable.

   c. The date of record is the date used to determine to whom the dividend will be paid.

   d. The date of payment is the date on which the actual payment is made.

   e. Dividends are generally distributed from retained earnings.

      (1) When the dividend (or dividends) is declared, Retained Earnings is debited and Dividends Payable is credited.

      (2) When the dividend is paid, the payable is debited and the appropriate asset account (usually Cash) is credited.

STOCK DIVIDENDS

6. Stock dividends involve the distribution of additional shares of capital stock.

   a. Stock dividends are declared for several reasons:

      (1) Retained earnings may be large, but cash may be low, precluding the payment of cash dividends.

      (2) The corporation may want to permanently capitalize some of the retained earnings.

      (3) The firm may wish to increase the number of shares outstanding and thereby decrease the market price if it is currently too high.

   b. The distributions usually involve the same class of stock as that held by the stockholders.

c. Total stockholders' equity is not affected; retained earnings is decreased and paid-in capital is increased by equal amounts.

d. A stockholders' percentage ownership in the corporation is not affected.

e. Small stock dividends of less than 20-25% of the previously outstanding shares are recorded at the fair market value of the shares issued.

   (1) When the dividend is declared, a Stock Dividend Distributable account is credited for the par or stated value of the shares, if any, or for the total amount of shares without par or stated value.

   (2) A Paid-In Capital—Stock Dividend account is credited for any amount above par or stated value.

   (3) A Dividends account is debited for the total fair market value of the shares issued.

   (4) When the dividend is issued, the distributable account is debited and a stock account is credited.

   (5) The stock dividend distributable is not a liability but is part of the stockholders' equity.

7. Large stock dividends of greater than 20-25% of the previously outstanding shares are assumed to have the primary objective of reducing the market price of the stock and are recorded at the par or stated value of shares issued.

STOCK SPLITS

8. Stock splits are distributions of additional shares of an issuing corporation's stock for which the corporation receives no assets. Usually the par value per share is reduced so that total par value of outstanding shares remains the same.

LIQUIDATING DIVIDENDS

9. Dividends from permanent capital, rather than retained earnings, are allowed in certain cases and are known as liquidating dividends. The legality of a dividend generally depends upon the amount of retained earnings available for dividends.

10. A statement of retained earnings is prepared to explain the changes in retained earnings that occurred between two balance sheet dates.

TREASURY STOCK

11. Treasury stock is capital stock that has been issued and then reacquired by the issuing corporation. It has not been canceled and may be reissued.

a. Treasury stock may be acquired by purchase or in settlement of a debt owed to the corporation.

b. Dividends should not be paid on treasury stock, nor is the stock voting stock.

c. In many cases, an amount of retained earnings equal to the cost of treasury stock is legally unavailable for dividends until the stock is reissued.

d. When the stock is reacquired by purchase, a Treasury Stock account is debited for the cost of the shares.

e. Reissues are credited to a Treasury Stock account.

   (1) If the reissue price is above cost, the difference is credited to Paid-In Capital—Treasury Stock Transactions.

   (2) If the reissue price is less than cost, the difference is debited to Paid-In Capital—Treasury Stock Transactions up to the amount of any credit balance in that account. The remainder is debited to Retained Earnings.

NET INCOME INCLUSIONS AND EXCLUSIONS

12. The net income for a period includes extraordinary items and the cumulative effect on prior years' income of an accounting change and excludes prior period adjustments.

a. A discontinued operation occurs when a segment, usually unprofitable, is sold or abandoned. The income or loss, net of tax effect, from the segment's operations for the portion of the current year before it was discontinued is shown. The gain or loss, net of tax effect, on disposal of the segment is shown. Discontinued operations appear on the income statement after income from continuing operations and before extraordinary items.

b. Extraordinary items are material, unusual, and nonrecurring items that have an income or loss effect. They are to be reported, net of their tax effects, if any, on the income statement after discontinued operations and before changes in accounting principle.

c. The cumulative effects on prior years of accounting changes are to be reported on the income statement after extraordinary items.

d. Prior period adjustments are material adjustments that are primarily recognizable by their easy identification with specific prior periods. They consist almost solely of the effects on prior years of corrections of accounting errors. Such effects are to be reported net of their tax effects, if any, in the statement of retained earnings as adjustments of the beginning retained earnings balance.

EARNINGS PER SHARE

13. Earnings per share (EPS) is a major item of interest to investors and potential investors. EPS is usually calculated and presented for each major category on the face of the income statement.

DEMONSTRATION PROBLEM

The following entries represent selected transactions that occurred during the year for Lewis Company.

Jan. 12 Purchased 2,000 shares of the company's own common stock at $18. There were 45,000 shares of $10 par common stock outstanding prior to the 2,000 share purchase.

Mar. 5 The board of directors declared a $5 per share semiannual dividend on the 5,000 shares of preferred stock and $2 per share dividend on the common stock to stockholders of record on March 15, payable on March 25.

Mar. 25 Paid the cash dividends.

May 10 Received cash for the sale of 700 shares of treasury stock at $21.

Sept. 5 The board of directors again declared $5 per share dividend on the outstanding preferred stock and $3 per share dividend on the common stock. The board also voted a 4% common stock dividend on the common stock outstanding. The fair market value of the common stock to be issued is estimated at $16 per share. The date of record for all dividends is October 1, and the date of payment is October 10.

Oct. 10 Paid the cash dividends and issued the stock certificates for the common stock dividend.

Required: Prepare the necessary journal entries to record the above transactions.

DATE	ACCOUNT TITLES AND EXPLANATION	POST. REF.	DEBIT	CREDIT

SOLUTION TO DEMONSTRATION PROBLEM

LEWIS COMPANY

Jan. 12	Treasury Stock—Common (2,000 × $18)	36,000	
	Cash		36,000
Mar. 5	Retained Earnings	111,000	
	Dividends Payable		111,000

$5 × 5,000   shares = $ 25,000
$2 × 43,000 shares =   86,000
                     $111,000

Mar. 25	Dividends Payable	111,000	
	Cash		111,000
May 10	Cash	14,700	
	Paid-In Capital—Common Treasury Stock Transactions		2,100
	Treasury Stock—Common (700 × $18)		12,600
Sept. 5	Retained Earnings	156,100	
	Dividends Payable		156,100

$5 × 5,000   shares = $ 25,000
$3 × 43,700 shares = 131,100
                     $156,100

	Retained Earnings (1,748 shares × $16)	27,968	
	Stock Dividend Distributable—Common		17,480
	Paid-In Capital—Stock Dividends (1,748 × $6)		10,488

43,700 × 4% = 1,748 shares

Oct. 10	Dividend Payable	156,100	
	Cash		156,100
	Stock Dividend Distributable—Common	17,480	
	Common Stock		17,480

MATCHING

Referring to the terms listed below, place the appropriate letter next to the corresponding description.

a. Liquidating dividends	e. Date of declaration of dividends	i. Prior period adjustments
b. Extraordinary items	f. Stock dividends	j. Stock Dividend Distributable
c. Treasury stock	g. Appropriation of retained earnings	k. Common Stock
d. Net-of-tax effect	h. Paid-in Capital—Treasury Stock Transactions	l. Date of record

_____ 1. An account created as a voluntary or contractual restriction on retained earnings and designed to inform readers of the existence of the restriction.

_____ 2. Dividends that are a return of contributed capital, not a distribution to be charged to retained earnings.

_____ 3. An account created when a corporation reacquires shares of its own outstanding capital stock at one price and later reissues them at a higher price.

_____ 4. The date on which the board of directors formally states the intention of the corporation to pay a dividend.

5. Material adjustments that have an income or loss effect and result from accounting errors made in prior accounting periods.

6. A dividend payable in additional shares of the declaring corporation's stock.

7. Used for discontinued operations, extraordinary items, accounting changes, and prior period adjustments whereby items are shown at the dollar amounts remaining after deducting the effects on such items of income tax obligations payable currently.

8. Shares of capital stock issued and reacquired by the issuing corporation that have not been formally canceled or retired and are available for reissue.

9. Gains and losses that are unusual in nature and nonrecurring.

10. A stockholders' equity account credited for the par or stated value of the shares to be distributed when a stock dividend is declared.

COMPLETION AND EXERCISES

1. A corporation has $100,000 of common stock ($10 par) outstanding. In July a stock dividend of one share for each five shares was issued. In November of the same year, a 20-cent cash dividend per share is paid to the stockholders. The total amount of cash dividends paid to the stockholders is _____ .

2. A company was authorized to issue 3,000 shares of no-par value common stock for which the directors voted to assign a stated value of $10 per share. In addition, the following transactions occurred for which you are asked to prepare journal entries.

May 1 Received a donation of 400 shares of the company's stock.
   10 Reacquired 100 shares of its stock at $12 per share. These shares were originally issued at $11 per share.
   20 Sold the donated treasury stock for $17 per share.
   28 Sold, for $15 per share, 70 shares of the treasury stock reacquired May 10.

DATE	ACCOUNT TITLES AND EXPLANATION	POST. REF.	DEBIT	CREDIT

3. The date of _____ is established by the board to determine which individual stockholders are entitled to any dividends that have been declared.

4. When a corporation reacquires some of its own previously issued and fully paid stock, which it does not cancel or reissue, such stock is termed _____ stock.

Chapter 14

5. The periodic payments made by a corporation to its stockholders are known as _____.

6. The _____ value is the price at which a share of stock is bought or sold at a particular moment.

7. What is treasury stock?

_____

_____

_____

8. When treasury stock is reissued, the excess of reissue price over cost is credited to _____

_____

_____.

9. A separate paid-in capital account is used for each _____ of capital.

10. A liquidating dividend returns a portion of the corporation's _____ capital to its stockholders.

11. An appropriation of retained earnings does not involve segregating a sum of _____.

12. The statement that summarizes part of the change in stockholders' equity (that part brought about by net income and the payment of dividends) is called the _____ _____ _____

_____.

13. Dividends paid in cash are usually debited to _____ _____.

14. What effect do stock dividends have on the total amount of stockholders' equity?

_____

_____

_____

15. When a corporation receives assets as donated capital, at what amount is the transaction recorded?

_____

16. Differentiate between small stock dividends and large stock dividends and the value used in recording each type of dividend. _____

_____

_____

_____

_____

_____

_____

17. a. A corporation that is being sued wishes to establish a retained earnings appropriation for $50,000. Show the required entry.

DATE	ACCOUNT TITLES AND EXPLANATION	POST. REF.	DEBIT	CREDIT

b. If the final judgment is for $25,000, show the entries for paying the judgment and closing the appropriation.

DATE	ACCOUNT TITLES AND EXPLANATION	POST. REF.	DEBIT	CREDIT

18. What are the two major elements of stockholders' equity in a corporation?

_____

19. When the Retained Earnings account has a debit balance it is called a _____.

20. What is the purpose of creating a retained earnings appropriation?

_____

_____

_____

21. On January 1, 1994, the Appropriation for Plant Expansion and Retained Earnings accounts for Sanders, Inc., appeared as follows:

Appropriation for Plant Expansion .... $ 90,000
Retained Earnings 950,000

The essential facts that related to retained earnings during the year are as follows:

Cash dividends declared $170,000
Increase in appropriation for plant expansion 50,000
Net income for year 410,000
Stock dividends declared 190,000

Prepare a statement of retained earnings for the current year. (Use the form on the next page.)

22. Prepare the necessary general journal entries required in the following transactions of Smitt Company:

1. Increased the retained earnings appropriation for plant expansion by $20,000.
2. The Board of Directors declared a regular quarterly dividend of $5 per share. 24,000 shares have been issued but 4,000 shares have been acquired as treasury stock and are still retained.
3. The dividends were paid.
4. The par value per share of the common stock outstanding was reduced from $100 par to $50; each stockholder received two new shares for each old share held.

23. An item that has a material income or loss effect and is unusual and nonrecurring is called an _____ _____ and is reported in the _____ _____ net of its _____ _____.

24. A material adjustment that is characterized primarily as a correction of an error in a previously published financial statement is called a _____ _____ _____. It is reported in the _____ _____ _____ _____, net of its _____ _____.

25. Changes in accounting principle are changes in _____ _____, which are reported in the _____ _____, net of their tax effects.

26. Whether an item is unusual and nonrecurring is to be determined by reference to the _____ in which the firm operates. Thus, a loss on the sale of a plant asset probably _____ (would/would not) be classified as an extraordinary item.

27. From the following information on the Marilyn Corporation, prepare an income statement for the year 1994.

Expenses (not including federal income taxes) $32,000,000
Revenues 37,000,000
Loss from earthquake 675,000

Assume a 50% federal income tax rate. The earthquake causing the loss was the first experienced in the area in which the company operates.

(Use the form on the next page.)

28. From the following information pertaining to Brown Corporation, prepare the stockholders' equity section of the balance sheet. The information is as of December 31, 1994.

Total retained earnings	$505,000
Preferred stock—$50 par value; authorized 5,000 shares; issued and outstanding 3,000 shares	
Common stock—$5 par value; 1,000,000 shares authorized; 600,000 shares issued	
Retained earnings appropriated for pending litigation	$125,000
Cost of treasury stock held—common	$ 90,000
Number of shares of treasury stock held	15,000 shares
Paid-in capital in excess of par value—common	$675,000
Paid-in capital from treasury stock transactions	$ 25,000
Paid-in capital from stock dividend	$330,000

29. Trett Company's common stock has a par value of $200 per share, which was issued at $220 per share; it has no preferred stock. Trett Company reacquired 400 shares at a cost of $274 per share on January 5. On July 10 the company sold half of the shares for $300 per share. Later, on December 8, the company sold the remaining shares for $250 per share.

Required: Prepare journal entries to record the above transactions.

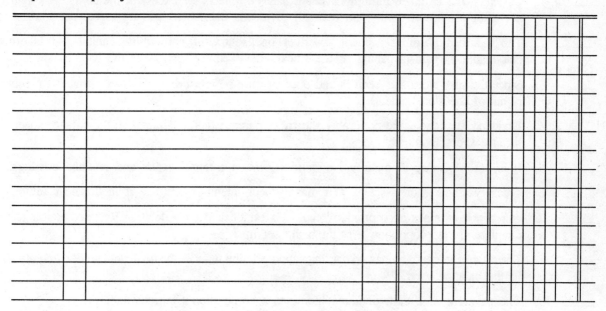

30. The Rug Company has authorized an outstanding 10,000 shares of $100 par value common stock. On June 1, 1994, the Rug Company declared a dividend of $2 per share to stockholders of record date on June 15, 1994, to be paid on July 15, 1994. Give the appropriate entries.

TRUE-FALSE QUESTIONS

Indicate whether each of the following statements is true or false by inserting a capital "T" or "F" in the blank space provided.

_____ 1. Basically, the Retained Earnings account balance reflects the excess of the company's aggregate net income since its formation over all dividends distributed and aggregate net losses.

_____ 2. The Retained Earnings account describes one source of corporation capital and is properly classifiable as paid-in capital in the stockholders' equity section of the balance sheet.

_____ 3. Since treasury stock has been issued once, it may be reissued without violating the preemptive rights of the stockholders.

_____ 4. Dividend restrictions are preferably shown by parenthetical comments in the balance sheet or by balance sheet footnotes.

_____ 5. It is not necessary to make a distinction between common stock and retained earnings.

_____ 6. Treasury stock is an asset only if management intends to reissue it in the near future.

_____ 7. A retained earnings appropriation account is established by a debit to Retained Earnings and a credit to the appropriation account being set up.

_____ 8. The establishment of a retained earnings appropriation reduces the total stockholders' equity shown in the balance sheet.

_____ 9. The payment of a cash dividend increases a corporation's current liabilities.

_____ 10. The date of declaration is the date used to determine to whom a dividend will be paid.

_____ 11. The declaration and issuance of a stock dividend does not change the total amount of stockholders' equity in the corporation.

_____ 12. The balance in the Treasury Stock account basically represents the cost of a company's own stock that was issued and then reacquired.

_____ 13. When treasury stock is purchased, the amount of issued stock is reduced.

_____ 14. A purchase of treasury stock does not affect stockholders' equity.

_____ 15. Dividends are expenses since they decrease stockholders' equity.

_____ 16. No-par stock may be more valuable than par value stock.

_____ 17. At the date of record of a cash dividend, an entry is made on the books of the corporation debiting Retained Earnings and crediting Dividends Payable for the total amount of dividends declared.

_____ 18. Par value, rather than market value, is used to indicate the legal capital of a corporation.

_____ 19. A "deficit" is an expression indicating a debit balance in the Common Stock account.

_____ 20. A statement of retained earnings for the current period itemizes revenues, expenses, and the net income or net loss for the period.

_____ 21. When treasury stock is purchased, the Retained Earnings account is reduced.

_____ 22. The par value of a share of stock is usually of more significance than book value or market value.

_____ 23. A loss suffered from destruction by a tornado of a firm's manufacturing plant is probably an extraordinary item.

24. A stock dividend declared from retained earnings reduces the retained earnings balance and permanently capitalizes a portion of the retained earnings.

25. Damage suffered by a Florida citrus grower's orange crop from a heavy frost would probably be reported as an extraordinary item.

26. The Paid-In Capital—Donations account is not the most common source of dividend distributions.

27. The retained earnings of a corporation are a part of its paid-in capital or capital surplus.

28. The entire proceeds from the disposal of donated treasury stock are credited to Gain from Donated Stock Transactions.

29. Stock dividends do not affect total stockholders' equity.

30. Treasury stock includes all the corporation's stock described in the company's articles of incorporation.

31. The Dividends account is closed to Income Summary at the end of the period.

32. If the Income Summary account shows a credit balance of $3,000 after all income and expense accounts have been closed, and the Dividends account shows a debit balance of $500, the net income is $2,500.

33. The date of declaration is the date when a liability for dividends becomes effective for the corporation.

34. At the time a company issues bonds payable, the board of directors may take action to disclose that a portion of retained earnings is unavailable for dividends.

MULTIPLE CHOICE QUESTIONS

For each of the following questions indicate the best answer by circling the appropriate letter.

Questions 1–2. Stockholders of Apple Co. donated 1,000 shares of no-par common stock to the corporation. The corporation issued these shares for cash at $40 per share.

1. The entry made for the receipt of the stock is:
   A. Common Stock Receivable
         Paid-In Capital—Donations
   B. Donated Stock
         Common Stock
   C. No entry made
   D. Memo entry made

2. The entry made for the issue of the stock described in Question (1) is:
   A. Cash
         Paid-In Capital—Donations
   B. Cash
         Common Stock
   C. Donated Receivable
         Common Stock
   D. No entry made
   E. Memo entry made

3. The balance sheet of the Brown Co. showed Common Stock (20,000 shares authorized) $25 par, $250,000; Paid-In Capital—Common Stock, $40,000; and Retained Earnings, $150,000. The board of directors declared a 10% stock dividend when the market price of the stock was $45 a share. The credit(s) to the journal entry to record the declaration of the dividend is (are):

   A. Stock Dividend Distributable $25,000
      Paid-In Capital—Common Stock Dividend $20,000
   B. Common Stock $25,000
      Paid-In Capital—Common Stock Dividend $20,000
   C. Retained Earnings $45,000
   D. Common Stock $25,000

4. An individual stockholder is entitled to any dividends that have been declared on stock owned, provided the stock is held on the:

   A. payment date.
   B. purchase date.
   C. date of record.
   D. None of the above.

5. An entry to increase the appropriation for plant expansion is:

   A. Dr. Appropriation for Plant Expansion
      Cr. Retained Earnings
   B. Dr. Retained Earnings
      Cr. Appropriation for Plant Expansion
   C. Dr. Retained Earnings
      Cr. Capital Contributed from Plant Expansion
   D. Dr. Appropriation for Plant Expansion
      Cr. Cash

6. Nancy Co. issued 50,000 shares of $20 par value common stock and subsequently acquired 1,000 shares, which it now holds as treasury stock. If the board of directors declares a cash dividend of $1 per share, what will be the total amount of the dividend?

   A. $50,000
   B. $49,000
   C. $51,000
   D. None of these.

7. The amount that a preferred stockholder will be entitled to receive per share if a corporation dissolves is known as:

   A. book value.
   B. redemption value.
   C. liquidation value.
   D. par value.
   E. market value.

8. Treasury stock should be shown on the balance sheet as a:

   A. reduction of the corporation's stockholders' equity.
   B. sundry asset.
   C. current asset.
   D. fixed asset.
   E. current liability.

9. The Board of Directors declared the regular quarterly dividend of $5 per share. The company had issued 12,000 shares, but now holds 2,000 shares as treasury stock. The entry for the dividend declaration is:

   A. Retained Earnings 50,000
       Dividends Payable 50,000
   B. Dividends Payable 50,000
       Cash 50,000
   C. Dividends Payable 60,000
       Cash 60,000
   D. Retained Earnings 60,000
       Dividends Payable 60,000
   E. (A) and (B) above.

10. The par value of a company's 1,000 shares of common stock outstanding has been reduced from $50 par to $25; an additional 1,000 shares are issued to stockholders. The entry is:

   A. Retained Earnings 25,000
       Common Stock 25,000
   B. Dividends Payable 50,000
       Common Stock 50,000
   C. Retained Earnings 25,000
       Contributed Capital from Reduction in Par Value of Stock 25,000
   D. None of these.

11–13. A company's 10,000 shares of $100 par value common stock outstanding were issued at $110 per share. It now reacquired 200 shares of its own stock at a cost of $137 per share.

11. The entry to record the reacquisition is:

   A. Premium on Stock 7,400
      Treasury Stock 20,000
       Cash 27,400
   B. Premium on Stock 5,400
      Treasury Stock 22,000
       Cash 27,400
   C. Treasury Stock 27,400
       Cash 27,400
   D. Paid-In Capital—Treasury Stock Transactions 7,400
      Treasury Stock 20,000
       Cash 27,400

12. The entry when the company reissued half of the shares for $150 per share is:

   A. Cash 15,000
      Treasury Stock—Common 13,700
      Paid-In Capital—Common Treasury Stock Transactions 1,300
   B. Cash 15,000
      Treasury Stock—Common 15,000
   C. Cash 15,000
      Treasury Stock—Common 13,700
      Retained Earnings 1,300
   D. Cash 13,700
      Treasury Stock—Common 13,700

13. The company reissued the remaining treasury shares for $125 per share. The entry is:

   A. Cash 12,500
       Treasury Stock—Common 12,500

   B. Cash 12,500
       Paid-In Capital—Common Treasury Stock Transactions 1,200
       Treasury Stock—Common 13,700

   C. Cash 12,500
       Retained Earnings 1,200
       Treasury Stock—Common 13,700

   D. None of these.

14. Atlanta Co. has been authorized to issue 100,000 shares of $100 par common stock. On May 10, ten years ago, it issued 5,000 shares; on July 20, four years later, it issued 3,000 shares; and on April 2 of the current year it reacquired 200 shares. On May 1 of the current year, a five-for-one stock split occurred in which the par value was decreased to $20. What is the number of shares outstanding after the last transaction?

   A. 101,000
   B. 100,000
   C. 40,000
   D. 39,000
   E. 125,000

15. New York Company declared a stock dividend amounting to 500 shares of common stock (10% of its outstanding shares). If at the declaration date the par value is $10 per share, the book value is $18 per share, and the market value is $20 per share, what will be the amount debited to Retained Earnings in recording the dividend distributable?

   A. $5,000
   B. $9,000
   C. $10,000
   D. None of these.

SOLUTIONS

Matching

1. g	5. i	8. c
2. a	6. f	9. b
3. h	7. d	10. j
4. e		

Completion and Exercises

1. $2,400; 10,000 shares outstanding × 20% = 2,000 shares in stock dividend. 10,000 shares + 2,000 shares = 12,000 × $.20 = $2,400 dividend.

2. May 1 Memorandum: Received donation of 400 shares common stock

    10 Treasury Stock 1,200
        Cash 1,200

    20 Cash 6,800
        Paid-In Capital—Donations 6,800

    28 Cash 1,050
        Treasury Stock 840
        Paid-In Capital—Common Treasury Stock Transactions 210

3. record
4. treasury
5. dividends
6. market
7. Treasury stock is stock that has been issued and then reacquired by the issuing corporation.
8. Paid-In Capital—Common (Preferred) Treasury Stock Transactions.
9. source
10. permanent (or contributed)
11. cash
12. statement of retained earnings
13. retained earnings
14. They have no effect. They usually increase paid-in capital and decrease retained earnings by the same amount.
15. the fair market value of the asset received
16. Small stock dividends are of less than 20 to 25% of the previously outstanding stock and are assumed to have little effect on the market value of shares. Small stock dividends are recorded at present market value of outstanding shares. Large stock dividends are those over 20 to 25% of the previously outstanding shares. Since they are assumed to reduce the market value of the stock, they are accounted for at their par or stated value.

17. a. Retained Earnings 50,000
        Appropriation for Possible Losses from Lawsuits 50,000
     To record Retained Earnings Appropriation.

   b. Loss from Lawsuits 25,000
        Cash 25,000
     To record payment of court awarded judgment.

     Appropriation for Possible Losses from Lawsuits 50,000
        Retained Earnings 50,000
     To eliminate appropriation of Retained Earnings.

18. Paid-in capital and retained earnings
19. deficit
20. To inform stockholders that a certain amount of the assets brought into the corporation through the earning process is not to be distributed as dividends.

21.   SANDERS, INC.
                    Statement of Retained Earnings
                  For the Year Ended December 31, 1994

Appropriated:		
Appropriated for plant expansion, balance January 1, 1994	$ 90,000	
Additional appropriation	50,000	
Retained earnings appropriated, December 31, 1994		$ 140,000
Unappropriated:		
Balance, January 1, 1994 .... $950,000		
Net income for year 410,000	1,360,000	
Cash dividends declared $170,000		
Stock dividends declared 190,000		
Appropriation for plant expansion 50,000	410,000	
Retained earnings unappropriated, December 31, 1994		950,000
Total retained earnings, December 31, 1994		$1,090,000

22. 1. Retained Earnings 20,000
       Appropriation for Plant Expansion 20,000

    2. Retained Earnings [(24,000 – 4,000 shares) × $5] 100,000
       Dividends Payable 100,000

    3. Dividends Payable 100,000
       Cash 100,000

    4. Memo: Increased shares to 40,000 shares outstanding and reduced par value to
       $50 per share.

23. extraordinary item; Income Statement; tax effects
24. prior period adjustment; statement of retained earnings; tax effects
25. accounting methods; income statement
26. environment; would not

27.   MARILYN CORPORATION
                                 Income Statement
                        For the Year Ended December 31, 1994

Revenues $37,000,000
Expenses $32,000,000
Federal income taxes   2,500,000   34,500,000
Net income before extraordinary items .... $ 2,500,000
Loss from earthquake (net of tax effect of $337,500)   337,500
Net income .... $ 2,162,500

28.   BROWN CORPORATION
                                Partial Balance Sheet
                                December 31, 1994

Stockholders' Equity:
  Paid-in capital:
    Preferred stock—$50 par value; 5,000 shares authorized, 3,000 shares
      issued and outstanding .... $ 150,000
    Common stock—$5 par value; 1,000,000 shares authorized, 600,000 shares
      issued and outstanding of which 15,000 shares are held in treasury   3,000,000
    Paid-in capital in excess of par value:
      From common stock issuances $675,000
      From capitalization of retained earnings through stock dividends ... 330,000
      From treasury stock transactions   25,000   1,030,000
        Total paid-in capital $4,180,000
  Retained Earnings:
    Appropriated for pending litigation $125,000
    Unappropriated (restricted to the extent of $90,000, the cost of treasury shares
      held)   380,000   505,000
                                                                         $4,685,000
Less: Treasury stock—common 15,000 shares at cost   90,000
  Total Stockholders' Equity $4,595,000

29.

Jan.	5	Treasury Stock—Common	109,600	
		Cash		109,600
July	10	Cash	60,000	
		Treasury Stock—Common		54,800
		Paid-In Capital—Common Treasury Stock Transactions		5,200
Dec.	8	Cash	50,000	
		Paid-In Capital—Common Treasury Stock Transactions	4,800	
		Treasury Stock—Common		54,800

30.

June	1	Retained Earnings	20,000	
		Dividends Payable		20,000
		Dividends declared: $2 on 10,000 shares, payable July 15, 1994, to stockholders on June 15, 1994.		
June	15	No entry.		
July	15	Dividends Payable	20,000	
		Cash		20,000
		Paid the dividend declared on June 1, 1994.		

True-False Questions

1. T
2. F   Although a source of corporate capital, retained earnings do not represent paid-in capital, that is, capital contributed by the owners. Retained earnings are classified separately from paid-in capital within the stockholders' equity section.
3. T   It may be reissued without violating the preemptive rights.
4. T
5. F   Stockholders' equity generally consists of two elements—paid-in capital, which includes common stock and retained earnings.
6. F   Treasury stock is never an asset because a corporation cannot own part of itself.
7. T
8. F   Setting up a retained earnings appropriation does not reduce the total stockholders' equity. It merely earmarks a portion of that equity to indicate that assets brought into the corporation through the earnings process are to be used for a specific purpose.
9. F   The declaration of a cash dividend increases a firm's current liabilities. The payment of the cash dividend decreases current liabilities.
10. F   The date of record is the date used to determine to whom the dividends will be paid. The date of declaration is the date the liability for dividends payable becomes effective.
11. T   The usual stock dividend merely decreases retained earnings and increases paid-in capital by an equal amount. Thus, there is no change in total stockholders' equity.
12. T
13. F   The amount of issued stock is not reduced; instead, the amount of outstanding shares is reduced. Treasury stock is not automatically canceled when it is purchased because the board of directors may intend to reissue it.
14. F   Treasury stock reduces total stockholders' equity.
15. F   Dividends are distributions of earnings and are not expenses.
16. T   No-par stock may be more valuable; but par or no-par is not the crucial factor. The market value, which reflects many economic factors, is a better indication of a stock's worth.

17. F No entry is made on the date of record; this date merely determines which stockholders are to receive the dividend.
18. T
19. F A deficit is a debit balance in the Retained Earnings account.
20. F A statement of retained earnings shows the changes in the Retained Earnings account during a stated period of time. These changes include additions such as net income and deductions such as dividends declared and net losses.
21. F Retained Earnings is not reduced; but the amount of retained earnings available for distribution as cash dividends is usually restricted by an amount equal to the cost of the treasury stock.
22. F
23. T Such losses are likely to be unusual in nature and nonrecurring.
24. T A stock dividend declared from retained earnings permanently capitalizes a portion of retained earnings by transferring an amount from retained earnings to paid-in capital.
25. F Such damage occurs too frequently to be considered nonrecurring.
26. T The usual source of dividend distributions is the Retained Earnings account.
27. F The paid-in capital of a corporation includes capital contributed by stockholders or others. It does not include retained earnings.
28. F Proceeds from donated treasury stock are credited to a paid-in capital account rather than a gain account that affects net income.
29. T
30. F Treasury stock does not include all authorized stock; only the stock that has been issued and reacquired.
31. F The Dividends account is closed to Retained Earnings. An alternative treatment is to debit Retained Earnings at the time dividends are declared and not use a Dividends account.
32. F The net income would be $3,000; dividends are not expenses and instead are distributions of income to stockholders.
33. T
34. T The board of directors may appropriate retained earnings at the time bonds are issued.

Multiple Choice Questions

1. D At the time the donated shares were received, a memo entry would be made.
2. A At the time of sale of donated shares, Paid-In Capital—Donations is credited.
3. A At the time of the stock dividend declaration, there are 10,000 shares of stock outstanding. As a result, 1,000 shares are to be distributed as a stock dividend; 1,000 shares × $25 par = $25,000 credited to Stock Dividend Distributable. Because the market value of the stock is $45 at the time of declaration, Paid-In Capital—Stock Dividend is credited for $20,000.
4. C
5. B The correct entry to increase the appropriation for plant expansion is to debit Retained Earnings and to credit Appropriation for Plant Expansion.
6. B 50,000 − 1,000 shares reacquired as treasury stock = 49,000 shares outstanding, on which $1 dividend per share is being paid.
7. C
8. A
9. A 12,000 shares − 2,000 shares reacquired as treasury shares = 10,000 shares outstanding, on which $5 dividends are being paid. The correct entry is to debit Retained Earnings and to credit Dividends Payable on the date of declaration.
10. D This is a stock split, and none of the entries listed is correct. A memo entry could be made or Common Stock, $50 par, would be debited and Common Stock, $25 par, would be credited.
11. C The Treasury Stock account is debited at cost, which is 200 shares × $137 per share.

12. A The Treasury Stock account is credited for the cost of the shares (100 shares × $137 per share). The difference between the cost and the amount received is credited to Paid-In Capital—Common Treasury Stock Transactions.

13. B The amount received is less than the cost of the treasury shares. The Treasury Stock—Common account is credited for the cost and the difference is debited to the Paid-In Capital—Common Treasury Stock Transactions, since that account has a credit balance.

14. D $(5,000 + 3,000 - 200) \times 5 = 39,000$ shares outstanding.

15. C Market value is used, which is 20×500 shares $= \$10,000$ debited to Retained Earnings.

15 BONDS PAYABLE AND BOND INVESTMENTS

Learning Objectives

1. Describe the features of bonds and tell how bonds differ from shares of stock.
2. List the advantages and disadvantages of financing with long-term debt and prepare examples showing how financial leverage is employed.
3. Prepare journal entries for bonds issued at face value.
4. Explain how interest rates affect bond prices and what causes a bond to sell at a premium or a discount.
5. Apply the concept of present value to compute the price of a bond.
6. Prepare journal entries for bonds issued at a discount or a premium.
7. Prepare journal entries for bond redemptions and bond conversions.
8. Prepare journal entries for bond investments.
9. Explain future value and present value concepts and make required calculations (Appendix).

CHAPTER OUTLINE

BONDS PAYABLE

1. Bonds are a common form of long-term financing and are a written instrument in the form of an unconditional promise, made under seal, wherein the borrower promises to pay a specified sum at a determinable future date and usually interest at a stated rate and on stated dates.

2. The bond certificate is physical evidence of the debt.

3. The borrower agrees to pay the face or principal amount of the bond on a specific maturity date and usually periodic interest at a specified rate on the face value at stated dates.

COMPARISON WITH STOCK

4. Bonds differ from stock in the following ways:

    a. A bond is a debt while stock represents ownership.
    b. Bonds have maturity dates, while stock does not mature.
    c. Bonds require stated periodic interest payments by the company; dividends to stockholders are payable only when declared.
    d. Bond interest is deductible by the issuer in computing both net income and taxable income, while dividends are not deductible in either computation.

SELLING (ISSUING) BONDS

5. An investment firm or banker, called an underwriter, usually sells a bond issue.

    a. The trustee usually is a bank or trust company that represents the bondholders.
    b. A bond indenture is the contract or loan agreement under which the bond is issued.

CHARACTERISTICS OF BONDS

6. All bonds have these two characteristics:

    a. They promise to pay cash or other assets.
    b. They come due or mature.

7. In other respects, bonds may differ as to features such as the following:

    a. Secured bonds are secured by a pledge against real estate, machinery, merchandise, investments, or personal property.
    b. Debenture bonds are unsecured bonds issued against the general credit of the corporation.
    c. Registered bonds are those for which interest is paid to the owner by check.
    d. Bearer bonds are unregistered and are assumed to be the property of the holder.
    e. Coupon bonds carry detachable coupons that are to be clipped and presented for payment of interest due.
    f. Term bonds mature on the same date as all other bonds in a given bond issue.
    g. Serial bonds mature in installments through time.
    h. Callable bonds contain a provision that gives the issuer the right to buy back the bond before its maturity date.
    i. Convertible bonds may be converted at the bondholder's option and under stated conditions into stock of the issuing corporation.
    j. Junk bonds with high interest rates were issued in the 1980s to finance corporate restructurings.

8. Bonds may be issued with stock warrants that allow the holder to purchase shares of stock at a fixed price for some stated period of time.

   a. A bond with nondetachable warrants is virtually the same as a convertible bond.

   b. Detachable warrants allow bondholders to keep their bonds and still purchase shares of stock through exercise of the warrants.

ADVANTAGES OF ISSUING DEBT

9. The advantages of issuing bonds when additional long-term funds are needed include the following:

   a. Stockholder ownership is not shared with the bondholders.

   b. The interest rate may be less than the dividend rate on the capital stock of the firm.

   c. Interest is deductible for tax purposes, whereas dividends are not.

   d. If borrowed funds can generate net income greater than their interest cost (favorable financial leverage), corporate earnings per share are enhanced, to the benefit of the stockholders.

   e. A firm is said to be trading on the equity when it issues bonds or is employing other financial leverage such as issuing preferred stock or long-term notes.

DISADVANTAGES OF ISSUING DEBT

10. Under certain conditions, there are also disadvantages to issuing bonds:

    a. The interest expense represents a contractual obligation that must be paid if default on the loan is to be avoided.

    b. The ability of the firm to absorb losses prior to becoming insolvent is reduced.

    c. If the borrowed funds generate net income less than their interest cost (unfavorable financial leverage), the additional amount of interest paid over the amount earned reduces the corporate earnings per share available. This reduction is to the detriment of the stockholders.

    d. A bond indenture may place restrictions on owners and managers, such as a restriction of dividends.

ACCOUNTING FOR BONDS

11. The bonds authorized may all be issued at one time, or a portion at one date and the remainder later, as a source of future funds.

12. When the bonds are issued, the appropriate asset account is debited for the amount received and Bonds Payable is credited for the face value on the bonds issued.

    a. The issue price comprises the sum of the present values of the principal due at maturity and the interest to be paid periodically; the interest rate involved being that demanded by the investors for bonds of that risk category.

    b. If bonds are issued between interest dates, the sales price must include accrued interest.

       1. The issuing company will debit Cash and credit Bonds Payable and Bond Interest Payable.

       2. At the next interest payment date, Bond Interest Payable and Bond Interest Expense are debited and Cash is credited.

BOND PRICES AND INTEREST RATES

13. If the interest rate on the bonds is lower than that demanded by the investors (the market rate), the bonds will be issued at a discount.

    a. The discount, the difference between the face value and the issue price, is debited to a Discount on Bonds Payable or Bonds Payable—Discount account.

    b. The discount represents a cost of using funds to the borrower and represents additional interest earnings to the investor.

    c. The total cost of borrowing is the sum of the total periodic interest payments plus the total discount.

    d. The discount is allocated or amortized, on the effective interest rate basis or on a straight-line basis, over the remaining life of the bonds. The discount account is credited, and Interest Expense is debited.

    e. When a balance sheet is prepared, the remaining balance of the discount account is shown as a deduction from bonds payable.

14. If the interest rate in the bonds is higher than that demanded by the investors (the market rate), the bonds will be issued at a premium.

    a. The premium, the difference between the face value and the issue price, is credited to a Premium on Bonds Payable or Bonds Payable—Premium account.

    b. The premium represents a reduction in the cost of using funds to the borrower and represents a reduction in interest earnings to the investor.

    c. The total cost of borrowing is the total periodic interest payments minus the total premium.

    d. The premium is allocated or amortized, on the effective interest rate basis or on a straight-line basis, over the remaining life of the bonds. The premium account is debited, and Interest Expense is credited.

    e. When a balance sheet is prepared, the remaining balance of the premium account is shown as an addition to bonds payable.

DISCOUNT/PREMIUM AMORTIZATION

15. The bond interest expense recorded each period differs from the cash payment for bond interest if bonds are issued at a premium or discount.

16. Two methods are available for amortizing a discount or premium on bonds: straight-line and effective rate of interest method.

    a. Under the straight-line method, interest expense is recorded at a constant amount.

    b. Under the effective rate of interest method, interest expense for any period is equal to the effective (market) rate of interest at date of issuance times the carrying value of the bonds at the beginning of that interest period.

REDEEMING BONDS PAYABLE

17. Redemption of bonds (or extinguishment of debt) may occur in the following ways:

    a. Paid at maturity.

    b. Called.

    c. Purchased in the market and retired.

18. When bonds are redeemed in total at maturity by direct payment from the cash of the issuing company, the journal entry is to debit Bonds Payable and credit Cash for the face amount.

SERIAL BONDS

19. Serial bonds mature over several dates and avoid the burden of redeeming an entire bond issue at one time.

    a. The amount maturing the next year is reported as a current liability.

    b. The entry to retire a serial bond is to debit Serial Bonds Payable and credit Cash.

BOND REDEMPTION OR SINKING FUNDS

20. Bond redemption funds or sinking funds are required in bond indentures to reduce the risk of default at maturity date. Cash deposited with the sinking fund trustee can only be used to redeem bonds.

    a. The entry to record a payment to the trustee is a debit to Sinking Fund and a credit to Cash.

    b. When bonds are redeemed out of the sinking fund, Bonds Payable and Bond Interest Expense on bonds redeemed are debited and Sinking Fund is credited.

    c. Expenses paid by the trustee are debited to Sinking Fund Expenses and credited to Cash.

CONVERTIBLE BONDS

21. Bonds may be convertible into shares of the issuer's common stock.

    a. The entry made when bonds are converted is to debit Bonds Payable and credit Common Stock. Unamortized discount or premium on the bonds is closed out.

    b. A Paid-in Capital account is established for the difference.

BOND INVESTMENTS

22. Bond investments may be either termed short term or long term and occur for several reasons.
    a. Short-term investments are usually made to earn income on idle cash.
    b. Long-term investments are usually made for reasons other than an investment of idle cash.
    c. Bond investments may be made to establish affiliation with another company.
    d. Bond investments may be made to secure a continuing stream of revenue from the investment over a period of years.

SHORT-TERM BOND INVESTMENTS

23. Short-term bond investments are recorded at cost, which includes price paid and any broker's commission.
    a. Premiums and discounts on short-term investments are not amortized because the length of time the bonds will be held is not known.
    b. A Temporary Investments account is debited for the cost, and Cash is credited. Any accrued bond interest that is paid for is debited to Bond Interest Receivable.

LONG-TERM BOND INVESTMENTS

24. Any premium or discount on long-term investments is not set up in a separate account, but the premium or discount is still amortized.

25. When bonds are purchased as a long-term investment, the Bond Investments account is debited for the amount *paid* for the bonds.

26. Bond Investments is shown at the book value of the account under the Investments heading of the balance sheet.

BONDS PURCHASED AT A DISCOUNT

27. If the bonds are purchased at a discount, the discount represents additional interest revenue that will be earned over the life of the bonds. The amount of the discount, although not formally set up in the statement of financial position, is allocated on the effective interest rate basis or the straight-line basis over the remaining life of the bonds. Bond Investments is debited, and Interest Revenue is credited.

BONDS PURCHASED AT A PREMIUM

28. If the bonds are purchased at a premium, the premium represents a reduction in interest revenue to be earned over the life of the investment. The premium is allocated on the effective interest rate basis or straight-line basis over the remaining life of the bonds. One way to accomplish this amortization is to debit the Interest Revenue account and credit Bond Investments.

29. When bonds are issued between interest dates, the investor usually pays for both the bond and the interest accrued from the last interest payment date.

SALE OF BOND INVESTMENTS

30. A gain or loss must be recorded when bond investments are sold. The gain or loss is computed as the difference between the price received and the carrying value of the bonds on the date sold.

VALUATION OF BOND INVESTMENTS

31. Short-term bond investments are carried at cost, and long-term bond investments are carried and reported at amortized cost.
    a. When a substantial, permanent decline occurs, bond investments are written down by debiting an account called Loss on Market Decline of Bond Investments and crediting Bond Investments.
    b. If bond investments are written down and the market price recovers, conservatism dictates that these bond investments not be written back up to their original cost.

APPENDIX—FUTURE VALUE AND PRESENT VALUE

32. Future value and present value concepts deal with the time value of money.

THE TIME VALUE OF MONEY

33. The time value of money concept is based on the preference for having a dollar today rather than at some future date because:

    a. there is risk that the future dollar will never be received.

    b. if the dollar is on hand now it can be invested resulting in an increase in total dollars possessed in the future.

FUTURE VALUE

34. The future value of an investment is the amount to which a sum of money invested today will grow in a stated time period at a specified interest rate.

    a. Simple interest is interest on principal only.

    b. Compound interest is interest on principal and on interest of prior periods.

FUTURE VALUE OF AN ANNUITY

35. An annuity is a series of equal cash flows spaced equally in time.

PRESENT VALUE

36. The present value concept is useful in determining the price of a bond and in amortizing a premium or accumulating a discount.

37. Present value is the current worth of a future cash receipt and is essentially the reverse of future value.

PRESENT VALUE OF AN ANNUITY

38. An annuity is a series of equal cash flows spaced equally in time; semiannual interest payments on a bond form a frequently encountered annuity.

DEMONSTRATION PROBLEM

On May 1, Macbeth purchased $100,000, 5-year, 8% bonds at a price to yield a 10% annual effective rate. Interest is to be paid May 1 and November 1. The fiscal year is the calendar year.

Required:

a. Prepare the entries for purchase of the bonds.
b. Using the effective interest rate method, present entries to recognize the interest received for the first six months.
c. Prepare entries to accrue interest and record discount amortization at year-end.

GENERAL JOURNAL

DATE	ACCOUNT TITLES AND EXPLANATION	POST. REF.	DEBIT	CREDIT

SOLUTION TO DEMONSTRATION PROBLEM

a. May 1 Present value of the promise to receive principal is $100,000 ×
the present value of $1 due in 10 periods at 5%. Using
Table E.3 $100,000 × .61391 .... $61,391.00
Present value of the promise to receive periodic interest is
$4,000 times the present value of an annuity of $1 for 10
periods at 5%—$4,000 × 7.72173 from Table E.4 ..... 30,886.92
$92,277.92

The discount is $100,000 − $92,277.92 = $7,722.08

Bond Investments	92,277.92	
Cash		92,277.92

b. November 1

Cash	4,000.00	
Bond Investments	613.90	
Bond Interest Revenue ($92,277.92 × 10% × 1/2 = $4,613.90; $4,613.90 − $4,000.00 = $613.90 discount)		4,613.90

c. December 31

Bond Interest Receivable	1,333.33	
Bond Investments	214.87	
Bond Interest Revenue		1,548.20

($92,891.82 × 10% × 2/12 = $1,548.20;
$1,548.20 − $1,333.33 = $214.87 discount)

MATCHING

Referring to the terms listed below, place the appropriate letter next to the corresponding description.

a. Bond
b. Bond indenture
c. Call premium
d. Carrying value
e. Coupon bonds

f. Convertible bonds
g. Effective rate of interest method
h. Favorable financial leverage
i. Market rate of interest
j. Registered bond

k. Serial bonds
l. Trustee
m. Underwriter
n Unsecured bond

_____ 1. Bonds that mature over several dates.
_____ 2. A debenture bond.
_____ 3. A bond in which the name of the owner appears on the bond certificate.
_____ 4. The addition to earnings of the owners from earning more with borrowed funds than the interest that must be paid for their use.
_____ 5. The $50 above face value per bond that a company paid when it redeemed all of a bond issue before its maturity date.
_____ 6. The bank or trust company selected to act for the bondholders.
_____ 7. The investment banking firm that aids a company in marketing a bond issue.
_____ 8. Bonds on which interest is paid by a means other than checks.
_____ 9. The rate of interest a bond is sold to yield.
_____ 10. The theoretically correct way of computing periodic interest expense on a bond.
_____ 11. Bonds that can be exchanged for shares of the issuer's stock.
_____ 12. Face value of a bond issue, plus unamortized premium.
_____ 13. Substantially the same as a note.
_____ 14. The contract containing all of the provisions under which bonds were issued.

1. Favorable financial leverage exists when borrowed funds can generate net income _____ than their interest cost.

2. If the interest rate on the bonds is higher than the market rate of interest for bonds of that risk category, the bonds will be issued at a _____ .

3. Outland Company issued on January 1, 1994, $100,000, 10-year, 10% bonds at an effective rate of 8%. The interest payment is made on January 1, and July 1 every year.

   Required:

   a. What is the entry to record the sale of the bonds on January 1, 1994?
   b. Give the entry for the first interest payment. (Use straight-line amortization.)
   c. When may the straight-line method be used?

a.

b.

c.

4. Present entries, in general journal form, to record the selected transactions of Timon Company described below.
   a. Issued $1,000,000 of 10-year, 9% bonds at 101-1/2. The interest is paid semiannually.
   b. The payment of semiannual interest; the amortization of bond premium for this period is $750.
   c. Redemption of bonds at 101. The bonds were carried at $1,012,000 at the time of the redemption.

a.				
b.				
c.				

5. On August 1, 1994, Issuer Company issued for cash to Purchaser Company, at 100 plus accrued interest, $1,000,000 of 10-year, 9% bonds, dated January 1, 1994, which call for semi-annual interest payments on January 1 and July 1. What entries are necessary at issuance, and at December 31, 1994 (the accounting year-end for both companies)?

Issuer

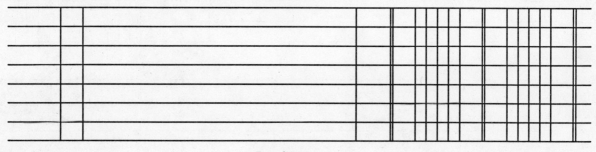

Purchaser

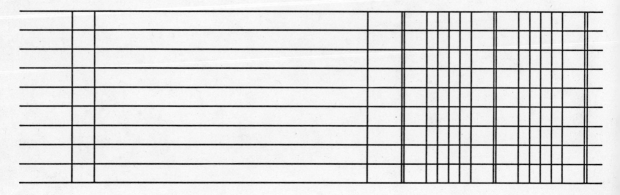

6. Assume the bonds in Question 5 were issued on January 1, 1994, for cash of $1,067,952—a price that yields 8%. Give the entries for 1994, including the December 31 adjusting entries, for both the Issuer Company and the Purchaser Company.

Issuer

Purchaser

7. The total cost of borrowing is the sum of the periodic interest payments _____ (plus/minus) the discount at issuance or _____ (plus/minus) the premium.

8. Discount and premium on bonds should be amortized using the _____ _____ _____ method.

9. When bonds are issued between interest dates, _____ _____ must be recorded on both the issuer's and purchaser's books.

10. A _____ bond has specific property that has been pledged to ensure its payment while a _____ bond is backed only by the general credit worthiness of the issuer and is not backed by a lien on any specific property. A _____ bond is unregistered and ownership is transferred by physical delivery of the bond.

11. The issue price of a bond is the total of the present values of the promises to pay the _____ at maturity and the _____ periodically throughout the life of the bonds.

12. Prove that a $1,000 face value bond, bearing interest at 8%, payable semiannually, and maturing in 10 years, will sell for $1,000 if sold to yield eight percent.

13. If $10,000 face value of 6%, 10-year bonds, interest payable semiannually, are issued to yield 8%, what price will they bring?

14. Give the entry to record the issuance of the bonds in Question 13 and the entry to record the first six months' interest expense.

15. Compute the present value of the bonds in Question 13 to yield 8% with 19 periods (9-1/2 years) of life remaining.

16. The difference between the present value computed in Question 15 and the present value (price) computed in Question 13 is $ _____ . This difference is equal (except for rounding difference) to an amount in one of the entries in Question 14 and is described as the amount of _____ _____ .

17. _____ _____ is the cash set aside regularly to pay outstanding bonds at maturity.

18. Leed Company plans to issue $200,000 face value of 12%, 10-year bonds that are dated January 31, 1994. These bonds have semiannual interest payments and mature on January 31, 2004.

Required: (Round all amounts to the nearest dollar)

a. At what price should the bonds sell if investors desire a 10% yield on these bonds?

b. Determine the first six months' interest expense assuming the bonds are issued at the price determined in (a).

c. Assume, instead, that the investor seeks a 14% yield.

   1. At what price should the bonds sell?
   2. What is the first six months' journal entry to record interest under these conditions?

a.

b.

c. 1.

2.

DATE	ACCOUNT TITLES AND EXPLANATION	POST. REF.	DEBIT	CREDIT

Chapter 15

19. a. On August 1, 1993, Titus Company issued for cash to Andrews Company, at 100 plus accrued interest, $150,000 of five-year, 8% bonds, dated January 1, 1993, that call for semiannual interest payments on January 1 and July 1. What entries are necessary at issuance, and at December 31, 1993, (the accounting year-end for both companies) for both Titus, the issuer, and Andrews, the purchaser?

Issuer

Purchaser

b. Assume instead Andrews Company purchased the bonds from Titus Company on January 1, 1993, for cash of $162,780—a price that yields 6%. Give the entries for 1993, including the December 31 adjusting entries for both the Titus Company and the Andrews Company. (Use the interest method.)

Issuer

20. Troilus Company plans to issue $100,000 face value of 10%, 10-year bonds that are dated January 31, 1994. These bonds have semiannual interest payments and mature on January 31, 2004.

Required: (Round all amounts to the nearest dollar)

a. At what price should the bonds sell if investors desire a 12% yield on these bonds?
b. Determine the first six months' interest expense assuming the bonds are issued at the price determined in (a).
c. If, instead, the investor seeks a 6% yield, at what price should the bonds sell?
d. Assuming the bonds are sold to yield a 6% yield, what is the first six months' journal entry to record interest on the books of the issuer?

a.		
b.		
c.		

d.

DATE		ACCOUNT TITLES AND EXPLANATION	POST. REF.	DEBIT	CREDIT

21. a. Prove that a $10,000 face value bond, bearing interest at 10%, payable semiannually, and maturing in 4 years, will sell for $10,000 if sold to yield ten percent.

b. If the same bond is issued to yield 8%, what price will it bring?

c. Give the entry to record the issuance of the bonds to yield 8% and the entry to record the first six months' interest expense.

DATE		ACCOUNT TITLES AND EXPLANATION	POST. REF.	DEBIT	CREDIT

d. Give the entry to record the second months' interest payment received by the purchaser.

DATE	ACCOUNT TITLES AND EXPLANATION	POST. REF.	DEBIT	CREDIT

e. Compute the present value of the bonds sold to yield 8% with 6 periods (3 years) of life remaining.

(The remaining questions are based on the chapter Appendix.)

22. Interest is compounded whenever the amount of _____ for a period is computed and is added to the _____ to serve as the basis for computing interest for the next period.

23. The future value of $10,000 five years from now if invested at 6% compounded annually is _____ _____ .

24. If the interest in Question 23 had been compounded semiannually, what would the future value have been? _____

25. Present value is the _____ of future value.

26. Prove that Question 25 is true by showing that the present value of $13,382.30 (the answer to Question 23) to be received five years from now at 6% is $10,000. (Hint: Multiply $13,382.30 by the reciprocal of the factor used to answer Question 23.)

27. What is the present value of an annuity of $2,000 to be received at the end of each of the next ten years at 8% interest?

TRUE-FALSE QUESTIONS

Indicate whether each of the following statements is true or false by inserting a capital "T" or "F" in the blank space provided.

_____ 1. Another term for determining present values is discounting.

_____ 2. The carrying value of bonds is the face value of the bonds plus any unamortized discount and less any unamortized premium.

_____ 3. Provisions in many bond indentures call for periodic payments to be made to a bond redemption fund, often called a petty cash fund.

_____ 4. Buyers of bearer bonds incur more risk through possible loss than do buyers of registered bonds.

_____ 5. Financial leverage is said to be favorable for an organization when borrowed funds are used to increase total assets of the organization.

_____ 6. The dividends received from investments in bonds should be debited to Cash and credited to Revenue from Bonds.

_____ 7. Investors will be less attracted to bonds offering a coupon rate greater than the market rate for such bonds and will generally only buy these at a discount.

_____ 8. Unfavorable financial leverage may result from trading on the equity.

_____ 9. Favorable financial leverage may result from trading on the equity.

_____ 10. The cost of a bond investment is recorded in a single account even if the bond is purchased at a premium.

_____ 11. Bonds acquired as a long-term investment may be correctly combined in the same account as those acquired as temporary investments on the books of the purchaser.

_____ 12. Short-term bond investments are recorded at cost, which includes any broker's commission.

_____ 13. Bond premium is amortized on the books of the investor by using a journal entry that debits Investments in Bonds and credits Bond Interest Revenue.

_____ 14. If bond interest is accrued, but not paid at the end of the accounting period, an adjusting entry should be made on the books of the issuer.

_____ 15. The recommended amortization procedure is the interest method, also referred to as the effective rate of interest method.

_____ 16. When Premium on Bonds Payable is amortized, an entry crediting this account is needed.

_____ 17. Under the interest method of amortization, interest expense is recorded at a constant amount.

_____ 18. A bond may have a life of 50 years and call for quarterly interest payments.

_____ 19. When bonds are redeemed before maturity and the original sales price was above face value, the entry required to record the redemption is to debit Bonds Payable and credit Cash for the call price.

_____ 20. A bond is likely to be called and redeemed with funds secured from new borrowing after a period of rising interest rates.

_____ 21. The contract rate of interest is used to determine the amount of interest payable currently.

_____ 22. Premium on bonds held as temporary investments is not amortized.

_____ 23. Bonds may be made more attractive by adding the convertible feature to them, which allows the bondholder to convert the bonds into shares of the issuer's common stock.

_____ 24. The amount a bond sells for above face value is called a discount.

_____ 25. Convertible bonds can be exchanged for other bonds issued by the same borrower.

MULTIPLE CHOICE QUESTIONS

For each of the following questions indicate the best answer by circling the appropriate letter.

1. Assuming no substantial, permanent decline, long-term bond investments are carried and reported on the balance sheet at:

   A. cost in the long-term liability section.
   B. cost in the stockholders' equity section.
   C. cost in the current asset section.
   D. amortized cost.
   E. None of the above.

2. The contract rate:

   A. is stated in the bond indenture and printed on the face of each bond.
   B. is also called the coupon, nominal, or stated rate.
   C. is the minimum rate of interest investors are willing to accept on bonds of a particular risk category.
   D. All of the above.
   E. (A) and (B) above.

Questions 3–5. On April 30, 1994, Dee Co. issued $100,000 of 10-year, 9% bonds dated April 30 for $94,000 to yield 12%. Interest is payable semiannually on April 30 and October 31. Present the entries in general journal form to record the following transactions.

3. Issuance of the bonds:

   A. Investment in Bonds 94,000
         Cash 94,000
   B. Cash 100,000
         Bonds Payable 100,000
   C. Cash 94,000
      Discount on Bonds Payable 6,000
         Bonds Payable 100,000
   D. Cash 94,000
      Premium on Bonds Payable 6,000
         Bonds Payable 100,000

4. Accrual of interest and amortization of bond discount on October 31, 1994, using the interest method is:

A. Interest Expense 4,500
   Premium on Bonds Payable 1,140
   Interest Payable   5,640

B. Interest Expense 5,640
   Interest Payable   4,500
   Discount on Bonds Payable   1,140

C. Interest Expense 6,000
   Discount on Bonds Payable   6,000

D. Interest Expense 9,000
   Interest Payable   9,000

5. Deposit of $6,000 in a bond sinking fund:

A. Sinking Fund 6,000
   Cash   6,000

B. Investment in Bonds 6,000
   Cash   6,000

C. Cash 6,000
   Sinking Fund   6,000

D. Investment in Bonds 6,000
   Bond Sinking Fund Income   6,000

6. On July 1, 1994, Brown Co. purchased as a long-term investment $200,000 of ABC Co. 10-year 10% bonds dated January 1, 1993, for $189,800. Interest is payable on June 30 and December 31. What is the journal entry to record the accrual of interest and amortization of discount on the bonds on December 31, 1994 using straight-line amortization on Brown Co.'s books?

A. Interest Receivable 10,000
   Interest Revenue   10,000

B. Interest Receivable 10,000
   Investment in ABC Co. Bonds   600
   Interest Revenue   10,000
   Discount in ABC Co. Bonds   600

C. Interest Receivable 10,000
   Investment in ABC Co. Bonds   600
   Interest Revenue   10,600

D. Investment in ABC Co. Bonds 600
   Interest Revenue   600

E. None of the above entries is correct.

7. Assume that bond investments were written down when a substantial permanent decline occurred two years ago and presently the market price of these bonds has recovered. The correct treatment to recognize this recovery is:

A. debit Bond Investments and credit Loss on Market Decline of Bond Investments for the amount originally written down.
B. debit Bond Investments and credit Retained Earnings for the amount originally written down.
C. debit Gain on Recovery of Bond Investments and credit Bond Investments for the amount originally written down.
D. debit Bond Investments and credit Gain on Recovery of Market Price for the amount originally written down.
E. do nothing because bond investments may not be written up once they have been written down.

8. When bonds are issued between interest dates at face value, the following is true:

   A. One reason for the delay may be due to higher interest rates on the bond than anticipated.
   B. Interest starts to accrue at the date of the bond sale.
   C. Investors purchasing such bonds after they begin to accrue interest have an option whether they pay for the accrued interest.
   D. The entry on the books of the issuer is a debit to Cash, a credit to Bonds Payable and a credit to Bond Interest Payable.
   E. All of the above.

9. If $100,000 of 10% bonds bearing semiannual interest are sold to yield an effective interest rate of 12%, the following is true:

   A. The bonds are issued at a discount.
   B. The bonds are issued at a premium.
   C. The Cash ledger account will be debited for $100,000.
   D. The discount amortized each period will be the difference between the carrying value of the bonds × 6% and $5,000.
   E. A and D.

10. Miller Corporation has a bond issue of $10,000 outstanding, on which there is an unamortized premium of $3,000. The corporation exercises its option of calling the bonds at 102. The entry is:

    A. Bonds Payable 10,000
       Premium on Bonds Payable 3,000
       Cash 13,000
    B. Bonds Payable 10,000
       Premium on Bonds Payable 3,000
       Cash 10,200
       Interest Revenue 2,800
    C. Bonds Payable 10,000
       Loss on Bond Redemption 200
       Cash 10,200
    D. Bonds Payable 10,000
       Premium on Bonds Payable 3,000
       Cash 10,200
       Gain on Bond Redemption 2,800

Question 11–13. Smith Corporation issued $1,000,000 of 9% 10-year convertible bonds for $985,000 to yield 10% on March 1, 1993; interest is payable March 1 and September 1. The conversion clause in the indenture granted the bondholders the right to convert the bonds before March 1, 1995 into shares of the company's common stock at the rate of 150 shares of $5 par value common stock for each $1,000 bond. The corporation completed the following transactions:

11. On September 1, 1993 paid the interest on the bonds and amortized the discount. The entry using the interest method is:

   A. Cash 985,000
       Discount on Bonds Payable 15,000
           Bonds Payable 1,000,000
   B. Bond Interest Expense 49,250
           Discount on Bonds Payable 4,250
           Cash 45,000
   C. Bond Interest Expense 45,000
           Cash 45,000
   D. Bond Interest Expense 45,000
           Discount on Bonds Payable 4,250
           Bond Interest Payable 40,750
   E. Bond Interest Expense 49,250
           Discount on Bonds Payable 1,250
           Cash 48,000

12. On March 1, 1994, after the semiannual interest on the bonds had been paid, converted bonds having a face value of $300,000 to common stock. Assume that the unamortized discount on the converted bonds at this time totaled $1,538. The entry is:

   A. Bonds Payable 300,000
           Common Stock 300,000
   B. Bonds Payable 300,000
           Discount on Bonds Payable 75,000
           Common Stock 225,000
   C. Bonds Payable 300,000
           Discount on Bonds Payable 1,538
           Paid-in Capital in Excess of Par Value—Common Stock 73,462
           Common Stock 225,000
   D. None of these.

13. On July 1, 1992, purchased on the open market and retired bonds having a $100,000 face value. The total cash outlay was $97,500. Assume that the unamortized discount on the bonds retired was $900.

   A. Bonds Payable 100,000
           Cash 97,500
           Gain on Bond Redemption 2,500
   B. Bonds Payable 97,500
           Cash 97,500
   C. Bonds Payable 100,000
           Cash 97,500
           Discount on Bonds Payable 2,500
   D. Bonds Payable 100,000
           Discount on Bonds Payable 900
           Gain on Bond Redemption 1,600
           Cash 97,500
   E. None of these.

14. What is(are) the credit(s) in the journal entry to record the issuance of $1,000,000 face value of 10-year 12% bonds dated October 31, 1993, at 103? Interest is payable semiannually on October 31 and April 30. Assume the effective interest is 11%.

A. Cash 1,030,000
B. Premium on Bonds Payable 30,000
   Bonds Payable 1,000,000
C. Bonds Payable 1,000,000
D. Discount on Bonds Payable 30,000
   Bonds Payable 1,000,000

15. What is the entry to record amortization of premium and interest payment on the above bonds on April 30, 1994?

A. Interest Expense 3,350
   Premium on Bonds Payable   3,350
B. Premium on Bonds Payable 3,350
   Interest Expense 60,000
   Cash   63,350
C. Interest Expense 60,000
   Premium on Bonds Payable   60,000
D. Premium on Bonds Payable 3,350
   Interest Expense 56,650
   Cash   60,000

SOLUTIONS

Matching

1.	k	8.	e
2.	n	9.	i
3.	j	10.	g
4.	h	11.	f
5.	c	12.	d
6.	l	13.	a
7.	m	14.	b

Completion and Exercises

1. greater
2. premium
3. a. Present value of principal: $100,000 × .45639 .... $ 45,639.00
      Present value of interest payments:
      $5,000 × 13.59033 ....   67,951.65
      Total price (present value) $113,590.65

      Cash 113,590.65
         Bonds Payable 100,000.00
         Premium on Bonds Payable 13,590.65

   b. Bond Interest Expense 4,320.47
      Premium on Bonds Payable 679.53
         Cash 5,000.00

   c.   The straight-line method may be used only when it does not differ materially from the interest method. The interest method is theoretically correct.

4. a. Cash 1,015,000
     Bonds Payable 1,000,000
     Premium on Bonds Payable 15,000

  b. Interest Expense 44,250
     Premium on Bonds Payable 750
     Cash 45,000

  c. Bonds Payable 1,000,000
     Premium on Bonds Payable 12,000
     Gain on Bond Redemption 2,000
     Cash 1,010,000

Issuer

5. Aug. 1, 1994   Cash 1,007,500
     Bonds Payable 1,000,000
     Interest Payable 7,500

  Dec. 31, 1994   Interest Expense 37,500
     Interest Payable 37,500

Purchaser

  Aug. 1, 1994   Bond Investments 1,000,000
     Interest Receivable 7,500
     Cash 1,007,500

  Dec. 31, 1994   Interest Receivable 37,500
     Interest Revenue 37,500

Issuer

6. Jan. 1, 1994   Cash 1,067,952
     Bonds Payable 1,000,000
     Premium on Bonds Payable 67,952

  July 1, 1994   Interest Expense ($1,067,952 × .04) 42,718
     Premium on Bonds Payable 2,282
     Cash 45,000

  Dec. 31, 1994   Interest Expense [($1,067,952 − $2,282) × .04] 42,627
     Premium on Bonds Payable 2,373
     Interest Payable 45,000

Purchaser

  Jan. 1, 1994   Bond Investments 1,067,952
     Cash 1,067,952

  July 1, 1994   Cash 45,000
     Bond Investments 2,282
     Interest Revenue 42,718

  Dec. 31, 1994   Interest Receivable 45,000
     Bond Investments 2,373
     Interest Revenue 42,627

7. plus; minus
8. effective rate of interest
9. accrued interest
10. secured, debenture, bearer
11. principal; interest

12. Present value of principal: $1,000 × .45639 .... $ 456.39
    Present value of interest: $40 × 13.59033 .... 543.61
        Total present value $1,000.00

13. Present value of principal: $10,000 × .45639 .... $4,563.90
    Present value of interest: $300 × 13.59033 .... 4,077.10
        Total price (present value) $8,641.00

14.   Cash 8,641.00
    Discount on Bonds Payable 1,359.00
        Bonds Payable 10,000.00

    Interest Expense ($8,641.00 × .04) 345.64
        Discount on Bonds Payable 45.64
        Cash 300.00

15. Present value of principal: $10,000 × .47464 .... $4,746.40
    Present value of interest: $300 × 13.13394 .... 3,940.18
        Total present value $8,686.58

16. $45.58; discount amortized
17. Sinking Fund

18.   LEED COMPANY

  a.   Price to yield 10% (5% per period)
       Present value of principal ($200,000 × .37689) .... $ 75,378
       Present value of interest ($12,000 × 12.46221) 149,547
       Present value (price to be offered) $224,925

  b.   First period's interest expense is $224,925 × 5% .... $ 11,246

  c. 1. Price to yield 14% (7% per period)
       Present value of principal ($200,000 × .25842) .... $ 51,684
       Present value of interest ($12,000 × 10.59401) 127,128
       Present value (price to be offered) $178,812

    2. Interest Expense ($178,812 × 7%) 12,517
        Cash 12,000
        Discount on Bonds Payable 517

Titus, Issuer

19. a. Aug. 1, 1993 Cash 151,000.00
                Bonds Payable 150,000.00
                Interest Payable (8% × $150,000 × 1/12) 1,000.00

      Dec. 31, 1993 Interest Expense 5,000.00
                Interest Payable 5,000.00

Andrews, Purchaser

      Aug. 1, 1993 Bond Investments 150,000.00
                Interest Receivable 1,000.00
                Cash 151,000.00

      Dec. 31, 1993 Interest Receivable 5,000.00
                Interest Revenue 5,000.00

Titus, Issuer

b. Jan. 1, 1993   Cash 162,780.00
                    Bonds Payable 150,000.00
                    Premium on Bonds Payable 12,780.00

    July 1, 1993   Interest Expense ($162,780.00 × .03) 4,883.40
                    Premium on Bonds Payable 1,116.60
                    Cash 6,000.00

    Dec. 31, 1993   Interest Expense [($162,780.00 − $1,116.60) × .03] ..   4,849.90
                    Premium on Bonds Payable 1,150.10
                    Interest Payable 6,000.00

Andrews, Purchaser

    Jan. 1, 1993   Bond Investments 162,780.00
                    Cash 162,780.00

    July 1, 1993   Cash 6,000.00
                    Bond Investments 1,116.60
                    Interest Revenue 4,883.40

    Dec. 31, 1993   Interest Receivable 6,000.00
                    Bond Investments 1,150.10
                    Interest Revenue 4,849.90

20. a. Price to yield 12% (6% per period)
        Present value of principal ($100,000 × .31180) $31,180.00
        Present value of interest ($5,000 × 11.46992) 57,349.60
        Present value (price to be offered) $88,529.60

    b. First period's interest expense is ($88,529.60 × 6%) .... $ 5,311.78

    c. Price to yield 6% (3% per period)
        Present value of principal ($100,000 × .55368) .... $ 55,368.00
        Present value of interest ($5,000 × 14.87747) 74,387.55
        Present value (price to be offered) $129,755.35

    d. Interest Expense ($129,755.35 × 3%) 3,892.66
        Premium on Bonds Payable 1,107.34
        Cash 5,000.00

21. a. Present value of principal ($10,000 × .67684) .... $ 6,768.40
        Present value of interest ($500 × 6.46321) 3,231.60
        Total present value $10,000.00

    b. Present value of principal ($10,000 × .73069) .... $ 7,306.90
        Present value of interest ($500 × 6.73274) 3,366.37
        Total price (present value) $10,673.27

    c. Cash 10,673.27
        Premium on Bond Payable 673.27
        Bonds Payable 10,000.00

        Interest Expense ($10,673.27 × .04) 426.93
        Premium on Bonds Payable 73.07
        Cash 500.00

    d. Cash 500.00
        Bond Investments 75.99
        Interest Revenue [($10,673.27 − $73.07) × .04] 424.01

352   Chapter 15

e. Present value of principal: $10,000 × .79031 .... $ 7,903.10
   Present value of interest: $500 × 5.24214 .... 2,621.07
      Total present value $10,524.17

22. interest; principal
23. $13,382.30. This can be found by looking in Table E.1 at the factor in the 5 periods row and 6% column (which is 1.33823). Multiply this factor times $10,000, and the answer is $13,382.30.
24. $13,439.16. This is found by looking at the factor in Table E.1 in the 10 periods row and 3% column (since there are 10 semiannual periods and the interest rate is 3% per period). 1.34392 × $10,000 = $13,439.20.
25. reciprocal or reverse
26. $13,382.30 × $\dfrac{1}{1.33823}$ = $10,000

Of course, this could also be found by using: $13,382.30 × 0.74726 = $10,000. Note that 1/1.33823 = 0.74726
27. $2,000 × 6.71008 = $13,420.16. The factor of 6.71008 is found in the 10 periods row and 8% column.

True-False Questions

1. T
2. F   The carrying value of bonds is the face value of the bonds less any unamortized discount and plus any unamortized premium.
3. F   The bond indenture may call for periodic payments to be made to a sinking fund, not a petty cash fund which is established for small expenditures.
4. T   If the bond is lost and it is a bearer bond, the finder can cash in the bond when due.
5. F   Favorable financial leverage occurs when the borrowed funds are used to increase earnings per share of common stock.
6. F   Dividends are not received from bonds, but are received from stock; interest is received from bonds. When interest is earned, the credit is to Interest Revenue.
7. F   Investors will be attracted to such bonds and will bid up the price of such bonds above the face value and the bonds will sell at a premium.
8. T
9. T
10. T
11. F   Long-term investments may not be combined with temporary investments on the books of the purchaser. Premium or discount on long-term investments is amortized on the purchaser's books even though the premium or discount is not usually set up in a separate account.
12. T   Premiums or discounts on short-term loans are not amortized because the length of the time the bonds will be held is not known.
13. F   Note the statement refers to bond premium.
14. T
15. T
16. F   A debit is needed to amortize Premium on Bonds Payable.
17. F   Interest expense is a constant amount under the straight-line procedure.
18. T
19. F   Bonds Payable is debited for the face value, any unamortized premium on bonds payable is debited, Cash is credited for the call price, and the difference is either a gain or loss on bond redemption.
20. F   Such a redemption is likely to happen in a period of declining interest rates.
21. T
22. T
23. T

24. F   A premium is the amount a bond sells for above face value.
25. F   See Answer 23.

Multiple Choice Questions

1. D
2. E
3. C   Bonds Payable is credited for the face of the bonds, and the discount is recorded as a debit of $6,000 (or $94,000 sales price − $100,000 face).
4. B   Using the interest method, Interest Expense is debited for $5,640 ($94,000 × 12% × 1/2); Interest Payable is credited for $4,500 (or $100,000 × 9% × 1/2); the difference is a credit to Discount on Bonds Payable of $1,140.
5. A
6. C   Interest Receivable is debited for $10,000 (or $200,000 × 10% × 1/2); the discount is amortized over 17 periods because the bonds were not sold at their date of January 1, 1993. This gives $10,200/17 periods = $600 discount amortization which is debited to Investment in ABC Co. Bonds. Interest Revenue is then credited for a total of $10,600.
7. E
8. D   One reason for the delay may be due to *lower* interest rates than expected. Interest starts to accrue from the date of the bonds, and investors are required to pay for the accrued interest.
9. E
10. D
11. B   Bond Interest Expense is debited for $49,250, which is 10% × $985,000 × 1/2. Cash is credited for $45,000, which is 9% × $1,000,000 × 1/2. The difference is credited to Discount on Bonds Payable.
12. C
13. D
14. B
15. D   Interest expense is debited for $56,650 (or $1,030,000 × 11% × 1/2), and Cash is credited for $60,000 (or $1,000,000 × 12% × 1/2). The difference is a debit to Premium on Bonds Payable.

16 STOCK INVESTMENTS—COST, EQUITY, AND CONSOLIDATIONS

Learning Objectives

1. Report stock investments and distinguish between the cost and equity methods of accounting for stock investments.
2. Prepare journal entries to account for short-term stock investments and for long-term stock investments of less than 20%.
3. Prepare journal entries to account for long-term investments of 20-50%.
4. Describe the nature of parent and subsidiary corporations.
5. Prepare consolidated financial statements through the use of a consolidated statement work sheet.
6. Identify the differences between purchase accounting and pooling of interests accounting.
7. Describe the uses and limitations of consolidated financial statements.

355   Chapter 16

CHAPTER OUTLINE

STOCK INVESTMENTS

1. Corporations invest funds in the securities of other corporations for any one of three reasons:
   a. to earn revenue on otherwise idle cash.
   b. to ensure a supply of a required raw material.
   c. to expand their business operations.

COST AND EQUITY METHODS

2. The two methods for accounting for investments in common stock are the cost and the equity methods. The Accounting Principles Board has identified the circumstances under which each method can be used.
   a. If the investor owns less than 20% of outstanding voting common stock and has no significant influence over the investee, the cost method is required.
   b. If the investor owns 20-50% of the outstanding voting common stock, the equity method is required.
   c. If the investor owns more than 50% of the outstanding voting common stock, the investor company may use either the cost or equity method, since consolidated financial statements must be prepared.

3. Using the cost method, the investor records the investment at the price paid at acquisition and does not adjust the investment account balance.

4. Using the equity method, the investor company adjusts the investment account periodically for the investor's share of the investee's earnings, losses, and dividends.
   a. The investor company records its share of the investee's earnings by debiting Investment in Investee Company and crediting Income of Investee Company for income.
      1. The debit to the Investment account increases the investor's equity in the investee company.
      2. Income of Investee Company is closed to Income Summary, which is then closed to the investor company's Retained Earnings.
   b. If the investee company incurs a loss, the investor company debits Loss of Investee Company and credits Investment in Investee Company for its share of the loss.
      1. The Loss of Investee Company is closed to Income Summary.
      2. The incurrence of a subsidiary loss reduces the investor's equity in the investee.
   c. When a subsidiary pays a cash dividend, the parent company debits Cash and credits the investment account, thereby reducing the parent's equity in the subsidiary.

COST METHOD FOR SHORT-TERM INVESTMENTS AND FOR LONG-TERM INVESTMENTS OF LESS THAN 20%

5. Using the cost method, Current Marketable Equity Securities is debited for the cash paid for the stock. Noncurrent Marketable Equity Securities is debited if the stock had been purchased as a long-term investment.

6. Income is not recognized upon the receipt of stock dividends; when a corporation declares a stock split, the investor would note the shares received and the reduction in the per-share cost.

7. Gain or loss on the sale of shares of stock is the difference between the net proceeds received and the carrying value of the shares sold.

356   Chapter 16

SUBSEQUENT VALUATION OF STOCK INVESTMENTS UNDER THE COST METHOD

8. The treatment differs for current and noncurrent marketable equity securities. Current marketable equity securities are valued at the lower of cost or market. When stock is to be written down, an unrealized loss account entitled Unrealized Loss on Current Marketable Equity Securities is debited, and Allowance for Market Decline of Current Marketable Equity Securities is credited.

9. The loss on current marketable equity securities is shown on the income statement and the Allowance for Market Decline of Current Marketable Equity Securities is a contra asset account.

10. Noncurrent marketable equity securities are also valued at the lower of cost or market. However, the reduction in value is debited to an unrealized loss account that is shown as a reduction in stockholders' equity, while the allowance is a contra account to the investment account.

11. If a loss on an individual noncurrent security is determined to be permanent, it is recorded as a realized loss and deducted in determining net income.

THE EQUITY METHOD FOR LONG-TERM INVESTMENTS OF BETWEEN 20% AND 50%

12. Owning between 20% and 50% of the outstanding stock of another company indicates significant influence. A company may have significant influence even when the investment is less than 20%. The equity method is used in either case.

REPORTING FOR STOCK INVESTMENT OF MORE THAN 50%

13. Companies expand by purchasing a major portion or all of another company's outstanding voting stock. The purpose of such purchases may be to acquire a source of raw material or to receive income on the investment.

PARENT AND SUBSIDIARY CORPORATIONS

14. A parent company is one that owns more than 50% of the outstanding voting common stock of another corporation.

15. A subsidiary company is the corporation acquired and controlled by the parent company.

16. Consolidated financial statements must be prepared when the following two conditions exist.
    a. One company owns a majority (which is more than 50%) of the outstanding voting common stock of another company.
    b. Unless control is likely to be temporary or if it does not rest with the majority owner (e.g., company is in legal reorganization or bankruptcy).

ELIMINATIONS

17. Consolidated entries are required so that the assets, liabilities, stockholders' equity, revenues, expenses, and dividends will appear as if the parent and its subsidiaries taken together constitute a single economic entity.
    a. To avoid double counting assets and owners' equity, the parent company's investment account and the subsidiary's capital accounts must be eliminated.
    b. Intercompany debt and other intercompany balances must also be eliminated.
    c. Elimination entries are made only on a consolidated statement work sheet; they are not posted to the parent's or the subsidiary's accounts.

CONSOLIDATED BALANCE SHEET AT TIME OF ACQUISITION

18. A consolidated work sheet is needed to combine assets and liabilities of a parent company and its subsidiaries.
    a. This informal statement includes the elimination entries necessary to show the parent and its subsidiaries as one economic enterprise.
    b. The first two columns show individual assets, liabilities, and stockholders' equity of the corporations involved.

c. The next column shows the eliminations that are needed to offset intercompany items.

d. A final column shows the amounts that will appear on the consolidated balance sheet.

ACQUISITION OF SUBSIDIARY AT BOOK VALUE

19. If the investment in the subsidiary is acquired at book value and represents 100% ownership, the elimination entry required is to debit Common Stock and debit Retained Earnings of the subsidiary and to credit Investment in Subsidiary at the original cost at the date of acquisition.

ACQUISITION OF SUBSIDIARY AT A COST ABOVE OR BELOW BOOK VALUE

20. Subsidiaries may be acquired at a cost greater than or less than book value.

   a. Where cost exceeds book value because of expected above-average earnings, the excess is labeled goodwill on the consolidated balance sheet.

   b. When the cost exceeds book value because assets of the subsidiary are undervalued, the asset values should be increased to the extent of the excess.

21. A parent may acquire a subsidiary at less than its book value.

   a. Any excess of book value over cost must be used first to reduce proportionately the value of the noncurrent assets acquired.

   b. After the noncurrent assets are reduced to zero, any remaining amount of excess should be reported as a deferred credit on the consolidated balance sheet.

ACQUISITION OF LESS THAN 100% OF SUBSIDIARY

22. When a parent acquires less than 100% of a subsidiary, minority stockholders or a minority interest exists.

   a. The minority stockholders have an interest in the subsidiary's net assets and share the subsidiary's earnings with the parent company.

   b. When a consolidated balance sheet is prepared for a partially owned subsidiary, only part of the subsidiary's stockholders' equity is eliminated.

ACCOUNTING FOR INCOME, LOSSES, AND DIVIDENDS OF A SUBSIDIARY

23. A subsidiary's net assets and retained earnings increase when a subsidiary is operating profitably. Both the parent company and minority stockholders share in the distribution when the subsidiary pays dividends.

COST METHOD FOR INVESTMENTS IN SUBSIDIARIES

24. Under the cost method, the parent company records its investment in a subsidiary at the cost or price paid at acquisition.

   a. The investment account is not adjusted subsequently.

   b. Dividends received from the subsidiary are recorded by debiting Cash and crediting Dividend Revenue.

EQUITY METHOD FOR INVESTMENTS IN SUBSIDIARIES

25. Under the equity method, the investment is recorded at cost, but the investment account is adjusted periodically for the parent company's share of the subsidiary's income, losses, and dividends as they are reported by the subsidiary.

CONSOLIDATED FINANCIAL STATEMENTS AT A DATE AFTER ACQUISITION

26. Under the equity method, the amounts eliminated on the consolidated statement work sheet will differ from year to year.

PURCHASE VERSUS POOLING OF INTERESTS

27. *APB Opinion No. 16* separates business combinations into two categories: purchases and pooling of interests.

   a. A purchase is a business combination in which cash, other assets, or debt securities are given up in exchange for a subsidiary's outstanding voting common stock. A purchase also occurs when common stock is exchanged for common stock and the resulting business combination does not satisfy the conditions specified in *APB Opinion No. 16*.

   b. A pooling of interests occurs when common stock is exchanged for common stock and the resulting business combination satisfies all of the conditions specified in *APB Opinion No. 16*.

28. The purchase method of accounting is used for business combinations classified as purchases.

   a. The parent company's investment is recorded at the amount of cash given up or at the fair market value of the assets or stock given up, or the fair market value of the stock received, whichever is the most clearly and objectively determinable.

   b. The subsidiary's retained earnings at date of acquisition do *not* become part of consolidated retained earnings.

   c. Only that portion of the subsidiary's net earnings that arises after the date of acquisition is included in consolidated net earnings.

29. The pooling of interests method of accounting is used for business combinations classified as a pooling of interests.

   a. The parent company records its investments at the book value of the subsidiary's net assets, with the result that there can be no goodwill or deferred credit from consolidation.

   b. The subsidiary's retained earnings on the date of acquisition become part of consolidated retained earnings.

   c. All the subsidiary's net earnings for the year of acquisitions are included in consolidated net earnings.

USES AND LIMITATIONS OF CONSOLIDATED STATEMENTS

30. Consolidated financial statements are of primary importance to the parent company's stockholders, managers, and directors, while the subsidiary's individual financial statements are more important to the subsidiary's creditors and minority stockholders.

31. Consolidated financial statements are of very limited use to creditors and minority stockholders of the subsidiary.

DEMONSTRATION PROBLEM

The Chris Company acquired all of the outstanding voting common stock of the JMA Corporation on July 1, 1994, for $900,000. The balance sheets for the two companies on the date of acquisition were as shown below:

Assets	Chris Company	JMA Corporation
Cash	$ 69,000	$ 45,000
Accounts receivable	135,000	116,700
Notes receivable	105,000	21,000
Merchandise inventory	180,000	75,000
Investment in JMA Corporation	900,000	
Building, net	450,000	468,000
Land	240,000	300,000
Total Assets	$2,079,000	$1,025,700
Liabilities		
Accounts payable	$ 195,000	$ 170,100
Notes payable	108,000	39,000
Common stock—$50 par	900,000	450,000
Retained earnings	876,000	366,600
Total Liabilities and Stockholders' Equity	$2,079,000	$1,025,700

Chris management believes that the building of JMA Corporation and the land on which it is sitting are undervalued by $15,000 and $30,000 respectively. The remainder of the excess of cost over book value is due to superior earnings potential.

On July 1, 1994, when the acquisition occurred, JMA Corporation borrowed $9,000 from Chris Company on a note.

Required:

a. Prepare a work sheet for a consolidated balance sheet on the date of acquisition.
b. Prepare a consolidated balance sheet for July 1, 1994.

a.

Accounts	Chris Co.	JMA Corp.	Eliminations		Consolidated Amounts
			Debit	Credit	
Assets					
Liabilities and Stockholders' Equity					

b.

SOLUTION TO DEMONSTRATION PROBLEM

a.

CHRIS COMPANY AND SUBSIDIARY JMA CORPORATION
Work Sheet for Consolidated Balance Sheet
July 1, 1994

Accounts	Chris Co.	JMA Corp.	Eliminations Debit	Eliminations Credit	Consolidated Amounts
Assets					
Cash	69,000	45,000			114,000
Accounts receivable	135,000	116,700			251,700
Notes receivable	105,000	21,000		(b) 9,000	117,000
Merchandise inventory	180,000	75,000			255,000
Investment in JMA Corp.	900,000			(a) 900,000	
Building, net	450,000	468,000	(a) 15,000		933,000
Land	240,000	300,000	(a) 30,000		570,000
Goodwill			(a) 38,400		38,400
	2,079,000	1,025,700			2,279,100
Liabilities and Stockholders' Equity					
Accounts payable	195,000	170,100			365,100
Notes payable	108,000	39,000	(b) 9,000		138,000
Common stock—$50 par	900,000	450,000	(a) 450,000		900,000
Retained earnings	876,000	366,600	(a) 366,600		876,000
	2,079,000	1,025,700	909,000	909,000	2,279,100

Chapter 16

b.

CHRIS COMPANY AND SUBSIDIARY JMA CORPORATION
Consolidated Balance Sheet
July 1, 1994

Assets

Current Assets:
Cash	$114,000	
Accounts receivable	251,700	
Notes receivable	117,000	
Merchandise inventory	255,000	
Total current assets		$ 737,700

Plant and equipment:
Building, net	$933,000	
Land	570,000	
Total plant and equipment		1,503,000
Goodwill		38,400
Total Assets		$2,279,100

Liabilities and Stockholders' Equity

Current Liabilities:
Accounts payable		$ 365,100
Notes payable		138,000
Total liabilities		$ 503,100

Stockholders' Equity:
Common stock—$50 par	$900,000	
Retained earnings	876,000	
Total stockholders' equity		1,776,000
Total Liabilities and Stockholders' Equity		$2,279,100

MATCHING

Referring to the terms listed below, place the appropriate letter next to the corresponding description. Not all terms may be used.

a. Consolidated statement work sheet
b. Consolidated statements
c. Cost method
d. Elimination entries

e. Equity method
f. Goodwill
g. Intercompany transactions
h. Marketable equity securities
i. Minority interest

j. Parent company
k. Pooling of interests
l. Purchase
m. Subsidiary company

_____ 1. A company acquired and controlled by a parent corporation, with control established by ownership of more than 50% of the subsidiary's outstanding voting common stock.

_____ 2. A method of accounting for stock investments in which the investor company records its investment at cost (price paid at acquisition) and does not adjust the investment account balance subsequently. Dividends received from investee are credited to a Dividend Revenue account.

_____ 3. A business combination in which the acquiring company usually issues cash or other assets.

_____ 4. Entries made on a consolidated statement work sheet to remove certain intercompany items and transactions.

_____ 5. An intangible value attaching to a business primarily due to above average income prospects.

_____ 6. The financial statements that result from combining the parent's financial statement amounts with those of its subsidiaries.

_____ 7. A corporation that owns more than 50% of the outstanding voting common stock of another corporation.

_____ 8. A method of accounting for stock investments in which the investor company records its investment at cost (price paid at acquisition) and subsequently adjusts the investment account balance for income and losses of the investee. Dividends received reduce the carrying amount of the investment account balance.

_____ 9. Financial transactions involving a parent and one of its subsidiaries or between two of the subsidiaries.

_____ 10. The claim or interest of the stockholders who own less than 50% of a subsidiary's outstanding voting common stock.

_____ 11. Shares of common stock of another company that can be easily sold.

_____ 12. A business combination that meets certain criteria specified in *APB Opinion No. 16*, including the issuance of common stock in exchange for common stock.

_____ 13. An informal statement on which elimination entries are made for the purpose of showing account balances as if the parent and its subsidiaries were a single economic enterprise.

COMPLETION AND EXERCISES

1. When a corporation invests in marketable equity securities of other corporations, what constitutes the cost of the securities?

_____

_____

2. If a cash dividend of $4,000 is declared on marketable equity securities held as investments in one period but paid in the next period, what is the form of the entry required at the end of the first period?

DATE		ACCOUNT TITLES AND EXPLANATION	POST. REF.	DEBIT	CREDIT

3. How is a stock dividend treated on marketable equity securities?

_____

_____

_____

4. Where is a realized gain or loss on the sale of marketable equity securities shown in the financial statements?

_____

_____

5. Marketable equity securities may be written down below cost when their _____ _____

is less than their _____ for a portfolio of securities classified as current assets and for a portfolio classified as noncurrent assets.

6. The account Unrealized Loss on Noncurrent Marketable Equity Securities would be shown as ____

_____

7. On December 31, 1993, Ace Co. has a portfolio of current marketable equity securities that has a total cost of $84,000, a market value of $80,000, and an Allowance for Market Decline of Current Marketable Equity Securities of $4,000. During 1994 the following occurred:

Purchased 100 shares of Mox Co. common stock at $50, plus a commission of $150.
Received 20 shares of Kahn Co. common stock as a stock dividend; market value is $20 per share.
Sold 200 shares of Lee Co. common stock at $40, less commissions and other charges of $200. Cost of securities sold was $4,000.
Cash dividends received, $5,600.
At the end of 1994, the cost of the securities in the portfolio is $3,200 greater than their market value. Prepare the necessary entries for 1994.

THE FORM FOR COMPLETION OF NO. 7 APPEARS ON THE FOLLOWING PAGE.

8. A parent company owns _____ _____ _____ _____ of the

outstanding voting common stock of another corporation which is referred to as a _____

_____.

DATE	ACCOUNT TITLES AND EXPLANATION	POST. REF.	DEBIT	CREDIT

9. Consolidated financial statements must be prepared when the following circumstances exist:

a. _____

_____

b. _____

_____

_____

10. Elimination entries are made only on a _____ _____

_____ _____.

11. The cost of an investment in a subsidiary may exceed the investment's book value for either or both of the following reasons:

a. _____

_____

b. _____

_____

12. When the cost of an investment exceeds its underlying book value and none of the subsidiary's assets is considered to be undervalued, the excess of cost over book value is labeled as _____* on the consolidated balance sheet.

13. What is the elimination entry needed if on the date of acquisition the parent company loaned the subsidiary company $8,000 on a note receivable?

14. A minority interest appears on the consolidated balance sheet when _____

_____.

15. If the equity method is being used, income of a subsidiary _____ (increases or decreases) the balance of the investment account, while losses incurred by a subsidiary _____ (increase or decrease) the investment account balance. Dividends paid by a subsidiary _____ (increase or decrease) the investment account balance.

16. Goodwill must be amortized over _____ _____ _____ years.

17. According to *APB Opinion No. 16*, business combinations can be classified into two categories:
(a) _____ and (b) _____ _____ _____. A _____
_____ _____ is a business combination that results when common stock is exchanged for common stock and the conditions specified in *APB Opinion No. 16* are satisfied. All other business combinations are classified as _____.

18. Book Company acquired 100% of the outstanding voting common stock of Sunny Company for $600,000. On the date of acquisition, Sunny Company's stockholders' equity consisted of common stock, $500,000, and retained earnings, $85,000. What journal entry should be made by Book Company to record the above transaction?

_____

_____

19. Refer back to Question 18. Assume that a consolidated statement work sheet is prepared on the date of acquisition. What elimination entry must be made? (The subsidiary's tangible assets are not overvalued or undervalued.)

_____

_____

_____

_____

20. The Sun Company acquired 80% of the outstanding voting common stock of the Meyers Company for $268,000 on January 2, 1994. During 1994, the Meyers Company had net income of $38,400 and paid out $18,800 in dividends on common stock. What journal entries should be made by Sun Company to record the above events assuming it uses the equity method? (The subsidiary's tangible assets are not overvalued or undervalued.)

21. Under the purchase method of accounting, a parent company records an investment in a subsidiary at the

_____

_____

_____

_____

_____

22. Under the pooling of interests method, what portion of the subsidiary's net income is included in consolidated net income for the year of acquisition?

_____

_____

23. Under the pooling of interests method, an investment in a subsidiary is recorded at the _____

_____.

24. Assume that the amount paid by a parent corporation for the stock of a subsidiary is either more or less than the book value of the subsidiary interest.

a. If the cost exceeds the book value:

1. Where will the amount be reported on the consolidated balance sheet?

_____

_____

2. Into what account on the work sheet is the excess classified?

_____

b. If the book value exceeds the cost:

1. What is the most logical explanation? _____

_____

2. In this case, what is the correct treatment? _____

_____

25. The consolidated statements are of primary importance to _____

_____.

26. The creditors and minority stockholders of a subsidiary are primarily interested in the _____

_____ financial statements.

27. Glove Company acquired 82% of the outstanding voting common stock of Hand Company for $201,000. On the date of acquisition, the minority interest in Hand Company amounts to $45,000. The book value of Glove Company's investment in Hand Company is _____. What is the relationship between the cost and the book value of the investment? _____

_____

28. On January 1, 1994, the Peach Company acquired 75% of the outstanding voting common stock of the Cream Company for $296,000. Also on January 1, 1994, the Cream Company borrowed $24,000 from the Peach Company. The debt is evidenced by a note. Complete the consolidated statement work sheet shown below. The subsidiary's tangible assets are neither overvalued nor undervalued.

PEACH COMPANY AND SUBSIDIARY CREAM COMPANY
Work Sheet for Consolidated Balance Sheet
January 1, 1994

	Peach Company	Cream Company	Eliminations		Consolidated Amounts
			Debit	Credit	
Assets:					
Cash	72,000	36,000			
Notes receivable	24,000				
Accounts receivable, net	58,000	38,000			
Merchandise inventory	68,000	54,000			
Investment in Cream Co.	296,000				
Equipment, net	94,000	100,000			
Buildings, net	166,000	148,000			
Land	56,000	44,000			
	834,000	420,000			
Liabilities and Stockholders' Equity:					
Notes payable		24,000			
Accounts payable	52,000	20,000			
Common stock	500,000	220,000			
Retained earnings	282,000	156,000			
	834,000	420,000			

29. Using the consolidated statement work sheet prepared for Question 28, prepare a consolidated balance sheet in the space provided below.

Chapter 16

Indicate whether each of the following statements is true or false by inserting a capital "T" or "F" in the blank space provided.

_____ 1. Unrealized losses on current marketable equity securities are reported in the income statement.

_____ 2. Unrealized losses on noncurrent marketable equity securities are reported in the income statement.

_____ 3. Realized gains on noncurrent marketable equity securities are shown in the income statement.

_____ 4. When the parent and subsidiary are engaged in similar or related businesses, consolidated financial statements must be prepared.

_____ 5. In the consolidating process of preparing financial statements for the parent and subsidiaries, elimination entries are made in the subsidiaries' respective journals.

_____ 6. One of the purposes of consolidated financial statements is to show a parent and its subsidiaries as one economic enterprise.

_____ 7. The reason that the elimination entry is needed crediting the Investment in Subsidiary Company is that if both the investment account and the subsidiary's assets appear on the consolidated balance sheet, the same resources will be counted twice.

_____ 8. When a subsidiary is acquired at a cost above its book value and its assets are undervalued, Goodwill is recognized in the elimination entries.

_____ 9. When a parent company pays less than the book value of the subsidiary's net assets, it generally indicates that the parent has acquired a "bargain" purchase.

_____ 10. Because minority stockholders own less than 50% of the subsidiary's outstanding voting common stock, they do not share in subsidiary earnings with the parent company.

_____ 11. There is lack of agreement among accountants as to whether the minority interest is a liability or a part of stockholders' equity.

_____ 12. When a subsidiary pays dividends, both the parent company and the minority stockholders share in the dividend.

_____ 13. When a subsidiary is acquired at a cost less than its book value and its assets are overvalued, the Accounting Principles Board requires that the excess of book value over cost be used to reduce proportionately the value of the noncurrent assets acquired.

_____ 14. When a subsidiary incurs a loss, the parent company debits a loss account and credits an investment account for the parent's share of the loss.

_____ 15. Consolidated statements are of great use to creditors and minority stockholders of the subsidiary because these creditors can look to the parent company for payment.

_____ 16. When cost exceeds book value and the purchase method is used, more depreciation (or amortization) will be recorded under the purchase method than under the pooling of interests method.

_____ 17. When a subsidiary reports net earnings and the parent uses the equity method, the parent company debits the investment account and credits a revenue account for the parent's share of the net income.

_____ 18. Subsidiary creditors are more interested in the consolidated statements than in the individual financial statements of the subsidiary.

MULTIPLE CHOICE QUESTIONS

For each of the following questions indicate the best answer by circling the appropriate letter.

1. An unrealized loss on noncurrent marketable equity securities is shown in the:
   A. Income Statement.
   B. Balance Sheet.
   C. Statement of Retained Earnings.
   D. None of the above.

2. The book value of stock is:
   A. accumulated depreciation less the related plant asset's original cost.
   B. total stockholders' equity.
   C. net assets.
   D. the price at which the corporation's stock is selling on the market.
   E. (B) and (C) above.

3. Bid Company acquired the stock of Bet Company for $125,000. The entry needed is:

   A. Investment in Bid Company 125,000
      Cash 125,000
   B. Investment in Bet Company 125,000
      Cash 125,000
   C. Cash 125,000
      Investment Income 125,000
   D. Cash 125,000
      Investment in Bet Company 125,000
   E. None of the above.

4. If the following balances exist prior to the preparation of a consolidated balance sheet, what elimination entry is needed if the parent owns 100% of the subsidiary (S Company)?

	Parent Company	Subsidiary Company
Common Stock	476,000	70,000
Investment in S Company	105,000	
Retained Earnings	252,000	35,000

   A. Investment in S Company 105,000
      Retained Earnings 35,000
      Common Stock 70,000
   B. Common Stock 546,000
      Retained Earnings 287,000
      Investment in S Company 259,000
   C. Retained Earnings 35,000
      Common Stock 70,000
      Investment in S Company 105,000
   D. Gain from Elimination of S Company 105,000
      Investment in S Company 105,000
   E. None of the above.

5. P Company acquires 100% ownership of S Company for $400,000 after evaluating its assets and finding that its building is undervalued by $4,000 and that its prospects of above-industry earnings are good. P Company management attaches $30,000 value to these earnings prospects. S Company's Common Stock has a balance of $250,000 and its Retained Earnings, a balance of $116,000. P Company's Common Stock has a balance of $360,000 and its Retained Earnings, $130,000. The elimination entry needed is:

A. Investment is S Company 400,000
   Retained Earnings   40,000
   Common Stock   360,000

B. Common Stock 610,000
   Retained Earnings 256,000
   Investment in S Company   400,000
   Goodwill   466,000

C. Common Stock 250,000
   Retained Earnings 116,000
   Building   4,000
   Goodwill   30,000
   Investment in S Company   400,000

D. Common Stock 250,000
   Retained Earnings 116,000
   Investment in S Company   366,000

E. Common Stock 250,000
   Retained Earnings 116,000
   Excess of Cost Over Book Value   34,000
   Investment in S Company   400,000

6. P Company purchases 70% of S Company's stock for $45,000 at a time when S Company's Common Stock balance was $45,000 and its Retained Earnings balance was $15,000. P Company attributes any excess to the excellent prospects of above-average earnings. The *credits* needed in the elimination entry are:

A. Investment in S Company   45,000
   Minority Interest   18,000
B. Goodwill   3,000
   Investment in S Company   45,000
C. Minority Interest   25,000
   Investment in S Company   45,000
D. Common Stock   45,000
   Retained Earnings   15,000
E. Goodwill   45,000
   Investment in S Company   45,000

SOLUTIONS

Matching

1.	m	8.	e
2.	c	9.	g
3.	l	10.	i
4.	d	11.	h
5.	f	12.	k
6.	b	13.	a
7.	j		

Completion and Exercises

1. The cost of securities is the actual price of the securities plus any brokerage fee.

2.
Dividends Receivable	4,000	
Dividends Revenue		4,000

3. A notation is made of the larger number of shares held and the smaller per share cost.
4. Such gains or losses are shown in the nonoperating portion of the income statement.
5. market value; cost
6. a deduction from total stockholders' equity or from total paid-in capital.

7.
Current Marketable Equity Securities	5,150	
Cash		5,150

Note: Received 20 shares of Kahn Co. common stock as a stock dividend.

Cash	7,800	
Current Marketable Equity Securities		4,000
Gain on Sale of Securities		3,800
Cash	5,600	
Dividend Revenue		5,600
Allowance for Market Decline in Current Marketable Equity Securities	800	
Recovery of Market Value of Current Marketable Equity Securities		800

8. more than 50% (a majority); subsidiary company
9. (a) one company owns more than 50% of the outstanding voting common stock of another company and (b) unless control is likely to be temporary or if it does not rest with the majority owner (e.g., company is in legal reorganization or bankruptcy).
10. consolidated statement work sheet
11. a. The parent may think the subsidiary's assets are undervalued.
    b. The parent may believe the subsidiary's income prospects justify paying a price greater than book value.
12. goodwill

13.
Note Payable	8,000	
Note Receivable		8,000

14. a parent owns less than 100% of a subsidiary (but more than 50%)
15. increases; decrease; decrease
16. 40 or fewer
17. (a) purchases; (b) poolings of interests; pooling of interests; purchases

18.
Investment in Sunny Company	600,000	
Cash		600,000

19.
Common Stock	500,000	
Retained Earnings	85,000	
Excess of Cost over Book Value (or Goodwill)	15,000	
Investment in Sunny Company		600,000

20.
Investment in Meyers Company	268,000	
Cash		268,000

To record investment of 80% in subsidiary.

Investment in Meyers Company	30,720	
Income of Meyers Company		30,720

To record 80% of subsidiary's income.

Cash	15,040	
Investment in Meyers Company		15,040

To record dividend paid by subsidiary.

21. amount of cash given up, or at the fair market value of the assets or stock given up, or the fair market value of the stock received, whichever can be the most clearly and objectively determined.

22. all the subsidiary's net income for the year of acquisition

23. book value of the subsidiary's net assets

24. a. 1. In the asset section, usually as the last item on the consolidated balance sheet.
    2. Goodwill.
    b. 1. Some of the subsidiary's assets are overvalued.
    2. The excess of book value over cost should be used to reduce proportionately the value of the noncurrent assets acquired.

25. the stockholders, managers, and directors of the parent company

26. subsidiary's

27. $205,000 (or $45,000 ÷ 0.18 = $250,000; $250,000 − $45,000 = $205,000);
Book value exceeds cost by $4,000 (or $205,000 − $201,000).

28.
PEACH COMPANY AND SUBSIDIARY CREAM COMPANY
Work Sheet for Consolidated Balance Sheet
January 1, 1994

| | Peach Company | Cream Company | Eliminations | | Consolidated Amounts |
			Debit	Credit	
Assets:					
Cash	72,000	36,000			108,000
Notes receivable	24,000			(b) 24,000	
Accounts receivable, net	58,000	38,000			96,000
Merchandise inventory	68,000	54,000			122,000
Investment in Cream Co.	296,000			(a) 296,000	
Equipment, net	94,000	100,000			194,000
Buildings, net	166,000	148,000			314,000
Land	56,000	44,000			100,000
Goodwill			(a) 14,000		14,000
	834,000	420,000			948,000
Liabilities and Stockholders' Equity:					
Notes payable		24,000	(b) 24,000		
Accounts payable	52,000	20,000			72,000
Common stock	500,000	220,000	(a) 220,000		500,000
Retained earnings	282,000	156,000	(a) 156,000		282,000
Minority interest				(a) 94,000	94,000
	834,000	420,000	414,000	414,000	948,000

29.

PEACH COMPANY AND SUBSIDIARY CREAM COMPANY
Consolidated Balance Sheet
January 1, 1994

Assets

Current Assets:

Cash	$108,000	
Accounts receivable, net	96,000	
Merchandise inventory	122,000	
Total Current Assets		$326,000

Plant and Equipment:

Equipment, net	$194,000	
Buildings, net	314,000	
Land	100,000	
Total Plant and Equipment		608,000
Goodwill		14,000
Total Assets		$948,000

Liabilities and Stockholders' Equity

Current Liabilities:

Accounts payable		$ 72,000
Minority Interest		94,000

Stockholders' Equity:

Common stock	$500,000	
Retained earnings	282,000	
Total Stockholders' Equity		782,000
Total Liabilities and Stockholders' Equity		$948,000

True-False Questions

1. T
2. F
3. T
4. T
5. F Elimination entries are not made in the accounting records of the parent or subsidiary; they are made only on a consolidated work sheet.
6. T
7. T
8. F Goodwill is recognized only when there are prospects of above-average earnings. In this case, the asset values should be increased to their fair market value.
9. F It generally means that the subsidiary's assets are overvalued.
10. F Minority stockholders do share in subsidiary earnings.
11. T
12. T
13. T
14. T
15. F Creditors and minority stockholders of the subsidiary cannot look to the parent for payment.
16. T
17. T
18. F Subsidiary creditors cannot look to parent company investments as a means to satisfy their debts; as a result they are more interested in subsidiary individual financial statements.

1. B
2. E
3. B
4. C
5. C
6. A The complete journal entry is:

Common Stock	45,000	
Retained Earnings	15,000	
Goodwill	3,000	
Investment in S Company		45,000
Minority Interest (30% × $60,000)		18,000

17 ANALYSIS AND INTERPRETATION OF FINANCIAL STATEMENTS

Learning Objectives

1. *Describe and explain the objectives of financial statement analysis.*
2. *Calculate and explain changes in financial statements using horizontal analysis, vertical analysis, and trend analysis.*
3. *Perform ratio analysis on financial statements using liquidity ratios, long-term solvency ratios, profitability tests, and market tests.*
4. *Describe the considerations used in financial statement analysis.*

CHAPTER OUTLINE

OBJECTIVES OF FINANCIAL STATEMENT ANALYSIS

1. Financial statements are issued primarily to communicate useful financial information to interested parties to aid them in making decisions regarding the company.

   a. Analysis of the statements usually clarifies and magnifies their significance.

   b. The purpose of statement analysis is to establish and present the relationships and trends found in the data contained in the statements.

FINANCIAL STATEMENT ANALYSIS

2. Comparative financial statements present financial data for a number of accounting periods for the same firm, and the analysis commonly includes:

   a. absolute increases and decreases in individual items.

   b. percentage increases and decreases in individual items.

      (1) Such percentage analysis facilitates analysis of widely varying dollar amounts.

      (2) Both dollar and percentage changes should be presented.

   c. trend percentages.

   d. percentage analysis of category totals (for example, current assets or current liabilities).

   e. ratios of significant figures.

RATIO ANALYSIS

3. Ratios can be broadly classified as liquidity ratios, equity or solvency ratios, profitability tests, and market tests.

LIQUIDITY RATIOS

4. Liquidity ratios are used to indicate a company's debt-paying ability.

5. The current ratio (total current assets ÷ total current liabilities) helps measure the company's ability to meet maturing current liabilities.

   a. Working capital is equal to the excess of current assets over current liabilities.

b. Current assets are cash and any other assets reasonably expected to be realized in cash, or sold, or consumed in the course of normal operations during the normal operating cycle or one year, whichever is longer.

6. The acid-test or quick ratio (quick assets ÷ current liabilities) is a more severe test of immediate debt-paying ability.

   a. Quick assets include cash, net receivables, and marketable securities. They are assets that are cash or can be converted into cash quickly.

   b. The quality of the receivables and marketable securities should be considered before determining whether the existing ratio is adequate.

7. Turnover ratios express the number of times during the period that an asset or group of assets was disposed of or converted into another asset or group of assets and generally measures the efficiency with which the assets are used.

   a. Accounts receivable turnover = Sales ÷ Net accounts receivable (preferably the average of end-of-month or end-of-week balances).

      (1) A high ratio usually means that the accounts have a relatively short average life.
      (2) The ratio size depends upon credit and collection policies and general business conditions.
      (3) Generally, a high ratio is desirable, but one should be careful when attempting to increase it so as not to discourage future sales.

   b. Average life (or collection period) of accounts receivable: the number of days in the year divided by accounts receivable turnover ratio.

   c. Inventory turnover = Cost of goods sold ÷ Average inventory for the period.

      (1) The ratio indicates the rapidity of inventory turnover.
      (2) The smaller the inventory required, the smaller the capital needed to produce a given volume of sales.
      (3) A rapid turnover tends to prevent the accumulation of obsolete items.
      (4) Shortages may result if the inventory is too small.

   d. Turnover of total assets = Net sales ÷ Average total assets during the period.

      (1) It is a measure of the efficiency of the use of the capital invested in assets.
      (2) Specific problems can be identified only by computing the turnover of specific assets.

EQUITY, OR LONG-TERM SOLVENCY RATIOS

8. Equity or solvency ratios indicate the financial structure of a company by showing the relationship of debt and equity financing.

9. Owners and creditors are both sources of assets.

   a. Owners invest capital and permit income to be retained.
   b. Creditors provide both long-term and short-term funds.
   c. The equity ratio (stockholders' equity ÷ total equity) indicates the portion of assets secured from stockholders and thereby the size of the protective buffer provided to creditors.

      (1) A high ratio is desirable to creditors because of the protection provided.
      (2) A low ratio is desirable to stockholders if borrowed funds can be put to work earning more than their cost.

PROFITABILITY TESTS

10. In judging profitability, two areas of concern are (1) the relationships of items on the income statement that indicate a company's ability to recover costs and expenses, and (2) the relationship of income to some balance sheet measure, which indicates the relative ability to earn income on assets employed.

11. Rate of return on operating assets = Net operating margin × Turnover of operating assets.

    a. Net operating margin = Net operating income ÷ Net sales.
    b. Turnover of operating assets = Net sales ÷ Operating assets.

c. Therefore, rate of return on operating assets also equals net operating income divided by the balance of operating assets.

    (1) Net operating income excludes nonoperating revenues and expenses and federal income taxes.
    (2) Operating assets are all those assets actively used in producing operating revenue.

d. This is the best measure of income performance without regard to the sources of assets.
e. High turnover tends to be associated with low margin; low turnover with high margin.

12. Stockholders are interested in net income as a percentage of average stockholders' equity and in earnings per share of common stock.

   a. If preferred stock is outstanding, a portion of net income must be assigned to these shares before earnings per share of common stock outstanding is computed.
   b. If shares were issued for assets during the year, the average number of shares during the year must be computed by recognizing the various dates on which the shares were issued.

13. Times interest earned = Income before interest and income taxes ÷ Interest for the period; it provides an indication of the likelihood that interest payments will continue to be met.

14. Times preferred dividends earned = Net income after income taxes ÷ Preferred dividends.

MARKET TESTS

15. Market tests help investors and potential investors assess the relative merits of the various stocks in the marketplace.

16. Earnings rate on market price = Earnings per share ÷ Market price per share; if the ratio is inverted, it becomes the price-earnings ratio.

17. Earnings yield on common stock = Earnings per share ÷ Market price per share. Dividend yield on common stock = Dividends per share ÷ Market price per share.

18. Payout ratio = Dividends per share ÷ Earnings per share; it indicates the percentage of the income which is paid out as dividends.

19. Yield on preferred stock = Dividends per share ÷ Market price per share.

FINAL CONSIDERATIONS IN FINANCIAL STATEMENT ANALYSIS

20. Ratios should be used only as clues that focus attention on certain relationships that might require further investigation.

21. The data used should be comparable in terms of the accounting practices followed.

22. External factors, such as general business conditions, may exert great influence on the firm's operations and should be taken into consideration when interpreting the statements.

23. Relationships between financial statement items become much more meaningful when appropriate standards are available for comparison.

24. Comparability of financial statements may be seriously impaired by fluctuations in the general price level or in specific prices. The effects of inflation must be considered when analyzing financial statements.

DEMONSTRATION PROBLEM

1. Common-size percentages are often used to compare the statements of companies of unequal size. The condensed income statements of companies A and B are given below. Enter in the spaces provided the amounts expressed in common-size percentages.

COMPANY A AND COMPANY B
Income Statements for Year Ended December 31, 1994

| | Dollar Amounts | | Common-Size Percentages | |
	Company A	Company B	Company A	Company B
Sales	$225,000	$262,500	_____%	_____%
Cost of goods sold	130,500	105,000	_____%	_____%
Gross margin	$ 94,500	$157,500	_____%	_____%
Selling expenses	$ 40,500	$ 44,626	_____%	_____%
Administrative expenses	22,500	26,250	_____%	_____%
Total operating expenses	$ 63,000	$ 70,876	_____%	_____%
Income	$ 31,500	$ 86,624	_____%	_____%

2. After expressing the amounts of the income statements in common-size percentages, examine them and write in this space (_____) the name of the company that operated more efficiently.

SOLUTION TO DEMONSTRATION PROBLEM

1.
COMPANY A AND COMPANY B
Income Statements for Year Ended December 31, 1994

| | Dollar Amounts | | Common-Size Percentages | |
	Company A	Company B	Company A	Company B
Sales	$225,000	$262,500	100%	100%
Cost of goods sold	130,500	105,000	58%	40%
Gross margin	$ 94,500	$157,500	42%	60%
Selling expenses	$ 40,500	$ 44,626	18%	17%
Administrative expenses	22,500	26,250	10%	10%
Total operating expenses	$ 63,000	$ 70,876	28%	27%
Income	$ 31,500	$ 86,624	14%	33%

2. Company B operated more efficiently.

MATCHING

Referring to the terms listed below, place the appropriate letter next to the corresponding description. Not all terms may be used.

a. Accounts receivable turnover
b. Acid-test (quick) ratio
c. Common-size statements
d. Current ratio
e. Debt-to-equity ratio
f. Dividend yield
g. Earnings per share
h. Equity ratio
i. Horizontal analysis
j. Inventory turnover
k. Liquidity
l. Operating margin
m. Price-earnings ratio
n. Total assets turnover
o. Vertical analysis
p. Working capital ratio

_____ 1. The ratio of stockholders' equity to total assets (or total equities).

_____ 2. The study of a single financial statement in which each item is expressed as a percentage of a significant total.

_____ 3. Show only percentages and no absolute dollar amounts.

_____ 4. Usually computed for common stock; net income less required preferred dividends, which equals earnings available to common stockholders, divided by weighted average number of shares of common stock outstanding.

_____ 5. Net sales divided by average total assets.

_____ 6. Same as current ratio.

_____ 7. The ratio of current market price per share divided by the earnings per share of the stock.

_____ 8. Dividend per share divided by current market price per share.

_____ 9. Net sales divided by average net accounts receivable.

_____ 10. Relates current assets to current liabilities.

_____ 11. Net operating income divided by net sales.

_____ 12. State of possessing liquid assets, such as cash and other assets that will soon be converted into cash.

_____ 13. Ratio of quick assets (cash, marketable securities, net receivables) to current liabilities.

_____ 14. Cost of goods sold divided by average inventory.

_____ 15. Total debt divided by stockholders' equity.

_____ 16. Analysis of a company's financial statements for two or more successive periods showing percentage and/or absolute changes from prior year. This type of analysis helps detect changes in a company's performance and highlights trends.

COMPLETION AND EXERCISES

1. Statement analysis is the selection and use of data presented in the financial statements to establish significant _____ and _____.

2. What are comparative financial statements? _____

_____

3. What are net assets? _____ _____ – _____ _____ =

_____ _____.

4. What is the definition of working capital? _____ _____ – _____

_____.

5. How is the current ratio computed? _____ _____ ÷ _____ _____.

6. What is the purpose of the current ratio? _____
   _____
   _____
   _____

7. What is the definition of current assets? _____
   _____
   _____
   _____
   _____

8. Does the payment of a current liability leave the current ratio unchanged? _____
   Why? _____
   _____
   _____
   _____
   _____

9. If a company borrows money from a bank on a one-year note, what effect does this have on the working
   capital of a company? _____ Why? _____
   _____
   _____

10. What items are included in "quick assets" for the purpose of computing the acid-test or quick ratio?
    _____
    _____

11. _____ and _____ are the two sources of assets for a business enterprise.

12. How is the equity ratio computed? _____ _____ ÷ _____ _____ .

13. Fill in the blank spaces below.

	December 31		Increase or (Decrease) 1994 over 1993	
	1994	1993	Dollars	Percentage
Current Assets:				
Cash	$ 81,000	$ 72,000	_____	_____
Accounts receivable, net	159,000	120,000	_____	_____
Inventories	138,000	126,000	_____	_____
Prepaid expenses	39,000	54,000	_____	_____
	$417,000	$372,000	_____	_____

14. What do turnover ratios express and what do they measure? _____
_____
_____
_____
_____
_____

15. What can be interpreted from the accounts receivable turnover ratio? _____
_____
_____
_____
_____
_____

16. What does the inventory turnover ratio show? _____
_____
_____
_____
_____
_____

17. What does the turnover of total assets show? _____
_____
_____
_____
_____
_____
_____

18. The price-earnings ratio is computed by dividing _____ _____ per share by
_____ per share.

19. The dividend yield on stock is computed by dividing _____ per share by the _____
_____ _____ .

20. The payout ratio is equal to _____ _____ _____ ÷ _____ per share.

21. Compute the requested figures for 1994 from the financial statements of the Sol Company presented on the following pages. (Assume all assets are operating assets.)

   a. Accounts receivable turnover = _____ ÷ _____ = _____.

   b. Average life of accounts receivable = _____ ÷ _____ = _____.

   c. Inventory turnover = _____ ÷ _____ = _____.

   d. Total asset turnover = _____ ÷ _____ = _____.

   e. Percentage of net income to net sales = _____ ÷ _____ = _____.

   f. Rate of return on operating assets = _____ × _____ = _____.

   g. Percentage of net income to stockholders' equity = _____ ÷ _____ = _____.

   h. Earnings per share of common stock = _____ ÷ _____ = _____.

   i. Number of times interest is earned = _____ ÷ _____ = _____.

SOL COMPANY
Comparative Balance Sheets
December 31, 1993 and 1994

	December 31 1994	December 31 1993
Assets		
Current Assets:		
Cash	$ 56,000	$ 48,000
Accounts receivable	76,800	67,200
Merchandise inventory	81,600	75,200
Prepaid expenses	8,000	6,400
Total Current Assets	$222,400	$196,800
Plant and equipment (net)	444,800	400,000
Intangible assets	20,800	24,000
Total Assets	$688,000	$620,800
Liabilities and Stockholders' Equity		
Liabilities:		
Current liabilities	$115,200	$112,000
9% first-mortgage bonds	144,000	144,000
Total Liabilities	$259,200	$256,000
Stockholders' Equity:		
6% preferred stock, par $200, 400 shares authorized and outstanding	$ 80,000	$ 80,000
Common stock, par $20	144,000	144,000
Paid-in capital in excess of par value—common	27,200	27,200
Retained earnings	177,600	113,600
Total Stockholders' Equity	$428,800	$364,800
Total Liabilities and Stockholders' Equity	$688,000	$620,800

SOL COMPANY
Income Statement
For the Year Ended December 31, 1994

Sales		$984,000
Less: Sales returns and allowances		24,000
Net sales		$960,000
Cost of goods sold:		
Beginning inventory		$ 75,200
Purchases		608,000
Goods available for sale		$683,200
Less: Ending inventory		81,600
Cost of goods sold		601,600
Gross margin		$358,400
Operating expenses		246,240
Net operating income		$112,160
Interest expense		12,960
Net income before taxes		$ 99,200
Income taxes		32,000
Net income after income taxes		$ 67,200

TRUE-FALSE QUESTIONS

Indicate whether each of the following statements is true or false by inserting a capital "T" or "F" in the blank space provided.

_____ 1. A firm with an equity ratio of .75:1 has three times as much stockholders' equity as debt.

_____ 2. The best measure of the ability of a firm to use assets efficiently is its rate of return on stockholders' equity.

_____ 3. A firm with an accounts receivable turnover of four has approximately 90 days' sales that are uncollected.

_____ 4. Prepaid expenses are included in calculating the quick ratio.

_____ 5. A firm that has a net loss of one percent on net sales may be quite profitable if it has a high turnover of total assets.

_____ 6. Comparative statements consist of the financial statements of two firms recast into the same format.

_____ 7. Interfirm analysis of financial statements may be aided if the balance sheet amounts are expressed as percentages of total assets.

_____ 8. A firm may be quite profitable and yet find it difficult to pay its accounts payable.

_____ 9. An earnings per share amount typically is calculated for both preferred and common shares.

_____ 10. If earnings per share for 1993 was $4, and a 100% stock dividend was distributed in 1992, the revised earnings per share for 1993 is $2.

_____ 11. Common-size statements provide information so that readers can determine the dollar amounts of increases and decreases in accounts from the previous year.

_____ 12. Trend percentages are calculated by first assigning a weight of 100% to the amounts appearing on the base year financial statements and comparing later periods with these amounts.

Chapter 17

_____ 13. The amount of earnings per share is increased if a company introduces larger portions of debt into its capital structure.

_____ 14. If a company's common stock balance was $200,000, retained earnings, $300,000, and bonds payable was $150,000, and these were the only balances in its equities accounts, its debt-to-equity ratio would be 1.5:1.

_____ 15. A low stockholders' equity ratio is desirable to creditors because of the protection provided to them.

_____ 16. Operating assets are all assets actively used in producing operating revenues and would include land rented to another company.

MULTIPLE CHOICE QUESTIONS

For each of the following questions indicate the best answer by circling the appropriate letter.

Questions 1–3. Consider each of the following transactions separately and state the effect of each transaction on working capital, current ratio, and acid-test ratio. Assume the current ratio is 1:1 before these transactions occurred.

1. Purchased merchandise on account, $105,000.

   A. No effect on working capital, decrease both current ratio and acid-test ratio.
   B. No effect on working capital or current ratio, decrease acid-test ratio.
   C. No effect on all three financial analysis techniques.
   D. Decrease all three financial analysis techniques.
   E. Increase working capital, decrease current and acid-test ratios.

2. Paid cash for office supplies, $4,500.

   A. Increase working capital and current ratio, decrease acid-test ratio.
   B. No effect on all three financial analysis techniques.
   C. No effect on working capital and current ratio, decrease acid-test ratio.
   D. Decrease all three financial analysis techniques.

3. Paid short-term portion of notes payable, $37,500.

   A. Decrease working capital, current ratio, and acid-test ratios.
   B. Increase working capital, no effect on currrent and acid-test ratios.
   C. Increase working capital, decrease current and acid-test ratios.
   D. No effect on all three financial analysis techniques.
   E. No effect on working capital, increase current ratio and acid-test ratio.

Questions 4–5. The following data were abstracted from the balance sheet of BB Company:

Cash	$212,500
Marketable securities	100,000
Accounts and notes receivable, net	287,500
Merchandise inventory	381,250
Prepaid expenses	18,750
Accounts and notes payable, short term	400,000
Accrued liabilities	100,000

4. The current ratio is:
   A. 1:2
   B. 2:1
   C. 1.2:1
   D. 3:1
   E. 4:1

5. The acid-test ratio is:
   A. 1:2
   B. 2:1
   C. 1.2:1
   D. 3:1
   E. 4:1

Questions 6–8.   The balance sheet for Tri-Now Co. at the end of the current fiscal year indicated the following:

Total current liabilities (noninterest bearing)	$ 650,000
Bonds payable, 5% (issued in 1994, due in 20 years)	1,300,000
Preferred 6% stock, $200 par	520,000
Common stock, $20 par	1,040,000
Premium on common stock	260,000
Retained earnings	910,000

Income before income taxes was $390,000 and income taxes were $169,000 for the current year.

6. The rate earned on common stockholders' equity is:
   A. 7.0%.
   B. 8.6%.
   C. 9.1%.
   D. 8.1%.
   E. 6.1%.

7. The rate of return earned on total (operating) assets is:
   A. 7.0%.
   B. 8.6%.
   C. 9.1%.
   D. 8.1%.
   E. 6.1%.

8. The number of times preferred dividends were earned is:
   A. 7.1
   B. 8.6
   C. 9.1
   D. 8.1
   E. 6.1

Questions 9–11. In the following questions express the following income statement amounts in common-size percentages:

OMEGA COMPANY
Income Statement
For Year Ended December 31, 1994

Sales	$180,000
Cost of goods sold	117,360
Gross profit from sales	$ 62,640
Operating expenses	43,200
Net income	$ 19,440

9. Cost of goods sold expressed in a common-size percentage is:

   A. 66%.
   B. 100%.
   C. 65.2%.
   D. 6.03%.

10. Operating expenses expressed in a common-size percentage are:

   A. 69%.
   B. 24%.
   C. 28%.
   D. 2.22%.

11. Net income expressed in a common-size percentage is:

   A. 100%.
   B. 31%.
   C. 12%.
   D. 10.8%.

12. A company showed the following for a fiscal year ended December 31.

Accounts Receivable, January 1	$ 60,000
Accounts Receivable, December 31	80,000
Gross Sales	400,000
Sales Returns and Allowances	50,000
Net Sales	350,000

   The turnover of accounts receivable is:

   A. 5.257 times per year.
   B. 5.83 times per year.
   C. 5 times per year.
   D. 4.375 times per year.
   E. 4.6 times per year.

13. Which of the following transactions would result in an increase in the current ratio assuming that the ratio presently is 2:1?

   A. Customer paid its account receivable.
   B. Merchandise was purchased on account.
   C. Paid a long-term debt.
   D. Repaid a 90-day notes payable.
   E. None of the above transactions would increase the present current ratio.

14. Calhoun Company's records reveal the following:

Income before interest and taxes	$800,000
Less interest on bonds	80,000
Balance	$720,000
Income taxes at 45%	324,000
Income after taxes	$396,000
Less preferred dividends	27,200
Income available for common stockholders	$368,800

The number of times the interest is earned is:

A. 2.20 times.
B. 2.02 times.
C. 10 times.
D. 11.11 times.
E. 12.5 times.

15. What would be the effect of the following transaction on working capital?

Received $330 from a customer in payment of its account.

A. Increased current assets, thus increase in working capital.
B. Decreased working capital.
C. No effect.

SOLUTIONS

Matching

1.	h	7.	m	12.	k
2.	o	8.	f	13.	b
3.	c	9.	a	14.	j
4.	g	10.	d	15.	e
5.	n	11.	l	16.	i
6.	p				

Completion and Exercises

1. relationships; trends
2. Comparative financial statements present the statements of the same firm for each of two or more accounting periods.
3. Total assets − Total liabilities = Net assets
4. Current assets − Current liabilities
5. Current assets ÷ Current liabilities
6. The purpose of the current ratio is to measure the immediate debt-paying ability and the strength of the working capital position of a company.
7. Current assets are cash or other assets reasonably expected to be realized in cash, or sold or consumed, in the course of normal operations during the normal operating cycle of the business or one year, whichever is longer.
8. Not usually. If the current ratio is greater than one, the payment of a current liability will increase the current ratio. If the current ratio is less than one, the payment of a current liability will reduce the current ratio. Only if the ratio is equal to one will it remain unchanged.
9. None. The borrowing increases cash (current asset) and notes payable (current liability) by the same amount.
10. The "quick assets" consist of cash, net receivables, and martketable securities.

11. Stockholders, creditors
12. Owners' equity ÷ Total equities (or Total assets)

13.

Increase or (Decrease)
1994 over 1993

Dollars	Percentage
$ 9,000	12.5
39,000	32.5
12,000	9.5
(15,000)	(27.8)
$45,000	12.1

14. Turnover ratios express the number of times during a period that an asset or group of assets is disposed of or converted into another asset or group of assets. Turnover ratios measure the efficiency with which the asset or assets are used.
15. The accounts receivable turnover ratio shows the average age of accounts receivable. A high turnover rate means that funds are freed quickly for investment elsewhere. A low turnover rate means that funds are "tied up" in accounts receivable.
16. The inventory turnover ratio indicates the rapidity with which inventories are sold and replenished. The higher the turnover, the smaller the amount of capital needed to produce a given amount of sales.
17. The turnover of total assets shows the relationship between dollar volume of sales and total assets as a measure of efficiency of the use of capital invested in the assets.
18. market price; earnings
19. dividends; market price per share
20. Dividends per share ÷ Earnings per share

21. a. $\dfrac{\$960,000}{\$72,000} = 13.3$ times

b. $365 \div 13.3 = 27.4$ (if 360 days were used in the calculation the answer would be 27.1)

c. $\dfrac{\$601,600}{\$78,400} = 7.67$

d. $\dfrac{\$960,000}{\$654,400} = 1.47$

e. $\dfrac{\$67,200}{\$960,000} = 7\%$

f. $\dfrac{\$112,160}{\$960,000} \times \dfrac{\$960,000}{\$688,000} = 16.3\%$ or $\dfrac{\$112,160}{\$960,000} \times \dfrac{\$960,000}{\$654,400} = 17.1\%$

g. $\dfrac{\$67,200}{\$396,800} = 16.9\%$

h. $\dfrac{\$67,200 - (\$12 \times 400)^*}{7,200} = \$8.67$

i. $\dfrac{\$112,160}{\$12,960} = 8.65$ times

---

*Dividend on preferred stock must be deducted from earnings after taxes to arrive at the numerator of $62,400.

True-False Questions

1. T
2. F
3. T   365 days/4 = approximately 90 days
4. F
5. F
6. F
7. T
8. T   The accrual net income shown on the income statement is not cash income and does not have a direct relationship to the cash flow.
9. F   Earnings per share are calculated for common shares only.
10. T   A 100% stock dividend doubles the number of shares of stock outstanding, which reduces in half the earnings per share.
11. F   Common-size statements show no absolute amounts, only percentages.
12. T
13. T
14. F   The debt-to-equity ratio is 30% ($150,000/$500,000).
15. F   Only a high stockholders' equity ratio would be desirable to creditors because of its protection.
16. F   Land rented to another company is a nonoperating asset; but, the definition of operating assets is correct.

Multiple Choice Questions

1. B
2. C
3. D
4. B $212,500 + $100,000 + $287,500 + $381,250 + $18,750 = $1,000,000 current assets
   $400,000 + $100,000 = $500,000 current liabilities
   $1,000,000/$500,000 = 2:1
5. C $212,500 + $100,000 + $287,500 = $600,000 quick assets
   $600,000 quick assets/$500,000 current liabilities = 1.2:1
6. B $221,000 net income − $31,200 preferred dividends = $189,800
   $189,800/$2,210,000 common stockholders' equity = 8.6
7. E $221,000 net income + $65,000 interest expense = $286,000
   $286,000/$4,680,000 = 6.1%
8. A $221,000 net income/$31,200 preferred dividends = 7.1.
9. C
10. B
11. D
12. C $350,000 net sales/$70,000 average accounts receivable
13. D
14. C $800,000/$80,000 = 10 times
15. C

18   STATEMENT OF CASH FLOWS

Learning Objectives

1. *Explain the purposes and uses of the statement of cash flows.*
2. *Describe the content of the statement of cash flows and where certain items would appear on the statement.*
3. *Describe how to calculate cash flows from operating activities under both the direct and indirect methods.*
4. *Prepare a statement of cash flows under both the direct and indirect methods showing cash flows from operating activities, investing activities, and financing activities.*
5. *Describe the historical development from a statement of changes in financial position to a statement of cash flows.*

PURPOSES OF THE STATEMENT OF CASH FLOWS

1. A statement of cash flows reports the flow of cash into and out of a business in an accounting period.

   a. Reports on cash receipts and cash disbursements of an entity.

   b. Reports on the entity's investing and financing activities for the period.

   c. Such a statement is required each time a balance sheet and an income statement are presented.

USES OF THE STATEMENT OF CASH FLOWS

2. The statement of cash flows summarizes the effects of the operating, investing, and financing activities of a company for a period.

   a. The statement of cash flows reports on past management decisions on such matters as issuance of capital stock or sale of long-term bonds.

   b. Cash flow information is available only in bits and pieces on other financial statements.

MANAGEMENT USES

3. A statement of cash flows provides feedback to management on results of past management decisions.

   a. May reveal that the flow of cash from operations is large enough to make proposed external financing unnecessary.

   b. May show why cash shortages, if any, exist.

   c. May cause management to change its dividend policy to conserve funds.

INVESTOR AND CREDITOR USES

4. The statement may provide creditors and investors with valuable information on the:

   a. Enterprise's ability to generate positive future net cash flows.

   b. Enterprise's ability to pay debts.

   c. Enterprise's ability to pay dividends.

   d. Enterprise's need for external financing.

   e. Reasons for differences between net income and associated cash receipts and payments.

   f. Effects on an enterprise's financial position of its cash investing and financing transactions during the period.

INFORMATION IN THE STATEMENT OF CASH FLOWS

5. The statement of cash flows presents cash receipts and cash disbursements in three major categories: operating, investing, and financing cash flows.

   a. Operating activities include events that enter into the determination of income.

      (1) Cash received from operating activities includes cash received from producing and selling goods, providing services, interest, dividends, and other sources that are not from investing and financing activities.

      (2) Cash paid for operating activities includes cash paid for raw materials or inventory, salaries and wages, interest, and other expenses not considered investing or financing activities.

   b. Investing activities generally include transactions involving the acquisition or disposal of noncurrent assets.

      (1) Cash received from investing activities includes cash received from the sale of property, plant, and equipment; sale of marketable securities; and collection of loans made to others.

      (2) Cash paid for investing activities includes cash paid to purchase plant, property, and equipment and market securities and cash paid to make loans to others.

c. Financing activities generally include the cash effects of transactions and other events involving creditors and owners.

   (1) Cash received from financing activities includes cash received from issuing capital stock and bonds, mortgages, notes, and from other short- or long-term borrowing.

   (2) Cash paid for financing activities includes cash paid for cash dividends, purchase of treasury stock, and repayments of amounts borrowed.

d. Investing and financing activities that do not involve actual cash flows must be reported in a separate schedule.

CASH FLOWS FROM OPERATING ACTIVITIES

6. Cash flows from operating activities can be calculated using either the direct or indirect method.

   a. The direct method deducts only those expenses using cash from those revenues yielding cash.

   b. The indirect method starts with net income and adjusts it for items that affected reported net income but did not involve cash.

      (1) Analyze changes that occurred in current accounts other than cash. Net income must be adjusted for differences between accrual basis and cash basis accounting.

         (a) Add decreases and subtract increases in accounts receivable, inventories, prepaid expenses, and other current assets (except cash).

         (b) Add increases and deduct decreases in accounts payable, accrued liabilities, and other current liabilities.

      (2) Add back expenses or losses that did not reduce cash; examples are depreciation and loss from sale of noncurrent assets.

      (3) Deduct noncash credits or revenues; examples are gains from sale of noncurrent assets and income recorded for investments accounted for by the equity method.

      (4) The residual is net cash flow from operating activities.

   c. The FASB encourages the use of the direct method, but permits the use of the indirect method.

STEPS IN PREPARING THE STATEMENT OF CASH FLOWS

7. The first step is to determine cash flows from operating activities and present these items in the "Cash flows from operating activities" section.

8. The second step is to analyze all noncurrent accounts for charges resulting from investing and financing activities.

9. The third step involves arranging the information in the format required for the statement of cash flows.

STEP 1: DETERMINING NET CASH FLOW FROM OPERATING ACTIVITIES—DIRECT METHOD

10. The income statement must be converted from the accrual basis to the cash basis.

   a. Changes in balance sheet accounts that are related to items on the income statement are considered.

   b. Generally, an increase in a current asset decreases cash inflow or increases cash outflow.

   c. An increase in a current liability increases cash inflow or decreases cash outflow.

ALTERNATIVE STEP 1: DETERMINING CASH FLOWS FROM OPERATING ACTIVITIES—INDIRECT METHOD

11. Using the indirect method, certain adjustments are necessary to convert net income to cash flows from operating activities.

   a. To convert accrual basis net income to cash basis net income, add decreases in current assets and deduct decreases in current liabilities.

   b. Changes that occurred in current accounts other than cash must be analyzed for their effects on cash.

STEP 2: ANALYZING THE NONCURRENT ACCOUNTS

12. Analyze noncurrent accounts for cause of the change in cash. Examine the difference between the amount at the beginning of the period and the amount at the end of the period.

    a. Begin by reviewing the Retained Earnings account, so that net income and dividend amounts can be determined.

    b. Classify the differences as either "cash flows from investing activities" or "cash flows from financing activities."

    c. Arrange information in the statement of cash flows.

STEP 3: ARRANGING INFORMATION IN THE STATEMENT OF CASH FLOWS

13. The three major sections of a completed statement of cash flows are:

    a. Cash flows from operating activities.
    b. Cash flows from investing activities.
    c. Cash flows from financing activities.

14. The format in the operating activities section differs for the direct and indirect methods.

15. The direct method adjusts each item in the income statement to a cash basis.

16. The indirect method makes these same adjustments but makes them to net income rather than to each item in the income statement.

COMPREHENSIVE ILLUSTRATION

17. A comprehensive illustration of the use of a working paper to aid in the preparation of a statement of cash flows is presented.

    a. The working paper develops the information needed for a statement of cash flows, first showing how the effects of changes in current accounts on cash are entered. The working paper technique used makes this a mechanical process—if accounts receivable increased, a debit is entered on the accounts receivable line, and a credit must be entered in "increase in accounts receivable." This increase is a deduction from net income to convert income to cash flows from operating activities.

    b. Then the changes in every noncurrent account are entered in the working paper.

    c. Analyzing entries must be made for every change, even those that do not affect cash—such as a stock dividend—to show that no change was overlooked. The entries define the changes and serve to separate the changes into the three classifications on the statement.

    d. Include significant noncash financing and investing transactions at the bottom of the work sheet so that they will not be overlooked when a separate schedule is prepared.

COMPLETING THE WORKING PAPER

18. The focus of the working paper is on cash, and every change in cash is accompanied by a change in a noncash balance sheet account.

PREPARING THE STATEMENT OF CASH FLOWS

19. The information on the working paper is used to prepare the statement of cash flows.

WORKING CAPITAL OR CASH FLOWS

20. The trend went from the working capital statement of changes in financial position to the cash basis statement of changes in financial position before the statement of cash flows replaced this former statement. Working capital was reported in the past because composition of working capital was not considered significant: if working capital was not in cash form currently, the assumption was that it would be shortly.

THE SHIFT TOWARD CASH FLOWS

21. The shift to the cash definition of funds occurred because many companies experienced severe cash flow problems.

22. Modern finance supports the idea that cash flows are more useful than changes in working capital.
    a. Management, creditors, and investors all need information to make predictions of the amounts, timing, and uncertainty of future cash flows.
    b. Information on prior cash flows is a better basis than information on working capital for predicting future cash flows.
23. Current financial theory holds that investment decisions should involve comparisons of cash outlays with expected cash returns.
24. Past cash flows have often differed sharply from past working capital flows.

DEMONSTRATION PROBLEM

The 1993 and 1994 year-end balance sheet of Gibson, Inc., carried these debit and credit amounts:

	Debits	
	1994	*1993*
Cash	$12,000	$ 7,500
Accounts receivable, net	12,000	18,000
Merchandise inventory	33,000	27,000
Equipment	42,000	39,000
Totals	$99,000	$91,500

	Credits	
Accumulated depreciation, equipment	$ 9,000	$10,500
Accounts payable	12,000	15,000
Taxes payable	9,000	6,000
Common stock, $20 par value	40,500	37,500
Paid-in capital in excess of par value	1,500	
Retained earnings	27,000	22,500
Total	$99,000	$91,500

Analysis of the 1994 income statement and accounts revealed:

1. Equipment costing $9,000 was purchased.
2. Fully depreciated equipment that cost $6,000 was discarded, and its cost and accumulated depreciation were removed from the accounts.
3. The company's equipment was depreciated $4,500 during the year.
4. The company's income statement showed a $15,000 net income for 1994.
5. One hundred fifty shares of the company's common stock were issued at $30 per share.
6. Dividends totaling $10,500 were declared and paid during the year.

Required:

a. Prepare a working paper for the 1994 statement of cash flows.
b. Prepare a statement of cash flows under the indirect method.

GIBSON, INC.

Working Paper for Statement of Cash Flows

For the Year Ended December 31, 1994

	Account Balances 12/31/93	Analysis of Transactions for 1994		Account Balances 12/31/94
		Debit	Credit	

b.

GIBSON, INC.
Statement of Cash Flows
For the Year Ended December 31, 1994

SOLUTION TO DEMONSTRATION PROBLEM

a.

GIBSON, INC.
Working Paper for Statement of Cash Flows
For Year Ended December 31, 1994

	Account Balances December 31, 1993	Analysis of Transactions for 1994		Account Balances December 31, 1994
		Debit	Credit	
Debits:				
Cash	$ 7,500	(0) 4,500		$12,000
Accounts receivable	18,000		(2) 6,000	12,000
Merchandise inventory	27,000	(3) 6,000		33,000
Equipment	39,000	(7) 9,000	(8) 6,000	42,000
Totals	$91,500			$99,000
Credits:				
Accumulated depreciation equipment	10,500	(8) 6,000	(6) 4,500	$ 9,000
Accounts payable	15,000	(4) 3,000		12,000
Taxes payable	6,000		(5) 3,000	9,000
Common stock, $20 par value	37,500		(9) 3,000	40,500
Paid-in capital in excess of par value			(9) 1,500	1,500
Retained earnings	22,500	(10) 10,500	(1) 15,000	27,000
Totals	$91,500			$99,000
Cash Flows from Operating Activities:				
Net income		(1) 15,000		
Decrease in Accounts Receivable		(2) 6,000		
Increase in Merchandise Inventory			(3) 6,000	
Decrease in Accounts Payable			(4) 3,000	
Increase in Taxes Payable		(5) 3,000		
Depreciation		(6) 4,500		
Cash Flows from Investing Activities:				
Purchase of Equipment			(7) 9,000	
Cash Flows from Financing Activities:				
Sale of Common Stock		(9) 4,500		
Paid Dividends			(10) 10,500	
Increase in cash			(0) 4,500	
Totals		$72,000	$72,000	

b.

GIBSON, INC.
Statement of Cash Flows
For Year Ended December 31, 1994

Cash flows from operating activities:

Net income		$15,000
Noncash expenses, revenues, losses, and gains included in net income:		
Decrease in accounts receivable	6,000	
Increase in merchandise inventory	(6,000)	
Decrease in accounts payable	(3,000)	
Increase in taxes payable	3,000	
Depreciation	4,500	
Cash provided by operating activities		$19,500

Cash flows from investing activities:

Purchase of equipment	$(9,000)	
Net cash used by investing activities		(9,000)

Cash flows from financing activities:

Sale of common stock	$ 4,500	
Paid dividends	(10,500)	
Net cash used by financing activities		(6,000)
Net increase in cash		$ 4,500

MATCHING

Referring to the terms listed below, place the appropriate letter next to the corresponding description. All terms might not be used.

a.	Direct method	f.	Noncash charges/expenses	j.	Statement of cash flows
b.	Financing activities	g.	Noncash credits/revenues	k.	Statement of changes in
c.	Indirect method	h.	Operating activities		financial position
d.	Investing activities	i.	Separate schedule	l.	Working capital
e.	Cash flows from operating activities				

_____ 1. Generally include the cash effects of transactions and other events that enter into the determination of net income.

_____ 2. Replaced by statements of cash flows.

_____ 3. Reports the flow of cash into and out of a business in a given period.

_____ 4. Current assets minus current liabilities.

_____ 5. Include obtaining resources from owners and providing them with a return on their investment and obtaining resources from creditors and repaying or otherwise settling the debt.

_____ 6. Shows significant financing and investing activities that did not affect cash.

_____ 7. A way of determining cash flows from operating activities that starts with net income and adjusts for expenses and revenues that do not affect cash.

_____ 8. Include lending money and collecting the principal on those loans; acquiring and selling or disposing of securities of other companies; and acquiring or disposing of property, plant, and equipment.

_____ 9. Deducts from cash sales only those operating expenses that consumed cash.

_____ 10. Revenues and gains included in arriving at net income that do not provide cash.

_____ 11. Expenses and losses that are added back to net income because they do not actually use cash of the company.

_____ 12. Cash generated by the regular operations of a business; usually computed as net income plus or minus the effects of other current assets and current liabilities on cash flows, plus noncash expenses deducted in arriving at net income, minus noncash revenues included, less certain gains and plus any losses that are included in the total proceeds received from sale of fixed assets.

COMPLETION AND EXERCISES

1. The increases and decreases in the individual current asset and current liability accounts are reflected in the aggregate as a change in the company's _____.

2. A statement of cash flows shows the _____ of the net change in cash between two dates.

3. The former statement of changes in financial position showed the _____ and _____ of financial resources.

4. Deterioration in the company's _____ position due to inadequate planning by management leads to a company's inability to meet short-run financial requirements.

5. The main source of cash of a business enterprise is usually _____
   _____.

6. What are three main sources of cash that result from financing or investing activities?

   a. _____

   b. _____

   c. _____

7. What are four main uses of cash that result from operating, financing, or investing activities?

   a. _____

   b. _____

   c. _____

   d. _____

8. What is a "noncash financing or investing activity"?

   _____

   _____

   _____

9. From the following condensed income statement show how these items would be presented in a statement of cash flows prepared under the indirect method.

Sales		$162,500
Expenses (except depreciation and amortization)		113,750
		$ 48,750
Depreciation	$16,250	
Amortization of patent	6,500	22,750
Net Income		$ 26,000

10. This question concerns the adjustment or conversion procedure used to adjust accrual basis net income to obtain the cash flows from operating activities. Add the plus or minus signs to complete the table in the space.

Accrual basis net income + or − Changes in other current asset and current liability accounts

a. _____ Expenses and losses not reducing cash
b. _____ Revenues and gains not producing cash
  = Cash flows from operating activities

11. The current assets and current liabilities sections for 1993 and 1994 are given below for Carter Corporation.

	December 31 1994	December 31 1993
Current Assets:		
Cash	$11,000	$ 8,250
Accounts receivable (net)	23,100	20,625
Inventories	28,160	26,180
Prepaid expenses	1,210	1,375
Total Current Assets	$63,470	$56,430
Current Liabilities:		
Accounts payable	$14,300	$12,650
Notes payable	17,050	19,250
Accrued liabilities	13,750	12,650
Total Current Liabilities	$45,100	$44,550

Using these current accounts and the following information, prepare a statement of cash flows for the Carter Corporation for 1994 under the indirect method.

Net income for 1994 .... $44,000
Depreciation expense $16,500

An analysis of changes in noncurrent accounts revealed the following:

a. Sold equipment for $2,750; original cost, $11,000, accumulated depreciation, $8,800.
b. Purchased equipment for $13,750.
c. Sold capital stock; 55 shares at $50 per share.
d. Purchased land and building for $34,210.
e. Paid cash dividends of $11,000.

12. An adequate working capital position does not ensure an adequate _____ position for meeting payments.

13. The income statement does not measure net cash flows from operating activities because it is prepared on a(n) _____ basis.

14. Assume an income statement shows sales of $243,750. The accounts receivable balance was $21,000 on January 1 and $16,500 on December 31. Given only this information, how much cash was collected from customers?

15. The income statement shows that cost of goods sold for the year amounted to $187,500. Accounts payable on January 1 were $27,000, and on December 31 they were $31,500. Inventory was $30,000 on January 1 and $35,000 on December 31. Given only this information how much was cost of goods sold on a cash basis?

16. To derive the cash flow from operating activities for the period under the direct method, net income on an accrual basis must be converted to net income on a _____ basis.

17. Cash flows from operating activities equals net income on an accrual basis

    plus decreases in (a) _____.

    plus increases in (b) _____.

    minus decreases in (c) _____.

    and minus increases in (d) _____.

    plus (e) _____.

    minus (f) _____.

TRUE-FALSE QUESTIONS

Indicate whether each of the following statements is true or false by inserting a capital "T" or "F" in the blank space provided.

_____ 1. When a building is purchased by issuing bonds, the transaction would not be reported in the statement of cash flows or in a separate schedule.

_____ 2. The excess of total assets over total liabilities is called working capital.

_____ 3. When a statement of cash flows is prepared, dividends paid are reported as an investing activity.

_____ 4. The indirect method of computing cash flows from operating activities adjusts net income rather than each income statement item to a cash basis.

_____ 5. A corporation may elect not to prepare a statement of cash flows.

_____ 6. The statement of cash flows explains how changes in noncurrent assets reported on last year's balance sheet and this year's balance sheet affect cash flows.

_____ 7. If accounts receivable increased from $12,000 to $15,000 during the year and if sales amounted to $100,000 for the year, cash receipts from customers amounted to $103,000.

_____ 8. A company must publish a statement of cash flows for each period for which it publishes an income statement.

_____ 9. The amount of goodwill amortized in a period is added back to net income under the indirect method.

_____ 10. The most important reason for preparing a statement of cash flows is to compute the change in cash.

_____ 11. Depreciation provides cash for replacing plant assets; and this is the reason depreciation is shown as an inflow of cash on the statement of cash flows.

_____ 12. If a company issues its common stock for equipment, this transaction would not be disclosed on the statement of cash flows or in a separate schedule.

_____ 13. Borrowing of funds through use of a mortgage would not be reflected on a statement of cash flows because it involves a long-term liability.

_____ 14. A stock split would be reported in a separate schedule.

_____ 15. The former statement of changes in financial position presented information on the flow of financial resources into and out of a business.

_____ 16. The former statement of changes in financial position set forth the sources and applications of financial resources for a given period.

_____ 17. When net income is used as a starting point in measuring cash flows from operating activities, there is no need to add depreciation expense to net income.

_____ 18. The collection of accounts receivable is a financing activity.

_____ 19. Capital stock issued as a stock dividend is reported in a statement of cash flows.

_____ 20. Collections of loans are a financing activity.

_____ 21. If capital stock is split three for one, this transaction is reported on a statement of cash flows.

_____ 22. Cash received from the issuance of long-term debt is a financing activity.

MULTIPLE CHOICE QUESTIONS

For each of the following questions indicate the best answer by circling the appropriate letter.

Using the following information, answer questions 1–3 concerning a statement of cash flows.

1. The company reported $35,000 of net income for 1994.
2. The company recorded $7,000 depreciation on its store equipment.
3. Store equipment that cost $2,800 and had depreciated $1,400 was sold for $700.
4. Fully depreciated store equipment that cost $4,900 was discarded.
5. $5,600 of new store equipment was purchased during the year.
6. $6,720 of cash dividends were declared and paid during the year.
7. A 1,000-share stock dividend was declared and distributed at a time when the stock was selling for $15 per share.

1. Which of the above data will be used to determine cash flows from operating activities?

   A. 1, 5, 6
   B. 1, 2, 3
   C. 5, 3, 2
   D. 1, 2, 7
   E. 2, 3

2. Which of the above data will be used to determine cash flows from investing activities?

   A. 7
   B. 1, 2, 3
   C. 6
   D. 3, 5
   E. 4, 5

3. Which of the above data will be used to determine cash flows from financing activities?
   A. 4, 5
   B. 1, 2, 3
   C. 6
   D. 6, 7
   E. 7

Questions 4–6. How would the following transactions be shown on a statement of cash flows?

4. Treasury stock was purchased for $6,500 cash during the year.

   A. Shown as a positive cash flow from investing activities.
   B. Shown as a negative cash flow from investing activities.
   C. Shown as a negative cash flow from financing activities.
   D. Not shown on the statement.
   E. Shown as an operating activity item.

5. Equipment was purchased for $41,250 during the year.

   A. Shown as a negative cash flow from investing activities.
   B. Shown as a negative cash flow from financing activities.
   C. Shown as a negative cash flow from operating activities.
   D. Shown as a positive cash flow from financing activities.
   E. Not shown on the statement.

6. A five-year, 6% mortgage note payable for $87,500 was issued to the bank to acquire additional land and building from a contractor.

   A. Shown in a separate schedule.
   B. Not shown at all since cash was not affected.
   C. Shown as a cash flow from operating activities.
   D. (A) and (C) are both correct.
   E. None of the above statements is correct.

7. Which of the following is true concerning depreciation, amortization of patents, amortization of bond discount, interest expense, and salary expense?

   A. All are added to income to determine cash flows from operating activities.
   B. Only interest and salary expense are added to income to determine cash flows from operating activities.
   C. Depreciation, amortization of patents, and bond discounts are added to income to determine cash from operating activities.
   D. Only depreciation and interest expense are added to income to determine cash flows from operating activities.

8. Indicate the effect on the statement of cash flows if fully depreciated office equipment costing $4,800 was discarded and its cost and accumulated depreciation were removed from the books.

   A. The transaction would be shown as an investing activity.
   B. The transaction would be shown as a financing activity.
   C. The transaction would be shown in determining cash flows from operating activities.
   D. The transaction would not be shown on a statement of cash flows.

9. Machinery with a cost of $13,500 and accumulated depreciation of $11,970 was sold for $1,800 cash. How would the proceeds of sale be reported in the statement of cash flows?

   A. Cash flows from investing activities; Sale of machinery of $270
   B. Cash flows from financing activities; $1,800
   C. Would be shown as a decrease in a current asset
   D. Cash flows from investing activities; Sale of machinery of $1,800
   E. Not shown on statement of cash flows

10. A corporation issued $2,000,000 of 10-year bonds for cash at 95. How would the transaction be shown on the statement of cash flows?

   A. Positive cash inflow from financing activities, $1,900,000
   B. Positive cash inflow from financing activities, $2,000,000
   C. Negative cash flow from investing activities, $1,900,000
   D. Negative cash flow from investing activities, $2,000,000
   E. Not shown on the statement of cash flows

11. A company paid the following dividends during the year:

Cash Dividends .... $ 6,000
Stock Dividends 15,000

The correct statement concerning a statement of cash flows is:

A. Neither dividend is shown on the statement.
B. Both dividends are shown on the statement.
C. Cash dividends are shown, while stock dividends are not shown.
D. Stock dividends are shown while cash dividends are not.
E. None of the above statements is true.

12. On a statement of cash flows, the correct statement concerning a gain of $1,440 from the sale of a patent is:

A. The gain appears as an investing activity of $1,440.
B. The gain is used to adjust the income reported.
C. The gain does not appear on the statement.
D. None of the above statements is true.

13. You are given the following data concerning the Land account:

Land

Date			Debit	Credit	Balance
July	1	Balance			337,500
Aug.	8	Sold for $75,000 cash		45,000	292,500
Sept.	1	Purchased for cash	37,500		330,000
Oct.	31	Purchased for cash	112,500		442,500

The above data would be shown on the statement of cash flows as:

A. Cash flows from investing activities; sale of land, $75,000.
B. Cash flows from investing activities; sale of land, $45,000.
C. Cash flows from financing activities; purchase of land, $37,500.
D. Cash flows from financing activities; purchase of land, $112,500.
E. None of the above is correct.

SOLUTIONS

Matching

1.	h		7.	c
2.	k		8.	d
3.	j		9.	a
4.	l		10.	g
5.	b		11.	f
6.	i		12.	e

Completion and Exercises

1. working capital
2. causes
3. sources; uses (or disposition)
4. cash
5. profitable operations (net income)
6. (a) capital stock issues; (b) bond or other long-term debt issues, (c) sales of noncurrent assets
7. (a) net loss existing after adjustment for noncash items; (b) dividends paid; (c) debt repayment; (d) purchase of noncurrent assets

8. A noncash financing or investing activity is one that neither provides nor consumes cash.

9. *cash flows from operating activities:*

Net income $26,000
Adjustments to reconcile net income to net cash provided by operating activities:
    Depreciation $16,250
    Amortization of patent 6,500

10. a. +
    b. −

11.

CARTER CORPORATION
Statement of Cash Flows
For the Year Ended December 31, 1994

Net cash flow from operating activities:

Net income	$44,000	
Adjustments to reconcile net income to net cash provided by operating activities:		
Increase in accounts receivable	(2,475)	
Increase in inventories	(1,980)	
Decrease in prepaid expenses	165	
Increase in accounts payable	1,650	
Decrease in notes payable	(2,200)	
Increase in accrued liabilities	1,100	
Depreciation	16,500	
Gain on sale of equipment	(550)	
Net cash flow provided by operating activities		$56,210

Cash flows from investing activities:

Sale of equipment	$ 2,750	
Purchase of equipment	(13,750)	
Purchase of land and building	(34,210)	
Net cash used by investing activities		(45,210)

Cash flows from financing activities:

Sale of capital stock	$ 2,750	
Payment of dividends	(11,000)	
Net cash used by financing activities		(8,250)
Net increase in cash		$ 2,750

12. cash
13. accrual

14.
Sales on accrual basis	$243,750
Add decrease in Accounts Receivable	4,500
Cash collected from customers	$248,250

15.
Cost of goods sold on accrual basis	$187,500
Deduct increase in Accounts Payable	4,500
	$183,000
Add increase in inventory	5,000
Cost of goods sold on a cash basis	$188,000

16. cash

17. (a) current assets; (b) current liabilities;(c) current liabilities; (d) current assets; (e) noncash expenses and losses; (f) noncash revenues and gains.

True-False Questions

1. F   This transaction is a significant investing activity and must be reported in a separate schedule.
2. F   Working capital is the difference between current assets and current liabilities.
3. F   Dividends paid are shown as a financing activity.
4. T
5. F   The Financial Accounting Standards Board specified that a statement of cash flows is required for each period for which an income statement and balance sheet are presented.
6. T
7. F   Cash receipts from customers would total $97,000.
8. T
9. T
10. F
11. F   Depreciation is not a source of cash for replacing plant assets; depreciation is shown as a noncash capital expense and is added to net income.
12. F   According to the FASB, a firm must disclose all significant financing and investing activities regardless of whether cash is used. The transaction is significant even if it did not change the amount of cash and would be reported in a separate schedule.
13. F   Cash is increased, and this transaction would be reported on a statement of cash flows.
14. F   A stock split is not considered to be a significant financing or investing activity.
15. T
16. T
17. F
18. F   The collection of accounts receivable is an exchange of one current asset (cash) for another current asset (accounts receivable). The net change in accounts receivable affects the cash flows from operating activities.
19. F   This transaction does not involve cash.
20. F   Collections of loans are an investing activity.
21. F
22. T

Multiple Choice Questions

1. B
2. D
3. C
4. C
5. A
6. A
7. C   Interest expense and salaries expense, unlike the other expenses listed, involve an outflow of cash.
8. D   There would be no effect on cash because Accumulated Depreciation would be debited for the same amount that Office Equipment would be credited. If significant, this item would be shown on a separate schedule.
9. D
10. A
11. C
12. B
13. A

a.

THE OVERLOOK SHOP
Work Sheet
For the Year Ended December 31, 1993

ACCOUNT TITLE	TRIAL BALANCE		ADJUSTMENTS		ADJUSTED TRIAL BALANCE		INCOME STATEMENT		STATEMENT OF RETAINED EARNINGS		BALANCE SHEET	
	DR.	CR.	DR.	CR.	DR.	CR.	DR.	CR.	DR.	CR.	DR	CR.

419

THE OVERLOOK SHOP

Work Sheet

For the Year Ended December 31, 1993

ACCOUNT TITLE	TRIAL BALANCE		ADJUSTMENTS		ADJUSTED TRIAL BALANCE		INCOME STATEMENT		STATEMENT OF RETAINED EARNINGS		BALANCE SHEET	
	DR.	CR.	DR.	CR.	DR.	CR.	DR.	CR.	DR.	CR.	DR.	CR.